Praise for *The Great Pretenders*

'The Great Pretenders *is a timely and critical intervention in current public discussions on race and racism. Pertinently, it brings into sharp relief important historical continuities in the ANC's problematic politics on these questions. This book by public intellectual, Ebrahim Harvey, will certainly provoke much debate on the crucial nexus of race and class, as well as on the state of contemporary South Africa.*'

NOOR NIEFTAGODIEN, SA RESEARCH CHAIR (SARCH): LOCAL HISTORIES, PRESENT REALITIES AND HEAD OF HISTORY WORKSHOP, UNIVERSITY OF THE WITWATERSRAND

'*Ebrahim Harvey provides a stinging critique of the failings of the ANC and its animating nationalist philosophy from the time of its founding to the present day. His chief concern is its failure to rise to the historical challenge posed by South Africa's system of racial capitalism. Harvey insists that race and racism constitute a central theme of that history. But he is equally insistent that race and racism are not free-floating facts of life: they are functionally embedded in the way economy and society are organised at a material level, and they will not be uprooted by changing hearts and minds alone. He brings much sophisticated theoretical and historical analysis to bear in support of his argument. This is a study that is fierce, passionate and provocative. It provides a challenge to liberationist rhetoric that serves to disguise the class interests that still hold the state in thrall. Harvey does not pull his punches and is unforgiving in his judgements. The book is a cri de coeur for radical root-and-branch thinking about where South Africa finds itself and where we are heading a quarter century after democracy.*'

TIMOTHY KEEGAN, AUTHOR OF *COLONIAL SOUTH AFRICA* AND *THE MAKING OF THE RACIAL ORDER*

'Veteran political analyst Ebrahim Harvey has written a provocative and partisan book. It is full of uncomfortable insights on race and racism. It raises tough questions that need to be urgently addressed if we are to create the shared society that we proclaim. An essential read on a neglected perspective.'

EDWARD WEBSTER, PROFESSOR EMERITUS, UNIVERSITY OF WITWATERSRAND AND DISTINGUISHED RESEARCH PROFESSOR SOUTHERN CENTRE FOR INEQUALITY STUDIES (SCIS)

'In his latest book, author, political analyst and trade unionist Ebrahim Harvey analyses the metamorphosis of the ANC from a national liberation movement to a neoliberal ruling party with unparalleled fidelity to established facts. He provides a historical, ideological and political critique of the ANC's handling of the race and class aspects of the struggle in South Africa with admirable intellectual and political insight.

'Harvey is able to clearly identify the confluence of the key strategic, ideological, organisational and ethnic factors in ways that clearly account for the persistence of the racial and class dimensions of apartheid in post-apartheid South Africa. In his inimitable style and intellectual depth, Harvey opens the ANC to unparalleled scrutiny.'

GAUTA KOMANE, FORMER ANC OFFICIAL AND POLITICAL COMMENTATOR

'This is a brilliant and provocative study of the historical development of South Africa's race-class history. This book delves into the past and the present in such a way that it provides an indispensable guide to the future.

'While it delves into the origins of the racial capitalist system through the growth of the cheap black labour system of the mineral revolution and its concomitant racial political expression in segregation and apartheid, the focus of the book is on the ANC and the race/class question.

'It is a must-read for historians, academics, students but mainly activists in the trade union movement, social movements and leftwing organisations. He has ruffled many feathers and much of what he says will not go down well with those in power. There is no doubt that this book will be the primary reader on race and class in South Africa for the foreseeable future.'

SHAHEEN KHAN, SOCIALIST REVOLUTIONARY WORKERS PARTY

'Harvey tackles the proverbial bull by the horns in this account of the pernicious issue of race relations in South Africa. In addition to an historical overview that sets the scene, he takes on and lays the blame for worsening racialised social conflict and the failure to address the "National Question" squarely at the door of the ruling African National Congress. The Rainbow Nation approach, advocated by SA's Nobel laureates, Mandela and Tutu, comes in for a real beating.'

MARTIN JANSEN, DIRECTOR OF WORKERS WORLD MEDIA PRODUCTIONS

'In this interesting, important and provocative book, Harvey argues a simple yet powerful thesis. The durability of South Africa's notoriously rapacious form of capitalism since 1994 dooms African nationalism to corruption, condemns ANC governments to failure and reproduces racism. Agree or disagree, Harvey's thesis must be engaged.'

MICHAEL MACDONALD, AUTHOR OF *WHY RACE MATTERS IN SOUTH AFRICA*

'Ebrahim Harvey uses a skilful and erudite, but uncompromising, scalpel to undertake an autopsy of the living corpse that has become the hopes for, and dreams of, substantive radical change in the post-1994 South Africa, especially for the increasingly impoverished masses. The book is an evisceration of the ANC and its record in office, including its use of the "master's tools" in its recourse to a colonialist nativisation of "African" and clearly shows that the ANC has failed to adequately address the matter of racism which still exists, for the most part, in its apartheid form. Class and race are the two dominative axes of oppression and exploitation around which Harvey conducts his interrogation, laying bare the way in which expediency, ignorance and corruption have squandered the potential for socialist progress.'

NEVILLE ADAMS, INDEPENDENT RACE EQUALITY SCHOLAR, LONDON

'The ANC dominated South Africa's liberation struggle and continues to dominate post-apartheid politics. Ebrahim Harvey's The Great Pretenders *challenges conventional wisdom about the party. Harvey challenges the ANC's claim to revolutionary leadership of the black masses and critiques its race politics. This book is sure to provoke controversy. In doing so, it will enrich public debate about South Africa's political history and possible futures.*'

SEAN JACOBS, EDITOR AND FOUNDER OF *AFRICA IS A COUNTRY*, AND AUTHOR OF *MEDIA IN POST-APARTHEID SOUTH AFRICA: POSTCOLONIAL POLITICS IN THE AGE OF GLOBALIZATION*

'The Great Pretenders *reveals in stark detail the failure of the ANC to address the National Question. Harvey documents the failure of the ANC to roll back the race and class divide in SA.*'

ABDUL KARRIEM MATHEWS, COMMUNITY ACTIVIST

'Just as the ANC enters its terminal crisis, Ebrahim Harvey has produced a powerful and richly detailed analysis of the path that led to the crisis and its likely results. A tour de force!'

ANDREW NASH, EMERITUS ASSOCIATE PROFESSOR, POLITICAL STUDIES, UNIVERSITY OF CAPE TOWN AND AUTHOR OF *THE DIALECTICAL TRADITION IN SOUTH AFRICA*

'Harvey seeks to unravel the unholy epistemological and political alliance between (African) nationalism as espoused by the ANC and the manifestations of "white monopoly capitalism". In his assessment, the contemporary context is marked "by a very complex, fluid, ambiguous, contradictory and revealing race-class-gender greyness that has socially reconfigured SA, but still under capitalist hegemony." The reasons for this alliance, the author argues, are "lessons" gleaned from South Africa's colonial past under British imperialist rule; are to be found in a misreading of this history by the (early) leaders of the ANC who saw a resolution of the historical convulsions of racism and capitalism in a liberal "non-racial bourgeois democracy", as we have had since 1994. Against this background, it has been of no surprise to the author that post-apartheid South Africa as governed by the ANC remains enmeshed in a "race" quagmire and in a globalised capitalism which goes roughshod across "the corpses of Marikana", the poor and the marginalised. In essence, Harvey states, the ANC in 1994 was ill-prepared to govern and to proffer viable social justice-driven alternatives to the capitalist crisis which it had inherited from the Nationalist Party.

'This book is essential reading for those seeking a just resolution to the multiple ambiguities in contemporary South Africa.'

ROBERT KRIGER, RETIRED EXECUTIVE DIRECTOR FOR INTERNATIONAL RELATIONS AT THE NATIONAL RESEARCH FOUNDATION (NRF)

'A sizzling, insightful, brave, mince-no-words and take-no-prisoners devastating critique of ANC rule in post-apartheid capitalist South Africa. At the centre of the critique is the undeniable worsening of the material conditions of black working-class South Africans on the one hand and, on the other hand, the rampant, self-enrichment, state-looting machinations of a black elite intent on grabbing a share of the enormous wealth stolen by White Monopoly Capital. Harvey explains this sorry development as reflecting "that old racial-class nexus and its related variables" that has plagued this part of the world and created so much suffering for black working-class people as a condition for the making of great fortunes. The "great pretenders" are the petty bourgeois ANC leaders whose forked-tongued, politico-economic double dealings in the course of waging and consummating the national liberation struggle Harvey identifies as ultimately responsible for this debacle. I agree with Harvey that unless capitalism is overthrown, the black working-class in particular will continue to bear the brunt of the exponentially rising cost that humanity everywhere must pay for the system's continued crisis-ridden existence.'

TREVOR NGWANE, DIRECTOR OF THE CENTRE FOR SOCIOLOGICAL RESEARCH, UNIVERSITY OF JOHANNESBURG AND PRESIDENT OF THE SOUTH AFRICAN SOCIOLOGICAL ASSOCIATION

The Great Pretenders:
Race and Class under ANC Rule

Ebrahim Harvey

First published by Jacana Media (Pty) Ltd in 2021

10 Orange Street
Sunnyside
Auckland Park, 2092
Johannesburg
+2711 628 3200
www.jacana.co.za

© Ebrahim Harvey, 2021

All rights reserved.

ISBN 978-1-4314-3056-7

Cover design by publicide
Cover photograph © Gallo Images
Editing by Colin Bundy
Proofreading by Russell Martin and Lara Jacob
Set in Ehrhardt 11/14.5pt
Printed by ABC Press, Cape Town
Job number 003754

For a complete list of Jacana titles visit www.jacana.co.za

Contents

Acronyms 9
Preface 11
Introductory reflections 17
1 The historical origins of the concept of race 41
2 Race, racialism and racism: Definitions and theoretical reflections 67
3 Race, class and gender in South African history 107
4 Towards understanding the African National Congress 145
5 Mandela, negotiations and the rise to power of the ANC 197
6 Some notes on the National Question 259
7 The 'New South Africa' unravels: Race, class and gender
   struggles 305
8 The vengeance of 'history'? 359
Bibliography 415
Index 429

Acronyms

4IR	Fourth Industrial Revolution
AA	Affirmative Action
AAC	Anglo American Corporation
Amcu	Association of Mineworkers and Construction Union
ANC	African National Congress
ANCWL	African National Congress Women's League
ANCYL	African National Congress Youth League
APO	African Peoples Organisation
Azapo	Azanian People's Organisation
BC	Black Consciousness
BEE	Black Economic Empowerment
BFLF	Black First Land First
BPC	Black Peoples Convention
Codesa	Convention for a Democratic South Africa
Contralesa	Congress of Traditional Leaders of South Africa
Cosatu	Congress of South African Trade Unions
CPSA	Communist Party of South Africa
CST	colonialism of a special type
DA	Democratic Alliance
DEIC	Dutch East India Company
EFF	Economic Freedom Fighters
FC	Freedom Charter
GDE	Gauteng Department of Education

Gear	Growth, Employment & Redistribution
HSRC	Human Sciences Research Council
ICU	Industrial and Commercial Workers Union
MERG	Macroeconomic Research Group
NDR	National Democratic Revolution
NEC	national executive committee
NEUM	Non-European Unity Movement
NNC	Natal Native Congress
NP	National Party
NPA	National Prosecuting Authority
NQ	National Question
NUM	New Unity Movement
Numsa	National Union of Metalworkers of South Africa
PAC	Pan Africanist Congress
PIC	Public Investment Corpration
RDP	Reconstruction and Development Programme
RET	Radical Economic Transformation
SACP	South African Communist Party
SACTU	South African Congress of Trade Unions
SADTU	South African Democratic Teachers' Union
Saftu	South African Federation of Trade Unions
SAHRC	South African Human Rights Commission
Sanco	South African National Civic Organisation
SANNC	South African National Native Congress
SASO	South African Students Organisation
SOE	state owned enterprise
SRWP	Socialist Revolutionary Workers Party
TRC	Truth and Reconciliation Commission
UCT	University of Cape Town
UDF	United Democratic Front
UDS	Urban Development Strategy
UF	Urban Foundation
Wits	University of the Witwatersrand
WLP	Worker's List Party
WMC	white monopoly capital
Wosa	Workers Organisation for Socialist Action
ZCE	Zondo Commission of Enquiry

Preface

IT WAS IN PARTICULAR the Marikana massacre in August 2012 which made me decide to write this book.[1] This decision was strengthened in March 2015 with the onset of the momentous student risings that began at the University of Cape Town (UCT) and spread like wildfire across the country. Those combustible events and the saliency of the issues they gave rise to, especially since they occurred so long after the 1994 watershed democratic elections, made this study imperative for several reasons. There had been numerous other indications of the legacy of racism and apartheid, and the historical links of race and class, after the 1993 negotiated settlement; but the circumstances under which Marikana and the student protests occurred were the actual trigger for this book.

The Marikana massacre shook this country as nothing has since 1994: 34 black miners shot dead during a strike and many more injured by black policemen, under a black-majority government of the African National Congress (ANC). The halo of the supposedly 'democratic' and 'non-racial' society and the 'miracle transition' many in the media raved about was shattered by Marikana. Much has been written about Marikana but I don't think the full implications for race and the race–class nexus were sufficiently teased out of what was the biggest tragedy to occur in this country since 1994.

However, the importance of Marikana and the Fallist protests was greatly magnified against the background of what had happened or not happened since the 1994 democratic breakthrough. In fact, those events threw into sharp relief the preceding 21 years (1994–2015), during which we were poignantly reminded many times not only of the centuries-long struggles waged by the black working-class majority for their liberation and the enormous hardships and sacrifices they suffered as a result, but therefore of the deep and palpable disappointment many justifiably felt at the questionable compromises made by the ANC before and after 1994. Such compromises included the failure to honour the demands of the Freedom Charter (FC), the provisions of the Reconstruction and Development Programme (RDP), and, even on its own limited terms, the National Democratic Revolution (NDR), after they won the 1994 elections.[2]

This is not in the least to suggest that no major political changes and gains were made by the negotiated settlement. The total removal of all racist legislation from the statute books, the first-ever free, open, democratic and non-racial elections, and the much-heralded 1996 constitution were of immense political and to a degree social importance. Neither do I underestimate the enormous difficulties the ANC government faced in rebuilding a country racked with centuries of brutal racism, political repression and economic exploitation in one form or another since the early days of the Cape Colony.[3]

However, because of the sensitive and controversial nature of the fundamental compromises the ANC made during the negotiations process, the 1996 constitution and the adoption of distinctly neoliberal economic and social policies since 1994, there have been massive and irreconcilable differences between the progressive and historic political changes of 1994 and the ongoing and in some respects deepening poverty, unemployment and class inequalities afflicting the majority black population. A whole host of related social miseries has severely tarnished and undermined the undoubted political revolution that occurred since 1994.

Essentially, these compromises and their devastating consequences, on the back of the neoliberal economic and social policies the ANC adopted, revolve around the fact that the capitalist economic system with which racism and apartheid, in its various forms, were inextricably intertwined for centuries, to a greater or lesser degree, was seemingly effortlessly perpetuated after 1994.[4] Research for this book began more seriously in January 2017. While initially my intention was that it would consist of a treatment of race and class in both our longer history and post-apartheid South Africa, as the study progressed two realisations became increasingly important. One was the necessity to approach race and racism both historically and globally, before a concentrated focus on SA; and, secondly, a need to include a stronger focus on gender. Though gender was always going to feature, it became increasingly more important as the study progressed, in the light of events and developments on the ground in SA. In fact, the title of this book speaks to the equally forceful convergence of the features of race, class and gender over undoubtedly the most critical period in post-apartheid history: 2012–2019.

What do I seek to mainly accomplish with this work? Firstly, of inestimable importance is a brief excavation of the history of this country, in which the narratives of race, racism, white superiority, white supremacy and 'racial capitalism'[5] were forged, in ways that were intertwined, even symbiotically so. I am convinced that the ANC never really understood how systemically – especially after the mineral revolution of the 19th century – various political, economic and social factors intertwined to decisively shape not only our history since then, but also, and probably most importantly, what was possible and indeed necessary to achieve during the liberation struggles in the 20th century and indeed during the negotiations between 1991 and 1993.

Secondly, and relatedly, I question and critique several narratives the ANC has peddled for over a century, both before and after the 1994 watershed elections, about what it represents in the broad liberation movement. Particularly, I critically examine its understanding of the key issues facing our society and its performance in the interrelated areas of race, racism, class, gender and capitalist social relations after it won the 1994 elections. Thirdly, while not necessarily intending to set the country aflame with this book, I do want it, without the slightest concession to 'political correctness', to confront and challenge some decades-old myths and some outright fallacies the ANC has peddled, many in fact since its birth. We need to go back to the roots of the ANC to really understand its problems, weaknesses, limitations and contradictions. I argue that, contrary to popular wisdom, the ANC was never really a powerful mass organisation.

One of those enduring myths is the ANC's claim to the revolutionary leadership of the black masses. There is an abundance of literature to dispel that myth; and in making this case, I arrive at what are arguably inevitable conclusions about the reformist and sometimes ultimately reactionary and counterrevolutionary character of the ANC.

The ANC, since its birth, has not properly understood South African history. It has failed dismally in terms of revolutionary theory, organisation, strategy and programme. It has also confused and misled the black working-class majority since its inception. This book intends to prove that. The fact that the ANC was the strongest component of the broad national liberation movement is a testament not to its strengths but to the political weaknesses of the black and especially African masses. A serious combination of problems from that time prevailed – illiteracy, lack of political and formal education, tribalism, cultural backwardness and, related to those matters, a conspicuous lack of class consciousness, in the revolutionary Marxist sense.

It is those factors too that we must examine to find out how it is possible that, despite an abysmal record in office, the ANC still holds power in SA, though it has been in serious decline at the polls over the past decade, indicating that the black masses are finally waking up in their own interests after a long slumber, during which time they were seduced by the fervour and tenacity of the African nationalism of the ANC and the many promises, often solemnly made. Despite the high levels of militancy it has produced in various and ongoing struggles, especially the township protests since 2004, the hold of African nationalism and the ANC is still strong, but the many disappointments since 1994 have opened the eyes of a significant size of the black electorate beyond the ANC; how that prospect plays itself out we will see over the next decade.

However, one point which is critical to this book must be made now: the revolutionary conclusions the ANC should have drawn about both the nature of South African society in 1912 and the kind of analysis and programme which logically flowed from it, its leadership consciously avoided drawing. It was not in the interests of its reformist African middle-class leadership, who all along desired a seat at the negotiations table and a 'non-racial' place in the capitalist order, to draw anti-capitalist conclusions. In other words, even if we completely leave aside the other 'minorities' who were also exploited and oppressed, namely Coloureds and Indians, if we follow the contours and trajectory of the 19th-century mineral revolution, of which the African masses were largely the slaves, then even on its own terms, namely 'blacks in general and Africans in particular', it has betrayed the most basic needs and aspirations of the African majority. Those truths post-apartheid South Africa have inscribed with their blood, sweat and tears.

There are many citations in the literature of the ANC itself which make it very clear that its leadership has misled the black masses or betrayed its own stated mission or did both. But there are also many mistakes and much confusion in both its analyses and programmes, such as I will show later in the case of the FC. For now, one example will suffice. In 1969, at its Morogoro conference the ANC pledged that 'In the last resort it is only the success of the national democratic revolution – by destroying the existing social and economic relationships – (that) will bring with (it) a correction of the historical injustices.'[6] Obviously, given the inextricable links between apartheid/white racism and capitalism, that statement could only be construed as inherently anti-capitalist. But the NDR was always effectively seen as the first (anti-apartheid) stage of a two-stage revolutionary theory, to be followed at an indeterminate and vague future that by an explicitly socialist stage, which over twenty-five years since the watershed 1994 democratic and non-racial elections we are still waiting for.

I need to heartily thank my publisher, Jacana Media, for their consistent support and encouragement since I started this project in 2017 and Colin Bundy for how he most skilfully edited and coherently pulled together a too lengthy and as a result in parts a bit unwieldy manuscript. I also need to thank two other readers of the manuscript, Martin Jansen and Neville Adams, for very useful comments which opened some interesting perspectives that served to strengthen the overall work.

Finally, I need to thank the funders of this book, namely the Ford Foundation (FF) and the Oppenheimer Memorial Trust (OMT). The FF has been very kind to me and supportive of my work over many years. They earlier also funded my PhD studies. The OMT also partly funded my earlier authorised biography of the former president, Kgalema Motlanthe. I need to specifically thank Nicolette Naylor, the Southern Africa representative of the FF, and Bobby Godsell of the OMT for their consistent support. This book would not have been possible without their financial support, for which I am highly appreciative.

Endnotes

1 There is, I believe, a deep historical connection between Marikana and the conditions under which British imperialism rooted itself in this country, following the mineral revolution of the 19th century and which essentially continued after the negotiated settlement between the ANC and the apartheid regime in 1993.
2 As will become clear later, the NDR, according to the ANC itself, was not only about achieving political democracy in South Africa, but equally about changes to the socioeconomic conditions of the majority black masses. In fact, it is in this regard that the ANC arguably failed dismally after 1994. On the contrary, as we will see later, conditions instead deteriorated, especially as regards basic services in black townships.
3 I argue that in fact aside from aspects of political democracy, like the right to vote and many other such basic 'bourgeois' democratic rights, important as they certainly are, SA is basically the same country as it was in the days of the Cape Colony and especially in the first decade or two after the mineral revolution of the second half of the 19th century. This is particularly so as regards what is arguably the heart of any genuine 'people's democracy', the adequate satisfaction of the basic daily needs of human beings. For a brilliant argument about how under capitalism democracy is in fact hollowed out, see D. Smith, *Capitalist Democracy on Trial* (London & New York: Routledge, 1990).
4 See N. Alexander, *An Ordinary Country: Issues in the Transition from Apartheid to Democracy in South Africa* (Pietermaritzburg: University of KwaZulu-Natal Press, 2002). The thrust of Alexander's analysis is that after black people won the right to vote and many other liberal democratic rights in 1994 and in the 1996 constitution, it was just like any other capitalist democracy in Europe or elsewhere, in which capitalist rule is still not only firmly entrenched but as a result determines the quality of life and standards of living of the populace, but done now on a putatively 'non-racial' basis. I critically analyse these matters in chapter 2.
5 'Racial capitalism' was a very interesting and in fact intriguing concept under apartheid. In chapter 2, which deals with theory, I examine it, because it is in post-apartheid SA that its validity and salience, especially because in political, analytical and programmatic terms it insisted on the inextricable intertwining of racism and capitalism under apartheid, became more questionable and debatable, following the installation of a putatively non-racial democracy. The key question in this regard is whether the post-apartheid experience undermines or invalidates the racism–capitalism nexus in SA.
6 See 'First National Consultative Conference: Report on the Strategy and Tactics of the ANC', 26 April 1969, at www.sahistory.org.za.

Introductory reflections

THIS INTRODUCTION IS NECESSARILY LONG. The aim is to set out the parameters of this work as clearly as possible. I believe that an introduction to a book must set out its contents as clearly and comprehensively as space permits. In this way readers should be able to see clearly what lies ahead in the book, chapter by chapter. The idea is also to give a very limited sense of the core thinking which informs the various themes and chapters. There must ideally be no surprises.

However, it is apt to begin it with the thoughtful, prescient and stirring words of Friedrich Engels on the significance of Karl Marx's materialistic conception of history, delivered at his grave, when he was buried on 17 March 1883:

> Just as Darwin discovered the law of development of organic nature, so Marx discovered the law of development of human history: the simple fact, hitherto concealed by an overgrowth of ideology, that mankind must first of all eat, drink, have shelter and clothing, therefore must work, before they can fight for domination, pursue politics, religion, philosophy, etc.; that therefore the production of the immediate material means, and therefore the degree of economic development attained in a given period or during a given epoch, form the foundation upon which the state institutions, the legal conceptions, art, and even the ideas of religion, of the people concerned have been evolved, and in the light of which they must therefore be explained, instead of vice versa, as had hitherto been the case.

As will become clearer in chapters 1 and 2, which respectively deal with history and theory, so inextricably intertwined for centuries have questions of economic development, society and history itself been with race, racism, class, gender and culture that it is today imperative to situate all of these interrelated factors within that wider context. And so almost symbiotically interrelated were these factors in South African history that this approach could arguably apply better in SA than in most other countries.

This historical materialist conception is of great explanatory significance in this work, which is a critical analysis of the oppression and exploitation wrought by racism, class and gender under the rule of the African National Congress (ANC) in SA since 1994, in the post-apartheid period, but which had its roots in the system that developed in SA both before and especially after the mineral revolution of the 19th century. I therefore constantly view race and the struggles against racism and class and gender exploitation and oppression as part and parcel and in fact a continuation of the struggles for liberation that were first waged in this country by the Khoikhoi shortly after Jan van Riebeeck, the Dutch coloniser, arrived at Table Bay in the Cape in 1652.

I therefore approach race, racism, class and gender within the context of the origins of racist slavery, colonialism and the later development of mining and industrial capitalism in SA. The logic, practice and history of race and racism, in its various forms, since the days of the Cape Colony, cannot at all be understood outside of that context, and therefore all the anti-racist struggles could not succeed outside of that historical context, which gave rise to systemic and institutional racism and which in SA overwhelmingly merged racist segregation and, later, apartheid with the capitalist system.[1]

This system, especially following the mineral revolution of the 19th century, not only developed racial-colonialist forms of both political domination and economic exploitation after then but it is essentially still in existence in SA under the present rule of the ANC, shorn, however, of the apartheid-era legalised and overt racism. There was in fact never a time since 1652 that race, colour and racism were not in some way and to some degree associated with the economic and, later, more specific class interests of initially Dutch and subsequently British colonialism and imperialism. In fact, as I will argue, throughout the period of colonialism in SA, from the very outset of the establishment of a refreshment station at Table Bay in the Cape, the introduction of slavery there, the motives for the Great Trek, the establishment of the Boer colonies of Orange Free State and Transvaal, the Anglo-Boer War, the establishment of the Union of SA in 1910 and finally the apartheid regime from 1948 onwards, were consistently and in the final analysis all driven by economic and material interests.

Never once have white racism, superiority and supremacy operated on their own. No matter how racist they were, the interests of Afrikaner nationalism, including its later National Party (NP) form, were always driven by economic, financial and material motives. In fact, a study of the development of the old Cape Colony shows clearly, including the stated reasons for the Great Trek, these factors at play, at each and every step of the way. It is indeed a very consistent theme in South African history, in fact right up until the release of Nelson Mandela and the beginning of negotiations between the National Party and the African National Congress, which led to the settlement agreement in 1993.

Intrinsic to my explanation of what happened in SA both before and especially after the release from prison of Mandela, South Africa's first black president, is a strong focus on how and why the then ruling NP decided to begin a process of negotiations with the ANC. Aside from delving into the history of SA and the global and historical origins of race and racism, imperative for this study, I focus on the systemic and structural reasons why the NP moved in that direction after the militant black mass struggles of the 1980s, combined with a deep economic crisis and growing pressure for serious and significant reform by various Western countries, led by Britain and the United States.

An understanding of those critical factors which drove the negotiations process over the period 1987–1993 is of inestimable importance in understanding not only why the NP moved in that direction, which was inconceivable a decade earlier, but why and how such political moves directly and indirectly emerge from and relate to the historical practice of imperialism in moments of deep, troubling and destabilising crisis. How British imperialism in particular reacted in such similar moments of deep structural crises in much earlier periods, including its role in South African history, is very instructive about the ulterior aims of the reformist designs of the NP in initiating the negotiation talks with the

ANC, which in fact began already in the mid-1980s at Pollsmoor, where Mandela was then imprisoned. It is precisely with this approach in mind that I deal with the abolition of statutory apartheid and racism, beginning in the 1980s and continuing into the 1990s.

All these reformist moves were very carefully calculated and calibrated, especially before and after the release of Mandela. The singular most vitally important goal then was to preserve the capitalist economy in SA, no matter what in *political terms* became necessary for the NP to concede in its negotiations with the ANC. However, even in political terms, the NP got more than enough guarantees of structural protections of both its political and economic interests in the final settlement of 1993, which was in 1996 enshrined in the constitution.

While I delve into theoretical matters in chapter 2, I wish to note now how both the British and later the white Afrikaners, in the form of the NP, moved towards significant reforms – how serious and significant they were is debatable – at various points during the 1970s and 1980s in order to stabilise and save the capitalist system, with which their economic interests were indeed inseparably intertwined. This is one of the secrets of the centuries-old global capitalist system and how, though in a long, deep structural crisis, it perpetuates and reinvents itself continuously. But it is vitally important to realise that this would not have been possible without the numerous failures and sometimes treachery of the revolutionary Marxist parties in various European countries during the 20th century.

There is also much in the literature which shows that far from the NP being a hideously and inflexibly racist party, bent on the total domination of black people at all times, in every respect, and nothing less, what really happened between 1948 and 1990, when Mandela was released from prison and the NP began negotiations with the ANC, shows a very different picture which strongly contradicts the notion of a totalitarian racist tyranny. I return to an assessment of the significance of these reforms, but in ways which discuss the inextricable racism–capitalism nexus and ask whether such conflation is schematic and does not recognise the perpetual and permanently 'contingent' nature of the relationship between racism and capitalism. However, I attempt to deal with this contingency, which is one of the most important theoretical and practical issues in capitalist societies in which racism has historically and structurally struck deep roots.

I argue that the NP in fact learnt a lot from earlier British rule in SA and when the crisis it confronted in the 1970s and 1980s became very threatening under the racial capitalism that had developed here historically, the NP politically, strategically and discursively did what British colonial rule tried to do in the 19th century, in relation to the 'Native Question': introduce politically significant reforms in order to avoid serious destabilisation of the capitalist system, especially since the struggle for liberation in the 1970s and 1980s was far stronger and more threatening than at any earlier time in our history.

And so much had the mineral revolution of the 19th century decisively and irrevocably changed SA and its future that whatever political regime existed needed to be aligned decisively to serving the needs of mining and industrial capitalism which had been hegemonic since then. In this regard a study of the relationship between Afrikanerdom, especially when in one form or another or to some degree or another it was in power, and British rule inside SA, particularly after the Anglo-Boer War, shows distinctly that the interests of the British were largely dominant, though British and Afrikaner capital became much closer in various ways towards the end of the 1980s.

The struggles waged by the black masses between 1976 and 1989 in SA were the most powerful and sustained in SA's history. The reformist wing of the NP began to realise the necessity of some kind of non-racial political settlement in order to prevent cataclysmic social explosions of a magnitude that would threaten to overwhelm NP rule and, with it, 'racial capitalism'. Furthermore, in a country with such startling demographic racial contrasts as SA, in which the 'whites' represented less than a tenth of the population, major political changes became necessary, no matter what even the conservative white electorate felt, especially in that same period, which was arguably the most severe political crisis ever in SA. This crisis was arguably worse, in structural and political terms, than was the crisis between Boer and Briton in the late 19th century, which led to the Anglo-Boer War, between 1899–1902. There was incomparably more at stake for a future SA, given the overwhelming black majority we have and have always had. But the 1993 political settlement between the NP and the ANC found a way around that central problem of South African politics: black people had been deprived of the right to vote and other 'democratic' rights whites enjoyed.

But it is crucially important to stress, yet again, that all this became ultimately necessary in order to save the capitalist system, which was historically configured to benefit whites in general, though unevenly and unequally, a sociological and political fact not often stated and interrogated in the literature. As with the case of 'blacks', never at any point in time since the earliest days of the Cape Colony were 'whites' homogeneous. I explore these dynamics in chapters 2 and 3, drawing substantially from the very useful work by Timothy Keegan, *Colonial South Africa and the Origins of the Racial Order* and another, as useful work by Michael MacDonald, *Why Race Matters in South Africa*.

However, of pivotal importance, it was not the reformist wing of the NP which took the initiative to meet with the exiled ANC leadership and begin a protracted process of negotiations, which culminated in the watershed 1994 elections. It was instead Harry Oppenheimer and his most senior leadership in the Anglo American Corporation (AAC), especially Gordon Waddell, who initiated these reconciliatory and settlement talks with the ANC in 1985. I return to a critically important period, between 1985 and the 2 February 1990 release from prison of Mandela, in chapter 5 in order to demonstrate that the NP had the same capacity and willingness as the British to reform its system of rule when circumstances made it imperative in order to preserve an economic order which was bound hand and foot to racism since the days of the old Cape Colony. There took place a liberal change of heart and mind when the social and political crisis engulfed the NP and SA in the 1970s and 1980s and seriously threatened white monopoly capital (WMC), led by the Anglo American Corporation.

Furthermore, and very importantly, it appeared that major interests abroad, including relatively conservative forces, such as the Republican Party in the US, also wanted 'change' and had already instituted sanctions against SA, making the 'writing on the wall' abundantly clear for the NP. It was only a question of preparing and waiting for the most propitious moment to make a decisive political shift towards a 'non-racial democracy', with built-in constitutional guarantees, both economically and politically. The release of Mandela best symbolised such a shift, seismic but only in the broadest democratic political terms: it posed no major threat to the hegemonic domination of capitalism in general and

WMC in particular. In fact, it served, as purportedly 'post'-apartheid SA has conclusively shown, to secure and stabilise and reimpose its domination of the economy.

And given that SA was the powerhouse of production in the whole of southern Africa and critically important for global capitalism, due to the treasure-house of strategic minerals it possessed, both the NP and the leaders of Britain, the US and other important Western countries reached agreement on the necessity of significant political changes. But this was necessary, not to change the economic system fundamentally, but essentially to retain it under different political conditions, in which liberal democratic rights would prevail, legally and constitutionally, but under the firm white ownership and control of the capitalist economy. That is essentially how Britain dealt with chronic political problems, unrest and instability in its colonies in the mid-20th century, as it began to realise that it would be much better for long-term economic stability that its colonies were granted formal political independence.

I repeat again, only because it is of the greatest political significance to this work, that British imperialism was the most sophisticated and advanced of all the colonial powers: it set out to grant the colonies political independence and thereby transfer the costs of running the country to the pro-independence liberation movements who came to power, and in formal terms free themselves – so they thought – from all the hatred colonialism had fostered among the African people. But most important of all their strategic interests was the retention of capitalism in the post-colonial governments, which is economically and systemically the essential feature of all forms of neo-colonialism in Africa and in fact the entire 'Third World'.

That was the genius of British colonialism, but the socioeconomic crisis which is so grossly evident today has seriously undermined political independence, just as the stability and feasibility of our 'non-racial democracy' in SA have been seriously undermined by the capitalist crisis and the stark lack of social justice since 1994. However, it is much worse today than it was in earlier decades with African 'independence', with unprecedented levels of poverty, unemployment and related social miseries. But it is crucial to understand that the essence of neo-colonialism was a very strategic adaptive political smartness calculated to retain economic power and control. The heart of this strategy was to disconnect formal political independence from the political economy and exploitative capitalist framework in which colonialism was enveloped and embedded for decades. But as we have seen, that systemic lopsidedness cannot be sustained over the medium to longer term without threatening to dislodge the entire economic system upon which neo-colonialism was crafted.

The same argument can be mounted about what happened in SA after the release of Mandela and the ANC taking office in 1994. Today we have a multifaceted but especially deep socioeconomic and political crisis. I will show that the political crisis engulfing the ruling ANC today is to a large extent the inevitable consequence of the economic, social and public policies it chose after taking office in 1994, which have left the majority of the black masses in worse poverty, unemployment and socio-class inequalities than under apartheid, especially in the wake of the widespread destruction wrought by Covid-19.

However, the neo-colonialism which followed independence in Africa involved both economic and political control of these 'independent' states. The only way in which the colonisers could retain economic control was through the political manipulation of these 'states', which were often little more than satellite states of these imperial powers, especially Britain, following independence. In *The Black Man's Burden: Africa and the Curse of the Nation State*,[2] Basil Davidson explored the many ways in which neo-colonialism, after independence, prevented the development of the economies, including even the growth of an African capitalist class, as in Ghana, and how utterly ruthless the former colonial masters were in this regard, notwithstanding their purported independence, their newfound democratic status and, most of all, the severe underdevelopment by colonialism-imperialism those economies suffered over long periods, which was perpetuated by neo-colonialism.

The key point in this decolonisation drive in Africa, and later the active support of the Western countries for the abolition of apartheid, was that capitalism, as a system, not only did not need institutional and legalised racism, but that its existence was endangered where it mattered most in the final analysis: the availability and supply of cheap labour to drive its accumulation regimes in these colonies. If that critical and indispensable requirement could be depoliticised by being deracialised and African people granted democratic and civil liberties, the perpetuation of capitalism over the longer term would be much better assured. This is what basically happened in SA, between 1990 and 1993, when the negotiated settlement was being hammered out.

But given the power and popularity then of the ANC and the hugely strategic importance of SA for global capitalism, the party was given more political leeway than the newly independent states in the rest of Africa decades earlier. This was also due to the fact that the NP in particular, and imperialism in general, could rely on the ANC to sustain the capitalist economic order, as this was a key and critical requirement of the negotiated settlement. Those economic interests were embodied in the 1996 constitution, embracing the right to private property, which is nothing less than a vote of confidence in and protection of the capitalist system in SA. However, most writers and thinkers on these matters have not shown why the ANC was also wedded to the capitalist system during the negotiations: it is only within that same system that space could be created for those aspiring to an upper black middle-class and bourgeois existence in post-apartheid SA. That, however, was both a blessing and a curse for them, as can be seen by the fact that SA is statistically the protest capital of the world and ANC rule has become extremely unstable and indeed unpredictable over the past decade.

Ours is a complex, intriguing and contradictory country. It was the current president of SA, Cyril Ramaphosa, who, representing the ANC, negotiated the content of the constitution. That the key and critical private property clause was included in the constitution, which was what the NP wanted, was perhaps also due to the close relationship he has had for many years with the white economic elite, especially with the AAC and its inner circles, which started already in 1978, when he was placed on the board of the Urban Foundation. The UF was started by Harry Oppenheimer himself, in 1977, a year after the 1976 student uprisings. It was specifically meant to build a black middle class and tiny elite with which to try to stabilise the country, but most of all to prevent any serious disruptions to the profitable functioning of the capitalist order. It was therefore only a matter of course that it was the AAC which initiated talks with the ANC in 1985, when it organised a group of white liberal business leaders, politicians and others to go and meet and have 'talks' with the ANC in Lusaka, Zambia, much to the chagrin of the ruling NP.

However, as with the neo-colonial regimes in the rest of Africa which followed independence and which were premised on liberal democracies, the post-apartheid state has been very unstable in office, especially over the past decade of ANC rule. Unstable because, as elsewhere in Africa, it proved very difficult, if not impossible, to deracialise and democratise politics and society at large without restructuring the capitalist economy, which was systematically intertwined with the historical denial of those political and constitutional rights. Here lies the gist of the very deep socioeconomic and political crisis and conundrum facing the ANC today.

The most intelligent of the imperialist ruling classes of Europe were the British, who in fact shaped SA in their imperialist interests more than did the white Afrikaner political parties, including the NP. Of the former colonial powers, the whole thrust towards political decolonisation was led by Britain, when in 1957 it granted Ghana its independence and all other British colonies followed suit. And the entire discourse of neo-colonialism that followed was based on the numerous pitfalls of such political 'independence'. But even such 'independence' was a dangerous myth, because the heart of neo-colonialism was the truth that though nominally independent, these states were dominated and controlled by local political elites, largely in the interests, especially economically, of the former colonial masters. Frantz Fanon best articulates the phenomenon of neo-colonialism in Africa.[3]

The reason why the British ruling classes had the power and acquired the intelligence to hold sway for such a long period of time, stretching across the globe, and prevent successful revolutions against such rule there or at home, has to do with the accumulated knowledge it gained over several centuries of slavery and colonialism. The British have excelled not only at divide-and-rule policies and tactics, better than any other colonial power, but in maintaining their rule through a wide variety of reforms, to stave off and compromise revolutionary struggles, and there is absolutely no doubt that they have been extremely successful at it since the late 19th century. This is what comes through very clearly in how they ruled in SA, though faced with many daunting challenges and contradictions at various stages, until that strategy ended after the Anglo-Boer War, except for the retention of the qualified franchise for blacks in the Cape, which ended in 1936 for Africans and in 1956 for Coloureds, under NP rule.

But how Britain ultimately responded to both slavery and colonialism is most instructive about the relationship between racism and capitalism and the way the British ruled and managed SA, especially in opposition to Afrikaner nationalism and its more overt racist oppression and exploitation of black people. I argue that the liberal constitutional democracy – in the form of the 1994 elections and the 1996 constitution – is in fact basically similar to what the British liberals wanted much earlier.

However, it must be stated clearly that much of this book is a comprehensive analysis and critique of African nationalism, as presented by the ANC. While it begins in chapter 4, by reflecting on its birth in 1912, I return to this theme to a greater or lesser extent in all the remaining chapters, which is a measure of how important a factor it has been in terms of what happened in this country both before and after 1994. I analyse all the major problems the ANC encountered since it took office in 1994, especially those that occurred under the presidency of Jacob Zuma, between 2009 and early 2018, such as the Marikana massacre, the Nkandla scandal, the #FeesMustFall student movement and the Esidimeni tragedy, in which many African mental patients died as a result of blatant and criminal negligence by the Gauteng Department of Health. I explain at length why I attribute those unfortunate and revealing developments to the petit bourgeois African nationalism of the ANC, its consistently middle-class leadership, the policies it held since its birth in 1912 and especially the policies it chose or was compelled to choose after winning the 1994 elections. There are various linkages here which are shown in chapters 7 and 8.

It is important to see that the ANC not only failed to adopt policies which reflected the interests and needs of its historically chief constituency, the black working class, both before and especially after 1994, but failed even to implement its own stated tasks of the National Democratic Revolution (NDR), which, it had articulated extensively during the 1960s, 1970s and 1980s, when it won state power in 1994. I demonstrate at length in this work that the ANC moved in the opposite direction, betraying the most basic needs, wishes and aspirations of the poor black masses, the overwhelming majority of whom loyally supported it for decades. So glaring and palpable was this betrayal and disappointment that I have penned many columns and articles on it since 1999, some of which I cite.

An analytical review of race and racism in both social and mainstream media left me absolutely in no doubt about the very poor and ill-informed understanding of race and racism, by both white and black people. However, once again demographic factors showed that Africans were in this regard more prominent, often appearing with appalling ignorance and confusion about matters of race and racism, especially on social media. Most of this I attribute to the centuries-long denial of basic democratic rights, and the exposure to very inferior education, especially in the form of Bantu education between the 1950s and 1994. While race and racism appear to spontaneously release great and often pent-up emotions, due to a very long history of every imaginable form of hideous racism in SA, to properly understand what are in fact very complex matters, which can be engaged with at various levels of abstraction and complexity, serious study is required.

Therefore, the single most important lesson of this study is that the furthest thing from the real truth about race and racism discourses is to approach it with a white–black dichotomous binary in mind, especially as regards what has happened in SA and to black people after 1994 under ANC rule. The historical black–white dichotomous racial divide has been replaced since shortly after Mandela's release in 1990 by a very complex, fluid, ambiguous, contradictory and revealing race-class-gender greyness that has politically reconfigured SA, but still under capitalist hegemony. Those changes were necessary for the survival of capitalism in SA after 1994. They make absolutely no sense and purpose outside of this strategy, which WMC began pursuing as early as 1977, with the formation of the Urban Foundation, following the 1976 black student uprisings.

More importantly, in this regard, is the total fallacy, peddled arrogantly by many in the black middle and upper classes, in all forms of the media, but especially print, that black people (meaning African really) have some ontological prerogative to pronounce on matters of race and racism, that they collectively constitute a repository in fact, while other people, such as white and Coloured and Indian people, in that racial pecking order, decidedly do not. Nowhere more crassly have I seen this unscientific falsehood peddled with regularity, by crude implication, than on social media, which was one of the main reasons why I withdrew from it, especially Facebook. For example, my study made it abundantly clear, somewhat ironically many might argue, that 'whites' were among the best theoreticians, scholars and writers on race and racism. There is arguably nothing that more powerfully demonstrates the fallacy of approaching race, racism and the related factors of class and gender from a dichotomous and racialist white–black approach.

These are not sentimental facts. They are, I argue, an inevitable expression of the centuries-old fact that race and epistemology are very strongly and causally linked. You can see this in every single academic discipline and all areas of scientific and especially technological inquiry and discovery over centuries. However, this study will show that it was in fact the accumulated profits, from the times of racist slavery, colonialism, neo-colonialism and global imperialism, which continues to this day, that laid the material basis for these developments in all the fields of scientific inquiry and discovery, led by white or European scientists and scholars. This means that over several centuries white people have for those reasons utterly dominated every conceivable area of the modern economy and society. This includes every societal sphere, including the arts, which is what the overwhelming domination of the economy by capitalism inevitably leads to, whether we talk about SA, Britain, France or the USA.

But the vast masses of people simply don't have the time, inclination or the means in many ways to conduct such studies. That is why what the leaders in various constituencies know and understand about race and racism is so very important and what they in turn tell their members and supporters. I will show, again with irrefutable evidence, how the ANC leadership and emergent black bourgeoisie and middle class consciously utilised race and colour after 1994 to advance themselves and their class interests, either in politics or the corporate world, at the same time that their policies left the black masses empty-handed, weakened and betrayed as electoral promises were repeatedly broken after 1994.

I demonstrate that there is an interesting connection between knowledge about race and racism and race itself, as there is generally in this country and wider world between epistemology and race, in every academic discipline and every field of scientific inquiry and production. I embarked on this book saying that the last thing I would do is to play along with any notion of 'political correctness', especially as it applies to the ANC and its policies and actions, both before and especially after 1994. I expose many myths and outright fallacies of the ANC and African nationalism since its origins in 1912. I intend to demonstrate that in fact the African leadership of the ANC, from its inception in 1912, and as a result of these same factors at play, seriously lacked the knowledge and understanding of the nature of South African society, especially after the 19th-century mineral revolution. That is why they had an almost exclusive focus on race and racism and very little on very important sociological and political issues, like class and gender, especially since race always intersects with the latter in our history. It is indeed time for new confrontations.

The multifaceted, very deep and serious social crisis we are in right now, of which the biggest victims are that same constituency the ANC claimed was the 'motor force of the revolution', the black working class, has been nakedly betrayed by it over and over since 1994. I will provide much evidence of such betrayals, including of the poorest African people, by the ANC and its leaders. The media have been saturated with such reports over the past decade, but often without the knowledge to conduct a critical analysis which explores its roots, including the corruption that has been oozing out of the pores of the ANC with such stunning regularity over the past few years. To such an extent has corruption occurred that we have become almost desensitised to it, as is the case with the untrammelled violence that has been exploding all around the country, with which it is to a large extent causally linked. It is as well easily arguable that the stark lack of social justice and worsening poverty, unemployment and social inequalities are causally linked to the neoliberal policy trajectory the ANC moved onto after 1994.

So palpably deep is the current socioeconomic and political crisis that I believe we are at the most important crossroads ever in post-apartheid SA. The conjuncture we currently inhabit is starkly worrying. What we do and which way we turn is going to have consequences for many years ahead, especially with the onset of Covid-19. I am not particularly optimistic about our future. I provide startling evidence of how ANC rule has taken this country so far backwards from 1994, and much more starkly over the past decade, that there are not many grounds for an optimistic outlook. I also confront the convenient, almost pathologic tendency of the ANC to attribute numerous failures and disappointment to the consequences of the apartheid era.

At its heart this work seeks to demonstrate that the serious social crisis we have today in SA can be traced back to the fundamentally false understanding and analysis of our society and its history by the ANC, from the time of the Cape Colony and especially since the mineral revolution of the 19th century. It is because of such a fundamentally false or mistaken understanding and analysis of our society and history that there are serious problems and limitations not only in the realm of analysis but more importantly how that informed the programmatic deficiencies in all the major documents the ANC produced, either on its own or jointly with other organisations, such as African Claims (1943), the Freedom Charter (1955), the Reconstruction & Development Programme (1993) and the South African Constitution (1996).

But it is at a theoretical level that the failure to both know and understand the kind of capitalist society already existed by the time of the Anglo-Boer War of 1899-1902, which is captured best in the critique of colonialism of a special type (CST), which originated in the Stalinist Third International or Communist International (Comintern) 1928 conference, under the theme of the Colonial Revolutions. As further discussed in chapters 3 and 4, the Comintern, out of a combination of ignorance of SA and the counterrevolutionary role it began to play from the mid-1920s onwards, after the death of Lenin and under the leadership of Joseph Stalin, made this false theory plausible to both the ANC and especially the South African Communist Party (SACP), with which it is most associated.

However, I do state in the conclusion what I think are the things we would need to urgently address in order to give sustainable hope for the future, without which I predict we are going to descend into a very uncertain and chaotic future, in which unresolved and combustible race-related issues, especially those which intersect with resources and social justice narratives, will feature prominently. What forms that will take is very uncertain, but what is not uncertain is that our collective future is going to be seriously compromised and imperilled as a result, unless we urgently address the root causes of the crisis. With the impending floodgates of the Fourth Industrial Revolution (4IR) opening upon SA, that future will in fact be far more imperilled, especially for black workers and youth, who already are in the doldrums of massive unemployment, poverty and related social miseries. Not just for SA, but for the entire world, especially the 'Third World', that future, to be frank, looks bleak, unless our leaders do what Angela Davis said many years ago: 'To be radical means to seize things by their roots.'

My earnest aim is to provide an understanding of what has really happened in SA, both before and after 1994. I explore the major historical developments since the days of the old Cape Colony up to 1994, when we had our first-ever democratic and non-racial elections. It is a remarkable and revealing fact that since 1652, when Jan van Riebeeck first arrived at Table Bay, up until the 1994 elections, black people in SA were not only largely denied the right to vote but also subjected to an avalanche of overtly racist legislation which controlled every single aspect of their lives. There is indeed no other country in the world where black people were so totally dominated, oppressed, controlled and exploited. Except for the qualified franchise in the Cape, until it was abolished in 1936 for Africans and for Coloureds in 1956, that was the situation of black people in SA.

Afrikaner history has always fascinated me, to the extent that I did some research on Van Riebeeck and the men who docked with him at Table Bay in April 1652, where they came from and what Dutch society was like in those years. Were they already racists when they arrived or did they become so after their arrival? Was there racism in Dutch society and other European countries at that time, before the contact they made with the Khoi and San? Did the fact that Spain, which had for long colonised Holland, influence the latter in its own later colonisation of many countries, including SA? I deal with these issues in chapters 1 and 3. Though it is Portugal which first made contact with the indigenous Khoi and San peoples, it appears that they probably learnt much about 'race' and colour from their Spanish neighbours.

Finally, the deeper I went into the study the more fascinated I became with the colonial history of SA, but also with the historical and global origins of race and the state of Dutch society before Van Riebeeck arrived in the Cape in 1652. There are ideological and discursive links over centuries from the early emergence of race and racism in antiquity, to early modern Europe, and also – interestingly, intriguingly and somewhat ironically – in India. Those links not only fascinated me but demonstrated beyond the slightest doubt that the race and racism discourses that have exploded in SA over the past few years have sorely but understandably lacked the knowledge of just how complex, complicated, ambiguous and contradictory race and racism phenomena are in fact, and that the woeful ignorance and confusion on social media left much to be desired.

Chapter outline

In **chapter 1**, I review and reflect on the historical origins and development of race and racism in the wider world, long before the Dutch colonised the Cape in 1652. I trace the origins of the notion of 'race' – especially from the 16th century on – out of which discursively and politically grew racialisation discourses and later the powerful system of racism, which, more often than not, lived cheek by jowl with capitalist exploitation of black labour in all the colonies, especially those of Portugal, Spain, Holland and Britain.

I must acknowledge the stress which the historian Timothy Keegan in an interview placed on the key importance of a historical understanding in any study of race and racism. He lamented the serious lack of historical knowledge in SA on matters of race and racism, and more generally. He kept on repeating during an interview that 'we don't know our history.' Having written one of the best works on the origins of race and racism in SA, dating back to the time of the Cape Colony, I paid serious attention to what he had to say in this regard.[4]

There is an abundant literature which I briefly draw on in **chapter 2** which critically explores the ontological, discursive, ideological and political origins of race and racism. In a country where my own study convinced me that people generally know little about race and racism, even in the most heated debates, beginning this work against the background of that ontological history was absolutely necessary, with the result that I spent a lot of time in my research on race and racism in antiquity and its emergence and re-emergence over the past five centuries, in one form or another. Such strong connections between race and racism in SA and that global history of race and racism exist, in so many ways, that I realised that I could not write this book without devoting significant time and space to it.

The chapter therefore focuses on theory, including the origins of the very notion of 'race', racialism and racism (and, though related, the important differences between the two); the immense complexities in all these themes and how they (particularly in relation to class and gender) articulate with one another. This indicates the need for much greater knowledge and caution in how we approach relevant discussions and debates. I also show that scientifically speaking race and racism, and especially the race–class or racism–capitalism nexus, is very far from the simple white-and-black dichotomous approach, which is so rampant in SA, especially on social media. A cursory glance at social media often reflects an overwhelmingly primitive understanding of race and racism.

But perhaps most importantly, I show in this chapter why a knowledge and understanding of our history, which the ANC seriously lacked, is so crucial. In fact, we are in many ways reliving our history, because the ANC failed spectacularly not only to know and understand it, but as a result have been utterly unable to draw lessons from it. There exists nothing in the abundant literature over the past century where the ANC concedes such a lack of knowledge and understanding and acknowledges its mistaken analysis of South African history and society.

On the other hand, it could be persuasively argued that such an approach is mistaken, and that the ANC knows very well our history, but that its petit bourgeois and reformist nature, since its inception, outweighed the anti-capitalist interests and policies which flowed logically from such a history. And from that point of view in the present SA we are reliving our history, and are captive to its racist-capitalist trajectory, instead of having used that same history to seriously transform the capitalist economy and thereby gain the capacity and required resources to fundamentally change the lives of the black working-class majority, a task that has been sorely neglected in post-apartheid SA, for which the ANC must directly take responsibility. That we have become the protest capital of the world is itself testimony to such failures by the ANC.

Like Keegan with his stress on the importance of history in a study of race and racism, so too Crain Soudien emphasised from a different but closely related field of study the key importance of theory in any study of race and racism. He also lamented the lack of theoretical knowledge in SA on these issues, especially in how race and racism intersect with class and gender. As in the case of Keegan, I completely agreed with Soudien, in terms of my own research and writings on these topics over the years. I delve into the reasons for this abysmal lack of both historical and theoretical knowledge of race and racism in chapters 3 and 4.

I argue that we have reached the stage, in the current very deep crisis in SA, where it is now abundantly clear that any attempt to reform or eradicate racism or extricate it from the capitalist system in SA, where it has existed for centuries in one form or another, is completely impossible. Reformist attempts to deal with the racist apartheid legacy, especially in its socioeconomic ramifications, are bound to repeatedly fail. This raises serious problems in theoretical and political terms about the future of SA. I argue at length that only an anti-capitalist and necessarily socialist approach to the ongoing institutional and social legacy of racism can succeed in eradicating this scourge by its systemic roots. Only such a radical approach will be able finally to secure a future free of the terrible poverty, joblessness, myriad social justices and the deepening class inequalities.

In **chapter 3**, having laid an essential basis in chapters 1 and 2, I critically explore the race, class and gender dimensions of South African history. I show how race and racism were woven into economic development and exploitation from the earliest days of the Cape Colony, and that the stress by some writers on religion and class, and far less on race, is somewhat overplayed, perhaps for ideological and political reasons. However, and whichever way that tension is played out, how the mineral revolution not only altered fundamentally the future of SA, but also overtook those discursive and ideological tensions about the formative period of the Cape Colony.

In this chapter I critically explore the ANC's history as regards its approach to and understanding of gender, especially as it relates to race and class. Going back to its origins in 1912, this study reflects some intriguing, contradictory and revealing aspects about the ANC and gender. If it was validly accused of neglecting the specific interests and aspirations of the black working class over the years, of which African women are the majority, then aside from its populist rhetoric in this regard, its record is much worse in fact regarding black gender issues. I also explore the ANC's treatment of African female members and comrades during the exile years.

Chapter 4 focuses on a critical analysis of the origins of the ANC in 1912, the politics and ideology of its membership, and on a brief history of its performance since the 1940s, when it shifted to a more radical orientation, which began with the programme of the ANCYL in 1949. I dwell on how the ANC understood and conceptualised the oppressed and exploited peoples of SA and how it approached and prosecuted the liberation struggle in SA, in relation to the major issues of race, racism, class, gender and capitalism. I examine their theoretical and political outlooks, their analytical perspectives, their programmes, and their achievements or lack thereof from 1912 until they won the 1994 election and took office.

Chapter 5 provides a critical review of the release from prison of Nelson Mandela in 1990 and the subsequent negotiations in which he led the ANC; it interrogates the nature of the settlement reached in 1993 and the subsequent economic, social and public policies the ANC adopted after 1994. It assesses and analyses the legacy of the Mandela era and shows that, contrary to the conventional populist wisdom about Mandela and that era, our current social crisis has its roots in that period and the unpalatable compromises he and the ANC made, which seriously compromised the most basic needs and interests of the vast majority of black people. At the same time Mandela and the ANC paved the way, through BEE and AA, for the growth of a sizeable black middle class and tiny elite, ever more distant from the vast impoverished black majority, who 25 years later are still struggling for the fulfilment of the most basic needs and rights.[5]

This chapter also deals with the 1994 elections, the Coloured Question and related aspects of culture vis-à-vis ANC rule, African nationalism and specifically the growth of an Africanist majoritarian chauvinism in post-apartheid SA. I assess the lead-up to the 1994 elections and the conquest of state power by the ANC. Note that the ANC took 'office' in 1994 and did not really win power to do with it as it saw fit in order to deal with the enormous and devastating apartheid socioeconomic legacy. But it could be argued that that was not the goal of the ANC, in terms of its agreement with the SACP's two-stage theory of revolution, in which only in the second undefined stage would questions of economic and social justice and the struggle against capitalism begin. But the ANC, through the sheer weight of demography, in terms of which Africans were the overwhelming majority of the population, won the 1994 watershed elections and secured important liberal democratic rights for all black people, who had been denied these before.

But as a result of that programmatic approach which artificially drew a distinction between the struggles for a non-racial or anti-racist political democracy from control of the economy and its resources, the ANC from the outset lacked the economic power after 1994 to carry through the fundamental transformation of the capitalist economy. To do so was essential in order to give full effect to the absolutely necessary social justice and arguably socialist order, without which even the most basic daily needs would remain unfulfilled. I conduct a critical analysis of the policies the ANC started adopting soon after it came to office, which continued unabated over the next decade along distinctly neoliberal lines. I also explore the negative impacts those policies had, and continue to have, on the black working-class majority, which was the historical support base of the ANC since the 1950s. This chapter provides a solid enough basis for the critical analysis of major developments in post-apartheid SA in the last two chapters, 7 and 8.

In **chapter 6,** I attempt to place the National Question (NQ) in perspective, from specific angles, namely the ANC's 'blacks in general and Africans in particular' narrative, non-racialism after 1994 and a particular intervention by Dali Mpofu when the EFF in parliament was involved in a race debacle in parliament, when they attacked Ismail Momoniat, the deputy director-general in the finance ministry. I chose these specific foci because they best illustrate the pitfalls of the African nationalism of both the ANC and the EFF. I unreservedly believe that the EFF itself, a breakaway product of the ANC, is just another but more radical version of African nationalism. I demonstrate why this is the case and how this has manifested itself since the EFF's birth in 2014.[6]

I also briefly return to the ANC's 'Four-Nation Thesis' of the 1950s and 1960s, which basically persisted into the post-apartheid period; I criticise the ANC's African nationalism and its understanding of 'non-racialism'; I assess the NQ in relation to questions of economic power and control and social justice after 1994; I briefly assess the race–class nexus in relation to the NQ and show the serious pitfalls in the ANC's conceptualisation of the NQ. I also critically review the ANC's attitude towards and relationship with traditional leaders after 1994.

In **chapter 7,** I turn to arguably the most contentious and controversial events – which in many ways most severely indicted the ANC since it took office – namely the catastrophic HIV/Aids crisis under the Mbeki regime, the 2012 Marikana massacre, the Nkandla scandal, the 2015 student uprisings, the 2016 Esidimeni health crisis, and the scandalous looting of funds in the VBS saga. These dramatic and in many ways tragic developments of post-apartheid SA tell us much about the ANC's policies before and after taking office in 1994. There are historical, political, ideological and programmatic threads which link these and the other major developments to the history of the ANC earlier dealt with. But even this perspective has to reckon with the severe constraints, both internally and globally, the ANC faced after its unbanning and during the negotiations between 1990 and 1993. Any analysis of that period would have to engage with those constraints.

In **chapter 8** I also critically appraise other developments over the past decade which, as with the events in chapter 7, dramatically revealed some of the most serious limitations of post-apartheid SA and how and why in many ways we are in fact reliving our history because the ruling ANC has not learnt and imbibed the most basic facts of that history in order to shape the kind of economic, social and public policies required after 1994. It considers how the minimum wage debacle, the contentious notion of WMC, the Guptas and 'state capture', the raging Land Question, and the very worrying implications of climate change, all seem bent on worsening the lot of the black majority in post-apartheid SA. In the last regard I find it very significant that white leftist scholars either often omit race from their work on climate change or downplay its significance. I earlier very briefly offered an explanation why this is the case, not only in climate change discourses, but why they tend to play down race generally.

This chapter, titled the 'Vengeance of History?', indicates how our history is replaying itself in the present period. All those contentious and combustible events and discourses are the logical outcome of the decisions the ANC took in the first decade after 1994, and the adverse social consequences they had, and continue to have, for the majority black working class, which has had to pay a very high price for it. I end this chapter with the key and critical question: 'Whither South Africa?' The question's urgency has been intensified by the devastating consequences of the coronavirus pandemic. The full enormity of this crisis can only be grasped if we realise that it comes on the back of the already deepening crisis in global capitalism, the climate crisis and the imminent further declines in employment, wages and living standards in the wake of the 4IR. This simultaneous convergence of the worst crises of our age is a distinguishing feature of the current period in global capitalism.

On the important matter of racial terminology, I decided for purposes of historical and social specificity and continuity (undesirable as that might be) to utilise the apartheid-era population registration's racial, racialist and in fact racist framework, which the ANC government woefully continued to use after 1994 on the pretext that it was the only way in which Affirmative Action (AA) and BEE could be used to secure redress and remedy for the past injustices. In fact, it is the ANC's decision to retain this apartheid-era terminology which compelled me to do likewise, and not in the least because I subscribe to it.

I therefore refer to the demographic majority as 'African', but in instances where I am referring to all the oppressed and exploited under apartheid, which included Coloured and Indian people, I use the term 'black'. However, where I disaggregate 'black' into its constituents, and need to distinguish between them, I refer to Africans, Coloureds and Indians. I retain 'whites' as a demographic category, though in chapter 2, dealing with theory, I critically dissect both 'whiteness' and 'blackness'. In fact, I criticise all attempts to categorise race and ethnicity homogeneously, as must be done too with the categories of class and gender, especially given our history and its myriad and complex intersections of race, class and gender.

In chapter 6 I explain the grounds upon which I and many other writers totally reject the decision by the ANC to retain that framework after 1994 and show that there were feasible alternatives. I show too why it was convenient for the ANC to continue using that racialist and racist framework, including for the reason that it suited their own class aspirations, both middle class and capitalist, relying on the race-driven AA and BEE policies and legislation. Both the late Neville Alexander and Jonathan Jansen rejected the stance of the ANC in this regard and argued that there were alternative approaches for such redress, especially to secure social justice for the black working-class majority after 1994. Instead, those policies were geared to hugely expand the black middle class and create a small black capitalist class, which in fact created a buffer zone between the interests of WMC and the ANC regime and the black masses, who still yearn for the much-heralded 'better life' the ANC promised repeatedly in elections but failed as repeatedly too to deliver thereafter.

Finally, given the extensive nature of this study, which I believe was necessary, and the space limitations, my writing in all the chapters is as condensed as possible. I doubt that it will undermine the overall coherence and integrity of the work. To condense many different but often-linked themes into one book is not an easy task, but that is what I've attempted to do with this work.

Endnotes

1. So overwhelming is the historical evidence which shows systemic links between racism, apartheid and capitalism throughout SA, especially after the 19th-century mineral revolution, that there are many scholarly works to refer to. But for my purposes I regard the following as among the best: Darcy du Toit, *Capital and Labour in South Africa: Class Struggles in the 1970s* (London & Boston: Keagan Paul International, 1980); Timothy Keegan, *Colonial South Africa and the Origins of the Racial Order* (Cape Town: David Philip, 1996); Michael MacDonald, *Why Race Matters in South Africa* (Cambridge, MA & London: Harvard University Press, 2006).
2. Basil Davidson, *The Black Man's Burden: Africa and the Curse of the Nation State* (London: James Currey, 1992).
3. Fanon deals with the strategy and effects of colonialism in various works, but it is best articulated in *The Wretched of the Earth* (London: Penguin Books, 1990).
4. See Keegan, *Colonial South Africa*.
5. Having completed my MA and PhD on various aspects of the ANC's policy decisions to commercialise, corporatise and commodify basic public services in the city of Johannesburg, including the devastating effects it has had on black working-class communities in the townships, I am firmly and irreconcilably of the view that nowhere are the very negative effects of neoliberalism more nakedly evident than in these vitally important basic services. I dwell on these issues in chapter 6.
6. Several attempts to interview some EFF leaders were in vain. I received no response to my requests.

One

The historical origins of the concept of race

THE INTENTION OF THIS chapter is to provide a brief historical overview of the global origins of race and racism, and to comment on its relevance to the South African experience. The next chapter then proceeds to define the concepts of race, racialism and racism, and to provide a theoretical perspective on how race, class and gender intersect within capitalist societies.

Ancient Greece and Rome
The origins of the concept of race in antiquity, in particular in Greece and Rome, and its subsequent reworkings in early modern Europe are important to comprehend. Although space does not allow me to explore it here, it is worth noting in passing that skin colour and related caste prejudices and oppression in India were pervasive for many centuries, and persist today, although in significantly diminished forms. This is an important point to imbibe because skin colour prejudice and related racism are usually associated primarily with Europe and the West.

The ignorance of our history in SA is shared with our ignorance and lack of understanding of race and racism in the wider world, with which it is linked by many threads. That we do not treat it with the seriousness it deserves affects not only what we know and understand, but how its witting or unwitting distortions, as a result, go unchallenged in post-apartheid SA. I am certain that if the public's knowledge of the history of race and racism, both in SA and wider world, was better, social media would not so often project abysmal lack of knowledge of our history, and we could engage in public debates more constructively and meaningfully.

Some knowledge of the historical and global origins of race, racialism and racism not only allows more meaningful discussion and debates, but also very importantly allows us to begin to define them more correctly and clearly in theoretical terms, and for example to distinguish between racialism and racism, which is crucially important, I believe, not only in scholarship, but in our daily debates about these matters. These debates are also important for the understandings we have and the decisions we make and take about race and racism and especially about the race–class dynamics and the future society we want to build.

Arguably, nowhere other than in post-apartheid SA has this task been more important in our public discourses. In fact, this was one of the reasons for this book. I was struck by the utter crudity and lack of knowledge of these issues in SA, especially over the past five years, when race, racialism and racism exploded in various public areas and in various ways with an intensity never seen before in post-apartheid SA.

Knowledge of slavery and the ontology of race, skin colour and the notion of the 'other' in ancient Greece and in the Roman Empire, alongside the explicitly class issues which were already then intersecting with those matters and which simultaneously governed those twin developments, is very important for this study. This is especially important because there is no doubt at all that the very history of centuries of racialism and racism in SA, including the dire lack of education about it at all levels of whatever schooling that existed, is the primary institutional, pedagogical, structural and systemic reason for such ignorance and paltry understanding, both in historical and theoretical terms, and is starkly visible in post-apartheid SA.

In *The History of White People*, Nell Painter considers whether the notion of white people and 'race' grew out of and alongside Greek and Roman slavery. While she discusses Greek and Roman slavery, and acknowledges that there were people with light skin, their contemporaries did not regard them as 'white' nor believe that their character was related to their colour. They could not: for 'neither the idea of race nor the idea of "white" people had been invented, and people's skin color did not carry useful meaning'.[1] Instead, she maintains that the question of whites, whiteness and the notion of race only took significant shape after the decline of the Roman Empire. The ancient Greeks 'did not think in terms of race (later translators would put that word in their mouths); instead, Greeks thought of place. Africa meant Egypt and Libya. Asia meant Persia or India, Europe meant Greece and neighboring lands as far as Sicily.'[2] The 'others' in Greek history were defined as 'barbarians' or attracted prejudices towards other nationalities and peoples in other countries, and certainly not racial difference as we understand it today.

Painter traces the history of slavery as an institution, emphasising its centrality to Greek and Roman societies. She lays stress on the major shift that took place from the enslavement of predominantly 'white' people in the Middle Ages to the 16th-century Atlantic slave trade of exclusively black people. Slavery throughout the years was an institution directly and indirectly linked to material, economic and class interests.

However, there remain scholarly differences about these matters. Not everyone agrees that race or racial perceptions, based on skin colour and other phenotypical features, played no role in ancient Greek society. McCoskey has a more cautious and nuanced approach to the key historical question about whether race played a part in ancient Greek and Roman society; and if so, to what extent and how formative it was for the structuring of those societies. She argues that 'race existed as a structure for organising human differences (including by writers like Voltaire and Kant) long before particular and modern forms took hold'.[3] But did that exist at all in ancient Greece? The evidence suggests it did not. There were no structured societal, political, economic, ideological and institutional forms of *racist* discrimination, oppression and exploitation, but public perceptions of colour differences began to take shape.

However, regarding the earliest origins of the notion of race and its phenotypical characteristics, McCoskey argues that these had their roots in the Greek and later the Roman Empires. McCoskey cites the work of Audrey Diller, *Race Mixture among the Greeks before Alexander*: 'The problem begins and ends in history. For it was first raised when it began to appear that races had a history and functioned in history, and the result of that argument must in turn be applied to the interpretation of history'. However, far from regarding the case as clear-cut, Diller adds: 'All combatants in the field of race theory recognise Greece and Rome as their chief bone of contention.'[4]

In their role in the origins of race discourses, Rome appears to have exhibited stronger racial connotations. Even so, as Lloyd Thompson argued in his work, *Romans and Blacks*: 'Roman attitudes ... even at their most negative, have nothing to do with the familiar modern phenomenon of race (sic) and are of a kind very different from those commonly described by social scientists by the terms "racist", "racial prejudice", "colour prejudice" and "racism".'[5] However, McCoskey is not convinced that skin colour discrimination, which later became a key signifier of modern racism, was not manifested in antiquity. She demonstrates that ancient Greek literature and art contain many references to skin colour and other phenotypical features. 'For one, such scholarship, in unanimously arguing for the insignificance of skin colour, did not in point of fact demonstrate that the ancients did not think racially, only that they did not endorse one particular brand of racial ideology.' She then asks a most pertinent question: 'If skin colour was not the basis of racial difference in antiquity, what forms or versions of racial formation might the Greeks and Romans have actually used?'[6]

Robert Miles has a position close to McCoskey's. 'There was a definite colour symbolism within Greco-Roman culture, by which whiteness was positively evaluated and blackness negatively evaluated. But the characteristics of Africans as having a black skin and the negative evaluation of blackness did not cohere to sustain either a negative stereotype or to constitute a legitimacy of slavery.'[7]

While I later return at length to the race–class nexus in SA, for me the most relevant point of this very brief historical excavation of race is that (although not in their modern forms) skin colour identity, and its more explicit racial associations later on, were evident many centuries ago in Greek society. When it came to race and territorial expansion, McCoskey concludes that 'Whether racism was also more negligible in antiquity is a difficult question, for even if racism was not the explicit engine of Greek conquest perceptions of racial difference patently shaped Greek views of the world and their conduct within it.'[8] Overall, it seems to me that the school of thought which totally denies the existence and validity of skin colour and race, however conceived, in ancient Greece and Rome has overplayed that approach, as McCoskey suggests.

The final section of McCoskey's book, titled 'Whose History?', provides a history of how ancient racial and ethnic ideas were received and reworked in early modern Europe. The Greek concepts of *genos* and *ethnos* were recast in more recognisably modern ideas about race and skin colour. This stemmed in part from the Renaissance view of Greece and Rome as epitomes of European civilisation and culture. It meant that modern racist thought could, and did, invoke Greek and Roman precedents to justify colonisation and imperialism. The next section deals with these important developments.

Spain and Portugal

The history of SA and the beginnings of colonialism there had little or nothing to do with the Greek and Roman empires, but a great deal to do with seafaring European powers such as Portugal, Spain, Holland and Britain. In Painter's history of racial thought, she emphasises the role of trade, the voyages of discovery, and slavery in creating new dynamics in Europe:

> Trade made all the difference. Trade in people as well as spices, silk, cotton, dyestuffs, salt and increasingly sugar. First the seafaring nations Pisa, Genoa and most gloriously Venice controlled the Asian trade. After the Ottoman conquest of Constantinople in 1453, Venice again began to decline. Iberian kingdoms in the Far West fattened on trade with Africa and the newly discovered Americas. In Italy and Iberia, wealth and peoples from immense trading networks met and fornicated within a polyglot, multi-coloured and religiously diverse population.[9]

There were, in other words, powerful and compelling economic, financial and material factors in the most brutal slavery and racism the world has seen over centuries It is important to bear in mind that before the emergence and later industrial and economic dominance of northern Europe and especially England from the 17th century onwards, the Mediterranean countries of southern Europe were the centres of civilisation and culture in Europe. They were more advanced than northern Europe, economically, intellectually and scientifically; and even further advanced in those terms than any of the African countries. My analysis begins with the neighbouring Iberian powers, Spain and Portugal, where the ideological roots of race and racism first took more systematic form. Shared experiences were partly responsible for this. Firstly, during the Middle Ages, both countries were partly under Moorish rule for several centuries, and both took part in the *Reconquista* – which involved retaking territory from the Moors (originally Muslims from North Africa), and the conversion or expulsion of much of the Muslim (and Jewish) population of the Iberian peninsula. The last Moorish state fell in 1492. Heightened race awareness was initially religious in form – hostility to Jews and Muslims – but particularly in Spain developed around the concept of purity of blood, or direct descent. 'The idea of the "purity of blood" developed in Christian Spain to denote those without the "taint" of Jewish or Muslim heritage ("blood"). It was directly linked to religion and notions of legitimacy, lineage and honour, following Spain's reconquest of Moorish territory.'[10]

Secondly, in the 15th century, both Portugal and Spain emerged as pioneer seafaring powers which played an important role in the voyages of discovery; and by the 16th century both were involved in the Atlantic slave trade, transporting Africans to the Americas. The slave trade sought justification in racist notions that Africans were backward, barbaric, inferior – and unalterably 'different'. The specific form taken by initial contact with black people in Africa was the congenital origin of a bolder and more nakedly discriminatory and oppressive approach to and perception of skin colour, race and privilege.

Portugal's role in the history of South Africa is significant. Though Portugal did not colonise SA, its importance lies in the fact that it was the first European country to make contact with the indigenous Khoikhoi and San peoples. The question of whether Africa contained mineral treasures waiting to be unearthed occupied for centuries the minds of European maritime explorers. Thomas Pakenham puts this question thus: 'Were there boundless treasures in the interior or was Africa the most barren continent in the world?'[11] But indeed Africa was long the source of great treasures, in which was rooted the colonial desire to dispossess countries of their natural mineral wealth. We see later how this thinking dominated the discovery of diamonds and gold in SA in the 19th century and decisively influenced the British presence here and their plans.

Pakenham is conclusive: 'In the Middle Ages Africa had been the El Dorado, the gilded place. And not merely the gilded place of the imagination. To African wealth the great medieval city states of Europe – Genoa and Venice especially – owed much of their own. Two thirds of the world's supply of gold in the Middle Ages came from West Africa.' Turning to Portugal, Pakenham had this to say: 'To tap this West African gold was one of the principal aims of the Portuguese navigators of the 15th century.'[12]

While it may be that the ideology and politics of race, colour and racism had a more fertile soil in Spain for its seeding and growth, it was its neighbour, Portugal, that was the first European power to develop into a centre of expansionist activity in the search for wealth. Portuguese sailors and explorers first made contact with SA in the 15th century, which ultimately led, by a twist of circumstantial fate, to the Dutch settling at the Cape in 1652. The geographical location of Portugal has certainly played a big and determinate role in its seafaring explorations for centuries, more so than even its neighbour Spain. But here too the stark commercial, economic and financial interests predominated from the outset as the primary motives of these exploratory missions around the world. As with the Dutch, the insatiable search and appetite for spices and minerals drove Portugal incessantly on these voyages.

It was that same exploratory zeal of the Portuguese, clearly driven by material and financial interests, but always with a mixture of seductive Christianity, which drove them into the waters of southern Africa. As Boxer notes: 'This close association between God and Mammon formed the hallmark of the empire founded by the Portuguese in the East, and for that matter in Africa and in Brazil as well.' The anti-Islamic fervour of Portugal's King João I was used to promote not only Christianity but always commercial expansion too, ostensibly against the Islamic 'infidels'. 'There was always with all colonial forces, but especially the Portuguese, a curious mixture of commerce, colonial plunder and Christianity.'[13]

It is against that background that the Portuguese became the first circumnavigators of Africa and Bartolomeu Dias in December 1487 sailed along the Namib coast of South West Africa, visited Walvis Bay and entered the bay later known as Lüderitz Bay. In early 1488 Dias, for the first time, had sight of the African coast east of Cape Point. As Muller reported: 'for the first time, south of the equator, the coast ran in a new direction, which indicated that the "southern shore" of this African continent had finally been reached after more than seventy years, and that the passage to the India of the priest king and the glorious riches of the East was now in sight.' This was the scene of the first contact between Europeans and the native Khoikhoi, a meeting 'which was unfortunately marred by violence'.[14]

But following the death of Dias, it was Vasco da Gama who first met black people, 'probably a Tsonga tribe, north of the mouth of the Limpopo, and a half a century passed before a shipwreck on the Natal coast brought the Portuguese in contact with the Nguni people'. Five years later, in 1503, Da Gama, 'sailed, through a navigational error, into the bay that is now called Table Bay'.

Table Bay is the historic place where Jan van Riebeeck arrived on 6 April 1652. Muller makes an interesting point: 'The Cape sea from the Natal coast to Cape Point, with its unpredictable storms and dangerous currents, was as perilous ... as the indigenous population of the Cape was hostile'.[15] Hostile, because every step of the way of the brutally enforced colonisation of SA there was resistance, initially from the Khoikhoi and San peoples, and later the Bantu-speaking 'African' people.

However, it is important that the stormy dangers which explorers such as Dias and Da Gama regularly encountered be considered. Muller captures this point well: 'The land discovered by Dias and Da Gama was a nightmare to the sailor. Its storms, from Natal to Agulhas, were a constant threat to every Portuguese who fought to pass the stormy Cape. This land was merely there to by-pass, not to visit and get to know.'[16] But that was until the Dutch settlement, which soon became a colony, and subsequently a British colony. Later still, the mineral wealth of SA was discovered in the late 19th century after the brutal colonisation of SA. We shall see how Britain, the predominant presence in what is now South Africa from the early 19th century, quickly prioritised and deepened its interests in this country, after diamonds and gold were discovered. The mineral revolution, like nothing before, made SA of the greatest strategic importance to Britain.

But the significance of such immense and constant dangers the colonisers encountered must be seen in relation to what they had to and were prepared to endure in order to discover the riches they sought. In the case of SA, the minerals discovered in the 19th century and the revolution they inaugurated were to dramatically change the face and future of SA for good. But we cannot ignore or minimise those dangers, especially since in the real world of that time, as of today, the discovery of such vast mineral wealth enabled the growth and development of resources with which to change people's lives for the better. The problem, however, was that white people, across classes, were the beneficiaries ultimately of such discoveries and black people, especially miners and later other workers, were the oppressed and exploited victims of it.

As brutal as colonialism and capitalism were, they also brought about changes, some of which promoted social and economic development. The ability to distinguish between the negative and positive effects is crucially important. Black slaves built the first roads in Cape Town, as they built other important infrastructure there and elsewhere in the world of slavery. In terms of their purpose, the roads built from slave labour are not any less roads. Here again, the need to distinguish between means and ends in discourses about colonialism is important. I find that throughout all periods of history this discursive and analytical ability is of crucial importance.

It is vitally important that this situation be recognised for what it was, especially the social, cultural and developmental consequences that European hegemony had for Africa and the Third World. These are not sentimental matters but of profoundly objective importance. It is only against that historical background of European supremacy that the carving up of Africa among colonial and imperialist powers could have been possible at the Berlin Conference of 1885. It is also against that background and the hegemonic powers of global capitalism that, despite all the anti-racist and anti-imperialist revolutionary struggles, no successful socialist revolution took place in any advanced capitalist country in Europe, till today. That is incontrovertibly a formidable fact we have to contend with, no matter how the broad left attempts to answer that hard and undiluted fact.

The Dutch and Jan van Riebeeck

Though by the early 17th century England had tentative designs on southern Africa, it was the Dutch who in 1652 established the first European colonial presence in what is now South Africa. After protracted battles with Portugal for the dominance of the Indian Ocean – by the mid-17th century Holland had ended the Portuguese nation's monopoly of trade in the East Indies. But it was an accidental circumstance, when in 1647 the Dutch *Nieuw Haerlem* ship was stranded at Table Bay, that the Dutch East India Company (DEIC) began to consider establishing a refreshment station for its ships. In July 1649, following strong recommendations to that effect, a decision was taken in Holland to build such a station. But there was no intention to establish a colony. However, Muller captures the moment when Van Riebeeck was appointed commander of the mission towards the end of 1651: 'That the humble task delegated to Van Riebeeck in 1651 would lead to the birth of a nation and the development of a country with vast natural resources was something only the future would reveal.'[17]

A considerable literature has debated the extent to which the Dutch settlers in the 17th century imported racial ideas and institutions from the Netherlands. Elphick and Giliomee, in an overview, concluded that 'Like all colonizing peoples of the period, the Dutch were convinced of the superiority of their culture and religion. Cultural chauvinism was an important component of racism; even before 1652 the Dutch had developed a strong aversion to Africans.' They brought with them views of human appearances and differences. Compared with Spanish or Portuguese colonists, the Dutch (and the English) were less accepting of people of mixed ancestry; they 'stigmatized any person with the slightest trace of black ancestry'.[18]

It is important to note how advanced Dutch society was in Europe at the time and how keenly, following the dislodging of Portugal's monopoly of trade in the Indian Ocean, Holland was driven by colonialist adventures. Dutch control of the Indian Ocean trade in spices and other goods, and the colonial presence of the DEIC, enriched the Dutch so much that the following lengthy quotation is necessary:

> The trading energies in the far east and in the Americas are reflected in the growing prosperity of the towns of the United Provinces. Wealth accumulates in Holland and other provinces at an extraordinary rate during the 17th century, creating an entirely new form of society and one with great significance for later centuries. These towns of the northern Netherlands are the first middle class communities, a foretaste of what is often described as the bourgeoisie. In this respect

the United Provinces differ profoundly from another republic founded on trade. The institutions of Venice, in origin a medieval power, are aristocratic. The States General of the Netherlands, acquiring its independence in the 17th century, is no less an oligarchy than the Venetian senate. It too is the preserve of a small ruling class. But the Dutch ruling class is made up of energetic merchants with eminently practical concerns. They are pillars of their community, in Amsterdam and in many lesser towns. And they are Protestants. These characteristics profoundly affect the style of life emerging in Holland at this time. How much the Protestant ethic of Calvinism is linked with this capitalist society is a matter of debate. But a new departure is evident in many observable details.[19]

This is a very useful description of the Dutch republic in the 17th century, around the time that Van Riebeeck landed in Table Bay. Its value lies in identifying the overall capitalist economic character of these developments already apparent in the 17th century. The same source notes of the Dutch: 'In the 17th century they are by far the most urban Europeans: two thirds of them live in towns.'[20] Clearly, urbanisation has always been a key measurement of economic and industrial development of a country. Comparatively, at this same time every black person (Khoikhoi, San and Bantu-speaking people) lived in rural areas, while in Holland two-thirds of the population were already living in towns. This highlights the incomparable differences between the level of economic, social and cultural development in Europe and Africa.

It is important for my purposes to show the level of development of the Dutch settlers at that time, in comparison with the conditions they found in the Cape. If we consider, along these lines, the wider global context, then the differences between Africa and Europe are vast, multilayered and stark. That the European Renaissance, the Reformation, the British Industrial Revolution and other major scientific discoveries of the 17th and 18th centuries in Europe largely bypassed Africa on the whole is an irrefutable fact, with huge global significance, in economic, social, political, cultural, pedagogic, scientific, intellectual and developmental terms. No politics, ideology or revolutionary fervour in fact can ignore those facts and realities. They have affected many things, including why white people globally and historically have been in the forefront of various kinds of scientific, technological and theoretical advances.[21]

The Dutch not only brought with them all these differences, compared to the Khoikhoi, San and other black people who lived here, but they applied that knowledge in colonising SA, including the economic and military means at their disposal in the many conflicts which took place between them, and the distinct and obvious advantages that these gave them. Further details of the impact of Dutch colonisation on black people at the Cape are explored in chapter 2.

But the significance of these events goes much wider: it shows how capitalism as a system, even when it is vulnerably intertwined with racism, is capable of reform, in order that this exploitative and profitable economic system be maintained, no matter how devastating its results have been for the working classes of the world and in fact for the survival of humanity itself. This raises many questions about how necessary racism is to capitalism for its functioning and survival, but also how too systemic racism over centuries can, as in SA, which affected every facet of social and human life, be neatly extricated from capitalism. This study in many ways shows that it is virtually impossible for racism, especially when it has been for two centuries intertwined in great detail with capitalism, to be eliminated without transforming capitalism itself.

Did English imperialism in its lengthy battles with Afrikaner nationalists learn in the 19th and 20th centuries that it could yield much to them politically and culturally, as long as their economic dominance could be assured, not just of capitalism as a system, but Britain's dominance of it? Yes, it did, it appears from that history. The singular most important lesson that I have seen from this study is that capitalism is far more adaptable and flexible than Marxists have ever imagined it could be, as long as those reformist shifts, which might even appear to be in conflict with the logic of the system itself, do not upset the power equation upon which the system rests. A system which has been in existence for over half a millennium has learnt a great deal about the strategy and tactics and cleverness of staying in power. There is not a great deal in the literature which deals with how this system and the people who work it at various levels, in different ways and geographical spaces, learn how to remain in power, amidst all the struggles against its existence. But this is how I believe the NP equipped itself with the wherewithal to retain the capitalist system in the tumultuous transition which took place in SA in the 1990s.

That is exactly how the NP dealt with the decision to release Mandela and begin the lengthy process of negotiations in 1990. Its own rule since 1948 and the centuries-long conflict with the English taught it to not only craftily survive but to give the impression that it had fundamentally changed course in 1990 and was dedicated to building a prosperous, united and non-racial country. But that is the language too that the ANC has spoken of for decades. I return to these matters in chapter 5, where I critically interrogate and analyse the numerous pitfalls of the settlement reached between the NP and ANC in 1993.

There is a key matter which requires ventilation at this point, because it is always the elephant in the room when it concerns questions of race, civilisation, culture and human development. I earlier pointed out that in these interrelated matters, it was what happened after the British Industrial Revolution which did most to define the future of the world, not what previously happened in Africa, the East or the Mediterranean region. The critical lesson here, which is palpably evident throughout human history, is the centrality of economics, in the final analysis. It is industrialisation and economic development which have both defined and determined human culture and the civilisational sweeps which have occurred in its wake.

Herein are the enormous forces at work which forced people off the land and into industry and the new cities and which accelerated the formation of social classes. These are the indisputable and implacable trends not only of British or South African history but of world history. In fact, so powerful are these forces in shaping and reshaping the world that the history of the Khoikhoi and African people and of the ANC itself was irrevocably shaped by it. And it is to the Marxist theory of society that we owe this key understanding of how the world and history have worked and evolved, notwithstanding the poor results of this theory in the real world of the 20th and 21st centuries.

A very brief definition of civilisation, however, is necessary for this discussion. This is how Grayling defines civilisation: 'It is the condition of a people who have attained a relatively high level of development in culture, technology and organization.'[22] But this definition must be seen within the context of the prevailing conditions in society and the world at large. In this regard one reality defines that global context since the 17th century: the untrammelled dominance of capitalism. It has indeed been the greater leveller of the world and its cultures and people since then. I would assert, however, that the level of 'material culture' is even more important to consider.

This is because there is a direct relationship between capitalism and the material culture of people, expressed largely in hierarchical socio-class terms. I will later write about the impact which Dutch colonialism, in its first few decades, had on the African people in the rural areas, who were very eager to obtain the products which the Dutch imported from the Netherlands and elsewhere in Europe. This is an important point to make, which might offer a necessary understanding of the complex and contradictory impact of colonisation.

The British in South Africa

No country has shaped SA more than Britain, especially in terms of what has been the real engine of history, economic development. I have always been fascinated by the adaptive intelligence of the British ruling classes. The biggest test of any ruling class, anywhere, is its ability to stay in power. The ruling political parties might and do change from time to time, as in Britain and the US, but the capitalist system has been in the saddle for centuries after the Industrial Revolution in Britain, which had profound consequences around the world.

Although older historical works emphasised the role of Dutch settlers in creating the racial order of the Cape Colony, more recent scholarship has suggested that it was in fact the arrival of British administration and of British settlers that was crucial in embedding and extending relations of racial dominance and subjugation.[23] Keegan writes that the [British] 'ideology of racial supremacy in the industrial age sought to impose quite new forms of exploitation' so that 'the scope, intensity, the ideological underpinnings of racial hegemony changed dramatically'. Legassick and Ross agree: British rule brought 'the radically new idea that African societies should be subjugated and ruled in the interests of the colonial economy'.[24] In short, it was a distortion of the truth to cast the Afrikaners as the real racists towards black people and the British as good, liberal, progressive and non-racial. It was the British, as we shall see later in chapter 23, who enacted some of the most racist and draconian laws in SA when they were in power.

If we study those countries in which, as in SA, racism has been so intertwined with capitalism for centuries, in one form or another, there is one remarkable fact common to all of them: the economic system of capitalism still dominates those countries, with a formally and legally deracialised political and constitutional system of rule. The fact is that no country more than Britain has upheld that system for so long and so steadfastly.

Up to the present, Britain has faced no serious revolutionary threat and try as much as the Marxist left has done to organise to overthrow it for long, it still stands as a bold testimony to the resilience of the capitalist system, often swallowing up, demoralising or neutralising its opponents, from one decade to the next. It was Britain and the US which played the biggest foreign role in the ending of apartheid and the crafting of the negotiated neoliberal settlement in SA in the 1990s.[25] Britain brought into play its centuries-old knowledge of how to pursue talks with whoever was required, with the overriding objective of preventing a revolutionary overthrow or transformation of capitalism. That has always been the chief role Britain has skilfully played throughout the 20th century and all over the world, when faced with opposition to its rule.

A general history of SA made this point well about the situation in the Cape Colony soon after the British took over it:

> The British, masters at placating conquered people, moved quickly to win the confidence of their new [white] subjects: language rights and religious freedoms were guaranteed; the monetary and legal systems (Dutch) were retained; and some key Dutch officials were absorbed into the new administrative structure. But the masterstroke of this public relations exercise was a decision to abolish some of the worst aspects of trading monopoly previously enjoyed by the Dutch East India Company.[26]

It is very clear that Britain's leading role and extensive experience in colonialism globally equipped it to deal adroitly with its subjects, but always strategically directed to refashion power relations in ways which served to stabilise its rule by absorption of elements among the colonised and oppressed into the system. Every such strategy, from one country to another, was pivoted around the necessity to preserve the capitalist order.

Much of what Britain did in the 19th century in SA was a naked and irrefutable demonstration of overt racism and authoritarianism. But the most despicable hypocrisy of Britain was its flagrant contradiction of all the many solemn promises it made to black people who supported the British cause, against the Afrikaner nationalists, in the Anglo-Boer War: that if they won the war, they would grant black people political and other civil rights. This betrayal took place when Britain conceded to the white delegates at the National Convention in 1908–9 who were hostile to the extension of political rights for black people and therefore supported their exclusion (apart from those in the Cape Province who retained a qualified franchise) from the constitutional ambit of the Union of SA. But it is the role Britain played in rapidly catapulting SA into the orbit of global capitalism, after the mineral revolution, and especially the discovery of gold, which did most to shape South Africa's economy, society and history. This is expanded upon in subsequent chapters.

After 1795, and more especially after the second British occupation of the Cape in 1806, British liberalism and culture steadily descended on SA, impacting on and influencing not only the economic development of this country, but also the political ideas and thinking of the national liberation movement, including the ANC, and in fact Afrikaner nationalism itself, especially in the closing decades of the 20th century. One could argue that British parliamentary liberalism began to resonate with and find an audience among the black middle-class intelligentsia from the mid-19th century onwards, until the birth of the ANC in 1912, and even more so thereafter, right into the transition period of the 1990s, and beyond. This is explored in chapters 3 and 4.

The Necessity of a Global Perspective

Just as we cannot discuss race and racism without simultaneously discussing class and gender, we also cannot understand these issues without a knowledge of the global history which ultimately informed their existence. Everything in this world, as it is currently constituted, has a historical genealogy, be it race, racism, colour or class or gender, and all of these factors have various points of intersection, both within a country and on a more global scale.

What serves to strengthen this global and historical outlook, from the outset, are the extensive and pervasive consequences of racist slavery and colonialism and the nexus of both with class and gender throughout our history. In fact, those intersections have proven stubbornly enduring, only because our history is a reflection of how our society and world have 'worked' over the centuries. In other words, presenting this historical background becomes imperative, more so when the author is black or a person of colour who has lived in that world and knows from such experiences how it has 'worked', aside from studying it. The embeddedness of such matters within the historical structures of capitalism has over centuries since its origins penetrated every nook and cranny of our society.

It is my contention that the major developments and phases in world history – such as ancient Greek and Roman society, the European Renaissance, the Atlantic slave trade, the British Industrial Revolution, the French Revolution, and the 1885 Berlin Conference – before we even get to the history of SA, are critically important to this study. All those global and historical developments have a lot to do with the society that evolved and developed in SA after the arrival of Van Rieebeck in 1652. For example, it matters a great deal that the 'West African slave trade paid Europe substantial profits from the beginning', as much as it matters that the Portuguese were constantly motivated by the search for gold and other mineral riches by their journeys into West Africa, from the 15th century.[27] Our history in SA was made from those interests. It matters because it is through such steady primitive accumulation of wealth over centuries that European colonialism occurred and a specifically British-led global capitalist system developed from the 17th century. There is now nothing that has escaped the calculus, reach and logic of global capitalism, which was the fate of race and racism itself for centuries in this country.

The globalised shrinkage of the world over the past two decades in particular and the technological impact of the impending Fourth Industrial Revolution (4IR) will shrink the world even much more in the coming years. That is why this study begins by looking back at the history of SA and the wider world. But it is not only that this global history has shaped us, but that as a result our future cannot be conceptualised and visualised without considering that wider global history.

But why is the history of Europe very important, despite the horrific results of racism and colonialism over centuries? Western Europe in particular (despite the fact that it was in Africa, the Middle East and the

Mediterranean region where the initial stirrings of civilisation, culture and development first occurred), became the centre of the world, as a direct result of the Industrial Revolution in Britain in the 18th century.

Just as the discovery of diamonds and gold irrevocably changed SA and reduced all prior history to less importance, so can we not ignore or undermine the global significance of the European Renaissance for world history. I have serious problems with an Afrocentrism which on the one hand seeks to glorify Africa's ancient past and neglects to deal critically with it, and on the other hand chooses to ignore key developments in European history, such as the European Renaissance. Similarly, the history of Germany cannot be reduced to Hitler and fascism, horrific as it was for Europe and the world. We must objectively appraise and appropriate all the major developments in world history for humanity at large. And as powerful and stirring as race and racism narratives often were, especially the virulent kind, we cannot allow them to obscure, undermine or belittle the historic achievements of Europe. That approach has nothing in common, however, with Eurocentrism.

The fact is that the European Renaissance had a major influence on the arts, culture, ideas and politics long before the British Industrial Revolution, beginning in the 14th century. Outstanding architecture, considered the best in the world, flourished and so did public libraries, which were 'places where ideas were exchanged and where scholarship and reading were considered pleasurable and beneficial to the mind and soul'.[28] Indeed, the scientific work of Copernicus, Galileo, Francis Bacon, and so many others were of crucial significance for the world and humanity at large.

So too was the influence of great political philosophers and thinkers, such as Thomas Hobbes, John Stuart Mill, G.W.F. Hegel, Karl Marx, John Locke, Jean-Jacques Rousseau and others. In the political, social and philosophical sciences we owe a great debt to these European or 'white' thinkers. I am irreconcilably opposed to any black or African nationalism which attempts to ignore or disparage these achievements, simply because these were white men, even though it is very evident that they dominated all these areas of scientific work. Neither can the gendered bias (only white males) detract from those great achievements. Nor can the fact that many leading thinkers, such as Locke and David Hume were racists, detract from the importance of recognising the hugely positive impact which they all had in shaping and reshaping history and humanity in many important respects.[29]

On the other hand, societies in sub-Saharan Africa remained pre-literate for many centuries. As Bahn put it: 'With the possible exception of the Egyptian Nile Valley, no part of Africa saw the rise of a wholly indigenous literate civilisation.'[30] However, an important point is made about the context within which these European scientists and thinkers made history: 'Great men of the Renaissance, such as Michelangelo and Leonardo da Vinci, arose not because of innate ability but because of "prevailing cultural conditions at the time".'[31] This is an important point to bear in mind, as all the great scientific and intellectual achievements were made in Europe over several centuries.

But this valuable and often wonderful European legacy also had consequences for how we appraise colonialism in Africa or elsewhere. Colonialism is discussed at various points in the chapters that follow. Colonialism is a many-sided complexity. While Greek colonisation was on a relatively small scale, 'Ancient writers considered the Romans' systematic opening up of the western landscape their most significant contribution to ancient geographic knowledge.'[32] This is besides the varied technical developments the Romans introduced through their rule in distant lands.

It was also not just that Europe was incomparably more knowledgeable, advanced and developed than Africa, but Europeans and whites who had such a head start over black people continually increased that gap over time. People are at a huge advantage when they are knowledgeable and skilled, not only in relation to those who are not, but when that knowledge is a kind of stepping stone to ever-higher forms of knowledge acquisition. The more knowledge a person has of something, the easier it is for him or her to accumulate more knowledge about and around it. This is how I see the relative historical advancement and advantages of white people in SA or the US or Europe.

These more complex forms of knowledge are progressively attained in order to be able to grasp matters which only deep study makes possible. The study of race and racism appears to fall into this approach, which means that there are different degrees and levels of knowledge and understanding. This especially applies to the complex race–class or racism–capitalism dynamic linkages. This point must be stressed, because of its discursive and political importance. But there is another, related reason. Many people seem to have a very mundane and crudely empiricist misunderstanding of race and colour: because a black person has suffered for very long under the whip of brutal racism, she/he – it is presumed – would understand race and racism. But that is an epistemological and empiricist fallacy, discussed later in this chapter.

I argue that we cannot seriously discuss race, class, gender and development without a recognition of that history, which is in fact critically important for social transformation and emancipation. Culture in the Netherlands at the end of the 15th century was itself influenced by the Italian Renaissance through trade. Today, the centrifugal forces of economic power and the technologies it unleashes are incomparably more powerful than they were in the 15th century, affecting virtually everything in our lives. It is the magnitude of this crisis which has thrown virtually everything together in a single global maelstrom of ever-expanding proportions, absorbing all the currents of life, in all facets of society. Virtually nothing is unaffected today by this crisis.

Global capital has arguably never enjoyed as much power as it does today. Often it appears rampant, unfettered and clearly unaccountable, subjecting states in various ways to its dictates. Civil society, the trade unions and the left have failed completely to confront and transform all the institutions of global capital, such as the World Bank and International Monetary Fund. It is in fact against the background of such failures that the Fourth Industrial Revolution is unchallenged in its designs in SA, even though it will lead to much further loss of jobs in all sectors. Such is the sad situation too of the 'independent left' in SA.

An important strand of global history – of direct relevance to South Africa – was slavery. The brief historical excavation in this chapter attempts to show how deeply intertwined the history of racist slavery has been with colonialism and the global capitalist system. Two books eloquently delve into this combined history: Martin Bernal's *Black Athena* and Cedric Robinson's *Black Marxism*.[33] They knit together the systemic geographical and historical strands which convincingly show how African slavery laid the basis for colonialism and capitalist imperialism, without which the global capitalist system could not have grown to dominate the world as it does, in virtually every area of life.

The important thing about both these books, and others which also deal with similar issues, is the commonality of white capital and black labour in all the major economic and societal developments they deal with. The widespread use of African slaves in the plantations of the New World was not just a racist regime, bent on enslaving, oppressing and exploiting black people, but it had profound economic significance for the development of the global capitalist system. In the colonies it created massive profits, out of which grew the capacity for technical innovation, scientific advancement and discoveries, and economic and industrial development. It was the profits from the abundance of super-exploitable black slave labour in many parts of the world which made these developments possible.

This high rate of exploitation of slave labour galvanised the rapid development of the capitalist system across the world and laid the basis for the historical low black-wage regime of industrial capitalism in modern times, in both Europe and its colonies around the world. Until today that low black-wage regime persists, including in SA after 1994. This empirical fact attests to the centrality of labour exploitation to slave, colonial and racist regimes the world over. It also contains the rationale and in fact almost the *raison d'être* of racism historically within global capitalism. This global historical trend deepens the conviction held strongly by many scholars and activists of the importance of the race–class and racism–capitalism nexus thesis, which is virtually universal. These trends not only uphold a systemic nexus between racism and capitalism but in theoretical terms serve to reinforce its tenacious strength and explanatory power.

What has emerged in a historical analysis of the structural relationship between slavery, racism, colonialism and capitalism is an abiding and overwhelmingly systemic symbiosis in those relations, to the extent that racism and capitalism, and gender too, can no longer be seen or dealt with separately, in theoretical, practical and especially political terms. Today, in the current unprecedented global capitalist crisis, in which each of these variables finds combined and coterminous expression, we have the undisputed face of the future. Intersectional theory and analysis tried to deal with these simultaneous intersections, but its grasp is limited and fragmentary.

There is an observation which must be made about these global linkages. If you travel in any country of Europe and look at the generally

'First World' infrastructure there and related standards of living, and compare them with those that you will find in the global South, the differences hit you between the eyes. It is similar to the differences between Alexandra township and Sandton in SA, which are separated by just one kilometre. Those differences will never change in any fundamental way unless the capitalist economy and underlying social relations which produced those differences in the first place are changed.

But there is a related fact that cannot evade us: both in SA and in Europe, the fortunes wrought from slavery, colonialism and imperialism over centuries have enabled white people at large to live as well as they do, subsidised by the huge profits made historically, directly and indirectly. That status quo too will not change for many years to come, even decades, until and unless capitalism is confronted and overturned. In this regard, we must bear in mind that what lends this perspective strength is that the white working classes of Europe, and in the US, though beneficiaries of past history, are today also suffering the effects of this exploitative system.

However, because of that same history, the unity of black and white workers will be very hard to achieve. History and its embedded effects relentlessly stalk us everywhere. It is therefore scary to think how such unity might become even more elusive in the wake of the centripetal effects of the oncoming Fourth Industrial Revolution, which will probably repeat that history, resulting in even greater race–class social disparities.

To conclude this overview of the history of race, there is ample historical evidence, across the globe in fact, to validate the slavery-racism-colonialism-capitalism thesis and trajectory. But in South African history those linkages are even more stark and stubbornly persistent, even well into the purportedly post-apartheid period. This – as argued subsequently – is primarily due to the inability or unwillingness of the ANC to confront and go beyond the capitalist framework it inherited from the NP. The political settlement between the ANC and the NP, as a result of negotiations between 1990 and 1993, left the capitalist economic underpinnings of those linkages intact, which accounts for the deep structural crisis today in SA.

This brief outline of the historical background of race and racism, both globally and in SA, demonstrates McCoskey's point: 'By gaining a more firm foothold on race historically, including its roots in classical antiquity (both real and invented), I think we can begin to combat its clandestine power and also see that our modern version of race is far from inevitable or neutral, it is simply a structure of belief that has been so powerful as to convince us that it is the only possible one.'[34] I would add that this historical background also illustrates and amplifies the materialist roots of race and racism globally and therefore the need to assert its political economy or the race–class or racism–capitalism systemic links.

From the outset, I have stressed the importance of history for me, and how I wished to approach this work. John Tosh puts it well: 'The business of historians is to apply theory, to refine it, and to develop new theory, always in the light of the evidence most broadly conceived. And they do so not in pursuit of the ultimate theory or "law" which will "solve" this or that problem of explanation, but because without theory they cannot come to grips with the really significant questions in history at all.'[35] Though not a professional academic historian, I am convinced that it is in history, though not in some fatalistic, deterministic manner and not neatly that we have the probable answers to the present crisis in this country and the rest of the world.

The deeper history of the past five centuries, briefly traversed above, shows beyond doubt that Europeans/white people have totally dominated the globe for that long period. John Lukacs suggests that 'Perhaps the entire 1500–1950 period ought to be called the European Age. For many reasons; among them "Europe" replacing the Mediterranean as the main theatre of history after 1500; and then because of the discovery and the possession and colonization and settlement of much of the globe by Europe's powers and by some of their peoples after 1500.'[36]

It was Cicero who said: 'To be ignorant of what happened before you were born is to remain a child always.'[37]

Endnotes

1 Nell Irvin Painter, *The History of White People* (New York & London: W.W Norton, 2010).
2 Painter, *History of White People*, p. 5.
3 Denise E. McCoskey, *Race: Antiquity and Its Legacy* (Oxford: Oxford University Press, 2012), p. 5.
4 Diller cited in McCoskey, *Race*, p. 6.
5 Thompson cited in McCoskey, *Race*, p. 9.
6 McCoskey, *Race*, p. 10.
7 Robert Miles, *Racism* (London and New York: Routledge, 1989), p. 15.
8 McCoskey, *Race*, p. 91.

9 Painter, *History of White People*, p. 32.
10 See 'Casta', at https://en.wikipedia.org/wiki/Casta.
11 Thomas Pakenham, *The Scramble for Africa* (Johannesburg: Jonathan Ball Publishers, 1990), p. 16.
12 Pakenham, *The Scramble*, pp. 16, 17.
13 Charles R. Boxer, *Four Centuries of Portuguese Expansion* (Johannesburg: Witwatersrand University Press, 1965), cited in Cedric Robinson, *Black Marxism: The Making of the Black Radical Tradition* (London: Zed Books, 1991), p. 49.
14 Cornelius F.J. Muller, *500 Years: A History of South Africa* (Pretoria & Cape Town: Academica, 1986), pp. 2, 6.
15 Muller, *500 Years*, pp. 10–11.
16 Muller, *500 Years*, p. 12.
17 Muller, *500 Years* p. 17.
18 Richard Elphick and Hermann Giliomee, 'The origins and entrenchment of European dominance at the Cape, 1652–c.1840', in *The Shaping of South African Society, 1652–1840*, 2nd edition, ed. Richard Elphick and Hermann Giliomee (Cape Town: Maskew Miller Longman, 1989), pp. 525–6.
19 See the History of the Netherlands, at www.historyworld.net/wrldhis/PlainTextHistories.asp?groupid=3102@HISTORYID=AC908gtrack=pthc.
20 History of the Netherlands.
21 See Ebrahim Harvey and Saliem Fakir, 'Decolonise science at your peril', *Mail & Guardian*, 21–27 October 2016 for comments on scientific knowledge and South African students.
22 Anthony C. Grayling, *Ideas That Matter: A Personal Guide for the 21st Century* (London: Weidenfeld & Nicolson, 2009), p. 77.
23 See Robert Ross, *Beyond the Pale: Essays on the History of Colonial South Africa* (Johannesburg: Witwatersrand University Press, 1994); Timothy Keegan, *Colonial South Africa and the Origins of the Racial Order* (Cape Town: David Philip, 1996); Martin Legassick and Robert Ross, 'From slave economy to settler capitalism', in *The Cambridge History of South Africa*, Vol. 1, ed. Carolyn Hamilton et al (Cambridge: Cambridge University Press, 2010).
24 Keegan, *Colonial South Africa*, pp. 13–14; Legassick and Ross, 'Slave economy to settler capitalism', p. 314.
25 Sue Onslow and Martin Plaut, 'Archive documents reveal the US and UK's role in the dying days of apartheid', *The Conversation*, 18 July 2018.
26 Dougie Oakes, *Illustrated History of South Africa: The Real Story* (Cape Town: The Reader's Digest Association of South Africa, 1988), p. 94.
27 Pakenham, *The Scramble*, pp. 17, 45.
28 Wikipedia, The Renaissance, https://Wikipedia.org.wik/Renaissance.
29 Martin Bernal, *Black Athena: The Afroasiatic Roots of Classical Civilisation* (London: Vintage, 1991), p. 27. While Bernal draws attention to the explicit racism of many scientists and thinkers, he recognises the importance of their work. We cannot dilute or belittle such recognition.
30 Paul Bahn, ed., *Ancient World in a Pocket* (New York: Barnes and Noble Books, 2007), p. 63.
31 Wikipedia, 'The Renaissance'.
32 McCoskey, *Race*, p. 37.
33 See endnotes Bernal, *Black Athena*; Cedric Robinson, *Black Marxism: The Making of the Black Radical Tradition* (London: Zed Books, 1991).
34 McCoskey, *Race*, p. 201.

35 John Tosh, *The Pursuit of History* (London and New York: Longman, 1999), p. 128.
36 John Lukacs, *The Future of History* (New Haven and London: Yale University Press, 2011), p. 161.
37 Cited in Lukacs, *Future of History*, p. 78.

TWO

Race, racialism and racism: Definitions and theoretical reflections

> Theory is nothing other than correctly considered and generalised practice. Theory does not overcome practice, but rather the thoughtless, purely empirical, crude approach to it. We have every right to say 'arm yourself with theory, since in the last analysis, theory wins out.'
> (Leon Trotsky, *Problems of Everyday Life*).

Race

WHILE I AM NOT sure that theory necessarily always 'wins out in the end', it is an indispensable tool for grasping complex phenomena, such as race, racialisation, racism and especially the race-class-gender intersections within a capitalist society. However, a few preliminary remarks are necessary. I want firstly to discuss these theoretical issues more generally and thereafter proceed to discuss how these theories relate to SA.

I decided to deal first with the historical and theoretical issues of race, racialism and racism globally before dealing with them in SA, including the race–class and racism–capitalism links, because of the paucity of knowledge and understanding of these issues in our daily discourses and debate, nowhere more evident than on social media and, to a slightly lesser extent, in the mainstream media. In scholarly works the knowledge and understanding is appreciably greater, though fiercely contested.

The approach I adopt in these theoretical discussions is to move from the global origins of race to its origins in SA, revealing clear threads of connection, discursively, ideologically and politically. One can begin to see these threads of connection very early on in the founding of the Cape Colony, in the struggles over race and slavery there between the Dutch/Afrikaners and the British, the reasons for the Great Trek and, more dramatically, after the mineral revolution of the 19th century, when cheap black labour was urgently required to operate the mines profitably. As a result this section moves between the global and the local, between the Netherlands and England – the two colonial powers which shaped our history – and SA itself.

My study of race and racism, and especially how it has intersected with and impacted on class and gender, has taught me that we cannot understand race and all its complex combinations with class, gender and culture without shedding light on its origins in Europe and how slavery, colonialism and the emergence of the global capitalist system are all connected to how slavery and colonialism were practised in SA, beginning in 1652. The key to this understanding lies not in race and racism per se, but in how capitalism as a system has utilised these instruments to constantly grow and expand in the frantic search for new markets, profits and wealth. Nothing shows this more clearly than in how this system developed after slavery was abolished in 1834.

Given this country's globally notorious history of racism over centuries, in one form or another, we know a great deal about white racism. But the current post-apartheid 'race' discourse in SA is not illuminating a path towards a genuinely non-racial and anti-racist ethos, practice and future. There are certain African politicians, political activists, writers and thinkers who are deliberately, consciously and dangerously stoking the fires of a narrow Africanist majoritarian chauvinism in relation to the so-called 'minorities', including Coloured and Indian people, who have historically been an organic part of the oppressed and exploited peoples of SA. I fear that if these racialist and arguably black racist trends continue unabated, the risk of a racial conflagration in this country must not be discounted. I argue that much of this naked chauvinism is born out of ignorance and a gross misunderstanding of what racism is and what has animated struggles since the early 19th century.

In addition, such a global historical background equips one much better to grasp race and racism and the intimately and often intricately related issues of class and gender in SA. There is an inherent logic to this approach, the wisdom of which we dare not ignore, irrespective of race. We need therefore to absolutely debunk the myth that if you are black or African you are therefore endowed, as victims, with a greater understanding of race, racialism and especially systemic racism than white people, who are largely the beneficiaries and perpetrators of racism both globally and historically. While at first glance that would appear to be empirically correct and understandable, it is far from the truth theoretically.

Nothing demonstrates this truth more than the undeniable and ironic fact that the global literature on these matters is dominated by white scholars and thinkers, who are also among the best theoreticians of race, racialism, racism and their intersections with class, gender and culture. It is an indisputable fact that they dominate the academic disciplines which deal with these interrelated issues. But given the racist history we come from globally and how it severely disadvantaged black people and privileged whites, it is perfectly understandable why this is the case, even if this fact might be resented by black thinkers, especially of the narrower Africanist kind.[1]

However, the first thing to do is to define as clearly as possible the terms which are most prevalent in the relevant discourses and literature, namely race, racialism and racism. There are discursive, ideological, political and even profoundly programmatic implications in these definitions, especially in that of racism, which I argue are derived in part from how we understand the notion of race, from which both the terms racialism and racism issue. But before proceeding, one observation must be made: the definitional relationship between race, racialism and racism is complex and it becomes much more so if the identities and analytical categories of gender and class are intertwined with those.

My focus is on notions of race in England, where it subsequently catalysed the racialisation and racism which was explicit in all its colonising missions. According to Miles, the idea of race as a people or nation emerged in the English language in the early 16th century and was used initially largely to explicate history and nation formation. As it appears in historical writing the idea of race referred to those groups which collectively constituted the populations of emergent nations such as England and France. For example, in the English case the Anglo Saxons were defined as a 'race' of people [which indicated] lineage or common origin and history and not a population with fixed biological characteristics.[2]

As Miles shows, the notion of race entered the English language and consciousness in order to distinguish between population groups and nations. It referred essentially to the sense of emerging and conflicting nationalisms among what would today be regarded as 'white' people and was not based on any biological and phenotypical characteristics, which later became the hallmark of race thinking, racialism and racism. Racial ideologies shifted and mutated over time; but initially differences, division and prejudices existed among white people, long before the development of more modern forms of race and racism. The dislike of and prejudice towards the Irish people by the British were a more extreme form of such bigoted nationalism.

The key point here is that race othering and racism, especially as it has been manifested between white and black people over centuries of brutal slavery, colonialism and imperialism, are not the only forms of oppression, discrimination and exploitation. There are many other forms in which societal scourges occur, most notably virulent and discriminatory and even hateful nationalism, tribalism, class exploitation, sexism, patriarchy, misogyny and so on. A heinous and destructive form of 'othering' is the caste-based hierarchical system in India, in which skin colour discrimination is still today a stark and haunting feature. How do we characterise such a caste system, in which the oppressive and exploitative elite are nowhere near white? Is it less pernicious because the elite are also Indian, but of fairer complexion? These are only some of the thorny questions that race and racism give rise to.

Miles argues – as do many other scholars – that from a scientific standpoint the idea of distinct and separate races is a fallacious myth, an ideological construction. 'Scientific' racism initially was based on biological and phenotypical differentiation between white and black people, but later mutated instead to an emphasis on cultural differentiation. However, aside from the debate about whether the notion of race and racial prejudice existed before capitalism took root in the 17th century, the literature makes it abundantly clear that the notion of race itself has absolutely no scientific foundation and credentials.

Yet even if race is a social construct, racial consciousness and 'othering' appear to be a reality. Miles makes an important point about the earlier origins of race. He argues that 'race' did not replace earlier conceptions of the Other. 'Ideas of savagery, barbarism and civilisation both predetermined the space that the idea of "race" occupied but were then reconstituted by it.'[3] This shows once again the discursive elasticity and adaptability of 'race' and 'othering', the various forms of which are not as important as their essence, which is a kind of rationale to exclude or oppress or exploit. History teaches us therefore to pay less attention to names, racial or otherwise, than to the underlying political purposes and social relations that they serve and embody. If forms of racial consciousness were present in ancient Greece and Rome, before the advent of industrial capitalism, does that not make it more likely that it will outlive capitalism, especially since it has to varying degrees and across different historical spaces and times been inseparably intertwined with it and often arguably had an existence independent of capitalism?

The numerous outbreaks of overt racism in the former Soviet Union over the past two decades were significant indications of this possibility. The nakedly violent forms of racism across Europe, including in former 'socialist' Eastern European countries, over this same period, have only served to reinforce the deep roots of race in the psyche and consciousness of even ordinary white European people. The key question of this massive outbreak of racism in Russia and other former Eastern European 'communist' countries is this: is it possible or even probable that deep in the underbelly and recesses of the consciousness of people in those societies there was for long suppressed racist impulses, but that after the collapse of Stalinism that lid of suppression was blown open?

Such experiences reinforce the validity of the thesis that racial consciousness and racism predate capitalism. Miles is emphatic about the pre-capitalist roots of race and racism:

> The evidence ... demonstrates that racialism and racism are not

exclusive 'products' of capitalism but have origins in European societies prior to the development of the capitalist mode of production and have a history of expression within social formations dominated by the non-capitalist mode of production in articulation with the capitalist mode. In other words, it is an ideology with conditions of existence which are, at least in part, independent of the interests of the bourgeoisie, a class specific to a certain period of history.[4]

He therefore criticises 'a history of economistic analysis where there is a strong tendency to present racism as "functional" to capitalist development in general and to the bourgeois in particular'.[5]

The universal persistence of race indicates that it is so stubbornly tenacious that it will probably, through far less destructively, continue in a post-capitalist and even explicitly anti-capitalist society. It appears that this prediction is rooted in the universal and historical inextricability of race–class and racism–capitalism, embedded for so very long that even when the systems and structures which lived and relied on it die, some of the ideological, behavioural and attitudinal elements will probably survive, but bereft of the power of capitalism and the state to use race as a tool to oppress, subjugate and exploit.

But there was no uniformity across countries in the way race and racism took root and manifested in different walks of life. Race and racism, historically and globally, were never at any point in time a simple and straightforward matter – and nor was colonialism or capitalism. How these phenomena occurred and impacted on societies and reshaped them has always been complex and contradictory, consisting of both negative and positive features and consequences – positive in the sense that economic development opened up new opportunities and vistas which were not there in the pre-capitalist past. Some of the most pioneering developments in science and technology took place during the years of slavery, colonialism and capitalism and, for that matter, racist apartheid in SA.

To cite Miles again:

Like 'nations', 'races' too are imagined, in the dual sense that they have no real biological foundation and that all those included by the signification can never know each other and are imagined as communities in the sense of a common feeling of fellowship. Moreover, they are also imagined as limited in the sense that a boundary is perceived beyond which lie other 'races'. Consequently, 'the ideas of 'race' and 'nation' are therefore both supra-class and supra-gender forms of categorisation with considerable potential for articulation.[6]

This is a key consideration, because hardly anywhere in the world have race and racism, however defined, manifested on their own. They are always, to a greater or lesser degree, combined with some or other aspects of class and gender.

Crucially, racial thinking in Europe was considerably affected by the encounters in Africa, Asia and the Americas that flowed from naval and mercantile expansion from the late 15th century. Even more so, the rise of the African slave trade was partly justified in Europe by negative stereotypes of African people. The fact of this transformation in racial thought, argues Miles, 'is more important than the precise time at which it occurred'.[7] This applies to the related concepts of 'racialisation' and 'racism' – discussed below – in the sense that the exact historical precision is far less important than the meanings we attach to them and how they dynamically operate and interact with each other, especially within the wider economic structures of society.

The ideological shift to which Miles referred was that 'the idea of race took on a new meaning with the development of science and its application to the natural world and, subsequently and more narrowly, to the social world from the late 18th century'. From this time it increasingly 'came to refer to a biological type of human being and science purported to demonstrate not only the number and characteristics of each race but also a hierarchical relationship between them. Moreover, science purported to demonstrate that the biological characteristics of each "race" determined a range of psychological and social capacities of each group, by which they could be ranked.'[8]

But Miles and other white writers on race and racism don't point out that at that time science itself was already highly racialised, racialist and arguably racist by virtue of the conclusions white people drew about black people or people of colour. While today the unscientific and racist nonsense of 'scientific racism' is probably rejected by most white people in SA and the world, it is important to stress that 'scientific racism' was peddled by white scientists.

The closest Miles, who is British, comes to this point is this:

> Not only did those who formulated the idea of 'race' consider themselves to be members of a 'race' but they also identified a hierarchy of 'races' in Europe. Efforts were made in the late 19th century to identify the different 'races' of which the British population was composed, using hair, skin and eye colour and later skull measurements. Concerning Europe as a whole, various classifications were devised, the most common being a distinction between Teutonic (or Nordic), Mediterranean and Alpine 'races'.

In the USA this classification was combined with an argument that human intelligence was 'a fixed and hereditary characteristic in order to ... produce a hierarchy of acceptable and unacceptable immigrants'.[9]

It is important to my arguments that Miles draws attention to this intra-European racialisation and the problems facing immigrants of colour in the US in order to show how wide and complex were the discriminatory parameters of racial discrimination, exclusion and subordination. Such racial and especially colour discrimination does not only occur between white and black but also among white people and especially between fair and dark-skinned black people. I cannot emphasise sufficiently the importance of such exposures for race discourses and for gaining a wider, deeper and more comprehensive perspective of the problems and challenges of race and racism. Such real complexities rupture the naïve white–black binary and open us up to the challenge of expanding our intellectual and political horizons accordingly. South Africans, black and white, need a more globally informed approach to notions of race and practices of racism in SA, so as to gain the knowledge with which to combat racism more effectively, as an integral part of a fundamental transformation of our society, without which racism will not be defeated.

There are questions about whether or not one's 'race' and related class position influence one's approach to 'race' discourses. I think it certainly does, which would arguably be in line with Marxist theories of historical materialism and political economy, especially that which grapples with race and racism within capitalism in the South African context. One of the most distinct manifestations of race discourse is that white Marxists, relatively, do not write much about it. While they write much about class and how, to them, it trumps race as the primary determinant of oppression and exploitation, seldom do left-wing white academics and intellectuals devote sufficient attention to race and racism. Indeed, as Neville Adams complains, they treat race and racism as 'epiphenomena, with class analysis the theoretical axis upon which they base their work'.[10]

Indeed, their approach is largely class reductionist, even when they appear to be entertaining race at times. What is very interesting is that this critique is overwhelmingly raised by black Marxists, which is why I think that one's 'race' and its past do influence one's approach to and analysis of such matters. On the other hand, it is largely white Marxists who critique 'essentialist' approaches to race and racism, which many black Marxists are accused of, because they treat race more seriously in their analysis. How to forge a delicate balance between these two theoretical approaches is a major challenge all Marxists face. Yet, there can be little or no doubt that of the two approaches it is the anti-essentialists, who stress class as ultimately the primary causal factor, that appear to have a stronger grasp of the dynamics of the race–class nexus.

A study of post-apartheid SA will confidently confirm this hypothesis. The organ grinder of black class formation after 1994 distinctly reflects the *class* aspirations of both the black bourgeoisie and the more numerous black middle class, but through the prism of 'race', via BEE and AA. In fact, it is such class forces, unleashed by the designs of WMC, which effectively constituted both the class compromises and betrayal of the needs and aspirations of the majority black working class, which led the struggles against apartheid.

It is also very important that we pause at this moment to make this point. Any study of post-colonial countries, of neo-colonialism, of the black civil rights movement in the US and, last but not least, of our own post-apartheid period will show the promotion of black middle and capitalist classes as universally inevitable, self-perpetuating strategies of the respective powers when it became impossible, for whatever reasons, to rule in the old ways. There is a deeper point to be made here: as well as reflecting the strategies of capital and white ruling parties – whether in Britain, the US or SA – it also often, if not always, coincided with what the aspiring black middle class itself wanted, after centuries of oppression and exploitation, in which the growth of these classes (black) was deliberately prevented and frustrated.

But a set of even deeper questions beckons about the existence and life of a middle class itself, especially under those historical circumstances: should it be frowned upon and resented as something 'white' and sometimes even as betrayers of the struggles over centuries of black people, dating back to the slavery period; or is it, independent of what the intentions of the white ruling classes are, only an inevitable social consequence of life as it exists? By this I mean that it appears globally that people who have been oppressed and exploited for centuries, as is the case with black people, inevitably strive for improvements and progressive changes in their lives.

Progressive in the sense that they want to live better and more meaningful lives for themselves and their children, after the long nightmares of slavery, colonialism, apartheid and capitalist exploitation. Is there anything 'wrong' with that aspiration and is it 'right' that such a basic aspiration be frowned upon by whomever and for whatever reason? These are fundamentally important matters for black people to discuss and debate, especially since these processes of class formation cut deep into families and have often created resentment and divisions within them.

The foundational problem, however, is this: it should ideally be the right of *everybody*, especially black people emerging from such a long history, to live different, better and more meaningful lives, to an extent that it would be both naïve and unrealistic to expect that people should not strive for such middle-class improvements and changes in the conditions of their lives until all can and are able to realise them. People will not avoid possible improvements in their lives for some abstract moral reasoning. They will utilise whatever opportunities arise, even if other family members do not share those opportunities. Such are the realities of life, especially for the black working class after 1994. For members of the working class to aspire to middle-class standards is not only inevitable but progressive.

It is also very important to ask why it is that after the underlying beliefs of 'scientific racism' have been scientifically refuted and convincingly discredited, 'a number of scientists continue to this day to assert the key ideas in various forms'.[11] A long history has shown globally not only how tenaciously race and racism continue to bedevil societies, especially for black people who continue to be its victims, but that its forms fluctuate constantly. Race and racism, both in SA and globally, will continue indefinitely to plague societies for as long as the capitalist system, which has for centuries benefited from it, continues to exist. Hence, in post-apartheid SA the stubbornness with which racial thought persists is a direct and indirect reflection of the wider systemic persistence of the capitalist system, with which race and racism lived cheek by jowl for so long.

But, as indicated earlier, not even this perspective necessarily means that race and racism will be eradicated automatically in a socialist society, but at least anti-capitalist structural changes to the economy will provide a basis and an impetus from which to build an anti-racist culture over the medium to longer term. This view is especially compelling due to the fact that capitalism and racism have for so very long cohabited that, as we are seeing in SA, it is virtually impossible to extricate race and racism from the capitalist system.

There is absolutely no need for the sciences to further seek to discredit race. More than enough has been done in this regard, so much so that in his book, *The Most Dangerous Myth: The Fallacy of Race*, Ashley Montague argued: 'Based as it is on unexamined facts and unjustifiable generalisations, it were better that the term "race", being so weighed down with false meaning, be dropped altogether from the vocabulary'.[12] But Miles argues that while 'race' is patently false, it cannot and should not be dropped from vocabulary and discourse. Instead he argues for a 'scientific language that allows for the deconstruction of the idea of "race" rather than a language which reifies and thereby legitimates it', such as the liberal notion of 'race relations'.[13]

The notion of race, as discussed above, has universal applicability, which is itself a measure of the great extent to which such discourses have permeated the globe over centuries and also the extent to which intersections of race–class and racism–capitalism systems are historical and global. SA is no exception. On the contrary, there is no country in the world which had as extensive a range of explicitly racist legislation on the statute books, oppressing, controlling and exploiting every single facet of black lives, as did apartheid.

South Africa's history directly and deeply resonates with what has been presented above in relation to race. This is how Crain Soudien assesses race in SA: 'Race and its consequences are truly virtually everywhere evident in SA', and race as an idea 'is so ubiquitous ... so dangerous that we need to discard it altogether'.[14]

I agree with Miles, who argues against the urge to drop usage of the term. The same issue arose with Neville Alexander, who felt that to even use the term race is to give it undeserved credibility. But if race is strongly tied to class and capitalism, we risk not only throwing out the baby with the bathwater by abandoning the term, but also obscuring the fact of its systemic linkages to capitalism, especially in SA. McDonald, in his book, *Why Race Matters in South Africa*,[15] uses race to comprehensively explain the entire system that prevailed not only before but also after 1994. But perhaps even more importantly, until and unless the oppressive and exploitative system underlying this term is eradicated, it is very unlikely that people will stop using it and the accompanying racial and even racist terms of African, Coloured, Indian and white.

Soudien goes further to assert that race as a 'master signifier is held up and invoked explicitly and implicitly – the often ineffable elephant in the room – to explain the mundane to the mysterious'. He then provides a possible or rather probable answer to the alienation of these race-saturated scenes: 'The hegemony of racial identity has made it extremely difficult for people to imagine and build for themselves, as they do in racial terms, identities which take their points of departure from senses of self which begin in the endless list of differences which actually constitute who they are.' He also refers approvingly to Helen Zille's qualm that 'race has become a "default identity"'.[16]

While I can understand Zille's eagerness to downplay race, as a white liberal leader, I don't understand why Soudien, a black socialist, supports her: 'The point she made is an anti-essentialist one. Our identities are not essentially this or that. As much as basic sociology now routinely explains, as human beings we have multiple identities, but we simplistically, almost everywhere in the world, reduce all the complexity embodied in our multiplicity to the single factor of race. This is what essentialism means.'[17] My point is not that one can and should avoid talking about 'race'. That is an impossible hope. Instead the point is that what we say about 'race' matters more than avoiding it. That we also have 'multiple identities' is a moot point. We need to deal with 'race' in ways which illuminate the structural issues in which it has found protracted, bitter and cruel expression. Soudien is so agonised by the term and its meaning that he asks 'if it is possible to live without race'.[18]

But this is hardly surprising, given our history and the fact that we are daily living out that history, because of what our much-vaunted 'rainbow nation' and the 'miracle transition' turned out to be: a miserable compromised settlement, which is now falling apart before our eyes, in a combination of ongoing gruelling black poverty, record levels of black unemployment and unprecedented class inequalities, especially intra-racial black inequality. Given what has happened or not happened after 1994, it would be surprising if race had not become a 'default identity', especially as a result of the palpable disappointment of the black masses with ANC rule.

It is that very concern of both Zille and Soudien about the apparent obsession with race which is a reflection of how dominant it has been both in our history and especially over the past few years, which coincide with an explosive social crisis that has left the black working-class majority reeling from its multi-faceted impact. The ordinary masses are doing what they did throughout the 20th century: they had recourse to race and colour when they were dissatisfied and angry with their lot, especially since for the overwhelming majority of them their bosses are not only still white, but it is what that whiteness has materially and socially meant that is the central problem. In other words, the exploitative social relations of the colonial-apartheid era have remained intact in SA after the 1994 political transition.

Besides, there is equally no doubt that, though often militant in action, the level of class consciousness of the black working class is not and in fact has never been really high and nowhere near 'being a class for itself', to use the Marxist terminology. I think the low rates of literacy among this working class, their lack of formal education, and being weighed down by poverty and low levels of trade union and political organisation were among the major factors contributing to this problem.

Another concern about the removal of the term 'race' is what word will replace it, especially when the socioeconomic realities embodied by it remain unchanged. In fact, 'post-racial', just like 'post-colonial' and 'post-apartheid', are fundamentally problematic, if not outrightly false concepts. All are based on varying degrees of 'bourgeois democracy' granted to former colonies, while leaving intact the respective economies, which remained in the hands of the metropolitan countries or, in the case of SA, the monopoly white owners. That was in fact what led to the emergence of 'neo-colonialism', a new form of colonialism in which the former colonial powers still owned or controlled those economies in their own interests, with the assistance of a tiny local comprador bourgeoisie, processes powerfully articulated in some of the writings of Frantz Fanon.[19]

Fanon captures the role of the local elites or 'comprador bourgeoise', as he calls it:

> The national bourgeoisie ... has totally assimilated colonialist thought in its most corrupt form, takes over from the Europeans and establishes in the continent a racial philosophy which is extremely harmful for the future of Africa. By its laziness and will to imitation, it promotes the ingrafting and stiffening of racism which was characteristic of the colonial era. Thus it is by no means astonishing to hear in a country that calls itself African remarks which are neither more nor less than racist, and to observe the existence of paternalist behaviour which gives you the bitter impression that you are in Paris, Brussels and London.[20]

As with colonialism in the rest of Africa, the colonisation of SA took place within the context of the emergence of the global capitalist system and specifically the interests of first Dutch and later British imperialism. Colonisation was imperialism in action. The only way in which colonialism could be defeated and the African people liberated in ways which address the crucial factor of the economy and their daily lives was to wage one united anti-colonial, anti-capitalist and anti-imperialist struggle. But as we well know, virtually all the national liberation movements either neglected the anti-capitalist dimensions of the struggle within their programmes or compromised on them during independence talks with their former colonial powers.

However, it is abundantly clear that all the various racial, racialist and racist terminology in SA, which accumulated over a long period of time, will not be eliminated unless the social relations under which they developed are fundamentally changed, which is very clearly what has not happened after 1994. Except for the formal de-racialisation across society, significant though this is, we basically still live in the same country which developed under British colonisation after the mineral revolution of the

19th century and under white minority rule in the 20th century.

And this is precisely the problem with most of the South African literature on race, including those that approach it from a Marxist perspective. They stop short, after lengthy and often convoluted historical and theoretical analyses, of drawing the necessary political conclusion: race and the racialisation and racism which ineluctably flow from it under the concrete historical conditions of SA show conclusively that it will be absolutely impossible to resolve even the most basic needs and interests of the black working-class majority without transforming capitalism. Race, because it is ontologically wedded to class and capital, cannot be sanitised or deracialised or rehabilitated to accommodate those needs and interests within a capitalist framework.

South African history, as it really happened, cannot be changed to suit those who wish to retain capitalism without race and racism. They are going to continue to fail repeatedly in their fervent endeavours to deracialise capitalism and extricate racism from it. Too much water has flowed under the bridge of history for such attempts to succeed. It is far too late in the day for the ANC and other liberals, white and black, to succeed in this regard. Race and capital were virtually symbiotically wedded for too long to be separated now because it is convenient to do so. And that is why this country has been burning from one year to the next since the township protests that began in the Free State in June 2004.

Simply put, as a result of the neoliberal economic policies the ANC has been wedded to since it came to power in 1994 and its inherently severe budgetary constraints, it cannot afford good and decent standards of living in housing, municipal services, education and health services for the black working-class majority. I am not necessarily talking about high standards of living, like those in Denmark and Sweden, but more average standards of living, like the average black middle-class family in SA today. The ANC cannot afford this, and they know this fact very well but are unable to say it openly because it will betray the neoliberalism to which they are captive.

Indeed, it is when we explore how race shapes class that we can also see how class in turn reshapes race, in a reciprocal interaction between the two. This reciprocal interaction is a result of the fact that racism and capitalism were historically intertwined. This is exactly what happened after 1994, when the floodgates of class formation opened, which in turn divided and fragmented the black population in unprecedented ways. Intra-racial class inequalities became more acute. These shifting class dynamics have been intriguing and revealing developments in post-apartheid SA.

How the black elite and middle classes have conducted themselves in relation to the state, white business and the black working class has vindicated a Marxist critique of the 1993 settlement, which has primarily been shown to have served their interests at the expense of working-class interests and needs. Very briefly, what that political transition did was to focus on reforming race and racism (understood as removing 'apartheid' laws), while leaving virtually intact the capitalist economic structures within which race and racism were embedded from the 19th century. This has meant the stubborn persistence of race, racialisation and racism after 1994.

A separate issue concerning race discourses is that of a specific 'black tradition' in the analysis of race. The American author Henry Louis Gates edited a collection of articles on race and writing; he proposed that 'we must turn to the *black tradition* itself to develop theories of criticism indigenous to our literatures' (emphasis added). In the same collection, Tzvetan Todorov responded: 'Is this not to say that the content of a thought depends on the colour of a thinker's skin – that is, to practice the very racism one was supposed to be combatting? This can only be described as cultural apartheid: in order to analyse black literature, one must use concepts formulated by black authors.'[21]

Todorov's point certainly seems to be valid. Besides, by now the saliency and usefulness of the 'black radical tradition' need to be questioned. There is no homogeneous 'black radical tradition' and there has never been. Even in Robinson's *Black Marxism: The Making of the Black Radical Tradition*, 'black radicalism' is certainly not homogeneous.[22] The key point is that class has come eventually to cut deep into all kinds of African and black nationalisms for over a century, even the radical versions of it. Because capitalism is so powerful, varying class interests penetrate, compromise and rupture even the most revolutionary discourses, which is why I found Todorov's remark insightful and appropriate: '... it is more important to know who are the masters and who are the slaves than whose skin is light and those whose is dark.'[23]

Robinson makes an important assertion: 'I have investigated the failed efforts to render the historical being of Black peoples into a construct of historical materialism, to signify our existence as merely an opposition to capitalist organisation. We are that (because we must be) but much more.'[24] Right there might be the crux of the matter in relations between race and class or racism and capitalism. He recognises the system of capitalism as ultimately the main target of the struggles of black people, but that race and racism also exist as independent factors, alongside and within that objective recognition.

He consequently argues that race cannot always be reduced to class. For example, he claims that in 'the intensely racial order of England's industrialising era, the phenomenology of the relations of production bred no objective basis for the extrication of the universality of class from the particularism of race.'[25] Therefore, historically, discursively and politically one cannot easily separate class from race or racism from capitalism.

A thoughtful South African commentary on race and racism was written by Enver Motala: 'Today "race" is often used in discussions about reclaiming and restoring the histories, identities and rights of black people who were victims of racist laws, practices and power. It is useful because it reminds us of the processes of slavery, colonialism, exploitation and oppression, and the criminality of racist regimes.' He further explains, importantly, that 'Racism as a historical practice is deeply related to the idea of "race"' and that it 'cannot be separated from the role of corporate global capitalism in the perpetuation of racist and exploitative practices. It is these practices, and the forms of power they are associated with, that give continuity and life to racism.' Race is 'an explanation of the material reality that has arisen from the political economy of southern Africa and colonisation more generally'.[26]

Motala asserts that '"race" remains critical for understanding the history and evolution of apartheid capitalism. Indeed, it is even more useful when understood together with other categories of oppressive social relations.' But while he acknowledges the reality of the 'race' discourse, he is strongly opposed to the contemporary usage of apartheid terminology: the racialised descriptions of 'Coloured', 'Indian', 'White' and 'African'. 'Those who use these terms seem to do so without being conscious of how contentious and offensive they are... they show a complete disregard for the struggles to discredit this kind of usage in the quest for "nationhood" and unity.'[27]

However, this section on 'race' would be incomplete without briefly assessing the views and analysis of Xolela Mangcu, the BC-oriented scholar. Mangcu, like Andile Mngxitama, the leader of Black First, Land First (BFLF), lays far greater emphasis on 'race' than on class in his approach to understanding both the history of the country and post-apartheid SA. Both writers criticise Marxists, whose approach to race and racism or the race–class equation – they allege – places a disproportionate and reductionist emphasis on class at the expense of race. In the case of Mangcu, the book that really captures the serious problems of his understanding of race is one he edited, *The Colour of Our Future: Does Race Matter in Post-Apartheid South Africa?*

He makes a number of problematic statements in this work, as he has in several other of his writings about race, but this one illustrates very clearly my criticism of his arguments: 'While scientists have discredited the concept of skin colour as the basis of racial differentiation, this does not invalidate the social reality of racialised groups.'[28] This flagrant race thinking, coming from a self-proclaimed BC supporter and thinker, is abundant in his work, which makes me wonder why he titled his chapter in the book 'What moving beyond race can actually mean: towards a joint culture'. For he is, by virtue of his own words, not moving forward at all but instead stuck very much in 'race' thinking in its crudest form.

He is actually defending the existence of 'races' when he defends the 'social reality of racialised groups', without even realising it. Ironically, this statement itself reeks of racialisation and indeed racialism, as earlier defined. I don't believe there is in the relevant scholarly literature on race a more blatant example of racialised thinking. You cannot become conscious of 'racialised groups' without being conscious of 'race'. That is the inescapable conclusion because the former can only be derived from the latter. That would be the conclusion of a basic analysis of that statement.

A major concern I have is what feeds the anti-Marxist black nationalist thrust of his arguments. He selects those things in our history which speak to and echo race and black nationalism, but largely ignores the ongoing and, in many respects, deepening salience of class after 1994. Because Mangcu is mired in race consciousness and the resultant racialisation, he likes to cite scholars who draw attention to the resilience of race. For example, he cites Achille Mbembe's observation that 'race has been a powerful, if destructive force in the modern world. It has separated masters from slaves, colonisers from colonised, rulers from their subjects',[29] which he says he concurs with, without placing it in a historical, social and discursive context. Mbembe[30] is himself a barely disguised African/black nationalist, though he sometimes critiques capitalism, which Mangcu hardly ever does.

The main problem with Mangcu is that he resists seriously engaging with the voluminous literature on race–class and racism–capitalism in SA, except to take pot shots at the Marxist treatment of race. But it is not only that he ignores class. He largely ignores gender too in his work. There is nothing substantial that he has written which relates race to gender, let alone class, in SA. While purportedly being anti-racist, he in fact actively defends race thinking in this chapter and generally in his work. In his warped critique of 'non-racialism', he ends up in bed with the overtly liberal notion of 'multiracialism'! Of Chief Albert Luthuli he says:

> Luthuli is interesting for me because his idea of a 'multi-racial society in a non-racial democracy' is not far from what I am about to suggest. I accept the multiracial in his formation because it seems to me a pragmatic recognition of the racialised identities that no amount of scientific rationality, left-liberalism or Marxism can diminish. I would substitute anti-racist democracy for 'non-racial democracy'. The ideal of a 'multi-racial society in an anti-racist democracy' is, interestingly, not very different from what Biko was proposing.[31]

But this is not at all surprising because historically African and black nationalism have ultimately, in the South African context, coincided with liberalism, primarily because both have not been anti-capitalist. That is why various shades of both African/black nationalism and liberalism have cohabited comfortably in South African history.

Mangcu's writing makes clear that he is himself a black middle-class liberal, who has never ever had any strong anti-capitalist views. He is wedded to race and racialisation, as black as he supposedly is. On why he is attracted to Luthuli's multiracialism he asserts: 'I accept his multi-racial in his formulation because it seems to me a pragmatic recognition of the racialised identities that no amount of scientific rationality, left-liberalism or Marxism can diminish.'[32] He also talks of the 'racial transformation' of South Africa.³³ What can that possibly mean in this day and age? You will hardly find Mangcu seriously discussing how class and capitalism have worked together with 'race' through most of our history, including in so-called post-apartheid or post-racial SA after 1994.

He writes in very general, populist and black nationalist tones, even after 1994, whereas class divisions among black people have exploded over this period. If it is not 'blacks' or blackness he is talking about, it is abstract generalities, like the pursuit of 'common public values',³⁴ which begs definition. He also speaks in the most abstract way about whites and blacks: 'This is a call ... for black people to embrace their past without being victims of it, and for white people to acknowledge the truth of their past as the only way to healing in the present and the future.'³⁵ How useful can that be for either white or black people today? It says absolutely nothing that is of any concrete significance that one can understand, relate to and act upon, especially for the black working-class majority steeped in poverty, joblessness and worsening inequalities.

He also does not seriously engage with the abundant race–class or racism–capitalism literature. In fact he seems to avoid it, except to make ill-informed criticisms of Marxist critiques and, while there are some serious limitations in the traditional Marxist critiques of race and racism – within a wider capitalist context – he does not constructively engage with those debates. He also pays no attention to the shifts from race to class which the BC movement made after the Azanian People's Organisation (Azapo) was formed in 1978. It is as if he deliberately sidesteps that important period in the ideological development of the BC movement, ignoring it because it did not suit his black middle-class tastes to identify and analyse those real ideological and political shifts from race to class. Even if the BC movement has seriously declined after 1994, its history cannot be erased. Azapo was founded in 1978 and one of its key objectives was the creation of a 'democratic socialist republic of Azania.'³⁶

Mangcu's main mission, typical of black nationalists, is to opportunistically lean on and distort any reference to the persistence of race or colour by Marxists as evidence that race cannot be analytically ignored – which is valid – but he treats race without class as its concomitant. But there is method in what he is doing here: an emphasis on 'race' serves to bolster his brand of opportunistic black nationalism and provides justification for him to undermine class analysis, even when it is abundantly clear from the literature that race and class and therefore racism and capitalism have, especially since the 19th-century mineral revolution, been largely inseparably linked, meaning that in theoretical and analytical terms one cannot at any point in time separate them. Analysis needs to consider to what extent and with which dynamics race, class and gender interact to produce similar patterns but with differential dynamics at different times. That these combined factors have shaped South African history is beyond the slightest doubt, and the post-apartheid period has in fact deepened and consolidated those linkages inexorably.

Mangcu's work is characterised by consistent evasion of a major theoretical and philosophical discourse of race and racism, which is capitalism and its class ramifications. He is notorious for his evasion of class. He also denies that the Pan Africanist Congress (PAC) was ever 'non-racial' and insists that 'racialised group identity remained central to its political characterisation of the struggle between the coloniser and the colonised'. But what is the point of this other than a racialist utterance itself? What is he trying to prove? This is the revealing answer he himself gives to that question:

> At the heart of BC was the argument that black people's oppression was not primarily economic. The most dehumanising aspect of colonial and apartheid rule was not even the fact that black people were paid starvation wages, terrible though that exploitation was. Even more fundamental was the cultural degradation that came from an ideology that systematically asserted that black people were less than human – that the development of their mental capacities had somehow been arrested in the process of human evolution.[37]

But it is ludicrous to draw such a convenient distinction between 'cultural degradation' and the role of capital in the oppression and exploitation of black people.

This links with another of Mangcu's forays into obscure and unscholarly generalities, this time into the important issue of culture, which is essential to understanding race in SA. His approach to 'culture' is strikingly haphazard and eclectic. If it is not the 'multi-racialism' of Luthuli he is attracted to, it is the 'joint culture' which Biko once referred to. 'Joint culture'? How does one even begin to engage with such obscurities, especially in scholarly works? Neither did Biko give us any clear definition of what he meant by it, other than it being some kind of osmosis of the cultures of black and white people. I return later to the subject of culture as an important part of the discourse of race in SA. For now, one myth must be dispelled: there is absolutely no such thing as black or white culture.

It is now abundantly clear that the terms 'race' and 'racism' are by their historical, literal and social meanings an inherent part of the discourses which attempt to define, make sense and understand the system of capitalism of which they have been analytical constituents. Race and racism have their meanings extended and clarified, despite their shifts in form from one period to the next.

What has not shifted is capitalism. It is the varying ideological tenets which have interacted and articulated with it that have changed in form from one period to the next and the dynamics within those. That is the essence of its constantly shifting complexities and how it impacts on and reshapes social relations, but constantly in motion and flux, with the systematic essence of capitalism remaining firmly in the saddle of power.

Capitalism is a powerful and resilient global system. Miles succinctly traces the key historical background of capitalism: 'The existing world capitalist system has its origins, in part, in the expansionary, trading activity of merchant capital in Western Europe from the 15th century. This gave way to colonial settlement and domination, and the subsequent incorporation of various parts of the world in an emergent capitalist system which until the early 20th century was centred in Europe and specifically, though not exclusively, in Britain.'[38]

In concluding the discussion on 'race', I want to mention the view of the late Neville Alexander. He proposed that 'There is no logical reason whatsoever to argue for the existence of entities called "races" or "ethnic groups" simply from racial prejudice or ethnic awareness of whatever kind. It is anti-scientific … to conclude that because a large number in the world believe in ghosts and hence behave as though ghosts really do exist … that therefore a category called ghosts has to be invented.'[39] But MacDonald counters this:

> The category of race may make no sense naturally and biogenetically, yet may make sense socially. If believers in God – or for that matter,

in ghosts – are organised, their communities are real, substantial and politically relevant. For political purposes, to be perceived *is* to be. Consequently, Alexander cannot sustain his line of argument. He reluctantly concedes that the racial group *does* exist (it is a 'social reality' ... a historical phenomenon that comes into being in the process of political, economic and cultural struggle under the aegis of the leading class in the nation).[40]

I am persuaded by MacDonald's line of argument. He adds that for Alexander it is not so much that 'racial groups do not exist, but that they *should* not and *need* not exist'. Indeed, 'denying the existence of race runs afoul of basic South African realities'.[41] Even illusions can become 'real' if they have been socially accepted and internalised.

Central to the concerns of this book is the historical relationship between race and class, in SA and elsewhere. Peter Hudis assesses Fanon's view of the relationship:

> Most important, Fanon held that while race is a product of class relations, which serves as their mask, it is not a secondary factor. While race *reflects* class formations, the reflection is not a one-way mirror image. The reflection is taken up in consciousness and performs a sort of doubling by mirroring its origin at the same time as *reshaping* it. Determinations of reflection are not passive but *actively* reconstructive. And since racial determinations are often not super-structural but integral to the logic of capital accumulation, efforts by people of colour to challenge them can serve as the catalyst for targeting and challenging class relations.[42]

I conclude this section on 'race' with an important point made by Hannah Arendt on how the colonisation of Africa influenced race thinking:

> It is highly probable that the thinking of race would have disappeared in due time together with other irresponsible opinions of the nineteenth century, if the 'scramble for Africa' and the new era of imperialism had not exposed Western humanity to new and shocking experiences. Imperialism would have necessitated the invention of racism as the only possible 'explanation' and excuse for its deeds, even if no race-thinking had ever existed in the civilised world.[43]

Racialism

The concept of 'racialism' is not often used in discourses of race and racism. Even in Miles's excellent book, *Racism*, he deals very briefly with racialism. However, it is clear from the literature that much of what is defined as 'racialism' is largely a logical extension of 'race', as it was defined by the 'scientific racism' of the 18th and 19th centuries. There appears to be a fairly direct connection between race, racialism, racism and capitalism – despite all the evidence of unevenness and contingencies.

Racialism explicated, expanded and generalised the fallacies inherent in the race thinking and beliefs of scientific racism, which were perpetuated, deepened and consolidated by colonisation, so that racism assumed more concrete structural and systemic forms. Sometimes it is defined as those beliefs and ideas which revolve around different phenotypical features, like skin colour and hair type, as the basis of prejudices towards those with dark skin colours or different hair types. At other times it is given a more materialist basis.

It is clear that sometimes 'racialism' is used as synonymous and interchangeably with 'racism'. Miles discusses the use by writers before the Second World War of the concept of racialism rather than racism to identify 'race thinking'. For example, writing in 1935 Huxley and Haddon declared: 'Racialism is a myth and a dangerous myth at that. It is a cloak for selfish economic aims which in their uncloaked nakedness would look ugly enough.'[44] However, after the war and with knowledge of the Holocaust, the explicit usage of the term 'racism' became dominant in the literature and relevant discourses, which remains the case. In Marxist literature 'race' and 'racism' dominate the discourses, with 'racialism' as a concept featuring infrequently in theoretical and analytical terms. The main reason for this is that the content of 'racialism' is much more descriptive.

Racialism appears to be the rationalising ideological architecture of the concept of race, as it was defined in the 'scientific racism' of the time. In important discursive ways 'race' informed the ideology of racialism, primarily as its signifying language, which basically attempted to rationalise its notion, characteristics and categories, as its *raison d'être*. Racialism may be defined to refer to all attempts to portray people in any way whatsoever as belonging to a particular 'race', exhibiting certain characteristics that are peculiar to it, whether negatively evaluated or not, be they physical, biological, genetic or even cultural, especially if it also connotes any form of conscious discrimination or exclusion of people on such bases. Miles cites Banton's use of the term 'racialism' in a more formal sense, to refer to 'the way in which scientific theories of racial typology were used to categorise populations'. Indeed, Miles himself uses the phrase as a synonym for the concept of 'racial categorisation'.[45] For MacDonald, 'the word "racialism" insinuates race as a defining human attribute, a central praxis of human society and political organisation'.[46]

However, the literature clearly reflects a conscious shift in the 20th century towards a racialism based on cultural differences. Todorov argued in the 1980s that the ideology of 'cultural differences' had replaced that of 'racialism', so that it is not 'race' per se that is the basis of differences but that black and white people inhabit different cultures.[47] In fact, this shift to a culturalist perspective dominates the discourse of race to such a high degree that the phenotypical, biological and physical features associated with the concept 'race' are hardly taken seriously any longer. But while the content of the racialisation shifted, the meaning of race did not, in the sense that the adherents of this move continued to believe in the existence of different races but for different reasons.

By its variegated and complex nature 'culture' was always bound to be a dubious criterion for drawing distinctions between people, especially between white and black people, particularly because its basis was bound to be vague, subjective and contested – unlike the real economic, social, material and class differences between them. In a world with a history which has been heavily racialised and racist for centuries, with wide-ranging attendant social injustices, it is also not very helpful to promote demographic, political and social illusions of universal commonalities of 'humanity'. Such collectivist approaches do not deal with and relate to the real world of multi-faceted, tangible and serious socioeconomic and class differences and divisions between people.

It is equally important to bear in mind that whites are not the sole repository of racial and ethnic consciousness and prejudices. These are in fact widespread among black people in SA, often combined with complex and complicated tribal differences, especially among African people. There are particular historical facts of our development as people in human societies which one has to call by their proper names. There are three interrelated areas of any society we cannot, and in fact dare not, be 'politically correct' about, namely the levels of economic, social and cultural development and associated factors. Those factors, and how they influenced and structured the development of societies, are indelibly etched into history. You can change the future but you cannot change that history.

The most important factor which has altered how society was organised and how it developed subsequently is capitalist urbanisation of people whose entire lives had been lived out in rural areas. Various South African historians – notably Charles van Onselen and other Wits History Workshop scholars – have studied these processes and analysed how urbanisation irrevocably changed people, their lives, priorities and values. The history of the entire world teaches us that the unleashing of the powerful forces of capitalist urbanisation is virtually impossible to resist. This was especially the case when it was sanctioned and enforced by a brutal racist state such as the Transvaal government of Paul Kruger in the late 1880s. But what made such enforcement much more powerful was the influence of British and other sections of global monopoly capital, which called the shots in the gold mining industry in Johannesburg, clearing any obstacles in its path.

It was impossible to stop the capitalist urbanisation of African people and as impossible to avoid the economic, social and cultural consequences in the rural areas. Relative to the emergent capitalist cultural forces of modernity, assembled in cities such as Johannesburg, Africans who moved to the city's slumyards or as migrant workers to the mining compounds at the behest of monopoly capital's cheap labour requirements, could do nothing to stop these processes. Legislation and taxation which compelled the migration of African men to the gold mines in Johannesburg to labour for the white mine bosses was a cruel baptism of the role the state in SA would continue to play. Through the instrument of the state, capitalism unleashed powerful forces which shaped and reshaped SA according to its requirements.

Racialism and racialisation took complex forms in SA, given the centuries-long divide-and-rule strategies and tactics of white rulers since the time of the Cape Colony. For example, there are real socio-cultural differences between 'Coloured' and 'African' people in SA, as there are between them and 'Indian' people, who first arrived in the country as indentured labourers in the 19th century. Such differences and how they might affect and influence perceptions of people's roles in actual struggles and in leadership of these struggles, especially during apartheid, were inadequately examined. Nor was it sufficiently specified what the minimum common requirements were for a post-apartheid SA, which would adequately satisfy the needs, interests and demands especially of the majority black working class.

This has bequeathed a serious legacy of race, racialism and racism in SA and the equally serious question of how we tackle it today, both from the National Question point of view and the intrinsic and serious lack of social justice in post-apartheid SA. Unfortunately, dealing with this legacy is not helped by the backward and ignorant rantings about race and racism of the sort encountered on social media. At such times I often recall the aphorism, where ignorance is bliss, it is folly to be wise. But that ignorance often extends to a crude claim, which itself can be construed as racist, that only the African majority know about racism and can talk about it with an authority born of the fact that they have been the most oppressed and exploited people in SA.

This kind of biological and racialist thinking is similar to that which typified white Afrikaner nationalist racist thinking under apartheid. It is the kind of crudely nativist approach which Soudien criticised when he observed: 'I want to insist, however, that a sense of community cannot be constructed simply on the basis of what we look like. If we were, if we automatically and instinctively see "connection" based on similarities of our appearance, we would be crafting our world in the most arbitrary way.'[48] Angelo Fick has argued that under Zuma in particular, SA has experienced a steady 're-racination' and 're-ethnicisation' of our politics and a 'retreat into cultural essentialism'.[49] But I trace this kind of race thinking back to the ANC, and especially to its decision to retain the apartheid-era racialist and racist population classification system.

MacDonald distinguishes between racists and racialists. 'Racialists ... do not necessarily claim that one person is better than another; they are content to claim that one person is different from another. The old segregationist precept in the US, of separate but equal, affected to be racialist.' However, he adds:

> Racialism usually derives from and abets racism, as the American example shows. Black and white might have been kept separate, but

they were not kept equal. Yet even when racialism serves the ends of racism, it elaborates a distinct logic. Racialists regard race as the source of identity and identities as the axis of political institutions. Racialists agree with racists that race is a critical human attribute, that it plays a constitutive role in making people who they are.[50]

But in order to know who blacks *are*, we need to ask why it is very important to know and recognise 'who *they are*'. This is a neglected but critical question in the literature. The question is even much more important to both pose and answer because 'blacks' have always been heterogeneous, disaggregated in terms of class, culture, religion and, ironically, even skin colour. But the thrust of the question should be who they *predominantly are* in class terms. The answer to that question in countries where they are the overwhelming demographic majority, as in SA, is that they are a working class primarily.

This point, I believe, should have analytical, political, programmatic and moral implications, especially in understanding the disastrous effects of capitalism on that black working-class majority, which continued after 1994. It is when we approach and disaggregate blacks and 'blackness' from this perspective that we can appreciate how unacceptable and intolerable the worsening socioeconomic conditions of the poor black majority have been, especially over the past decade. This is the class that the 'miracle transition' of the 1990s has left far behind.

Racism

It is racism, in the sense of its historical place in the systemic and structural ideological properties of global capitalism, of which it has been an integral part for centuries and with which it has intersected and articulated, that needs to be defined and dissected.

There is a vast international literature on racism, and I have selected two useful but contrasting definitions. For Robert Miles, in a general survey of the phenomenon, the task is to 'unravel the different forms and levels of determination, the articulation between racism, sexism, and nationalism and the extraordinary practices that are derived from these ideologies, in the context of the capitalist mode of production.' He considers racism exclusively as an ideological phenomenon: by ideology he means 'any discourse which ... represents human beings and the relations between human beings, in a distorted and misleading manner.' Racism is an 'ideology that takes a number of different forms' but always with a particular ideological content.[51] An example could be that the wages paid to workers are portrayed as a fair amount of money for a fair day's work, without critically examining the systemic capitalist exploitation of workers and considering that by far most of the wealth created goes to a few people who are the owners and managers of the company.

In a work on race in South Africa, MacDonald provides a succinct definition:

> Racism has members of one racial group, usually whites, dominating members of a different racial group, usually blacks, for material or expressive reasons. Asserting the superiority of one group and the inferiority of the other, racists prescribe supremacy for the superior population and subordination for the inferior one. Racism deems some people as *better* than other people on the basis of their membership of a race.[52]

Building on Miles and MacDonald, I briefly define racism in SA as follows: from a historical point of view, racism is a set of mutating ideological tools and policy regimes, which began under Dutch and later British colonial rule, intended to uphold and buttress the interests of capitalism through various measures, such as segregation, control over movements, cheap black labour and a host of other measures, particularly under apartheid.

Many of the legal measures implemented by Dutch and British colonialism had to do with access to and the subordination, exploitation and control of cheap black labour. Whether we are dealing with laws to uproot Africans from the land or the exploitation and control of their labour in the urban areas, these were designed to serve systemic and integrated purposes. All these measures were overtly racist. The whole thrust of racism was to oppress, exploit and dominate black people in every respect, and there was no aspect of social, economic and political life unscathed by race.

Apartheid laws intruded upon and controlled every facet of life, including sexual relations between black and white people, marriages, where black people lived and the conditions they lived under, what work they might do and what work was proscribed, where children were schooled and where students studied at tertiary level and under what conditions. Even churches were racially segregated. Generally, conditions were incomparably poorer for black people, and generated hardship and squalor. Life under apartheid was so absolutely dominated by the racist state that it can be described as a totalitarian – though not fascist – regime.

Apartheid excluded black people from that which white people enjoyed and were entitled to, such as good housing, education, wages, health care and so on. This is not to suggest that everybody who was white had a similar standard of living or that there was no class structure among whites. In fact, since the earliest days of the Cape Colony there were class and social divisions among them.

More important economically was how Afrikaner nationalism used access to state power, both before and after 1948, to favour the rapid growth of white Afrikaner capital vis-à-vis white English capital. As a result, there emerged large companies such as Sanlam, Volkskas, Rembrandt, Federale Mynbou and others. The NP also used access to state resources to finance the huge advances in living standards made by the white Afrikaner working class, resulting in their enjoying among the highest standards of living of any working class in the world, especially during the 1950s, 1960s and 1970s. All this and much more was made possible because white racism, anchored in the NP's control of the state, excluded the majority black population from similar standards.

It is important to note that the exclusion black people suffered in all these areas was not because no housing, municipal services and amenities were provided to them in the townships. No, it is that the incomparably superior infrastructure and services provided to whites reflected that they regarded themselves as superior to blacks. It exemplified Miles's observation that racism is a 'label attached to a set of beliefs about "race" that were used to justify exclusionary actions.'[53]

What makes racism systemically possible in the first place is the state power to introduce, enforce and sustain it, especially in a country where black people are overwhelmingly the majority of the population. Enormous state power – the army, police, parliament, the legislature and last, but not least, the white working class – was at hand to brutally enforce racism in every aspect of life. State power was frequently exercised to defend and maintain the class interests of WMC.

An accurate and objective definition of racism is important for educational, political, organisational and transformative purposes. As Miles puts it, 'The conceptual ability to make these distinctions is necessary not only in the interests of analytical accuracy but also, and therefore, in the interests of formulating potentially successful interventionist strategies intended to negate both racist ideologies and the disadvantage that accrues from exclusion.'[54] To know clearly and correctly what racism is also enables one to know what racism is not and thereby distinguish one from the other. This is of specific importance for SA, both before and especially after 1994.

In defining racism it is precisely when emphasis is laid on how it has historically informed, intersected and interacted with class exploitation and gender oppression that it assumes greater definitional clarity and explanatory power. That is why a definition of racism should emphasise its larger structural and systemic components, especially when it concerns how and under what conditions black people have worked and lived, under both apartheid and post-apartheid SA.

The importance of definitional precision is the crux of the problems with African or black nationalist definitions of racism, which are presented largely in binary and homogeneous terms because they ignore class among both white and black people; this is problematic when it comes to understanding multi-class alliances, which the nationalism of the ANC alliance represents. It neutralises, compromises and dissipates the independent organisational strength of the black working class, especially since its organisations, such as the SACP and Cosatu, are in a ruling alliance with the neoliberal ANC.

The African nationalist politics of the ANC in post-apartheid SA have conspicuously compromised the interests and needs of the black working class, on the one hand, and, on the other, have as conspicuously deferred to WMC after 1994. The worst manifestation of this was probably when it allowed WMC to list on the stock exchanges of London, New York and elsewhere, thus allowing many billions of rands of profits, produced over many decades by the black working class, to be repatriated abroad. This is partly the consequence of a politics of 'race' and the concentrated focus by the struggles waged by the ANC and many other organisations against racist apartheid, without raising strongly enough the political economy and social justice issues, inseparable from the anti-apartheid struggle, as the inextricable links between 'race' and class and racism and capitalism were clearly reflected in 20th-century SA.

Robert Miles firmly opposes binary black nationalist understandings of race and racism. He explicitly objects to those

> who maintain that racism is a 'black' experience which the 'white' person is unable to understand. This view is often defended with the claim that racism is an exclusive creation of, and an essential feature, of European, 'white' cultures and societies, and that all those who belong to those cultures and societies are therefore necessarily tainted with racism. It follows that 'white' people are themselves the origin or cause of the problem, and therefore 'white' people lack the capacity to understand, analyse and explain racism. I do not accept these arguments, at least not in their 'hard' form. ... it is mistaken to limit the parameters of racism to skin colour because various 'white' groups have been the object of racism.

Thus, although (indeed, because) 'whites' may have limited personal experience of racism compared with 'black' people,

> there is no single truth about racism which only 'blacks' can know. To assert that the latter is so is, in fact, to condemn 'white' people to a universal condition which implies possession of a permanent essence which inevitably sets them apart ... Armed with the notion that truth is relative and negotiated ... and hence the assumption that one may advance claims which will be shown subsequently to be wrong, there is no reason to believe that the colour of one's skin naturally or inevitably prevents one from contributing to an understanding of the nature and origin of racism.[55]

I find this perspective invaluably important and persuasive in the present South African context, especially to counter the emergence over the past decade in particular of a Africanist majoritarian chauvinism which not only dabbles in race and racism discourses with ignorance and arrogance, but also appears to think that because demography – in terms of biology, 'race' and skin colour – makes them the overwhelming majority of the population, that translates into a kind of prerogative for them to say all kinds of unacceptable things, including racialist and often even overtly racist utterance and actions.

Another crucially important matter raised by Miles is how 'racism became a relation of production because it was an ideology which shaped decisively the formation and reproduction of the relations between exploiter and exploited; it was one of those representational elements which became historically conducive to the constitution and reproduction of a system of commodity production.'[56] The utility of this point serves to reinforce, if that were necessary, that race and racism have been consciously utilised by initially the mining industry and later various manufacturing industries to impose a regime of super-exploitable cheap black labour in order to maximise profits which enabled the rapid expansion of the capitalist system.

In concluding this theme of 'racism', I point to the critically important matter of the effects which racism has on its victims, which in the case of SA must have amounted to an immensely destructive human toll. This point is well captured by Motala:

> Recognising the political and social effects of racism demands at the same time an acknowledgement of its impact on the lives of the exploited and oppressed peoples through centuries of human existence. Asserting this is a deliberate act which negates the violence of enslavement, colonial and post-colonial rule, human exploitation in the development of capitalism and the brutality associated with the reconstitution of the lives of millions of human beings through this.[57]

Amplification of this matter assumes much greater importance, even its theorisation, when we take a long historical view and trace what black people have been subjected to since the days of slavery and colonisation. The sheer devastation inflicted on black people, as summarised by Motala, over that long history is incalculable. The multiple ways in which they were affected and the systematic violence were a toxic combination. It involved punitive treatment and physical harshness with mass impoverishment, dispossession and brutal exploitation of black labour to create a history of extreme hardship and suffering. It is from this recognition that we need to anchor any moral notion of antiracist campaigns.

A striking feature of SA, which reveals the depth, extent and brutality of racism here, is the avalanche of increasingly overt racist legislation on the statute books, from the 18th century onward, climaxing after the NP 1948 electoral victory. Looking at the significance of this legislation and its purposes over the centuries, and how the key formative features of capitalism have basically remained intact after 1994, reminds one how in fact we are reliving our history, albeit shorn of the formal racism which motivated and accompanied that legislation.

Important though de-racialisation has been as a social advance, the same capitalist system is intact, dominating production, distribution and exchange in SA.

But there is a related question: why does racism survive, even after all racist laws are removed? The question is relevant not only to post-apartheid SA but much more generally in the world at large. As Todorov puts it, 'Virtually nobody in the scientific community today believes that whites or Europeans are superior, but racism thrives more than ever.'[58] Even if the entire white community held anti-racist beliefs, it would not encourage capitalism to discontinue exploiting the working class, white and black. What has changed is that capitalism no longer requires whites to believe in their superiority or supremacy for its operations. In fact, openly displayed racist beliefs would seriously destabilise capitalism.

However, my answer to this crucial question of the persistence of race and racism in purportedly 'post-racial' societies is that after a very long historical period in which racism and capitalism were inseparably intertwined, as in SA, the socioeconomic effects penetrate into the very fibre of everyday life. The working and living conditions which black people, now supposedly liberated from racism, continue to live under, to an overwhelming extent, make it clear that the consequences of that system cannot be eradicated within a continuing capitalist economic framework but only outside and, in fact, against it. This also serves to reinforce the necessity of always linking race and class, and racism and capitalism within the ongoing struggles of black people in such societies, especially that of the black working class.

Racism and Capitalism: Getting to Grips with the 'Contingency Thesis'

What I refer to as the 'contingency thesis' makes a basic assertion regarding the historical relationship between racism and capitalism in SA: that there were times when capitalism did not 'require' or 'need' racism to function profitably. The contingency thesis basically argues that there were periods when racism was useful to and, indeed, aided and abetted South African capitalism, but there were other periods when it became a hindrance and liability. One such period for WMC developed during the 1970s and 1980s, especially after the 1976 Soweto student uprisings. This appears in the literature to be the period during which the alleged contingent relationship between racism and capitalism first manifested itself. After Soweto and during the economic crisis of the 1970s and 1980s, unlike earlier periods, capitalism did not require racism, at least not the avalanche of laws and policies on the statute books. A succinct statement of the contingency thesis was provided by Harold Wolpe in 1988. He argued that elements within South African capitalism came 'to perceive apartheid as an obstacle to their further expansion' and proposed: 'That there is a contingent, not a necessary, relationship between capital and racism in South Africa is a correct starting point.'[59]

In criticising the contingency thesis, I argue that racism in its various forms (of which 'apartheid' was the last before the democratic political changes of the 1990s) had since the mineral revolution of the 19th century allowed capitalists to reap bigger profits than they would have done if racist laws and policies did not exist, which permitted the super-exploitation of an abundant supply of cheap black labour and its regimented social subordination and control. A large body of literature abundantly shows the systemic historical links between racism and capitalism in SA. The contingency thesis appears to hold that not only did WMC no longer want or need legalised and formal racism but that it was positively opposed to *all* forms of racism and discrimination, so that the apartheid system of systemic racism had to be abolished for good.

However, while aspects of racism which were enshrined in legislation were indeed formally abolished after 1994, the more important and serious socioeconomic effects of racism over a very long period not only remained intact but in some respects worsened. It is in this qualified sense that it can be argued that there was a necessary, not a contingent, relationship between racism and capitalism. The incontestable fact is that there has never been a historical period in SA when the race–class and racism–capitalism nexus did not hold sway to a greater or lesser extent. White racism was intimately and inextricably intertwined with South African capitalism as it had historically developed and this frames the racism–capitalism nexus, not some theoretical abstract model. There is no period in the 20th century – including the period of reforms after the 1976 black student uprisings – in which the key aspects of racial and racist capitalism were dislodged or dispensed with.

The limited and piecemeal reforms that followed the Wiehahn and Riekert Commissions, were critical to the interests of WMC and the NP to secure 'industrial peace' within a 'free market economy' and to be able to better control black labour and prevent wildcat strikes. Housing for black workers, their 'right' to be in urban areas, and the higher wages paid to skilled black workers were all important for stabilising the manufacturing sector and must also be seen against the low black wage base which until then characterised the racist-capitalist apartheid system. Capital needed more skilled, settled, better-paid workers and a viable industrial relations framework to manage, contain and try to prevent conflict.

However, it is not only at the formal and legal levels that we need to examine changes in conditions and progress. If we include a comparison of the social and material conditions of the lives of the black working-class majority before and after 1994 – which is in fact the analytical and political heart of the racism–capitalism nexus – then it is clear that the perpetuated poverty, unemployment and worsening social inequalities in post-apartheid SA are the accumulated results of that nexus in action, to a greater or lesser extent, since the mid-19th century.

Those who peddle the contingency thesis overplay the significance of political and legislative reforms in the 1970s and 1980s in order to argue that WMC and later the NP reformists were ready to ditch apartheid for a new democratic and non-racial political dispensation. But as I have indicated, all those political reformist moves were finely calculated and calibrated not to upset, disturb or threaten the capitalist system. And as we have seen, the deeply systemic social crisis after 1994 was a direct result of that process, which left intact, as did the negotiated 1993 political settlement, a highly monopolistic and powerful white-dominated and -controlled capitalist economy. It is there that we must locate the causes of the unstoppable black township protests since June 2004 and the current unprecedented social crisis.

An approach which rests on the contingency thesis effectively limits an understanding of racism to formality and legality. The implicit assumption of this approach is that with the abolition of racist laws in the 1990s, racism was systemically uprooted. This thesis is mistaken, false and misleading given the historically inextricable nature of the racism–capitalism relationship in SA. In the final analysis it is impossible to abolish racism within the framework of a capitalist system with which it coexisted since the mineral revolution began.

Today, 26 years since the 1994 watershed non-racial and democratic elections, poverty, unemployment, housing, basic services and much more are all still etched in the racial and racist colours of our history. The footprints and social legacy of race and racism are still embedded in the SA of today, notwithstanding the abolition of all racist laws and policies. Nothing more convincingly demonstrates the veracity of the racism–capitalism nexus and its virtually symbiotic nature than this incontestable fact of post-apartheid society. There is overwhelming evidence that in spite of efforts at deracialisation after 1994, the contingency thesis must be rejected. As I have tried to demonstrate, it was never a clear, coherent and compelling account of the dynamics of the racism–capitalism relationship, even under apartheid.

As indicated, the key problem appears to lie with a definition of racism which is limited to formal laws and policies, rather than one which recognises and deals with the systemic effects of the long historical period when racism and capitalism had a virtually symbiotic relationship. If we approach a definition of racism from that historical angle and link it to the working, living and social conditions of the black working-class majority, then we are arguably not less but more racist after 1994. Removing racism from our laws, without addressing its devastating socioeconomic effects is the heart of the problem of racism in purportedly *post*-apartheid SA. It is also the heart of the problem of the contingency thesis, which essentially suggests that the racism–capitalism nexus began to be eroded in the 1970s and no longer holds after 1994.

To present an argument for the essential continuity of racism after 1994 is not to fail to recognise that the relations between racism and capitalism are always uneven, asymmetrical, unstable and even contradictory. But that is not enough to sustain a contingency argument because the most visible and even visceral manifestation of the continuity of racism after 1994 is the ever-worsening social crisis of the past decade afflicting the poor black majority and now at its zenith with the impact of Covid-19.

Conclusions

We have seen how the notion of 'race' has been socially and ideologically constructed over a long historical period and under diverse conditions and in different manifestations, taking shape and form in different ways and under different circumstances, from one country to the next. An initial period – from the 15th century onwards – was when the ideology of race typology began to take root in Spain and Portugal and later spread to England, France and other countries. Crucially, racist ideas were linked to the voyages of discovery, an expansion of colonialism, and the onset of the African slave trade.

I have noted in passing the critical importance of India in any history of racism, precisely because it was not in the European world but in the East. In Asia, as subsequently in the West, skin colour prejudice presented itself – among predominantly black people or people of colour, not among whites or Europeans.

The case of India and skin colour prejudices in so many other parts of the world, even among black people themselves, must teach us something cardinally important about every form of enslavement, oppression, subjugation and exploitation that ever existed: we must critically examine what the ideological foundations and beliefs were. This will reveal that there is much in the world which is oppressive and exploitative that has nothing to do with 'white' people or even capitalism: cultural beliefs and practices, such as prearranged and forced marriages, genital mutilation of young women, caste atrocities in India and elsewhere, the stoning to death of people for cultural or religious reasons, and other similarly offensive practices.

A systematic study of various cultures, countries, and systems of government would reveal that racism, oppression and exploitation do not only occur in a binary white/black world. There are instances where the oppressors and exploiters are not white or European, but people of colour. In SA, black and 'African' people in particular have continued to suffer grinding poverty, unemployment and social inequality, at the hands of an African ANC government.

However, since 'racialism' and 'racialisation' have more to do with the ideological socialisation of the acceptance of race and its hierarchical stipulations according to differential population categories, by whatever shifting criteria, it is defining and dealing with racism as a system of oppression and exploitation, and how it articulates with class and gender, which is the crux of this work. The abundant literature shows that we have long ago passed the stages of scientific racism and of lame attempts to justify the proposition that white people are inherently better than and superior to black people. There have been thoroughly convincing scientific refutations of 'race' along those lines.

I believe that South African and world history have now set the stage for dealing with any ongoing 'race' and racism only in ways which confront the central questions of how people are living today. The kind of adverse socioeconomic conditions which confront the poor, mainly but not solely black people, must become the concentrated focus. The discourses and debates of 'race' and racism must now shift decisively to confronting those conditions of poverty, unemployment, inequality and social miseries.

Endnotes

1. Ebrahim Harvey, 'Breaking free from the white left', *Mail & Guardian*, 15–21 December 2000.
2. Robert Miles, *Racism* (London and New York: Routledge, 1989) p. 31.
3. Miles, *Racism*, p. 33.
4. Miles, *Racism*, p. 33.
5. Miles, *Racism*, p. 33.
6. Miles, *Racism*, p. 89.
7. Miles, *Racism*, p. 31.
8. Miles, *Racism*, p. 32.
9. Miles, *Racism*, p. 32.
10. Neville Adams email, 22 February 2018.
11. Miles, *Racism*, p. 36.
12. Cited in Miles, *Racism*, p. 45.
13. Miles, p. 73.
14. Crain Soudien, *Realising the Dream: Unlearning the Logic of Race in the South African School* (Cape Town: HSRC Press, 2012), p. 11.
15. Michael McDonald, *Why Race Matters in South Africa* (Cambridge MA: Harvard University Press, 2006).
16. Soudien, *Realising*, p. 11.
17. Soudien, *Realising*, p. 11.
18. Soudien, *Realising*, p. xi.
19. Frantz Fanon, *The Wretched of the Earth* (London: Penguin Books, 1990).
20. Fanon, *Wretched*, p. 130.
21. Tzvetan Todorov, '"Race", Writing and Culture', in *'Race', Writing and Difference*, ed. Henry Louis Gates (Chicago and London: University of Chicago Press, 1986), p. 371.

22 Cedric J. Robinson, *Black Marxism: The Making of the Black Radical Tradition* (London: Zed Books, 1983).
23 Todorov, 'Race', pp. 371–2.
24 Robinson, *Black Marxism*, p. xxxvi.
25 Robinson, *Black Marxism* p. 3.
26 Enver Motala, 'Racism, liberal confusion or material explanation?', *Amandla*, 45, 17 October 2016, at http://aidc.org.za/racism-liberal-confusion-material-explanation/.
27 Motala, 'Racism'.
28 Xolela Mangcu, ed., *The Colour of Our Future: Does Race Matter in Post-Apartheid South Africa?* (Johannesburg: Wits University Press, 2015), p. xix.
29 Mangcu, *Colour of Our Future*, p. xv.
30 Achille Mbembe, *Critique of Black Reason* (Johannesburg: Wits University Press, 2017).
31 Mangcu, *Colour of Our Future*, p. 9.
32 Mangcu, *Colour of Our Future*, pp. 9–10.
33 Mangcu, *Colour of Our Future*, p. xvii.
34 Mangcu, *Colour of Our Future*, p. xx.
35 Mangcu, *Colour of Our Future*, p. xviii.
36 Azanian People's Organisation (1978*)*, *Constitution* (Section 2(ix), see https://en.m.wikipedia.org.
37 Mangcu, *Colour of Our Future*, p. 8.
38 Miles, *Racism*, p. 2.
39 Cited in MacDonald, *Why Race Matters*, p. 93.
40 MacDonald, *Why Race Matters*, p. 94.
41 MacDonald, *Why Race Matters*, p. 94.
42 See Peter Hudis, 'Racism and the logic of capitalism: A Fanonian reconsideration', *Historical Materialism* 26, 1 (2018).
43 Cited in Valentin-Yves Mudimbe, *The Invention of Africa: Gnosis, Philosophy and the Order of Knowledge* (Bloomington: Indiana University Press & London: James Currey, 1988) p. 108.
44 Miles, *Racism*, pp. 42–3, 51–4; the quotation from Julian Huxley and Alfred C. Haddon, *We Europeans: A Survey of 'Racial' Problems* (London: Cape, 1935) is cited on p. 43.
45 Miles, *Racism*, p. 74.
46 MacDonald, *Why Race Matters*, p. 93.
47 Todorov, 'Race', p. 373.
48 Soudien, *Realising*, p. xi.
49 Angelo Fick, 'Ethnic boxes perpetuate colonialism', *Mail & Guardian*, 13 July 2018.
50 MacDonald, *Why Race Matters*, p. 7.
51 Miles, *Racism*, pp. 10, 48–9.
52 MacDonald, *Why Race Matters*, p. 6.
53 Miles, *Racism*, p. 48.
54 Miles, *Racism*, p. 77
55 Miles, *Racism*, pp. 6–7.
56 Miles, *Racism*, p. 111.
57 Motala, 'Racism'.
58 Todorov, 'Race', p. 372.
59 Harold Wolpe, *Race, Class and the Apartheid State* (Paris: UNESCO Press and London: James Currey, 1988), pp. 28, 32.

THREE

Race, class and gender in South African history

The Cape Colonial Origins of the South African Racial Order

THE FIRST SECTION OF this chapter briefly explores the colonial origins of the racial order in SA, from the landing of Van Riebeeck and his crew in 1652. But the Portuguese were the first Europeans to set foot on South African soil a century and a half earlier. In December 1497 Vasco da Gama landed with his men at St Helena Bay, about 100 miles north of Cape Town. King John II of Portugal, after the earlier first rounding of the Cape by Dias in 1488, called it the 'Cape of Good Hope', because of the optimism it engendered for the opening of a sea route to the spices of India and the East.

Why it was that the Portuguese were the first to set foot on South African soil is of absorbing interest and reveals many things. According to Muller, it was Henry the Navigator's work on the 'theory and art of navigation which ultimately resulted in the Portuguese becoming the first navigators of Africa'. Under orders from the Portuguese crown, mathematicians worked feverishly to improve measurements of the sun's altitude south of the equator, and as a result 'more efficient astrolabes were being taken on voyages to Africa'. Muller points out that by then

'African trade had already brought Lisbon considerable prosperity'.[1]

The second half of the chapter deals with SA from the start of the mineral revolution in 1867, when alluvial diamonds were found in the Northern Cape. The key purpose of this historical background is to better understand not only the distant past but also the powerful economic and industrial development of SA triggered by the mineral revolution, fundamentally transforming the country and the lives of those who lived there, including the black working-class majority whose labour made it the powerhouse of production in South and southern Africa. In other words, as a result of such enormous economic and industrial power, SA had the material and financial means to have secured a fundamental transformation of the lives of the working class who built it up over that period.

The central idea of this section of the chapter is to dig down a bit deeper into both the history of SA and the relevant theories and debates about the place of 'race', class and gender in shaping it, in preparation for moving into contemporary SA. In his book, *Colonial South Africa and the Origins of the Racial Order*, Timothy Keegan has done an excellent job in systematically tracing the history of SA. From this and many other works it is amply evident that the SA of today is powerfully shaped by its colonial history, especially in terms of the impact which 'race' and colour had on the initial growth of slavery and later on colonialism and capitalism. Keegan is clear about the key purpose of his work:

> The issue of race in South African history is at the centre of my concerns in this study. Here race is treated not simply as a derivative of relations of production or of economic class, but as an autonomous variable with a life of its own (though, in practice, race as a historical reality takes on meaning in the context of specific social and economic systems). For from the beginnings of settlement colonial society was built on a racial basis. It was unthinkable to the colonists in early South Africa, as it would be to those who exercised power and dominance in the industrially based state established in the 20th century, that the social order might be built on anything other than the foundations of racial or ethnic exclusiveness and hegemony.[2]

The Dutch at the Cape

Importantly, race and skin colour were inscribed from the very outset in the initial contact and subsequent conflict between the Dutch settlers and the indigenous San and Khoikhoi people, especially from the moment that the Dutch decided to create a permanent settlement in the country. The Dutch colonisers were 'white' and the San and Khoi were people of colour or 'yellowish brown'.[3] In this specific sense, much like the rest of the momentous history of SA, it is race and colour which coloured that initial conflict, first over land and livestock, and soon labour. It is also significant to recognise that none of the scholarly work on that initial period reflects hostility by the Khoi and San towards the Dutch. On the contrary, most historical accounts indicate that the Dutch were initially warmly, but cautiously, welcomed by the Khoikhoi and San people.

From the initial contact between the Portuguese mariners, who were the first Europeans to land at the Cape, and the pastoral Khoikhoi, they exchanged for cattle and sheep metal and other goods. Such bartering was done without any violence, but that changed once the Dutch began to settle permanently, to raise their own animals, and to compete for grazing land. Virtually everything that occurred from the outset of the Dutch establishment of a refreshment station at the Cape had to do with their need to obtain food, water, shelter, land and, later, labour. What all these factors did was to unalterably inscribe material and economic motivations to both slavery and colonialism in the Cape Colony. Slaves were imported from 1658 onwards as the Dutch could not secure labour in the Cape because the Khoi and San resisted proletarianisation. By 1692 the slaves outnumbered the settlers. Every system of oppression and exploitation has always been built indispensably on labour.

The Dutch presence at the Cape was initially intended by the Dutch East India Company (DEIC) to serve only as a refreshment station, providing food for the fleets on their way to the East Indies. But in 1657 Van Riebeeck persuaded the directors of the company to release some of its servants and allow them to become free burghers to provide a more regular and reliable supply of grain, vegetables and cattle for the ships. Each burgher was granted 26 acres of land on which to grow grain and tobacco and breed cattle. The land of the indigenous people was unilaterally allocated by Van Riebeeck to these burghers with absolutely no regard to the natural rights to the land of the indigenous people.

Some tried to resist but were overwhelmed by the military supremacy of the settlers – a pattern repeated in subsequent wars fought by the Dutch and later the British. To add insult to injury, after appropriating much of the Khoisan land, Van Riebeeck recorded in his journal that 'the Hollanders were not a nation to rob another of its property'.[4] The heart of this irony is that it was under Dutch rule that the violent and brutal land dispossession of black people began on an increasingly mass scale.

The DEIC was a chartered company, founded in 1602 by the Dutch government, initially to trade with India. It grew and diversified, enjoying monopoly access to the lucrative spice trade. The Company administered the Dutch colony at the Cape until 1795, when the British took over the Cape. Clare puts this point well: 'Trade soon became the monopoly of the DEIC ... the world's first venture in corporate capitalism and rapidly grew into a powerful state-within-a-state.'[5] Although they were different in form and content, the monopoly rights over mercantile capitalism can be seen as a forerunner of the monopoly capital mobilised when gold was discovered in Johannesburg in 1886. The bulk of the capital invested in the gold mines was from Britain and other European countries and the US.

This is an important historical fact because it expresses very clearly that the very birth of modern-day SA was at the hands of a multinational capitalist corporation. A global monopoly trading company, with the active support of the state in Holland, was brutally imposed on a defenceless, innocent and primitive people whose only crime was to have tried to defend themselves and their simple lives against conquest. There are strong connections between all those events, which in fact laid the basis for the very high concentration of white wealth in the South African economy, not only in mining but in every sector of the economy, evinced most clearly by the fact that even over three centuries later, in 1994, just five monopolies owned and controlled the JSE.

The DEIC constantly sought opportunities for trade and expansion. The Dutch Cape Colony was not only no exception to this history: once the DEIC imported slaves into the Colony, they acquired the means to rapidly grow the business side of their operations, so much so that François Le Vaillant, a French naturalist and explorer, who spent a few years at the Cape, said:

News of the Company's riches spread and attracted new colonists every day. It was decided, as is always the practice, that might was sufficient right to spread as much as one wanted to. This logic nullified the sacred and respectable rights of property. On several occasions, they grabbed indiscriminately more than was needed, taking all land that the government or individuals it favoured thought good and suited them.[6]

This trend remained constant from those early years right into the present period of post-apartheid South African history.

It should be noted that one of the early motivations by the Dutch to explore the interior of the Cape was the fervent hope of discovering minerals. The Company's officials organised expeditions in the hope of making profitable mineral discoveries. As proposed earlier, it was always material and financial interests driving navigation and exploration, especially by seafaring nations such as Spain, Portugal, England, Holland and France. The European explorers were incessantly in search of riches and resources, which is therefore also important in understanding the evolution of and expansion of capitalism globally.

In the colony established by the DEIC, the colonists were white and the indigenous peoples and slaves were black people or people of colour. As noted in the previous chapter, the Dutch brought to the Cape a strong sense of their cultural and religious superiority that would feed into more explicit racism. Early on we can see how race and colour, though mediated through cultural chauvinism, began to set the social and political template for relations between the Dutch and the Khoisan. A substantial literature has discussed the nature and timing of racial thought and behaviour among the colonists; its relation to religious beliefs; how it compared to awareness of social status or class; and so on. Giliomee is among those who contend that the burghers of the 18th-century Cape 'were not preoccupied with colour', that their 'racial consciousness was rudimentary', and that racial divisions were 'not rigid'.[7] A broad consensus appears to have emerged that issues of race and different skin colour and phenotypical features became more pronounced only during the later 18th century. As Michael MacDonald puts it, 'Whites came to identify themselves in racial and ethno-cultural terms *after* they had established domination and racialisation was abetted by the influx of settlers from Britain, the new colonial power.'[8]

There occurred an important and increasing conflict among the Dutch settlers themselves, once a few were allotted some land and allowed to farm, using slave labour, and to trade for themselves in order to increase food production. The axis of conflicts shifted from that between the settlers and the Khoisan, with the attendant racial connotations, to that between the Dutch officials and the burghers, over land, trade, markets and prices. Fierce competition between free burghers and officials over these matters was evident and often required the intervention of the most senior officials in Holland. But the key point about these events and processes is that they show that material, financial and class interests ruptured the apparent homogeneity of 'race'. The hostile relations between free burghers and Company officials show that 'whiteness', at any point in South African history, was never homogeneous. On the contrary and despite their conjunctural 'unity' against black people, there were always in fact deep differences and divisions among white people.

The conflict between the Patriots in the Cape Colony and the Dutch authorities not only shaped subsequent settler politics but it was the challenge the Patriots posed to the upper classes I find most interesting: 'The Patriots wished to end the economic domination of the small circle of officials and some privileged burghers. The privileged free burghers whom the Patriots called "Mamelukes", also enjoyed excessive privileges in the social and cultural spheres.'[9]

However, it might be asked why some historians and writers are strongly inclined to downplay race and colour in the first decade or two of the Cape Colony, even when much or most of the evidence points to its existence to a significant degree, even if it existed alongside religious or even social status or class differences. It appears that for some obscure reasons if it were socio–class differences and not so much race–colour differences, it would be more understandable, acceptable or palatable but not race or colour. What does it say and what is the significance of the matter, whether it is race *or* class, instead of race *and* class? The validity of this question is reinforced in the light of the historical fact that race and class have frequently around the world intersected. In fact, most of the relevant literature points to that preponderant universal nexus.

A key feature of relations between indigenous people and settlers involved armed conflict. For over a century, colonists and Khoisan were embroiled in clashes that ranged from local skirmishes to sustained confrontation such as the so-called Bushman War on the colony's northeast frontier in the 1770s. These were followed by the Frontier Wars, also known as 'Xhosa Wars' or, as the British called them, 'Kaffir Wars', waged for almost a century, over land and labour mainly. The last such war ended in 1878, after which military resistance by the Xhosa was smashed permanently. In short, SA was conquered by the Dutch and British between the 17th and 19th centuries by their sheer military and economic power against the indigenous majority who did not possess comparable economic or military power. Although whites were always a minority of the population – in the Cape and Natal colonies, in the Boer Republics, and in the state formed in 1910 – they were able to keep their jackboot on the necks of the vast majority of the population simply because the white racist state always ensured that it had the military might to smash any attempt to overthrow it. Economic power throughout history consistently determined a state's military capabilities.

But military power was strengthened by political support. From the earliest days of colonialism, the Dutch and later the British, in order to deal with any opposition from the black majority, required and received the active support of the privileged white working and middle classes, in return for the protection and advancement of their material and social interests. This serves to reinforce the cardinally important point about race and racism throughout history and in all countries: without exception, it served the material interests of white people, to a varying degree all classes among them, but differentially.

In the 1920s and 1930s, successive South African governments intervened extensively to win the support of the white working class. The job colour bar, employment on public works, and generous provision of housing, education, health and social welfare bought off the white working class. But that is why it was absolutely necessary that they continued to support the white racist state. There may be no other country in the world where such a high degree of mutual dependence between a state and a minority of the population existed in order to sustain and perpetuate white racist rule. It is this indispensable requirement of support of the white working class for the retention of the status quo which accounts for why they enjoyed relatively high standards of living. The white working class benefited from racism, while the black working class, at the same time, suffered heavily from it. The resources that went to white workers to maintain their support was denied to black workers. Their respective race-class positions were completely dependent on one another, without which neither could be what it was. White workers could only enjoy such high standards of living because black workers were denied it.

In fact, a study of South African history shows that at every step of that long journey all the major developments were characterised by economic, material and financial interests, virtually without exception. The decisions to establish a refreshment station, to allow the burghers to start their own farms, to extend the frontiers, to undertake the Great Trek, to establish the two Afrikaner republics, to wage nine wars against the Xhosa people and dispossess them of land, the Anglo-Boer War, were all in one way or another driven by the distinctly economic and material interests of land and labour. The key importance of this point is that there was always, if I can put it that way, 'method in the madness' of slavery, racism and capitalism: oppression, exploitation and profiteering.

The British at the Cape

In 1795, the British seized the Cape from the DEIC, which was far from the commanding presence it had earlier been. The colony was briefly returned to Holland, but in 1806 – with the onset of the Napoleonic Wars – the second, conclusive British occupation took place. It is important to recognise the big political and economic changes that occurred from 1806 onwards. Keegan summarises them:

> The early British governors at the Cape ruled in some ways more autocratically than their Dutch predecessors. Proclamations and laws were issued in the governor's name only; no formally constituted body of officials or settlers advised him; his executive powers were virtually unlimited; and appellate jurisdiction in the judicial sphere rested in his hands only. ... Under British rule, the possibilities for private profit from trade increased greatly ... the Cape's international trade was decisively oriented towards Britain and its empire – far and away the most dynamic mercantile network in the world.[10]

While a capitalist economy began in the Cape with the wine industry in the 18th century, it entered a far more dynamic phase with merino wool and ostrich farming in the Eastern Cape in the 19th century. The decisive change came after the discovery of diamonds and gold, the building of railroads, and the rapid growth of cities like Kimberley and Johannesburg. It was then that capitalism took off in SA.

A great deal more could be added about Britain's role in South African history to conclusively show that in fact it decisively shaped present-day South Africa far more than earlier Dutch colonialism. Moeletsi Mbeki made a similar point: 'In the brief five years from the signing of the Peace of Vereeniging in 1902 to the establishment of responsible government in the Transvaal and Orange River colonies in 1907, the British set South Africa on a political, economic and social trajectory that has survived virtually intact to this day'.[11] He also reminds us that it was under British rule that the Witwatersrand Native Labour Association, which recruited African mine labour from outside SA, and the Native Recruitment Corporation, which recruited men inside SA, were formed. Britain early on had its finger on the pulse of the vital mining industry, especially gold, for which purpose an abundant supply of cheap labour was crucial.

An important aspect of British rule in the Cape Colony was liberalism. The next chapter presents a critical analysis of the origins of the ANC, and liberalism was central to its formation in 1912. English liberalism in the Cape included the goal of establishing legal equality between white and black people. Nobody championed this cause more than Dr John Philip, the leading liberal figure from the London Missionary Society in the 19th century.

Philip was the most politically influential of the missionaries and their most powerful spokesperson. His greatest contribution to the liberal cause of human rights was the passage of Ordinance 50, which was passed by the British parliament in January 1829, and is for some the 'foundation stone of a proud tradition of liberalism which was to last into the twentieth century'.[12] But for the racist and conservative Dutch at the Cape, Ordinance 50 was seen 'to be the work of the devil', and Philip became 'an ogre in the eyes of the colonists generally'.[13]

Although Keegan thought its significance was exaggerated, he conceded that it did 'represent, on paper at least, a kind of charter of rights for the colony's Khoi working class'. The Ordinance scrapped pass laws, prohibited summary punishmen.t without benefit of trial, and abolished all forms of compulsory service. 'It affirmed the right of Khoi to buy or own land in the colony. All contracts of service were to be freely entered into by mutual consent. Oral contract could only hold from month to month and children would no longer be indentured without parental consent.'[14] But the Khoi people were hardly impressed with Ordinance 50, concludes Keegan. 'It is revealing that the Khoi themselves ... were not greatly excited by Ordinance 50, for by itself it did not hold out any promise of economic independence or an end to de facto discrimination. Without land, their newly won legal equality did not seem of great consequence.'[15]

On Philip and other leading liberals, Keegan was forthright: 'But despite their dislike of the concept of property in human beings, they also believed in the absolute and inalienable right to the privileges of property. For the rights of property were the foundations of the entire capitalist edifice and were clung to the more vehemently by the British middle classes as new populist, even socialist, ideas began to question them.'[16] This thread of liberal conservatism runs consistently through South African history. Under varying historical conditions, from the British occupation of the Cape into arguably the present-day SA, liberalism ultimately finds its succour within the free market system of capitalism, even if it began to see some limited role for the state in dealing with poverty alleviation and in securing reforms, but always far short of tackling the systemic roots of exploitation. Basically, what Philip wanted is similar to what the ANC wanted and what we have today in SA: a non-racial political democracy, with universal suffrage and other liberal democratic rights. But he never once questioned or critiqued capitalism in the Cape or elsewhere. Nor did Philip's reformism sink real roots in the Cape: 'In the end,' concluded Keegan, 'liberal humanitarianism turned out to be a shallow, tawdry, deceptive thing.'[17] Liberalism only re-established itself in political terms in the mid-20th century, with the formation of the Liberal Party and then the Progressive Party. They combined a commitment to civil rights with strong support for capitalism. So too has the DA, although it has stretched the boundaries of its liberalism over the past decade or two, in post-apartheid SA, towards a kind of social democracy. And despite the occasional radical rhetoric of the ANC, there is not much policy difference between the DA and the ANC.

But that role is not peculiar to white liberals. It is the creed of all liberals, including black middle-class liberals both before and after the 1994 political transition. In fact, the ANC has always been basically a liberal party, and embraced distinctly neoliberal policies after 1994. I argue later that under the conditions of the 1990s, when neoliberalism held sway globally and exerted considerable pressure on the ANC, this was an inevitable outcome, given the orientation of its own analysis and policy direction.

Before proceeding to the mineral revolution which decisively and irrevocably changed SA, I want to consider a major outcome of colonialism after 1652: the emergence and significance of the Coloured population at the Cape. As early as 1682, a leading official of the DEIC, Rijckloff van Goens, had instructed Governor Simon van der Stel to oppose all miscegenation at the Cape. Muller notes that 'There had been many marriages between Dutchmen and emancipated slaves at the Cape, but after 1685 these were prohibited, except when female slaves had Dutch fathers. A school established solely for the children of burghers and officials fitted well into this policy.'[18] This was a 17th-century precursor of laws forbidding marriage between white and black.

Yet those and other measures to prevent sexual relations between black and white in the late 17th century were hardly effective. By the end of the 1700s the Cape Colony had grown to include a large number of mixed-race Coloureds who were the offspring of extensive interracial relations between white, male Dutch settlers, Khoikhoi females and female slaves imported from Dutch colonies in the East. Members of this mixed-race community formed the core of what was to become the Griqua people. If the slaves who were imported from the East Indies, Madagascar, Mozambique and elsewhere are included, then perhaps the degree of sexual relations across racial and colour lines may have been unparalleled in the world. Nowhere more clearly can the result be seen of inter-mixing than in the physical features of the Coloured people, and skin colour of Coloured people, ranging from the fairest to the darkest skin complexions.

I argue that to understand the Coloured Question is crucial to our history and is in fact an inseparable and integral part of the wider National Question, especially the working class. The Khoi-Coloured people were used, abused and manipulated by Dutch, Afrikaner and British rulers, and as the 'stepchildren' of that history were torn between various groups of people. Their entire history of dispossession, enslavement, oppression and exploitation has left a legacy which affects today's Coloured people in numerous ways. It cannot be swept under the carpet of a majoritarian Africanist chauvinism, which has inverted the race hierarchical pyramid of apartheid, resulting in the intense and extensive alienation and demoralisation of Coloured people, especially the working class, just when they expected that their historical genealogy of slavery, oppression, exploitation and marginalisation for over three centuries would end.

Expectations of Coloured progress and protection at the hands of missionary liberalism ran into the sand. The Khoi servants' rebellion of 1799–1803 only ended because they were 'persuaded to lay down their arms in return for promises of independence and equality which never materialised, a belief which would form part of "Hottentot nationalism" and the basis of continuing appeals to British justice'.[19] As the 19th century proceeded, writes Keegan, and 'as the colonial bourgeoisie grew in size and self-confidence, so concerns for the place of Coloured people in colonial society receded as an obstacle to constitutional development, both in Cape Town and London'.[20] This was a further setback for the Khoi-Coloured population.

In recent decades, scholars have enlarged our knowledge of the Khoi and their struggles from the 17th-century Cape Colony onwards and how much the existence of the Coloured people and their ancestry had to do with the Khoi. Long before the Dutch and British waged recurring wars against the Xhosa, Zulu and other African people, it was the Khoi and San, especially the former, who bore the brunt of white racist colonialism. These historians have restored the Khoi to their rightful place in the Cape's history and rescued them from the relative obscurity to which a more dated scholarship relegated them. Keegan and other historians have shown that the Khoi were absorbed into the 18th-century colonial economy as a working class, forming an important component of the Coloured population. By the mid-19th century, the Masters and Servants Ordinance 'was aimed at the coloured working class and was universally so interpreted. The ordinance sought to buttress the racial hierarchy and to reinforce the subordination of coloured workers, as well as the subordination of women to men in labouring families.'[21]

The oppression of Khoi-Coloured people has deep roots in SA. Keegan explains how in the Cape Colony 'Khoi testimony was inadmissible as evidence in court' and that 'it had long been regarded as improper to teach Khoi to read and write, skills which were central to missionary education'.[22] Reflecting their own experiences and the influence of missionary liberal ideology, Keegan reports that in 1834 in 'the Kat River settlement meetings were held where Khoi spokesmen identified themselves as representing the Hottentot nation, robbed of its heritage, discriminated against and oppressed, but seeking equality of opportunity and status with white colonists, and above all, land'.[23] It is patently false and misleading to downplay, belittle or evade this specific history in the making of modern SA, which may be partly why Coloured people today are so terribly alienated from the ANC.

An important aspect of Keegan's narrative is to rupture not only the myth of homogeneous 'whiteness' in South African history, but also to show the stark hypocrisy of English liberalism from the inception of British rule in 1795. Nowhere is such hypocrisy more evident than in dealing with and satisfying the demands of black labour for social justice, which, given the historical conditions under which capitalism developed in SA, were and remain potentially revolutionary, even basic demands such as a 'living wage'. Under British rule, Keegan placed the fate of freed black labour in perspective after the abolition of slavery: the colonists in 'administering the apprenticeship system (in reality indenture rather than apprenticeship) introduced stringent measures to discipline ex-slaves and to appease employers' demands that their interests be secured'.[24]

As a result, 'The British were caught between the dictates of the free-labour ideology and the need to subordinate and control workers. Little wonder that ameliorative measures had unintended consequences'.[25] Brutal Khoi-Coloured working-class oppression and exploitation, despite all the apparently liberal legislation at the Cape, is made vividly evident in Keegan's pages.[26]

How the Mineral Revolution defined the South Africa of today

Much has been written about how SA was irrevocably changed after the discovery of alluvial diamonds in 1867 in the Northern Cape and later gold in Barberton and Johannesburg. Once the mineral revolution was under way, the oppression, subjugation and exploitation of black people, especially workers, became more systematic, deepened and widened increasingly. Virtually everything, in every facet of life, was sooner or later brought into the crucible of the mining revolution and what was required to unearth diamonds, gold and other precious minerals from the earth and to build the industries which grew around the needs of mining on a profitable basis. There was a conscious convergence of local and global capitalist forces, led by Britain, to invest in and build the gold mines, which, together with the profits from diamond mining and the manufacturing industries later built around them, turned SA into the most powerful economy in Africa.

One must also bear in mind that the period which combined the discovery of diamonds in 1867 and gold in 1886 occurred during an aggressive expansion of the global capitalist system, frequently dubbed 'the high age of imperialism'. That period extended into the 20th century and the First World War, which was basically an internecine capitalist war. Undoubtedly, that global context influenced the eagerness of several major powers to invest in and exploit the riches of the gold mines of Johannesburg, especially Britain, which had the huge advantage of being the colonial masters of SA then. But many countries were eager to exploit the 'golden' opportunities which the gold mines promised, the key to which was the abundant cheap black labour. Prospectors and workers from many countries across the world made their way to SA.

It was ultimately upon the backs of the black working class that most of the white people who came to SA, whether from Britain, France, Germany, Scotland, Ireland, the US or many other countries, secured protected employment and lived well and comfortable lives. Though there were distinct class divisions among white people, they all, to varying degrees, benefited from white supremacy. Similarly, the European working class was able to secure high standards of living in Europe because of the massive exploitation of the colonies by the respective colonial powers, at the expense of the workers in the colonies. The higher the rate of exploitation of black labour, the greater were the resources available for the benefit of the European working and middle classes.

However, from 1867 when diamonds were discovered, Britain's interests in SA increased dramatically, reflected not only in the annexation of the Transvaal in 1877, but also in a flurry of wars against African opponents, including the Zulu War in 1879. The annexation of the Transvaal happened three years after gold was discovered in

Barberton, in the Eastern Transvaal, in 1874. In the same year the first gold coins were minted from Barberton but revealingly this was done in London.[27] Quite clearly, British interest in gold far exceeded its earlier interest in diamonds, and even before the big gold discovery was made in Johannesburg in 1886, Sir Garnet Wolseley reported to London in 1878: 'The Transvaal is rich in minerals, gold has already been found in large quantities and there can be little doubt that larger and still more valuable gold-fields will sooner or later be discovered. Any such discovery will soon bring a large population here.'[28] How right his prediction proved to be.

Though not necessarily every single piece of legislation after the mineral revolution was to the benefit of capital, many laws which dealt with access to abundant land and labour, and their attendant structural and institutional requirements, certainly were. Massive profits and severe state repression allowed the owners of capital and their families to live in unbounded luxury, and over time the entire white middle and working classes were provided with high standards of living, at the expense of the overwhelming black majority of the population.

Probably, the law which most blatantly served the interests of white mining capital in the late 19th century was the Glen Grey Act of 1894, which was deliberately meant to place irresistible pressure on and compel African men to seek work in the cities, notably as migrant miners to Johannesburg. The Act was presented to the Cape parliament by Cecil John Rhodes. Referring to him and the mine owners, Merle Lipton asserted:

> They supported restrictions on black land ownership, as well as taxes to force them to work for cash wages. Cecil John Rhodes, leading mine owner and Premier of the Cape Colony, sponsored the Glen Grey Act. Its land tenure and tax provisions would, he said, act as a 'gentle stimulant' to blacks to work and 'remove them from that life of sloth and laziness ... teach them the dignity of labour ... and make them give some return for our wise and good government.[29]

Lipton argued that it was also mine owners who supported influx control and the pass laws: 'The pass laws introduced in the Transvaal Republic in 1895 were actually drafted by the Chamber and gave them, as their spokesman put it, "a hold on the native".'[30]

One also has to ask a pertinent question: since SA remained a dominion in the British Commonwealth after the 1910 Union of South Africa, did Britain not have the power to persuade the new South African state not to pass many pieces of legislation which deepened, extended and entrenched the oppression and exploitation of black people? It obviously did, but it never served their economic interests to oppose such legislation, which was in the interests of the mines and other employers, because it made cheap African labour more available.

Had it not been for the Johannesburg and later the Free State gold mines, the expanded economic power would not have materialised and been unleashed. Wheatcroft placed this situation in sobering perspective: 'What would have happened to Southern Africa without the mines is an imponderable of history. We can only know what happened. There came together three elements: the incomparable riches which nature had left beneath the soil of the Transvaal, European financial assistance and the lust for wealth and cheap labour. Together they transformed the country utterly.'[31]

The first half of the 20th century saw the expansion and consolidation of the minerals-based capitalist economy, with the growth of a strong manufacturing sector, beginning in the 1920s and enjoying explosive growth between the 1940s and 1960s. From the time of diamond mining in 1867 in Kimberley, all this economic growth, which made SA the most economically powerful and industrialised country in Africa, was made possible by an abundant supply of super-exploitable cheap black labour.

The impact of the mineral revolution on SA and its global repercussions dwarfed the agrarian capitalism of the Western and Eastern Cape. It directly and indirectly virtually determined everything of importance that happened in this country thereafter, including the Anglo-Boer War of 1899–1902 and its conclusion. After the Anglo-Boer War 'Britain "found it expedient to give the white inhabitants of the ex-republics a free hand to rule over blacks more or less according to the settlers' own traditions" – as if the South African state after 1910 was simply the old Boer republican state redivivus'.[32] As far as the defeated Boer republicans were concerned, 'The Boer General (General Louis Botha) accepted the British Commander-in-Chief's proposal to leave the question of the native franchise to be settled by a future representative government'.[33]

Why did Britain betray black hopes for the franchise, even if it was also going to be limited by the property qualification that prevailed in the Cape at that time? It was the lucrative gold mines which required lots of cheap black labour. To have granted even a limited franchise to black people in the new constitution for the 1910 Union of SA would have endangered the profits of the gold mines and perhaps led to more demands from blacks. There could not have been a more tragic betrayal than this by British colonialism and imperialism.

There is no city in the world which, as a result of the discovery of vast gold deposits, was baptised as thoroughly by British imperialism and flung into the vortex of global capitalism as Johannesburg, with cataclysmic consequences in SA and southern Africa. The early years of the new metropolis are important for understanding the significance of its future, and that of South Africa. Wheatcroft put it thus: 'Johannesburg was built as a modern industrial and commercial city, in which money and business efficiency came first. Characteristically, there were telephones long before there were mains sewers.'[34]

According to Wheatcroft it was important that the transition to and achievement of monopolistic mining took 'far less time in Johannesburg than it had in Kimberley, partly for the very fact of Kimberley having been first'. There was much more investment in gold mining in Johannesburg's early years compared to diamond mining in Kimberley. In addition, 'besides foreign investors there were now indigenous capitalists in Kimberley diamonds. With the advantage of proximity and expert advice they were much more adroit than European backers.'[35]

Quite clearly, prospectors and investors in the Johannesburg gold mines had learnt a lot from the Kimberley experience. As a result, 'The Witwatersrand gold rush was dominated not by a crowd of men who wished to make their fortunes but by a few who had already made them: the Rand imported its capitalists ready-made from Kimberley'. All of these factors combined, so that 'For the first time South African shares caught the public imagination in Europe. Shares shot up, higher and higher'.[36] Several internal and external factors converged to permanently reshape virtually everything in SA. But the question of the legacy of Dutch and British colonialism on these processes must be appraised dispassionately, otherwise we cannot provide an objective appraisal either of colonialism or the capitalist system in which it was embedded.

The capitalist development of SA, which the Boers and British initiated, represented in the life of black people both a racist hell and prospects for development, including literacy, education and cultural development. This was so despite the unalterable fact that black people generally, especially the working class, bore the brunt of capitalist development in SA. Understanding the march of history, its contours, complexities and contradictions, is essential notwithstanding the racist brutalities of that system over a long period. However, all those tremendous developments were possible only because the economy relied for its growth on cheap black labour, for which purpose a wide range of overtly racist legislation was imposed on black people after the discovery of diamonds. A brutally enforced proletarianisation took place in SA, as violent as anywhere else in the world.

But it is no exaggeration to assert that the foundations upon which SA was rebuilt after the mineral revolution of the 19th century are virtually still intact today, even alongside the extension of the franchise to black people and a wide range of constitutionally enshrined liberal democratic freedoms. In economic terms, it is still WMC which overwhelmingly owns and controls the economy, even 25 years into a 'democratic' SA, and despite the emergence of a significant black middle class and a small layer of black capitalists.

As described earlier, British interventions in southern Africa accelerated after the discovery of diamonds. The mineral discoveries had the immediate effect of placing SA at the centre of British imperial interests. The strategy of Britain was henceforth strategically commensurate with the vital importance of the mineral revolution. So too was the appointment of Lord Milner, a very experienced colonial administrator, in 1897 as governor. But nothing was of greater strategic significance for Britain than the Anglo-Boer War of 1899–1902. The huge costs of the war directly reflected how important the defence of Britain's control of the gold and diamond mines was and therefore nothing less than a military victory was required.

How British imperialism conducted itself in relation to Afrikaner nationalism, especially after the Great Trek began in 1836, was of profound importance in showing how little 'race' mattered in the final analysis, as did the brutalities of the Anglo-Boer War, particularly in how Afrikaner prisoners of war and civilians were treated. Nothing depicted those brutalities more than the scorched earth policy of the British and the concentration camps created to house women and children. No racial sentiment about sharing a common 'whiteness' mattered to either side during that costly and brutal war. Britain utilised its colonialist experience to the utmost in SA, especially after diamonds and gold were discovered. How it moved and strategised with the singular aim of securing total control of those assets is very clear.

Of great importance too is the recognition of the fact that after the discovery of diamonds and gold and the rise to power of Rhodes, he curtailed the multiracial franchise in the Cape and his expansionist policies in fact set the stage for the second Boer War. This change by Rhodes, though limited to the Cape, was extremely significant because it reflects sharply how a non-racial, though still class-based, franchise was realised by Rhodes not to be in the interests of the mining magnates for whom increasingly cheap black labour and land throughout the country became of paramount importance. Additionally, while the British promised that if they won the Anglo-Boer War the lot of blacks would change for the better, they did not want the qualified franchise of the Cape extended to blacks in the Boer republics.

English liberalism has undeniably had a woeful history in SA, which in fact is a manifestation of the historical fact that racism in all its political forms since the days of the Cape Colony, including mostly under apartheid, was inseparably intertwined with capitalism. I am reminded of the blurb of the book, *South Africa INC: The Oppenheimer Empire*: 'South Africa's fabulous wealth and the laws of the apartheid regime were built on diamonds and gold, which over the past seventy years have become concentrated in the hands of one of the richest families in the world – the Oppenheimers. The book explodes the reputation that the Oppenheimers have cultivated as the leading South African opponents of apartheid.'[37] Within the framework of capitalism, liberalism was constrained in its ability to strike deep roots within the black population, especially the working class. Yet, the ANC, with its African nationalist liberalism, had huge success in building a sizeable mass base of support among the working class, the dynamics of which I explore in the next chapter.

It is an indisputable fact that despite its rose-tinted ideology which professed to be free of racism and wedded to a future SA free of apartheid, the hands of South African liberalism are stained with the blood of black mine and later manufacturing workers. White liberalism did not question and criticise the appalling conditions of the migrant labour system and the hostels and compounds black miners lived in, not to mention the terribly low wages paid to those miners.

I conclude this section with three comments. Firstly, long gone are the days of fighting for political or civil rights, as happened in the US and SA. Today there are not many countries in the world where the right to vote and other 'bourgeois' democratic rights are not respected and constitutionally entrenched. 'We the People' of the American constitution and Robespierre's 'Every citizen has an equal claim to representation' are no longer in question or the focus of struggles. No, those are indeed 'bourgeois rights', in the very important sense that capitalism has long learnt how to live fairly comfortably with them, with no country showing this fact more than parliamentary British democracy, which itself decisively shaped post-apartheid SA.

We need only look at what has happened after black people won those rights in the US and SA to understand and appreciate this point. In fact, arguably in no country is the charade of enjoying such rights but continuing to suffer the same poverty, joblessness, homelessness and inequalities which characterised apartheid more evident than in SA after 1994. As a result, ironically we have experienced greater mass struggles in post-apartheid SA than we had under apartheid. The reason for that crucial irony resides in the nature of the ANC since its birth and its policies both before and after 1994.

Secondly, in South African history race, class and gender have been permanently embedded in its formative fabric, from which there can be no escape. A critical analysis of what happened during the negotiations process between 1990 and 1993 and after 1994, in the realm of economic, social and public policies, and how these events made SA the protest capital of the world, speaks volumes for how inextricably tied race, class and gender are. This is going to have profoundly important implications for anti-racist struggles into the future.

Thirdly, I want to mention the work of the late Bernard Magubane, the ANC-aligned historian who wrote a great deal on SA. While his work is very useful, especially on colonialism and the political economy of race and racism in SA, he avoids throughout his otherwise often brilliant work the key question of the ANC's approach to the revolution in SA. There is a serious disjuncture in his work between how he approaches race and racism, through Marxist political economy and recognition of the strong race–class links, and his failure to critique the two-stage approach of both the ANC and the SACP. He was a member of the ANC and had close relations with Mbeki and all the other ANC leaders in exile. There probably lies the answer to this disjuncture between his theoretical approach and his failure to adopt a socialist, permanent revolutionary solution towards the struggle in SA.

In a paper in 2001, he argued that 'In order to counter the ANC's National Democratic Revolution, the DP (Democratic Party, predecessor of the DA) counterrevolutionary strategy tries to conserve the dominance of capital at the expense of the poor, who are mostly Africans'.[38] But while Magubane criticised the DP, which was a pro-capitalist, mainly white party, he did not say a word about the NDR's two-stage approach which also conserves the dominance of capital. Instead of a socialist agenda the NDR sought to oppose apartheid and replace it with a non-racial democracy, within a capitalist economic framework.

Reflections on Colonialism

The previous section established that the discovery of diamonds and gold (and later other minerals) fundamentally changed SA. The mineral revolution galvanised capitalism in SA. Equally important was the subsequent industrialisation of SA. Those achievements made possible gigantic strides in productive capacity in every sector of the economy, on the basis of super-exploitable black labour on the mines and in agriculture at the glaring expense of the basic needs and interests of those workers.

However, we cannot ignore the indisputable fact that both the Dutch/Afrikaners and the British contributed enormously to the material development of SA, before and especially after the mineral revolution. Such development occurred alongside slavery, a harsh colonialism and an enforced proletarianisation. From the time of the old Cape Colony important technological changes were made by the Dutch: they provided access to clean water, carried out sanitary works and irrigation, promoted farming and viticulture, built roads, housing and schools, and made available a wide variety of imported products, which the indigenous peoples had never seen nor used before. All of these brought about profound and lasting changes to the culture of Khoisan peoples and, later, Africans from the Eastern Cape.

I argue that material culture brought by colonialism and capitalism to SA had positive aspects to it. To deny that significance is to deny history, as it happened, and not as we wish it did. For example, is it without significance that Rhodes introduced in the Cape Colony vine stock resistant to phylloxera, which destroys grapevines at its roots if untreated, introduced the ladybird to counteract a pest which attacked citrus fruit or pushed through the compulsory dipping of sheep against scab?[39] To close one's eyes to these developments, because they happened under racist colonialism, is to close one's eyes to history.

The craftsmanship and architecture of the old Cape Dutch houses, buildings and furniture, much of which still stand today, form an important heritage, which cannot be disregarded because of what the Dutch did to the Khoikhoi, San and later African peoples. History is history, no matter what happens at any particular point in time, as is the case with the unmitigated horrors of Nazism in Europe in the 1930s and 1940s. Hitler cannot be excised from history as a result of the murder of six million Jews or German technology frowned upon or boycotted. History is a complex, convoluted and contradictory phenomenon, from which we can learn not only about our past but about our present.

John Bond catalogued the significant infrastructural changes introduced to SA under British rule. The first education system and university in SA were established by the British. They also 'built the roads, opened the harbours and created the postal, telegraph and railway services. They revitalised agriculture, carried trade far into the interior, developed the first banks, opened mines in the wilderness, found great cities and launched an industrial revolution.' They built schools, churches and hospitals and created a public service, an administration system, a system of law and order, police, courts and so on.[40]

Transportation from the Cape to the Voortrekker Republics changed after the arrival of the British, going from ox-wagons to carts and horses, to public coach and later the motor car and lorry. The changes to transport 'transformed the whole of SA and not merely its farming, trade or administration'.[41] History is a zigzag process. This meant that material progress took place during colonialism, alongside the virulent racism, brutal oppression, and exploitation of the Khoisan and other

African people. The young Marx commented on this apparent paradox: 'England has to fulfil a double mission in India: one destructive, the other regenerating – the annihilation of old Asiatic society, and the laying of the material foundations of Western society in Asia.'

Unsurprisingly, questions about the legacy of colonialism remain contentious in SA. This was the case in 2017, when the former leader of the DA, Helen Zille, sent a controversial tweet: 'For those claiming that the legacy of colonialism was *only* negative, think of our independent judiciary, transport infrastructure, piped water, etc. Would we have had a transition into specialised health care and medication without colonial influence? Just be honest, please' (emphasis added). The qualifier 'only' is very important to note. When later, in 2019, someone on Twitter suggested that she had said that 'colonialism wasn't bad', she replied: 'I didn't say anything like that. Colonialism was terrible. But its legacy is not only negative. If you can't tell the difference between those two statements, I feel sorry for you.' Things were complicated for Zille when the then leader of the DA, Mmusi Maimane, replied on Twitter, without referring to Zille: 'Let's make this clear: Colonialism and Apartheid was a system of oppression and subjugation. It can never be justified.' I think Maimane only said that because as the black leader of the DA he would attract lots of criticism if he said nothing. But he missed the point. It would be a distortion to say that Zille sought to justify colonialism by her tweet.[42]

Predictably, Zille's original tweet unleashed a slew of angry condemnations, especially from African people. The DA KZN politician, Mbali Ntuli, responded: 'It was only negative!! Colonialism = development argument is trash as those subjugated can attest to.' Eusebius McKaiser condemned it as 'disgusting'.[43] Zille sought to defuse the situation by apologising 'unreservedly for a tweet that may have come across as a defence of colonialism. It was not.'[44] The problem with this reply was that it failed to clarify matters, leaving much that was important unsaid.

Zille certainly should have been far more careful in how she formulated her tweet when she praised colonialism for some of the progressive technical changes it introduced, especially under British rule, alongside the brutal oppression and exploitation of black people. But how can anybody even begin to deny the obvious usefulness, progress and benefits of some technological changes ushered in by colonialism? We need to separate issues in this debate, rather than indiscriminately lump everything together under the rubric of 'colonialism'.

I refuse to play the card of political correctness in a serious matter like this, to the point that I would differ even if every black person believed that Zille's tweet was necessarily racist, or that she was necessarily insensitive to the terrible suffering colonialism inflicted on black people, or that she simply praised colonialism. What she should have said was something along these lines: 'Despite all the horrors both Afrikaner and British colonialism perpetrated against black people it is also important to recognise that those colonial powers, especially Britain, did introduce certain technical changes, which benefited the society at large, namely access to clean and safe drinking water and safe and decent sanitation and so on.' Such a statement does not in the least amount to a condonation of colonialism. Perspective is very important in these matters.

Of course, how the material benefits during colonialism were experienced depended upon race and class. The gains provided by technological changes were rarely extended to black people at the time. But we need to adopt the same approach to the complex development of capitalism, recognising that – like colonialism – it had destructive and creative features. Marx praised the economic and technical achievements of the capitalist system many times. In fact, the technological revolution of the past three decades, especially in communications technology, has been breath-taking and extremely important for humanity at large and for future generations. There is nothing revolutionary whatsoever in disregarding the technical gains to society which were ushered in under colonialism and capitalism. On the contrary, we must welcome them, but turn them to the usage, advantage and benefit of all people.

At the same time, it is essential to bear in mind that technological change – modernisation in shorthand – comes at a high historical cost. Tim Keegan provides a most perceptive take on the relationship between modernisation and racism:

> Rather than a modernisation that philosophers held out moved in one direction of 'lifting the untutored masses out of their passivity into the rational light of day through the power of education and example', it was left to a later, more cynical generation, with an eye

on the lessons of history rather than the abstractions of philosophy, to point out that modernity is more likely built on what some have called primitive accumulation, the process whereby aggregations of productive resources (land, labour and capital), in the hands of the powerful few inevitably involved (at least in the short term) the dispossession and immiseration of the many. As we shall see all too clearly, the ideology and practice of racial supremacy ... were in the globalised world of the 19th century integral to that process.[45]

Far from such insights, the 'debate' precipitated by Zille's tweet evoked largely predictable race-based, knee-jerk responses, in particular the reaction of African people and Africanists, which did not serve to clarify the real issues but instead fatally obscured the matters that were really important in this 'race' debacle. Many black people seemed to think that Zille was wrong and must be wrong because she was not only 'white' but the leader of what was seen as a predominantly 'white' party and the official opposition to the ANC. She faced such a torrent of criticism and abuse that it seemed as if many of her critics would gladly have publicly burnt her at a stake.

In another intervention in 2019, Zille also attracted condemnation when she was reported saying that 'Black privilege is being able to loot a country and steal hundreds of billions and get re-elected' and that 'whiteness is a swear word used to stigmatise and marginalise'.[46] Why should anyone get upset when she criticises black privilege? Surely that is what ANC rule and its BEE and AA policies created. That is what the black elite and, to a lesser degree, the black middle class enjoy after all. Elitist black privilege of these layers, especially BEE businesses, is a conspicuous reality in post-apartheid SA. An attack on white privilege makes sense to people, but an attack on black privilege is wrong or in fact morally outrageous. But to deny black privilege is either ignorant or hypocritical. According to research in 2016 there are presently around 17,300 millionaires from 'previously disadvantaged' groups, which represents 45% of the total number of millionaires in SA.[47]

A central problem for SA is that any politics that is built and reliant upon a racial demographic majority, a mere matter of numbers, might ultimately be the worst enemy of a progressive revolutionary politics and a vibrant civil society, which is able to fearlessly 'talk truth to power'.

That is what this country desperately needs. I want to be able to listen to Zille or any other white person without always seeing her or him as a 'white' and belonging to a fictitious and racialist 'minority'. The very term 'minority', which has been used by African nationalists, especially of the narrow chauvinist type, for decades to refer to those groups who are not 'African', including Coloureds and Indians, could arguably be racist.

To conclude this section, it is important to note of colonialism in SA that we cannot speak about it in homogeneous terms. White people did not always share the same interests. Keegan draws attention to the existence already in the late 19th century of the 'resentment of the Afrikaner bourgeoisie towards the more established and prosperous British mercantile elite'.[48] Conflict between Afrikaner and English-speaking elites grew as the century unfolded. The point is that divisions among whites were always there under colonialism – especially around class, nationalism and culture – and persist to the present day. Today, the most glaring class divisions among black people are more visible than ever before in the entire history of this country. But we can only see and appreciate the importance of those factors, in which the intersecting hierarchies of gender and culture also feature, when we accordingly widen the lens of our assimilation, analysis and perspectives.

Equally, colonialism must not only be associated with its Dutch or British expressions. Too often we tend to whitewash history and present it in binary racial or black–white terms, and this applies to the term and meaning of colonialism. Khoi collaboration with Dutch settlers began in the first few years of the Cape Colony, when intra-Khoi conflicts resulted in some of them looking for support from the Dutch against other factions.[49] For the early 19th century, it has been pointed out, King Shaka was in effect a coloniser, conquering and incorporating neighbouring clans. Equally, there are many references to African leaders in SA and elsewhere in Africa who collaborated with their respective colonial powers, who sometimes sought their military support against other African leaders. In 1818, for instance, differences between two Xhosa leaders, Ndlambe and Ngqika, ended in the defeat of Ngqika, who thereafter appealed to the British for help against Ndlambe. Britain's eventual defeat of the Zulus was accomplished with the assistance of Zulu collaborators resentful of centralised royal authority. There were similar such divisions and collaboration with the apartheid state among Coloured and Indian communities. In fact, never at any point in time throughout the liberation struggles against slavery, colonialism and capitalism was there a fully homogeneous class of people, either perpetrating these systems or at their receiving end. Such centrifugal disunities have characterised all political struggles. There is an overwhelming convergence of similar stories and themes historically and globally, affecting both white and black peoples and their histories and struggles.

We also saw much of this in late 20th-century SA and, depending on what conclusions an analysis of the nature of the negotiated settlement in SA in 1993 reaches, the collaborationist analysis could easily extend to various aspects of the post-apartheid ANC government. Nothing depicts more this collaboration than the elitist compromises made there and especially what has happened in SA since 1994.

However, there is a very interesting but shocking story I must tell which was the most tragic expression of the persistence of the often brutal racist practices black people were subjected to since the days of slavery, but with a most hideous and macabre 'scholarly' twist to it gone mad. Upon its discovery I was taken back to what I said at the outset: how little knowledge of our history South Africans have, a fact which troubled me deeply while doing research for this book. Still it stunned me when I first discovered this story. World-renowned palaeoanthropologist Philip Tobias, who was greatly admired for long by white liberal South Africans and after 1994 by Mandela, Mbeki and many other luminaries of the ANC, not only believed under apartheid that race was a valid 'biological concept which helps bring order out of the otherwise meaningless range of human variations',[50] but for a long time while he worked at Wits University conducted experiments on the private parts of Khoisan women in the Northern Cape.

That the very popular Tobias, whom the white liberal media promoted as an anti-apartheid campaigner for many years and whose funeral was attended by Mbeki and many other ANC dignitaries in June 2012, had such a past, hardly anyone knew or talked about. There is no record of an apology by Tobias and other leading scientists from Wits University who also for many years wantonly violated the bodies of numerous Khoisan women in what was nothing less than racist research. As Christa Kuljian noted: 'They were not at European hospitals doing comparative research on young white adolescent girls.'[51] It was this and many other shocking details Kuljian presented about the practices of Tobias, his predecessor Raymond Dart, and other white scientists during the apartheid years which served to remind one how race, medicine, science, sports, the arts, education and so many more areas of life bowed before the master that white racist apartheid was.

What was particularly disturbing is that these scientists appeared strongly to have exploited those very dark days of racist apartheid in that they conducted their racist research on the bodies of Khoisan women without any regard for rules or laws that they needed to comply with. Kuljian writes about what was officially referred to as a particular 'Bushman female specimen'[52] from Oudtshoorn, whom they had worked on before and who was seriously ill. Even before she died Dart had arranged that her body be sent to him at Wits University, for which purpose he got someone to drive down to Oudtshoorn to fetch the corpse and load it in a bakkie. But like so many other countless atrocities during apartheid, this Khoisan woman and all the other Khoisan women these white scientists conducted their racist experiments on were never heard of again.

Their names did not even appear at the Truth and Reconciliation Commission (TRC). These most vulnerable women were victims of racist 'science' in the most damning and degradable manner imaginable, but there was not only no justice for them or their remaining families, but no memory of them either. I asked Kuljian why there was not much public controversy in the media about these utterly racist activities of Tobias after her book was published. I suppose I'd have been surprised if there was. There is no record anywhere either in which Tobias had admitted to these racist atrocities and apologised to the remaining families of these women and to black South Africans.

But it's also how Tobias was revered after 1994 by the ANC regime without the slightest knowledge of that past. Neither did Tobias and any of his colleagues appear before the TRC. Given the most shocking nature of the facts Kuljian disclosed, the media very clearly gave scant attention to it when the book was published in 2016. Not only did the TRC exclude, I believe deliberately, economic and social transformation from its agenda, but these kinds of non-military racist atrocities against black Khoisan women were also excluded, as were the systemic and multiple social injustices white supremacy and apartheid represented in the lives of black people, especially the majority black working class.

The Silence of Gender in Our History

Over a long and protracted period gender has been the real and most serious 'elephant in the room' in SA, sorely neglected especially in daily discourses. However, that picture has begun to change significantly over the past decade, especially in South African newspapers, which have paid increasing attention to gender issues, mainly involving African women, but mostly regarding the aspirations of middle-class women. What is required is a more concentrated focus on the needs, interests and aspirations of the majority black working-class women, arguably the most neglected constituency in SA after 1994.

This neglect and often silence about the interests and needs of such women are symptomatic of the situation which faced the black working class under apartheid, from which it must not be separated. These women are in fact the most oppressed and exploited people in South African history, but not only at the hands of the various white racist regimes since the 19th century. Though in different ways, these women, many often illiterate and uneducated, have been at the receiving end of multiple forms of oppression and exploitation. This has included employers of often ultra-exploitable cheap African women as domestic workers, whether they be white, Coloured, Indian or African. After 1994 many more middle-class Africans have also employed cheap black female domestic labour. Black working-class women remain the poorest people in SA, right at the bottom of the race–class capitalist-defined social hierarchy.

Not even the left outside the ANC alliance, even when they are supposedly gender-sensitive, have adequately probed the living and working conditions of these women, who arguably bore the brunt of various white racist regimes even more than black male workers. The wages paid to female domestic and farm workers have been historically the lowest wages paid to any workers in SA since the 19th century. On the farms of the Western Cape, Coloured women have been paid very low wages for centuries. Slave wages were also paid to women workers in the clothing and textile industries of SA. But that is only on the wage front. In addition, black women, whether as wives, sisters or daughters, have been subjected for centuries to a very oppressive system of traditional patriarchy in their own homes.

It is the combination of these various forms of oppression, discrimination and exploitation that black women, especially working-class women, have lived with for centuries across the country, often at the hands of black men who themselves constituted the exploitable backbone of the mining and manufacturing industries. Since the beginning of the industrial revolution in the mid-19th century, this has been their deplorable lot. But which scholars and thinkers of the ANC or any of the other black/African nationalist organisations have done research in this area and published works on it? After 1994, the rising black middle class increasingly employed black female domestic workers, behaving as middle classes across the world have behaved. In these cases, race, notwithstanding the previous solidarities apartheid generated among black people, was trumped by new class opportunities.

An interesting and revealing sociological development in post-apartheid SA is the expansion of the size and status of the black middle class. Sakhela Buhlungu put this point well: 'The opening up or deracialisation of society triggered class formation on a scale that has no precedent in black South African history.'[53] But it is important to temper this assessment with a related reality: there is a lower end of the black middle class which has not been much better off than the families they came from in the townships, including some who went to live in the city and areas like Hillbrow, Berea and so on. The black middle class is not a fixed, immutable phenomenon and is subject to a whole range of constantly fluctuating factors. Much of it is fragile, since it does not have the education, resources and stability the white middle class historically enjoyed because it was able to consolidate itself and advance due to the protections apartheid afforded it.

But it is not about race in the first instance. No, it is about class factors at play: the higher the wages workers earn the more they are able to live differently, enjoy higher standards of living and employ domestic workers, which frees them from the drudgery of domestic work. But the point is that the lot of domestic workers has hardly changed much after 1994. It is a disgrace that under ANC rule the minimum wage for domestic workers is a paltry R15 an hour, which is less than R3,000 a month. Under the soaring cost of living in SA, especially over the past few years, it is self-evident that this is cruelly inadequate.

Caught between the traditional patriarchal family and marital oppression and low wages and poor working conditions, the lot of black domestic workers is arguably the worst of all the oppression and exploitation that black people suffered before, during and after apartheid. African domestic and farm workers have been the worst off in SA: they and their families have been the 'niggers' of the South African labour market since the discovery of diamonds in Kimberley. This history the ANC knows very well, but if we study what has happened under its rule, it is probably the biggest disgrace of the ruling party. Even the ANC Women's League has not once drawn public attention to the plight of these workers and appealed to the ANC government to set a higher minimum wage for domestic and farm workers. But neither have they supported, for example, the resistance of black women in townships to the imposition of prepaid meters. They were nowhere to be seen when these women were in the forefront of the community fight against these meters.

But it is not only black female domestic workers who have suffered. All other black working-class women, especially African women, have suffered too. If truth be told, the ANC has neglected the position, needs and interests of these women since its inception, as it did with the broader black working class, who after 1994 have largely been convenient electoral cannon fodder for it. I believe that this was partly as a result of a strong patriarchal cultural tradition in the ANC which its leaders took with them into exile, returned with, and continued to embody since then, wittingly or unwittingly. The sad and deplorable lot of these women in post-apartheid SA is the result of that history and especially the neoliberal policies the party adopted over this period, which severely affected budgets for redress and transformation across society.

There have been media reports about how black female members of the ANC were ill-treated and disrespected in exile, including some who were sexually abused by fellow black male members, often senior.[54] Some women began to speak out about their experiences in exile, especially in the camps. One must try to picture the extreme vulnerability of these women while in exile. Often with little education, at the mercy of patriarchal party bosses in foreign countries and without supporting family structures, they were there as vulnerable as they always have been in South African history. Till today, and since they took office in 1994, the ANC has never been seriously and consistently committed to meeting even the basic needs of these women, despite having access to enormous state resources. In fact, I have never once heard an ANC leader speak about African working-class women, who are the vast majority of women in SA, in these terms, that their basic needs and interests deserve the highest priority, and then act accordingly.

It is also black working-class women, especially African, who have suffered most from the neoliberal budgetary constraints of the ANC government since 1994, particularly since Gear was adopted in 1996. They have borne the brunt of the commercialisation, corporatisation and commodification of basic services since the Municipal Systems Act (MSA) was passed in 2000. They have done so because it is they who perform all the tasks which require water and electricity, such as the washing of dishes or clothing or cooking and so on, as a result of centuries-old patriarchal social relations, in which they are traditionally expected to perform a wide range of domestic tasks, which is only possible because they are subordinated to the power and control of men in their homes, whether husbands or brothers or even sons.

Violence against black women, including widespread rape, is yet another acute social problem in modern SA. The people whose needs should have received the greatest attention have been the most neglected. Today they are the ones who suffer most from poverty, unemployment, staggering social inequalities and related social miseries. A similar situation will be seen in just about all other African countries.

Unemployment in townships has been gruelling for several years but reached its highest rate since 1994 in August 2019, when it was 29% (6.7 million people), but with the expanded definition (including people who are out of work but have stopped looking for work) being 38.5% (more than 10 million).[55] This is aside from the fact that even people who do have work are regarded as 'working poor' because they don't earn much. Webster also points out the gender dimension of unemployment: in SA 43.5% of women are out of work, while 35% of men are unemployed.[56]

It is therefore change in the conditions that these women face that best serves as a reliable yardstick with which to measure social progress and transformation in our society. This is a powerful and compelling approach the ANC must adopt and sustain if it is indeed committed to these changes, which must be reflected in appropriate budgetary provisions. This is not the approach the ANC has had towards black working-class women thus far. Instead these women have suffered various problems as a direct result of the neoliberal policies it adopted after 1994. Unless those policies are urgently addressed and changed, these women will remain trapped in conditions which are likely to worsen ever further in the future, along with the worsening economic crisis.

But the fact that the ANC has moved in a different and opposite direction has conclusively shown the serious limitations of its African nationalism and the resultant failure to understand that in order to build the better life it has repeatedly pledged itself to, these policies will have to be addressed. Unfortunately, there is not the slightest indication that the policies which have been responsible for the worsening lot of black women will be reviewed and changed. Instead, the limited free water and electricity they received in municipalities before was done away with in 2017 and replaced with an exclusive focus on indigency. Today, only households which have registered as indigents – a painfully stigmatising and demeaning bureaucratic procedure – receive a limited amount of water and electricity. So onerous and alienating has the process been that many, if not most, poor households have not registered.

What the unresolved issues of both race and gender have shown since 1994 is the necessity to draw a distinction between perceived offences which impinge on the personal dignity of black people, such as racist remarks made by white people, like Penny Sparrow, and a range of offensive conduct and behaviours and the material effects of race and racism. That is a critical distinction to make and sustain because it is completely impossible to eliminate such conduct given a very long history, but while those battles will continue indefinitely, we need a far greater focus on the systemic and institutional issues of racism, which have resulted in the perpetuation of mass black poverty, unemployment and inequalities.

It is significant that while we pay so much attention to the subjective expressions of race and racism, which is understandable, we pay so little attention to the structural causes of these massive social ills, the result of systemic features over a very long period of time. To deal with that legacy requires policies which the ANC has shown no willingness to adopt. The ANC, especially with Ramaphosa at the helm, will continue with a neoliberal policy regime for as long as organised workers and civil society allow it to. He has followed a conservative path on economic policies and his appointment of Tito Mboweni, who is a neoliberal hawk, as minister of finance, made it very clear what Ramaphosa wants to do.

The problems of race and racism have always in the history of this country been the legal framework which denied the black majority political and socioeconomic rights. Given our race–class historical nexus, we must strive at all times to weave socio-material measures into our discourses of race and racism and not be detained endlessly with the angst evoked by unadulterated racism. That is why linking race to social justice and questions of political economy is the most useful and practical approach to what could otherwise be very vexatious and combustible issues, especially given our history. Once we depart from that narrative, it is the easiest thing to find ourselves sucked into white or black nationalist zeal and its associated diatribes, which is the surest way of killing off further conversations.

The earlier solidarities which 'race' and blackness evoked during the anti-apartheid struggle no longer matter at all. Non-racial neoliberalism and a constitution with no trace of racial discrimination have altered the historical construction of the economy and society. But the problem is that the 1996 constitution – which is premised on the protection of private property and therefore of capitalism – whose praises were falsely sung across the world as a beacon of democracy, cannot change the history which ultimately produced the mass black poverty, unemployment and social inequalities we have today in SA, because the ANC–NP settlement left the systemic causal structures in place. The key and critical question that therefore arises is: just what has ANC rule, and its African nationalism, done for the black working-class majority or, to use its own racialist mantra, 'blacks in general and Africans in particular'?

But even if we defer to that racialist mantra, what has the ANC done for African people and specifically women, especially when they are materially worse off than Coloured and Indian people? To seek to deny the deplorable poverty, unemployment and inequalities which the African majority still suffers today is to add insult to injury and to further hoodwink the African masses. However, this palpable disappointment and in fact betrayal are accentuated when contrasted with the chasmic divide between the conditions of the black majority and that of the ANC elite in the state and those who quit politics and joined the white corporate world. These betrayals are etched into the fabric of our society with the blood, sweat and tears of those masses.

However, as complex as the situation has become in SA after 1994, one thing that is abundantly clear is that the black working-class majority has by default learnt much about race, class and gender and the power relations which underpin them. It is certainly no longer a simple white and black dichotomy, as the situation was perceived under apartheid. The much better life the ANC promised has not materialised, and in some respects, especially regarding basic services, things got worse, especially for African women. How this situation will change is hard to say, but we must not exclude the possibility that conditions might even worsen further, in the midst of the global crisis and the oncoming 4IR, which I suspect is going to accelerate the unemployment crisis.

The last word on the silence of gender in our history, especially of black working-class women, belongs to the late activist, feminist and academic, Phyllis Ntantala, mother of Pallo Jordan. Regarded by many as the greatest South African feminist intellectual, she was a most assertive, independent and militant black female voice in the broad liberation movement. On a visit to the Eastern Cape in 2006 she condemned the state of the public hospitals after she collapsed and was admitted to the Nelson Mandela Hospital.

> The state of public hospitals in the Eastern Cape is horrific. And I understand the conditions I encountered there also apply to similar hospitals in other parts of the country. In all my 80-plus years I have never felt as insulted as I did for those two days and nights lying naked in that bed. I relayed my experience and my feelings, in writing, to both the national and provincial ministers of health and only resolved to go public when I did not even receive the courtesy of a reply.[57]

Ntantala epitomises the kind of black feminist militancy we might have had much more of had it been paid more attention historically. It is very clear that the ANC has never consciously nurtured such voices. Paul Trewhela ended his tribute to Ntantala on a sombre note: 'Nothing was more foreign to this woman than the culture of cadre deployment, the party list and slate politics of the so-called New South Africa, by which women with not a fraction of her qualities are catapulted into the highest offices (provided they shut their mouths or are praise singers).' He ends by referring to the 'curse of patriarchal slavishness' under Zuma's rule.[58] But patriarchy, like sexism and Africanist chauvinism, has deep roots in the ANC.

Endnotes

1 Cornelius F. J. Muller, ed., *500 Years: A History of South Africa* (Pretoria: Academica, 1986), p. 8.
2 Timothy Keegan, *Colonial South Africa and the Origins of the Racial Order* (Cape Town & Johannesburg: David Philip, 1996), p. 13.
3 John Clare, ed., *Captured in Time: Five Centuries of South African Writing* (Johannesburg and Cape Town: Jonathan Ball, 2010), p. x.
4 Clare, *Captured in Time*, p. 18.
5 Clare, *Captured in Time*, p. 12.
6 Cited in Clare, *Captured in Time*, p. 53.
7 Hermann Giliomee, *The Afrikaners* (Charlottesville: University of Virginia Press, 2003), pp. 14, 18.
8 Michael MacDonald, *Why Race Matters in South Africa* (Cambridge, MA and London: Harvard University Press, 2006), p. 39.
9 Muller, *500 Years*, p. 81.
10 Muller, *500 Years*, p. 48.
11 Moeletsi Mbeki, *Architects of Poverty: Why African Capitalism Needs Changing* (Johannesburg: Picador Africa, 2009), p. 40.
12 Keegan, *Colonial South Africa*, p. 104.
13 Keegan, *Colonial South Africa*, p. 105.
14 Keegan, *Colonial South Africa*, pp. 103–4.
15 Keegan, *Colonial South Africa*, p. 117.
16 Keegan, *Colonial South Africa*, p. 112.
17 Keegan, *Colonial South Africa*, p. 127.
18 Muller, *500 Years*, p. 42.
19 Keegan, *Colonial South Africa*, p. 120.
20 Keegan, *Colonial South Africa*, p. 168.
21 Keegan, *Colonial South Africa*, p. 126.
22 Keegan, *Colonial South Africa*, p. 83.
23 Keegan, *Colonial South Africa*, pp. 120, 117.
24 Keegan, *Colonial South Africa*, p. 122.
25 Keegan, *Colonial South Africa*, p. 108.
26 Keegan, *Colonial South Africa*, see pp. 118–128.
27 Geoffrey Wheatcroft, *The Randlords: The Men Who Made South Africa* (London: Weidenfeld, 1985), p. 77.
28 Wheatcroft, *The Randlords*, p. 76.
29 Merle Lipton, *Capitalism and Apartheid: South Africa, 1910–1986* (London: Wildwood House, 1985), p. 119.
30 Lipton, *Capitalism and Apartheid*, p. 120.

31 Wheatcroft, *The Randlords*, p. 267.
32 Keegan, *Colonial South Africa*, p. 11; the quoted words are by the American historian George Frederickson.
33 Martin Plaut, *Promise and Despair: The First Struggle for a Non-Racial South Africa* (Johannesburg: Jacana Media, 2016).
34 Wheatcroft, *The Randlords*, p. 5.
35 Wheatcroft, *The Randlords*, pp .81, 85.
36 Wheatcroft, *The Randlords*, pp. 88, 84.
37 D. Pallister, S. Stewart and I. Lepper, *South Africa Inc: The Oppenheimer Empire* (Johannesburg: Lowry Publishers, 1987).
38 See Bernard Magubane, 'Social construction of race and citizenship', conference paper delivered at the United Nations Research Institute for Social Development, Durban, 3–5 September 2001.
39 Wheatcroft, *The Randlords*, p. 1.
40 John Bond, *They Were South Africans* (London and New York: Oxford University Press, 1971), pp. 4–5.
41 Bond, *They Were South Africans*, p. 116.
42 All quotations in this paragraph from 'Helen Zille defends colonialism tweets again', 8 April 2019, *Cape Times*.
43 'Helen Zille defends colonialism'.
44 Nic Andersen, 'Helen Zille has been tweeting about "colonialism" and people are furious', *The South African*, 16 March 2017, see www.thesouthafrican.com.
45 Tim Keegan, *Dr Philip's Empire: One Man's Struggle for Justice in Nineteenth Century South Africa* (Cape Town: Zebra Books, 2016), p. 2.
46 See 'Helen Zille unapologetic about "black privilege" message: 'Stop stigmatising whiteness', 20 May 2019, at www.timeslive.co.za.
47 'Black vs white millionaires in South Africa', *Businesstech*, 20 April 2016.
48 Keegan, *Colonial South Africa*, p. 106.
49 Muller, *500 Years*, p. 55.
50 See Christa Kuljian, *Darwin's Hunch: Science, Race and the Search for Human Origins* (Johannesburg: Jacana Media. 2016), p. 134. Anybody interested in the life of Philip Tobias will not find a more informative, better and more critical-minded book than this.
51 Kuljian, *Darwin's Hunch*, p. 136.
52 Kuljian, *Darwin's Hunch*, p. 78.
53 M Sakhela Bulhungu, 'Democracy and modernisation in the making of the South African trade union movement: The dilemma of leadership, 1973–2000', PhD thesis, University of the Witwatersrand, 2001, p. 295.
54 See 'Women freedom fighters tell of sexual abuse in camps', *Mail & Guardian*, 27 October 2017.
55 Dennis Webster, 'Unemployment in South Africa is worse than you think', *Mail & Guardian*, 5 August 2019.
56 Webster, 'Unemployment'.
57 See Paul Trewhela, 'Activist academic Phyllis Ntantala was surely the greatest South African feminist intellectual', *Daily Dispatch*, 23 July 2016.
58 Trewhela, 'Activist academic'.

Four

Towards understanding the African National Congress

> If history has nothing to say to us, then it wouldn't make much sense to study or teach it or read about it at all. History is important to us, and knowledge of the past can have a profound effect on our consciousness, on our sense of ourselves.
> Gordon S. Wood, *The Purpose of the Past*

The Origins of the ANC

IT HAS NEVER BEEN more urgent to turn our attention to what the ANC really consisted of and what lessons we can draw from it than this moment of crisis. In this regard Wood asserts that 'Perhaps there was always a tension between critical history and memory, between what historians write and what society chooses to remember'. But that tension has become much more conspicuous in recent years. The shocking things that have happened under ANC rule since 1994 demand that we go back to its own history to understand the roots of the widespread black poverty, joblessness and related social injustices. In this regard, Wood makes the crucial point that 'True history is basically destructive, for by its very nature it dissolves those simple, structural generalisations by which our forefathers interpreted the purpose of life in historical terms'.[1]

This chapter focuses on a critical analysis of the origins of the ANC in 1912 and the period leading up to it. The late Phil Bonner, an outstanding historian of SA, stated that 'history is a key political resource. You cannot do without it. It has to be controlled.' He further noted: 'As history becomes more instrumentalised, it tends to be more homogenised and stripped down. Inconsistencies, the ignoble, even the human, get airbrushed out. Most critically, failures cannot be adequately addressed because the grand narrative in struggle is ultimately heroic and correct.'² I start this chapter on this note in the light of how ANC leaders and scholars have portrayed the party, and how that weighs up against the historical facts.

Especially after 1994 the ANC, wittingly or unwittingly, has distorted, misrepresented and falsified its own history in many ways, which I hope to illustrate in this and following chapters. I believe that the tension between its popular leadership role and mass support and the weakness, failures and contradictions of its policies, analyses and programmes compelled it to resort to a fabrication of its own history, especially when its promises to the electorate of 'a better life' not only failed to materialise but black poverty, unemployment and inequalities worsened over the past decade.

It is an indisputable fact that the ANC dominated the broad national liberation movement during the past century but there are facts and features of its history that many writers and scholars hardly ever analyse, including how these facts have influenced and determined to a large extent what has happened in SA after 1994.

But for that attempt to be useful it is necessary to acknowledge and respect the historical record and in this regard what ANC leaders themselves have stated since its inception. If words carry meanings, which they are meant to do, we are compelled to abide by their meanings and not distort and misrepresent them, especially not for the purpose of political correctness, the need to remain in power or to seek to explain away or rationalise the bitter disappointments and compromises the ANC made without any mandate.

About the roots of the ANC in 1912 and the decade or two before its birth André Odendaal's book *The Founders: The Origins of the ANC and the Struggle for Democracy in South Africa* is indispensable reading. In numerous passages Odendaal makes it abundantly clear that the people who later became leaders of the ANC were already, through a narrow Africanist majoritarian nationalism, displaying both an aspiring middle-class liberalism and what might be called 'racial nationalism'. But it is the obsequious and liberal ideological character of the leadership of a forerunner to the ANC, the Natal Native Congress (NNC), that is most interesting and revealing. Etherington describes the NNC's formation in 1900:

> The inaugural meeting of the Natal Native Congress, NNC, had assumed the trappings of a state occasion. GH Hulett, a prominent Natal planter and son of the serving minister for native affairs, J Liege Hulett, took the chair of a meeting where 'after prayers and hymns, loyal resolutions were passed and a vote of thanks proposed to the Queen.' In this way the meeting accorded with the programme of Christianisation and civilisation articulated by missionaries and colonial officials over the previous half century.[3]

In 1908, the president of the NNC, Martin Lutuli and its secretary, Mark Radebe, called for some degree of representation, in similarly formal language:

> We, Natives of Natal, through loyal subjects of the Crown and sharing the burden of taxation, are labouring under serious disabilities by being excluded from free access to the franchise, and having no efficient means of making our wants known to parliament and no say in matters regarding our most vital interests, such as taxation and other things. We humbly beg, with regard to our future, for some degree of representation in the legislature. This would go far to remove all causes of complaint and make the Natives a more contented and devoted people under his Majesty's gracious rule.[4]

Very clearly, the NNC set the deferential tone for the ANC's birth in 1912. Similarly, in 1909, W. P. Letseleba of the Transvaal National Natives Union called on the white politicians negotiating the constitution for a new South African state to extend the Cape franchise to all provinces:

> We attribute the advancement in prosperity, contentment and loyalty, which is such a marked characterisation of the natives of the Cape Colony, to the generous policy which has permitted them to qualify themselves as citizens and to enjoy the privileges of citizenship. And we submit that the same happy result may be expected to follow the extension of the Cape franchise to our people throughout SA.[5]

This was the kind of discourse used by leading African figures, which subsequently influenced ANC delegations to Britain to plead for the ear of the monarchy. It is not so much the liberalism that stands out in these remarks, as the begging-bowl mentality of the early leaders of African nationalism in SA. But in clearer political terms, the ANC all along wanted the franchise of the Cape Colony to be extended to the rest of the country, which the majority of delegates to the National Convention refused to do. The ANC remained focused on the franchise and citizenship, paying far less attention to the economic structure and policies of the country, even when the hand of global capital was quickly, nakedly and brutally evident in both the diamond and gold mines.

Historically a middle class by its nature is important for any ruling class and serves various purposes. Most notably it acts to cushion the conflict between the working classes and the ruling class, and it also acts as a magnet of attraction for elements of the working class to 'work' their way into the ranks of the relatively better-paid and more comfortable middle classes, making them more politically pliable.

Odendaal identifies aspiring middle-class sentiments and values among Africans from around the mid-19th century, influenced by the missionary schools which some attended:

> Cosmopolitanism was one of the goals and attractions of the new African politics. The school people relished the opportunities to become acquainted with the wider world and find means to engage with it through education, work and politics in the new colonial states. They adapted readily to cosmopolitan ideas and ways of life and interacted easily with people and ideas overseas. Many travelled abroad, studied abroad and formed close ties with people overseas.

As an example, he points to Tiyo Soga:

> Until the last decade of the 19th century Britain was the main reference point for the pioneering African intellectuals, setting out to stake their claim in the global world. It was to Britain that a number of early figures went to study, the most notable being Tiyo Soga, who as an 18-year-old was taken in 1847 by the Rev. John Chalmers from Lovedale to further his education in Glasgow and later got married to a Scottish bride. He was to become the most

famous educated African of his day. In time Soga's own children would follow in their father's footsteps.⁶

In a nutshell, there you have the kind of material attractions which perfectly suited an aspiring African middle class. But that is why the missionary schools were a very important conduit for the educational advancement and personal progress which it made possible and indeed desirable, especially for African people.

This history, their own middle-class interests, and the influence of the British missionaries disposed the 'politically active Africans' to generally support Britain in the Anglo-Boer War, in which, according to Odendaal, 'They had hoped a British victory would result in the extension of the idealised British liberal values to the Afrikaner republics. This was best exemplified by the non-racial constitution of the Cape Colony and Cecil John Rhodes's opportunistic promise of "equal rights for all civilised men south of the Zambesi".'⁷ The British made many solemn promises to Africans at the time of the Anglo-Boer War in order to secure their support against the Afrikaners. But no sooner had the war ended than the British reneged on their promises, including abandoning the most important of those 'British liberal values', which African people most wanted: the franchise. Worst of all, they rejected in London several official black delegations from SA, which pleaded with them not to exclude them from the 1910 Union of SA.

British treachery is magnified by their pre-war pronouncements on the treatment of Africans by the Boers. The British Colonial Secretary, Joseph Chamberlain, said: 'The treatment of the Natives (in the Transvaal) has been disgraceful; it has been brutal; it has been unworthy of a civilised power.' Lord Salisbury, the Prime Minister, promised that if Britain was victorious in the war there would be improved treatment 'of these countless indigenous races of whose destiny I fear we have been too forgetful.' The High Commissioner to SA, Alfred Milner, in fact used the 'ill-treatment of black people' in the Transvaal as one of the reasons for British intervention.⁸ When it concerns colonialist treachery, nothing the Boers had done could rival that of the British, then the world's most powerful coloniser.

But back to Soga. There is an important point to be made here: everybody, especially given the conditions of black people at the time, would correctly jump at the opportunity to travel abroad and learn about other countries, cultures and peoples, which must have been a very edifying experience for him. This is relevant to a more careful, thoughtful, honest and balanced approach to colonialism. We need to weigh up and assess much more carefully the 'legacy' of colonialism. In this regard, the missionary schools, especially given the brutal conditions under which black people lived during Afrikaner nationalist rule, provided an opportunity to achieve English literacy, a basic education and even further study.

The missionary schools equipped African people with the literacy and basic education with which to begin to grasp, articulate and even write about the conditions of colonialism and the necessity of striving towards its abolition. In fact, several senior ANC leaders came through the missionary school system before they became politically conscious and active, but all such influences were consciously trimmed and tailored to suit liberal democracy and eschew any socialist radicalism, including by the most progressive and, for his times, radical of British missionaries, John Philip.

Odendaal captures the consequence of Africans who emerged from missionary schools well:

> Influenced by the trinity of African humanism or ubuntu, the egalitarian message of Christianity and mid-Victorian political liberalism and proceeding from a newly constructed base of schools, churches, newspapers and organisations at home, they engaged with metropolitan debates ... In the process their struggles and activities acquired an international dimension, which became a strong feature of twentieth-century political resistance in South Africa.[9]

By all accounts the ANC was strongly influenced ideologically and politically by British liberalism.

Odendaal also points out a related phenomenon: that between the 1830s and 1900 'several hundred Africans travelled to Britain and the US for educational, religious or political reasons, in the process experiencing the life and ideas of the great metropolitan centres directly. From these experiences and engagements arose new ideas which refined or challenged, through an African lens, the dominant western perspectives of the development of the world order'.[10] However, it is clear from the literature that the circles in which Africans moved abroad were linked to various missionaries and therefore predominantly of a liberal democratic persuasion, which also served to set the tone to some degree for the reformist politics of the ANC when it was born in 1912.

Among numerous visits to Britain, Odendaal tells the story of a Zulu choir's trip in 1892 to London. It included the future ANC president, Josiah Gumede, and members of the choir were drawn almost exclusively from the well-off *kholwa* who had dominated Natal African politics from the 1860s to the 1890s.[11] The *kholwa*, Christian converts who were fairly well educated and included many quite wealthy landowners, were aggrieved that they were not treated differently from the rest of the black population, and wanted to be exempted from racially restrictive legislation. They also demanded direct representation in the legislative assembly.[12] For example, in the late 1880s the monetary and cultural resources available to *kholwa* near Pietermaritzburg enabled them to establish their own newspaper, *Inkanyiso yase Natal*, and an organisation dedicated to protecting and advancing their own interests, the Funamalungelo Society.[13] The class status of the *kholwa* enabled them to be so well resourced and organised.

To a significant extent Christianity was used as a tool during colonisation, even by the liberal missionaries themselves. According to Etherington, a Natal law of 1865 was explicitly designed to serve the needs of Christians who denounced polygamy and other 'heathen customs', who were then allowed to apply for exemption from Native law. In practical terms, the law 'helped people acquire and hold property, manage business and accumulate capital'.[14] Religion and business were smartly blended not only to create and woo a black middle class but to use religion as a disciplinary force. From the outset of the Cape Colony and under Dutch rule, Christianity was used in various ways as a tool in the designs of colonialism.

Christian Africans in Natal had 'enjoyed a number of significant privileges since the mid-Victorian era. Africans who lived in square houses rather than round hut houses were exempted from the hut taxes paid by all other household heads.'[15] This is just yet another example of material differences among African people during the colonial era. A later chapter examines similar processes at work when the NP and WMC promoted the formation of a black middle class during the apartheid era. Those processes created real differences and divisions among black people. Class formation had a powerful impact on people's lives universally and historically. It creates a logic and momentum of its own to diffuse struggles and militancy and often succeeds in pacifying people who were once committed activists in the struggle. In this regard we need look no further than to what happened to some activists across the political spectrum in SA after 1994.

However, the key point about the class formation of the *kholwa* is that African communities were never at any stage totally homogeneous and free of any notion of social and even class differentiation among themselves. Precolonial African societies were strongly shaped by communal values such as reciprocity and prescribed responsibilities for others. Today, however, the whole notion of ubuntu has been torn to shreds within all black townships. Capitalism penetrates and ruptures all communities and societies, according to its own monetised logic, which has eroded the strongest cultural bonds among people over centuries and across the world. South Africa is no exception. More recently, class forces unleashed after 1994 have further eroded the earlier sense of togetherness and unity, which was born out of the collective anti-apartheid struggles.

Odendaal shows that from the mid-1890s onwards black South Africans began to visit the US in increasing numbers, including those 'from the cream of the new educated elite in southern Africa'.[16] Among the students who went to study in the US were John Langalibalele Dube, the founding president of the ANC, and Pixley Seme, also a future president of the ANC. They were profoundly influenced by experiences and ideas in the US, which, unlike the cosmopolitanism of Britain, housed a more assertive, separatist black narrative, influenced by the history of slavery and by 'Jim Crow' segregation, especially in the American south in the decades after the Civil War.[17] These formative experiences of African people who later became leaders of the ANC played a pivotal role both in shaping its birth in 1912 and in what became of it thereafter, including its beliefs, ideas and programmes during the decades of struggle, the compromises it made during the negotiations and the subsequent betrayals after 1994.

The key point is that there are numerous ideological, political and class links and continuities between the pre-history and the later history of the ANC. As Odendaal puts it:

The new elite of Africans were preparing to become global citizens and shapers of a new society in SA. The cosmopolitanism of these early intellectuals guided their local struggles in important ways. At the level of individuals, four of the five first ANC presidents had travelled abroad for education or other purposes before 1900. More generally, the patient development of an international solidarity network by black South Africans and their sympathisers, over many decades, forms at least part of the reason why the anti-apartheid struggle became one of the most important moral crusades since the abolition of slavery. Internationalism was deeply ingrained in the ANC from the beginning.[18]

The internationalism of the early years was a cosmopolitan liberalism. It obviously did not resemble the revolutionary internationalism of the Bolshevik party in Russia then. The ANC's leaders also lacked knowledge and understanding of revolutionary developments in Europe, such as the 1789 French Revolution, the 1848 European revolutions, the 1871 Paris Commune and the 1905 Russian Revolution. Nowhere will we find the ANC in those years even referring to or explaining the significance of those important international revolutionary developments, with which the struggles in SA were in fact linked by many threads, especially after global capital came to dominate the diamond and gold mining industries.

Another distinct strand emerged among early ANC leaders, influenced by their studies in the US. This was an Africanist stance, influenced by ideas encountered among African Americans. The most prominent public figure to emerge from the ranks of the *kholwa* in Natal in the first decade of the century was Dube, who returned from studying in the US in 1899. He returned from America with a 'strong belief in the idea of "Africa for the Africans"'. Coming from the founding president of the ANC, this was ideologically very significant and went on to fundamentally influence ANC thinking at the time and, later on, its membership, organisation and leadership. Dube also asserted that 'Justice will be done only when the African ruled the country'.[19] Already then, prior to the birth of the ANC, one can see in this belief of Dube the germ of a narrow Africanist chauvinism, which would have profoundly negative effects on political organisation against the white racist-imperialist regime and the wider National Question.

Dube started the first major independent African-controlled school in SA, the Ohlange Institute, at Inanda, north of Durban, where he was a minister.[20] Throughout the colonial period in SA, missionary work meant that religion was often inseparably linked to the education of the colonised. Several early ANC leaders were closely involved with the church and a few were Christian ministers. The mission schools certainly played an important part in the development of leaders, within political limits, because it was largely within a liberal framework which left intact capitalist social relations. This is exactly the basis upon which the ANC has ruled since 1994.

The historian Luli Callinicos made an important point about missionary education during colonialism: 'The missionaries not only brought literacy but also taught you to read and write. Such basic education opened up the mind to the experiences of life, politics and the ability to articulate one's views and opposition to colonialism, which the missionaries were often representatives of.'[21] This was an important component in the legacy of colonialism. In fact, several key leaders of the ANC were direct products of the missionary schools; it is important to emphasise this if one is to strike the necessary objective balance in an appraisal of colonialism.

The problem with the view that African nationalism was a progressive force because it called for the unity of Africans, especially against the nakedly divisive tribalism that colonialism fostered and imposed on African people,[22] is that it is very questionable, if it does not simultaneously assess and analyse it in relation to other considerations too, with which it is in fact inseparably intertwined. I refer to the deeply rooted and brutal exploitation of the black majority working class and the denial of the most basic human rights to decent housing, water, sanitation, electricity, education, health and so much more. I argue that no form of nationalism, especially one purportedly driven by the need for emancipation of the black masses from such conditions, can demand a whole range of democratic rights and freedoms, including the abolition of all racist legislation, without addressing vital questions of economic power and control, without which the human rights mentioned above cannot and will not materialise.

Enough has been said in this chapter about the origins of the ANC, especially in class terms. The relatively middle-class nature of the people who became the leaders of the ANC influenced and even perhaps determined also the class orientation of the organisation, in terms of its ideas and programmes. I conclude this section with MacDonald's comment on the ANC's 'Christian liberal phase', which ran from 1912 to about 1940:

> The ANC's principles were anchored in liberal ideals of legal and political equality, suffused with Christianity taught in missionary schools. For the ANC, South Africa was made of interdependent racial groups bound together by mutual respect, Christian brotherhood and liberality of spirit ... The ANC's Christian liberal politics was a patient politics, advancing moderate proposals, working with and often deferring to white liberals and accepting the values of British liberalism.[23]

However, I now want to turn to the critically important question of the membership policy of the ANC. There was much more than met the eye in 1912.

The Politics and Ideology of ANC Membership

I want to focus on the Africanist strand of the ANC, already mentioned, which became more explicit in the 1940s, as discussed in the next section, and its bearing on membership and leadership. Membership of the South African Native National Congress (SANNC) in 1912 was restricted to 'Natives' (black people who were not white, Coloured or Indian). In 1923 the SANNC changed its name to the African National Congress, as it sought to articulate a wider African nationalism.

According to the Camissa People 'heritage activist' group in Cape Town, the 1919 constitution of the ANC 'required that individual members were all required to belong to the aboriginal races of Africa'. They criticised this as 'not the congress way' in that it was 'moving in the direction of apartheid multiracialism as different to non-racialism or antiracism'.[24]

But it is the underlying ideology of a narrow Africanism which never really departed from an essentially tribal politics that is significant. For MacDonald, the SANNC and ANC never confronted tribalism even though they wanted to unite the tribes. In its 1919 constitution the then SANNC declared its intention:

> To encourage mutual understanding and to bring into common action as one political people all tribes and clans of various tribes or races and by means of combined effort and united political organisation to defend their freedom, rights and privileges;
>
> To discourage and contend against racialism and tribal feuds or to secure the elimination of racialism and tribal feuds, jealousy and petty quarrels by economic combination, education, goodwill and by other means.

While the unifying theme is clear, says MacDonald,

> Note the wording: the Congress spoke of bringing tribes together, of combining efforts, of discouraging feuds. Its constitution not only did not suggest getting rid of tribes; it spoke as if the 'people' was composed of tribes, as if they were its constituent units. The African people was conceived as standing above, but as made up of, particular tribes. The ANC's job was to join the various tribes into a united political organisation. The early ANC's idea was to eliminate tribal rivalries, not tribes themselves. Tribes were to remain centres of life, culture and community, but they were to be removed as loci of political loyalties and activities, superseded by the African people for the purpose of promoting 'common action as one political people'.[25]

What MacDonald is arguing has been vindicated in various ways since the inception of the ANC in 1912. Tribalism has been an 'elephant in the room' of South African politics, made possible by the demographic fact that the African people are the vast majority of the people. It is another reason why this country urgently needs to break with a demographic ideology and politics, in which sheer numbers are allowed to determine its direction and destiny. It is this phenomenon which in 1999 I called an 'arrogant majoritarian African chauvinism'.[26]

MacDonald notes that this approach of the early ANC was transformed by the Youth League (ANCYL) in the 1940s. It tried to move beyond tribal identities and differences, in favour of one united African people. 'Africans, in the old view, were connected through particular tribes. The ANCYL took the "nation" as the fount of collective identities, as the source of "nationalistic feeling", and suspected tribal loyalties as endangering racial unity'. However, this could only happen because 'the ANCYL, in equating races with "nations", took for granted both that South Africa's population consists of four races and that races – now called "national groups" – were constitutive units, that is, focal political organisation and participation'. As a result 'the ANCYL stated matter-of-factly, "South Africa is a country of four chief nationalities".' That is where the origins of the 'national group' in the Freedom Charter lies, an idea 'one laden with fundamental political implications'.[27]

Here are laid bare the roots of the mistaken and misleading approach of the ANCYL and the ANC to the National Question, with implications not only in terms of race and who or what constitutes the 'nation', but perhaps more importantly what this approach means for a resolution of the questions of the economy and social justice, without which it would be a mere shell. What is of further importance, which MacDonald draws attention to, is how the ANCYL, with that ethnic approach, went as far as criticising 'Coloureds for lacking a "national" organisation of their own ("Coloureds will never win their national freedom unless they organise a Coloured People's National Organisation to lead in the struggle for the National Freedom of Coloureds")'.[28] Similarly, the ANC in the 1950s supported the existence of a separate white Congress of Democrats and the Natal and Transvaal Indian Congresses.

Camissa reminds us that the common label of 'Coloured' includes the descendants of a wide range of indigenous tribes, such as the Nama, Korana, San, Griqua, Cape Khoi, as well as African slave and creole ancestry, together with Indian and Southeast Asian slave ancestry and some 'admixture of non-conformist Europeans'.[29] The Coloured people are as diverse phenotypically as any other group of people with similarly mixed ethnic ancestry.

This very wide range in physiognomy of Coloured people across SA, but especially in Cape Town, is important because for centuries, right into contemporary SA, a defining feature of racism against black people was based on skin colour. But in apartheid SA, even Coloureds who had very fair skin complexions, in many cases fairer than some registered as 'white', were oppressed, discriminated against and exploited. It was always one of the most bizarre and contradictory manifestations of apartheid ideology. No group of people in the history of SA reflects the phenotypical diversity of Coloured people. But there is also no group of people who have been more unhappy and alienated in post-apartheid SA. There has been much in the print media about this fact. That is why, I believe, the race–class predicament of Coloured people after 1994 reflects most sharply the agony of the unresolved Nation Question in SA.

Camissa does not fully interrogate race and ethnicity in the ANC since its inception. Even before the 1919 constitution with its clearly racialist and mistaken 'aboriginal races of Africa' language, nobody who was not 'African' could join. So, when they say that such restrictions and the language used are 'not the congress way', what do they mean? What is the 'congress way'? The truth is that there was never a 'Congress way' which was genuinely non-racial and anti-racist. The ANC started off on the membership issue on a mistaken, misguided and African chauvinist note. In other words, the 'Congress way' Camissa talks of is at best a myth and at worst an outright falsification of the history of the ANC.

But Camissa is clearly correct in asserting that 'Both the genocide and ethnocide faced by the indigenous tribes of the Cape and the crime against humanity – slavery – faced by these people are the well-documented worst experience of all Africans during the first two and a half centuries of colonisation in SA'.[30] No wonder the former president, Jacob Zuma, in his State of the Nation address in 2012 said: 'It is important to remember that the Khoi-San people were the most brutalised by colonialists who tried to make them extinct and undermined their language and identity. As a free and democratic South Africa, we cannot ignore to correct the past.'[31]

What Zuma said is significant because that has not been stated as strongly by any leader of the ANC and of the country before. But Camissa makes an important point about the ANC's stance towards Coloureds. The ANC 'in a sop to the ethno-nationalists in its ranks came up with a formulation still used today – "the oppression of blacks in general, Africans in particular"'. In a stroke it adopted the apartheid de-Africanisation of "Coloured" people'.[32] This is an effective rendering of an utterly racialist and divisive approach to Coloured and Indian people and is a clear expression of the 'narrow Africanist majoritarian chauvinism' I have criticised.

For if Africans were 'rightless', were Coloureds and Indians not too? They too were denied the franchise in an open, democratic and non-racial democracy, until the 1994 elections. That is at the political level. Regarding issues of social justice and standards of living, the vast majority of Coloured and Indian people belonged to the working class, especially the former. In Natal, as well as the indentured Indian labourers who arrived from 1860 onwards, there was also a stream of trader and merchant immigration and by the end of the 19th century a commercial and professional elite had taken shape.

The socioeconomic conditions of the majority of Coloured and Indian people during the 20th century were those of poverty, oppression and exploitation (though slightly less harsh than that of Africans). But this varied: in the Western Cape Coloured farm labour was hardly better off than African labour in other parts of the country. So, why were these people excluded from membership of the ANC? The ANC has never since 1912 fully and coherently addressed this issue. That is itself a serious indictment: that it failed to even explain and justify such a policy of exclusion for over a century. But much more than a policy failure, it reflected a leadership who were out of their depth on such basic issues as the criteria for membership of the organisation. As it stood in 1912, the only criterion was that you needed to be an African.

So wedded was the leadership of the SANNC (later the ANC) to a colonial-inspired racial and racialist paradigm that it took them 57 years to open up its ordinary membership to everyone at its 1969 Morogoro conference and another 17 years for the national executive committee to be opened to all in 1985 at its Kabwe conference. The first question that arises is this: why did the ANC firmly restrict membership to Africans, especially since the vast majority of Coloured and Indian people, who were workers, were also for long oppressed and exploited? This question is reinforced in the light of the obviously greater unity in the ranks of the working class there would have been if the ANC had a collective class approach to membership and not succumbed to the racist segregation of the Dutch and British.

The exclusion of Coloured and Indian people as members is instructive about the political and racialist thinking of the SANNC and later ANC leadership in the early years of the organisation. Bear in mind that this came from the African elite at that time and especially some who had studied at universities abroad, like Dube. We are not talking about uneducated people. This can only point to a lack of political understanding about the history not only of the mineral revolution, but of Dutch colonialism, and the history of Coloured people specifically.

However, the SANNC leaders could not have known and understood that history and still decided to restrict membership to Africans, especially on the basis that they comprised the overwhelming majority of the South African population. Even an elementary knowledge of the history of this country would have made those leaders realise that the Coloured and Indian workers were inherently part of the black working class and therefore should not only have been invited and welcomed as members but encouraged to join. What this omission by the SANNC and ANC shows us is that they never thought in historical and class terms. They were misguidedly consumed entirely by the plight of African people only, and even that was from a liberal middle-class point of view because it failed totally to deal with working-class interests and needs.

Ethnicity aside, their politics was confined to the franchise and appealing to British colonialism and imperialism for piecemeal reforms. Theirs was the voice of the African middle class and had virtually nothing to do with the conditions of African miners and other workers.

However, on the question of ANC membership policy, it was nothing less than shocking that only five years before Nelson Mandela was released from prison in 1990 did the ANC open membership of the leadership structures of the organisation to all. Today, it seems incredible. What is worse is that there was no official document produced by the ANC which cogently explained and defended this policy, which is to all intents and purposes not only racialist but racist, especially in relation to the Coloured and Indian working masses who were denied membership of the ANC on racial grounds. If not on racial grounds, on what conceivable basis were Coloured and Indian people excluded from membership? What the exclusion of Coloured and Indian people did was to internalise the racialisation and segregationist mentality of their white supremacist rulers. At a basic conceptual level the ANC and the ANCYL simply lacked the knowledge and comprehension of race in SA at the time, a serious ignorance and lack of understanding they perpetuated throughout the 20th century. But it is important to recall that the ANC was formed mainly in response to the Union of 1910, which excluded black people from the vote, except for those who retained their qualified franchise in the Cape.

Soudien narrates an interesting argument on Robben Island between

Neville Alexander and Nelson Mandela over race. Alexander objected strongly to the description of SA as consisting of four 'national groups and races' in the Freedom Charter. He denied that the people in SA consisted of such groups and said that they 'were just ordinary people and not national groups'. The debate, according to Soudien, turned to the notion of 'four races' in SA, in which Mandela insisted 'race' was a biological issue which defined character, whereas Alexander argued that 'race' was a sociological construction. However, the argument became heated when Alexander also denied that SA constituted a 'nation' but was still building one. Mandela got upset: 'We can stop this discussion immediately because African people are a nation and the rest are minority nations'.[33]

If somebody of Mandela's stature had such badly mistaken views, we can only imagine what other lesser known leaders of the ANC thought at that time. But as I have argued, race, knowledge and the sciences are closely related in SA's historical development. The striking thing is that this argument took place several decades after earlier leaders of the ANC in the early part of the 20th century held primitive views on race. Mandela's views in the 1970s were essentially similar to those of the early leaders of the ANC. This only serves to reinforce the serious problems of a lack of knowledge and understanding across the leadership of the ANC since its inception. You cannot even begin to seek to change a society of oppression and exploitation if you do not have a thorough, deep and scientific understanding of how it developed historically and defined the nature of both the problems and the solutions that are necessary.

It was not only Africans who were excluded from full citizenship in the 1910 Union of SA but Coloureds and Indians too, who were organically an inherent part of the oppressed and exploited people of SA. Historians tend to focus on the threat to Africans posed by the Union legislation as triggering the formation of the SANNC. They overlook the exclusion of others who were historically an organic part of the oppressed and exploited of this country. While this applies particularly to Coloured people, the vast majority of whom had long been members of an oppressed and exploited working class, it also applies to Indian people, especially during the decades of indentured labour in Natal. Odendaal points out that the Natal government made clear its intention that 'Indians were appreciated as labourers only and were not welcome as settlers and competitors'.[34]

Even South African History Online (SAHO), an important and informative progressive history project, does not even mention the ideology and politics of the membership of the SANNC and later ANC. However, they do point out why the issues of the non-racial unity of workers were not addressed at that time by the SANNC leadership:

> The group of men who assembled at Bloemfontein was well aware of the wider dimensions of the social tragedy enacted around them. But their particular concern, the fear of any petit bourgeois at the time of crisis, was being thrust back into the ranks of the urban and rural poor. The main aim of the SANNC was to represent the concerns and anxieties of the professional middle class which was mainly responsible for convening the Bloemfontein meeting.[35]

The middle-class character of the African elite also found expression in the aims of the South African Native Convention, which met in Bloemfontein in March 1909: 'Full and equal rights and privileges, subject only to the conditions and limitations established by law and applicable alike to all citizens without a distinction of class, colour or creed.' This was proposed for inclusion in the draft constitution for the Union of SA. The Convention simply wanted 'native and coloured people' to be included in the draft Act as citizens with the right to the franchise.[36] It is interesting to note that no reference to Indian people was made in their deliberations.

The important matter of membership is related to the notions of race, racialism and racism previously discussed. It is also primarily – but not only – concerned with the exclusion from membership of Coloureds and Indians. But for consistency's sake, it should be noted that white people were also excluded from membership. But the exclusion of other components of the black working class was a more grievous omission, especially as most of the white working class were racist, and almost certainly would not have joined the ANC.

But to exclude Coloureds and Indians was a completely different matter, not only in terms of race, but much more importantly in terms of non-racial and anti-racist class consciousness and class solidarity. However, was there perhaps 'method in the madness' of such exclusion? In an interview, I asked the historian Luli Callinicos about it. Her answer was significant:

In fact, I asked Rusty Bernstein why it is that we have four different organisations (the Congress of Democrats (COD) for whites); the Coloured People's Congress (CPC), the South African Indian Congress (SAIC); and the African National Congress) when we could all belong to one organisation. But Rusty said that Albert Luthuli, then president, said that if there was one organisation, the whites and Indians would dominate us.[37]

I asked if this meant that Luthuli was apprehensive because it was suggested that Indians and whites had more knowledge and education than Africans. She conceded that this could have been a factor, but what other explanation could there be behind Luthuli's fears?

In a follow-up question to Callinicos and Edward Webster, her husband, about the same matter, they responded: 'Yes, but it was not only knowledge the whites had but the power they held.'[38] True, but the line between such knowledge and power blurs and more often than not coincides. To the question of why Coloureds and Indians were not invited to the inaugural meeting of the SANNC/ANC in Bloemfontein and why they were excluded from membership of the SANNC, Callinicos and Webster's response was not convincing: 'Well, you have a point but the ANC said that they did not have to carry passes.'[39] This response is too facile, and requires interrogation, along the lines of the strong critique by Robert Fine and Dennis Davis. Several times in their book, *Beyond Apartheid* they criticised the left generally for deferring to African nationalism far too often since the inception of the ANC.

It appears to me that the views of Webster and Callinicos are an expression of such deference. The vitally important political principle of non-racial, anti-racist and working-class unity was reduced to one of who was required to carry passes or not. But that Coloured and Indian workers were not required to carry passes was part of the divide-and-rule strategy of the both the Dutch and British colonialists. This kind of reasoning comes close to blaming these people for not having to carry passes and letting the divisive strategy of the ruling class off the hook. Furthermore, were the leaders of the SANNC and ANC not aware that the first people who were forced to carry passes in the Cape Colony were the Khoi? Keegan notes: 'At the centre of the oppression and exploitation of the Khoi, Philip contended, was the system of passes. This severely restricted their rights of movement and rendered them liable to prosecution for vagrancy if caught passless; thereupon they could be contracted out to anyone at the whim of the local official.'[40]

There are various answers as to why the ANC did what it did. They excluded Coloured and Indian people because they were not required to carry passes; they also excluded them because their priority was uniting the tribes. This is an unhelpful approach, especially regarding important matters of principle. Membership policy is not a tactical matter; it is instead a profoundly important policy and organisational matter. The argument by Callinicos and others, that at the time the main purpose of forming the ANC was to create a united African organisation, bringing the different tribes into one organisation, was short-sighted and inward-looking. By confining themselves to African people and excluding Coloureds and Indians, especially the working classes, they started out on the wrong footing.

A country that was born with 'race' in the Cape in 1652 and one in which the oppressed and exploited masses were always racially divided and fragmented since the earliest days required a much greater unity at the very outset. I believe that short-sightedness set a precedent for intra-working class 'racial' divisions which still plague SA today. Besides, our history should have compelled the leaders of the SANNC to look beyond tribal antagonisms and the unity of tribes. After all, by 1912 SA already had the most advanced capitalist economy in Africa. Therefore, as important as the unity of the tribes was for the liberation of SA from colonialism and imperialism, arguably as important was linking that task to a broader unity with the other strata of the oppressed and exploited.

However, when I asked whether there was a restriction on membership because the leaders feared that they would be intellectually dominated by whites and Indians, Callinicos replied without hesitation: 'Yes, I think there was such a logic' and went on to mention that even Oliver Tambo, who was more 'open to non-racialism ... was however of the view that if whites were included, blacks won't get a chance to express themselves'.[41] This matter, I believe, is the elephant in the room around the question of why the ANC restricted membership to Africans. I believe it was deliberately not confronted by the SANNC/ANC leadership and probably as deliberately not pursued by white liberals and in fact many Marxists, to serve the purpose of political correctness, by deferring to hegemonic African nationalism. A sentiment, which I have heard many times, runs: 'they are the majority, so what can we do?' Besides smacking of intellectual prostration, this quantitative rendering is decidedly not what building a vibrant democracy is all about. We are not allowed to think, object and fight for our ideas because the African people have numbers on their side.

What we have here is an intriguing combination in the SANNC/ANC of a distinctly middle-class liberal politics with a narrowly chauvinistic Africanist approach to membership in order to ward off any challenges from 'minority' groups, who largely were better educated and had greater access to intellectual resources than Africans. This combination, in different forms, has fundamentally characterised the ANC since its inception. But that combination has been shrewdly played upon in ways which favoured the middle-class and elitist aspirations of the leadership and not the needs and interests even of its own working class, alongside its own majoritarian Africanist chauvinism. The demographic Africanist chauvinism was emphasised and played out in its membership rules, not to favour the needs and interests of African workers, but in the interests of their own middle-class and aspiring bourgeoisie. In one form or another and under fluctuating conditions since its birth, this has been the history of the ANC.

The PAC, formed in 1959, espoused a virulent form of what would today be called 'racial nationalism', which sharply eschews working-class politics, precisely because it is a class analysis that would clearly reveal their own class interests. Its journal, *The Africanist*, asserted in 1959 that 'Whites are steeped in Herrenvolk ideology, so much so that the idea of class struggle in which it is hoped to bring African workers alongside white workers in a common struggle against the capitalists can be escapist, illusory ... The Africanists say that the issue of class struggle in South Africa is so insignificant as to play no part at all.'[42] To which Fine and Davis responded: 'Its ultra-nationalism did not permit the PAC to penetrate the class contradictions at the heart of the struggle.'[43]

Furthermore, one is compelled, among other reasons, to interrogate the meaning of 'African' for the PAC. Answering Sobukwe's aim of Africanist exclusiveness in his call for a 'government of the African, by the African, for the African', Fine and Davis argued: 'The very idea of "African" was elusive: at one time counterposed to other groups in South

Africa and at another broadened out into "anybody who owes loyalty to Africa and who is prepared to accept the democratic rule of an African majority", being considered an African'.[44] But many valid questions arise in response to Sobukwe's definition of African. What is the 'democratic rule of an African majority'? It says very little indeed and leaves many questions about the kind of economic, social and public policies which would underpin such a government not only not unanswered but unasked.

There are various reasons why African nationalism since the birth of the ANC is so deeply engraved in African politics, but a lack of education, organisation and political alternatives among the African masses, when the ANC was formed, and the tenacious hold of cultural and religious traditions are among many factors. A lack of clear socialist influences and leadership must also count as important, especially against the background of the role the SACP has played, through its alliance with the ANC. Despite the efforts of many individual African socialists, no socialist organisation strong enough to rival the SACP emerged among African people throughout the 20th century.

So dominant was African nationalism that the late Neville Alexander criticised the 'pervasive reactionary nationalisms' of both apartheid and the liberation movements. He called them 'bogus nationalisms, the main purpose of which is to dissipate the force of the class struggle by deflecting into channels that will nurture the dominant classes'.[45] About the attitude of the SANNC and the ANC to the British, Alexander hit the problem on its head: the leadership of the ANC, the African People's Organisation (APO) and the NIC sought a 'betterment of their own particular group' and reflected a 'craven subservience to Anglo Saxon culture'.[46] But though I think that in certain respects it is mistaken to lump the ANC and APO indiscriminately together, no book shows more clearly the damaging effects of African nationalism than that of Fine and Davis. It is for me the greatest problem, weakness and contradiction of the 20th century within the South African national liberation movement. If we want to understand the tragedy of SA today, we must begin with the pitfalls of the ANC's African nationalism in that century.

However, in the absence of strong non-racial and anti-racist mass socialist alternatives to the ANC and PAC, they dominated liberation politics for several decades, until their unbanning in 1990. They did so, while airing some of the most unfortunate ideas. As Sobukwe ominously put it: 'The Africans constitute the indigenous group ... form the majority ... are the most ruthlessly exploited ... The African masses constitute the key to liberation and can be organised only under the banner of African nationalism ... They must decide on methods of struggle without interference from either so-called left-wing or right-wing groups of the minorities.'[47]

While it is true that Africans were the 'most ruthlessly exploited', the solutions Sobukwe sought and the political conclusions he drew were mistaken, misdirected and dangerous. He was also wrong as it was the Khoisan who were the aboriginals of this country – rooted here long before the arrival of Bantu-speaking people from central Africa – and were also the first who fought against Dutch colonialism. But you will hear nothing about the Khoisan people from Sobukwe and many other African nationalists, both inside and outside the ANC. They do the history of this country a serious disservice, which, however, cannot change that history.

Besides, there are countless other similar statements throughout this history of the ANC. Aside from the evident hostility of Sobukwe towards 'minorities' (which would include Coloured and Indian people), I argue that the very notion of 'minorities' is arguably both racialist and potentially even racist. This argument includes whites, who too have always had class, ideological and political differences among themselves. In fact, at no time were any of the 'minorities' homogeneous in socio-class terms. The importance of this point cannot be stressed enough. What it shows and reinforces is that no matter how fierce the oppression and brutal the exploitation of black people were, there were always, often deliberately created, social and material differences among them.

Though the literature does not capture this point, I have no doubt that it was such narrow, racialist and arguably racist views about 'minorities' which in 1912 determined the exclusion of Coloureds, Indians and whites from membership of the SANNC. There are also, I believe, discursive and political links between that fact and the related fact that the attitude of and approach towards the Coloured people by the ANC smack of such alienating Africanist majoritarian chauvinism, seen nowhere more evidently than what has happened to the 'Coloured vote' since the 1994 elections.

I argue that the ANC – in spite of the 1996 non-racial constitution and its Bill of Rights – perpetuated a narrow Africanist majoritarian chauvinism in its governance of SA. Mandela appears to have been concerned at the consequences of ethnic and majoritarian voting: 'It is clear that the majority within these national minorities continue to believe that the ANC represents the interests of the African majority and that their own perceived interests stand opposed to those of the African majority.'[48] ANC African leaders, by virtue of being the vast majority of the population, have treated Coloureds and Indians as less than their equals, politically speaking. Effectively, they utilised a demographic majoritarianism to marginalise all 'minorities'.

Fine and Davis point out that even during the height of apartheid oppression and exploitation, different sections of the African people, including workers, were treated differently: 'Compared to most black people, industrial workers were both materially and juridically better off: they had more rights; they earned higher wages; they were more exposed to political ideas of trade unionism, socialism and nationalism associated with modern labour movements.' They also cite Solly Sachs to this effect:

> African workers, although subjected to many restrictions, can change their jobs ... more freely than in mining and agriculture. A breach of contract is a criminal offence for Africans in industry, but contracts of service can be terminated by a week's or a month's notice, whereas in the mines these contracts are binding for about a year and on the farms for a maximum of six months. African workers in industry have possibilities of improving their skill and efficiency and obtain higher wages. The majority do not live in compounds and when they finish their day's work, they are free from the control of their employers.[49]

During the 1940s and 1950s, when manufacturing industries were established, there were many other differences among African people, especially around conditions of housing and standards of living. The conditions in which black workers lived in town were better than in the countryside, but 'nonetheless reminiscent of the conditions of the working class described by Engels in the early years of the industrial revolution in England'.[50] What all this means – and there is a great deal more such evidence – is that the whole notion of some homogeneous 'African' identity is not just a myth but an outright distortion and falsification of social realities.

MacDonald, in a discussion of the early ANC's conception of 'nation', points out that 'even the African people, a hybrid of clashing histories and peoples and consisting of those subjugated to the South African state, were mixed'.[51] But not only do the African people have an ethnically mixed ancestry, comprising Zulu, Xhosa, Bapedi, Basotho, Venda, Tsonga and Tswana peoples, but there is also a history of conflict and even wars between these groups, including prior to colonisation. No wonder Seme, one of the founders of the ANC and its president from 1930 to 1936, warned in 1911 that 'The demon of racialism, the aberrations of the Xhosa-Fingo feud, the animosity that exists between Zulu and Tsongas, between the Basotho and every other Native must be buried and forgotten; it has shed among us sufficient blood! We are one people. These divisions, these jealousies, are the cause of all our woes and all our backwardness and ignorance today.'[52]

Seme was writing long before the NP came to power in 1948. He did not claim that internecine African ethnic conflicts were all the result of Dutch or British divide-and-rule policies and was aware that such ethnic conflicts existed in pre-colonial times. But the fact that Seme not only points to the divisions and jealousies among Africans but that he also refers to their 'backwardness and ignorance' is an important acknowledgement by a future president of the ANC. That is why we need to address the real legacy of colonialism with much more nuance than many black people do. Colonialism left a mixed and contradictory legacy, which broke down many conservative, archaic and indeed oppressive cultural traditions in the countries which were colonised.

In contrast to the SANNC/ANC, the APO, formed a decade before the ANC, in 1902, never had a policy on membership which restricted it to Coloureds, although its membership and officials were overwhelmingly Coloured. The APO tended to attract a Coloured membership, probably because it was born in Cape Town and its leader, Abdullah Abdurahman, was a local Muslim political leader, but its membership was not restricted to Coloureds.

Odendaal notes that in its petition to the National Convention (which wrote the constitution of the Union of South Africa) 'the APO appealed to the Convention on behalf of all black people, reflecting a greater sense of solidarity that had developed after the Queenstown Conference of November 1907'. The petition of the APO urged that the principle of 'equal rights for all civilised persons in SA' should be respected and that no colour line should be drawn in the new constitution.[53] Despite the British elitist and often racist insinuation of 'civilised' people, this was the non-racial stance of the APO, while the SANNC only spoke of the plight of African people, without any serious mention of the Coloured and Indian people, especially their working classes. Despite having itself a distinctly middle-class leadership with a reformist programme, the APO was an interesting development in its formative years.

The APO 'grew into what was perhaps the first national party, open to persons of all races and with branches in all colonies. It failed to attract significant numbers of Africans and Indians, and remained predominantly Coloured, centred in the Western Cape and concerned mainly with coloured affairs.'[54] Though it disbanded many years ago, the APO was the earliest liberation movement, not the ANC. What makes this point much more important, especially in terms of the interests of the black working class, is the unalterable fact that the APO was incomparably more radical in its orientation than the SANNC/ANC ever was during those early years.

Whereas the SANNC never bothered to talk of the plight of African mine labour, Abdurahman condemned the 'cosmopolitan (British) exploiters', whose greed for gold had given rise to the system of indentured labour. He also argued that the Boer ex-republics under British rule were 'simply Imperial prisons for Coloured people, who are but goods and chattels in the hands of the country's exploiters'. So radical was his public image that the English press accused him of 'incendiary talk' and of 'stirring up the embers of race feud'. In consequence, the Johannesburg City Council refused him permission to address a Coloured audience in the City Hall. Unlike the SANNC, the 'need for unity was a constant theme in Abdurahman's speeches at that time'. He spared no effort before the Union of SA to stress the need for unity among black people, which included a public meeting in Queenstown in April 1910 at which 'Abduraman and [John Tengo] Jabavu appealed for a political union of all Coloured races'.[55]

Abdurahman made the appeals for unity of black people knowing that it would be a powerful weapon against white South African politicians and the British government, especially in light of the divide-and-rule policy and tactics of both, but such unity never materialised: 'If Europeans persist in their policy of repression, there will one day arise a solid mass of black and Coloured humanity whose demands will be irresistible'.[56] There is no statement made at that time by any African leader which comes even close to expressing the enormous potential power such unity could have achieved than this, but it fell on deaf ears. That the African people were the numerical majority in the country must have been a consistent consideration by Abdurahman in this quest.

But Simons and Simons point out the difficulties in attaining such unity: 'The contemplated union never took place. African and Coloured leaders joined in protest, but the political ties were never more than tenuous. Geographical isolation, barriers of language, custom and race, economic differences and inequalities of status restrained them from merging into a single organisation'.[57]

Though certainly not a theoretician and often sending mixed and confusing messages ideologically and politically, Abdurahman was incomparably more progressive, open and radical than any of the SANNC leaders. His grasp of the race–class nexus in the early years of the 20th century was impressive, especially in terms of an African–Coloured working-class unity which he and his organisation repeatedly advocated. Simons and Simons sum up the APO's understanding thus:

> It was a class tyranny as well as a racial tyranny. The word *kleurlyn* concealed the realities of capitalist exploitation behind the myth of racial inferiority. The colour line was a subterfuge used to persuade the world that the darker races were inferior and incapable of undertaking so-called white man's work. All employers took part in the exploitation. The capitalists hired 'kaffir drudges' because these worked for a scanty wage.[58]

That is very clearly a socialist voice in the first decade of the 20th century, whereas subsequently the SANNC leaders lacked a political vocabulary which included such radical language and meanings. Simons and Simons also point out that Abdurahman 'retained his faith in working class unity for many years in spite of rebuffs by white trade unionists who agitated for colour bars' and the APO newspaper insisted that 'Workers of all creeds and colours must stand together; must put an end to all divisions'.[59] Abdurahman's stance is hugely significant, and probably emanates from his background as a grandson of manumitted slaves. But like Mandela, he too harboured illusions about the virtues of British parliamentary democracy: the British constitution was 'the admiration of the world and one of the greatest blessings of mankind'.[60] However, the fact remains that he was the only black leader who in those early years called for non-racial working-class unity and criticised the mining-led capitalist system.

I have no doubt that Abdurahman was serious and sincere about black unity. In 1909, when members of the executive of the APO in the Orange River Colony attended the South African Native Convention in Bloemfontein, they had the 'full blessings of their national president, Dr. Abdurahman'. He informed the organisers that he had advised APO branches that they could attend if they so wished, 'for it matters not who initiates the movement as long as we attain our object'.[61]

Enough has been said of what African leaders of the SANNC and ANC wanted after its birth: a non-racial democracy, with all the same rights and freedoms whites had, but within a capitalist economic framework; hence the notion of 'bourgeois democratic rights.' Never, till today, in our current economic crisis, have ANC leaders said that the major problems the vast majority of black people experience in SA are due to capitalism and that we need to change this system in order to serve the interests and needs of the black working-class majority of our society.

What this shows conclusively is that at its birth in 1912 the ANC had two interrelated congenital weaknesses, which I maintain have basically remained intact. Firstly, its policy of restricting membership to Africans was to all intents and purposes arguably both racialist and racist. Secondly, its policy outlook was mild, liberal and moderate. The ANC took on new ideologies, new policies and new methods after 1950, yet these foundational features did not disappear. There has persisted a convergence, not necessarily conscious, between a narrow Africanism, arguably chauvinistic, and an explicitly liberal and middle-class orientation, which hardly espoused ideas and policies that reflected the interests of the black working-class majority.

An interrogation of the membership policy of the ANC leaves one with the startling conclusion – borne out by the facts – which reinforces the critical analysis I have made of that policy. After 1912 the ANC continued to exclude people who were not African from membership of the organisation, until its Morogoro conference in 1969, where it for the first time opened ordinary membership to all. But that deracialised opening was only for ordinary membership. The highest structure, the national executive committee, was still restricted to Africans. Only at its Kabwe conference in 1985 did the ANC open the NEC to all. This was not just a racialist and in fact racist exclusion of others, no matter what could be said in an attempt to justify or rationalise it, but it has all along been the ugly face of a narrow, inward-looking Africanist majoritarian chauvinism which has resurfaced in the ANC over the past decade.

This is possible because its mass base of African support has always, from the earliest days, suffered from ignorance, lack of education and, most importantly, lack a of sense of class consciousness, in the Marxist sense of a 'class-for-itself' and not just a 'class-in-itself'. There are various factors which have historically contributed to this low level of class consciousness, aside from the oppression, exploitation and racism of colonisation. There can be absolutely no doubt that the weight of tribal and traditional cultural and religious beliefs, often deeply ingrained, has played a part. As Marx once said, 'The tradition of all dead generations weighs like a nightmare on the brains of the living.' But there are hardly any writers and critical thinkers who have questioned and interrogated these issues.

It is an undeniable fact that given the history of SA there are very clear causal links between race and epistemology in every area of life and study, so much so that I devoted a column to this topic in 2000.[62] In fact, since then the gaps between white and black have become even wider, given the global effects of the technological revolution led by the Western countries, especially through social media. I specifically refer to scientific knowledge in the various fields of the economy and in every academic discipline.

The literature and scholarship dealing with race, class and gender is so overwhelmingly white around the world that this historical fact, inextricably related to the emergence of slavery, colonialism and imperialism, is stark and indisputable. Raising the consciousness and the educational and cultural level of the multitudes will require transformed social relations. Such an educational and epistemic revolution to empower the ordinary masses will require enormous resources, which under capitalism it is impossible to generate for that purpose. In short, for that prospect to be realised we would require an anti-capitalist solution to our problems in SA.

The historical oppression, subjugation and exploitation of black people took a heavy toll on their consciousness and development. In fact, black people were deliberately underdeveloped. Personal, educational, intellectual and social developments of various kinds were reserved for white people. That is why they absolutely dominate every academic discipline and field of science. In fact, arguably nowhere else has this race-class epistemic and technological chasm been as wide as it was and still is between white and black than in SA.

The matric results over the past two decades reflect the general historical epistemic hierarchy in SA: whites, Indians, Coloureds, Africans. And it is precisely because of this pattern that passing standards in schools was dropped in order to artificially boost the numbers of black students who obtain a pass, so that the ANC government can be made to look good in the crucial area of education. Although epistemic disparities were more acute in SA in the 19th and 20th centuries than they are today, the changes that have occurred in education and training after 1994 have not been enough to dispel that historical hierarchical legacy.

However, research for this book revealed a related problem which is derived from the lack of education and knowledge of the African masses. In this regard I underestimated the destructive power of many of the traditional systems and beliefs, especially among the ordinary people who have had little or no education. Various leading African people I interviewed gave me many examples of the serious problems some traditional belief systems pose for liberation movements in their struggles against oppression and exploitation. I will mention just two: Pali Lehohla,[63] the former statistician-general of SA, and Solly Mapaila,[64] deputy general secretary of the SACP. Both examples bear upon the status of African women in the cultural traditions they spoke of. Lehohla explained that at harvest time in the rural areas, women are not allowed to walk on or near the area harvested because it is believed that it will negatively affect the yield.

Not having known about this cultural tradition, I found it incredibly sad and revealing in the first place for people in this day and age, given the many progressive provisions in our constitution, to harbour such views, especially because of its nakedly backward sexist and patriarchal content. But as I mentioned earlier, in an environment that lacks the means of education and consciousness-raising, such views will survive, especially when they have existed unquestioned and unchallenged for very long under tribal and traditional rule in rural areas. Mapaila spoke about the disempowerment of African women in villages across SA, where they are not allowed to attend community meetings as a rule, because these are reserved only for men, even if the matters to be discussed, such as water use, are traditionally largely performed by them, such as the washing of clothing and watering of vegetables.

These issues are of critical importance from an emancipatory perspective and provide irrefutable evidence of what a genuinely progressive and liberationist movement would be up against, especially the engrained sexist and patriarchal beliefs of African men particularly. Given these vitally important issues, political correctness must be avoided like the plague. While there is no doubt that such sexist patriarchy also exists elsewhere in our society, it is indisputably more concentrated and rampantly evident in African communities, due to socio-cultural factors which have been embedded for centuries and their demographic dominance.

But even those problems of patriarchal and sexist power relations and its analysis assume greater importance when seen in relation to class issues and especially the historical triad of race, class and gender, which is the triple oppression black working-class women have suffered for very long. It is these intersecting and complex social realities and relations which make finding integrated solutions more difficult. For that purpose, we require a political leadership of the working class to draw those systemic links and organise upon them. But to be able to do that requires a much higher degree of knowledge, not just political, but scientific, of the kind that would clear the cobwebs of the mind in which ignorance enchains the masses, those who are either illiterate or with little formal education. Not surprisingly this ignorance extends to many activists.

Given the history of Dutch and British colonisation and racism and the systematic denial of basic rights to black people, there can be no doubt that illiteracy and lack of education would not only have been serious problems for the mass of African people but even its elected leadership would have had difficulties, including in communicating in both the Afrikaans and English languages. The lack of formal education and a culture of reading would have been great challenges for African members and activists of the ANC after its birth in 1912. Not many historians have investigated these educational and literacy issues, which would have profoundly affected the politics and organisation of black people, including their knowledge of and understanding of the system they were up against.

It is also crucially important to understand that none of the early ANC leaders wrote about or analysed the impact of Dutch and later British colonialism on the country and the lives of the Khoisan and African people, nor how the mineral revolution had drastically changed the country and the lives of its people. Neither did the ANC leaders capture how the race–class struggles, which began already in the diamond mines, had changed the character of the struggles which were developing within the industry and which became much more pronounced after gold was discovered.

The failure by the leadership of the early ANC to understand or analyse social and economic developments had consequences, which is why there exists no analysis by any ANC leaders of that crucially important period in the growth of the mining industry and capitalism in SA. This lack of leadership by the ANC was much more significant if one recalls that historically African societies south of the Sahara were not literate. Surely, this fact would have impacted negatively on the education and development of African people in these countries, including in SA.

The African people were the most oppressed, subjugated, exploited and humiliated in SA from the time of the mineral revolution, especially the working class and migrant labour from other countries. They lacked not only political rights but also basic education and the most basic labour rights to organisation and representation. But they were without any organised leadership until 1921 when the Industrial and Commercial Workers' Union was formed by Clements Kadalie in Cape Town. The early ANC leaders knew these facts and understood their political significance but were ideologically not oriented to the African and black working classes. It is for this reason that the ICU instead briefly became such a powerful force in SA.

In the first decades of the ANC's existence, Christianity and a distinctly middle-class liberalism coexisted happily, as the initial impetus of its leadership. These two themes intertwined to depict a very clear race–class politics in favour of a bourgeois liberalism, which is precisely why the ANC has never openly declared itself to be unambiguously anti-capitalist and pro-socialist. Even the mantra of the ANC decades later, that the 'working class was the motor force' of the struggle, was little more than rhetoric, its purpose to acquire a mass base for the ANC with which to win state power in SA. But who then understood these severe limitations of the SANNC and later ANC?

I have already dwelt on the main reason why I think the ANC began and persisted with its racialist and arguably racist membership restriction. I am persuaded by what Callinicos reported of Luthuli's explanation about why the ANC had restricted membership to Africans. It made sense given the strong historical relationship between race and skills, knowledge and science.

Bonner argues that after the First World War ended, conditions were very bad for all workers, including white workers. White supremacist politicians enacted a panoply of schemes to rehabilitate poor whites: 'road-relief work, agricultural settlements, forestry projects and railway employment'. Very clearly, although conditions were always worse for Africans, all other 'minorities' suffered too. The point of all this is to show that if the SANNC and later the ANC had had an open and non-racial policy on membership, it might have attracted the attention of a wider range of people, especially workers across racial divisions. However, Bonner also points out that 'The rise of poor white racism accompanied the economic decline of whites'. He adds, that 'White indigency and social distress all added to a mounting sense of desperation'.[65]

There are many stories of such conditions and even worse among the Coloured and Indian people, especially its working-class communities, ever since the mineral revolution. But a crude Africanist majoritarian chauvinism has made it appear that it is only the African masses who have suffered hardships and injustices in SA, which falsely determined the restriction of ordinary ANC membership to Africans from 1912 until 1969 and the exclusion of non-Africans from the executive leadership until its 1985 Kabwe conference. This is probably the most neglected but burning question of the ANC and Africanists in this country's history, but it is sorely neglected by historians in their work. I agree with the argument by Fine and Davis that the left in SA succumbed and deferred far too much to African nationalism, and think this applies equally to how they failed, probably due to the same majoritarian pressures, to identify, deal with and confront this chauvinism in their work.

I think that a narrow Africanism which excludes other black people or people of colour, such as Coloureds and Indians, was a reflection of a limited and limiting political consciousness which revolved around 'race', to the exclusion of two things. Firstly, it failed to appreciate and understand how race was configured in SA and systemically linked in many ways to class. Secondly, and in consequence, it failed to realise that in theoretical, political and organisational terms it was a major mistake to promote a narrow, especially chauvinist Africanism, which either excludes Coloureds and Indians or minimises their role, which is arbitrarily determined by their 'minority' status in the overall population.

I argue that the very term 'minority', whoever uses it, is arguably both racialist and racist, especially if it is devised by some racial or ethnic majority which holds power, either economic or political or both. There are many questions which arise with such divisive and stigmatising terminology, among which are the following. Is 'minoritisation' not itself a form of 'othering'? What power and right does a demographic majority have to identify other people as 'minorities', whether it be white racists under apartheid or these narrow African nationalists inside or outside the ruling ANC? To whom is a 'minority' related and for what purpose? Whose 'minority' is this? Does not the very term 'minority' smack of some form of Africanist-majoritarian chauvinistic politics? What are the values and interests that 'minority' proponents seek to promote with such 'majoritarian' language? Arguably the only plausible 'minority' and 'majority' identities are those which relate to politics and class, determined through votes in a constitutional democracy. Accordingly, we must abolish all talk of racial 'minorities' because it makes an already highly racialised society more prone to a perpetuation of racialism and racism.

In fact, the usage of the term 'minorities' is much worse when it is instrumentally deployed by an Africanist majoritarian chauvinism in order to gain advantage regarding jobs, resources and public services, especially in the form of BEE and AA legislation. The fact is that SA in 1994 moved from a 'minority' white racist exclusion of black people (including Coloureds and Indians) to an Africanist majoritarian chauvinism.

Another issue discussed by Bonner concerns land, race and class. After the Anglo-Boer War, particularly in the OFS, 'Many bywoners were squeezed out of arable land by more productive black tenants and slipped inexorably into the ranks of poor whites.'[66] In fact, throughout South African history, from the days of the Cape Colony, there were class divisions between both white and black people. After the 1913 Natives' Land Act there was a large buy-back of land in the Transvaal, headed by chiefs. They were assisted by 'many if not most of the major black political leaders of this period [who] doubled as estate agents, searching out plots for purchasable land. These included Seme, Dube, Kadalie, Gumede and Makgatho and others.'[67]

Once more we see evidence of the thoroughly middle-class interests of many leaders of the ANC, in order to remind us that we have had too romantic a view of the history of the ANC and in fact of all its leaders over the decades, including leaders like Mandela, Tambo and Sisulu, with some mythical halo surrounding their names. I argue later that those same class interests and forces, under very different political circumstances, have been at play in what has happened in SA under ANC rule after 1994. That is why I cannot reconcile what Mandela had to say about the birth of the ANC with how he describes it: 'Sometimes people point to the initial aims of the ANC and its early composition in order to suggest that it was a reformist organisation. The truth is that the birth of the ANC carried from the beginning profoundly revolutionary implications. The formation of the ANC was the first step towards the creation of a new South African nation.'[68] However, that attempt by Mandela to characterise the ANC as revolutionary had been flatly contradicted by himself writing three decades earlier: 'The breaking up and democratisation of these monopolies will open up free fields for the development of a prosperous non-European bourgeoisie class. For the first time in the history of this country the non-European will have the opportunity to own in their own name and right mills and factories, and trade and enterprise will boom and flourish as never before.'[69]

Bonner also explores the impact of urbanisation on the culture of Africans during the first few decades of the Union of SA, as people left the rural areas for the cities, to find work.[70] He showed how this process changed the culture, life and identity of both Africans and white Afrikaners, often irrevocably, as is always the case with urbanisation, when powerful economic and social forces rupture conditions and relations and fundamentally change life itself. In this respect, the history of capitalism in SA is very similar to what happened elsewhere in the world. The 'exceptionalism' of SA is vastly exaggerated, except that there is probably no country in the world which had as many explicitly racist laws as South Africa under apartheid.

Following Bonner, under the impact of capitalist urbanisation, cultural, religious, ethnic and social identities were transformed. This had been the case for the lives and cultural traditions of the Khoisan people ruptured by Dutch colonialism in the 17th century and later the Coloured people who became urbanised in the Western Cape. Similar processes were at play when the Indian indentured labourers, who arrived in Natal in the mid-19th century, later worked in cities, especially Durban and Johannesburg. Culture, social relations and identities are all transformed in the vortex that is capitalist urbanisation and modernity. This was true of cities like Kimberley and Johannesburg at the time the SANNC was formed. Between 1886 and 1912 Johannesburg was radically and irreversibly transformed. In such a racial and ethnic melting pot why would the SANNC have felt compelled to restrict membership to Africans, especially when they were themselves the product of many diverse cultural and religious identities? I can find no compelling argument, notwithstanding efforts by white liberals, and some Marxists, to rationalise it.

To conclude my discussion of the issue of membership: I found absolutely no credible basis for the insistence by the ANC for 57 years to exclude 'minorities' from membership of the ANC and for 73 years to bar them from occupying leadership positions in the organisation. Looking back over this long period it seems unnecessary, ludicrous and in fact counterproductive that the ANC had such policies. I have come to the firm conclusion that since its inception the ANC has had not only a racialist but racist policy on membership. To all intents and purposes the ANC's policy on membership was arguably both racialist and racist.

When the ANC opened ordinary membership to all in 1969 at the Morogoro conference, but still kept the top leadership structure, the national executive committee, open to Africans only, the progress was both half-hearted and contradictory. How can an organisation open its membership to all but reserve its most senior leadership structure only for Africans? This was a fundamental and untenable contradiction in terms. From time immemorial in political parties, the top leadership was always logically drawn from the membership. The resultant schism between the policy of non-racial membership and a racialist and racist restriction on membership of the ANC's NEC could only have occurred in an organisation whose knowledge and understanding of the National Question was very poor to begin with, let alone the wider socioeconomic questions of the National Question that arise within the context of colonialism and imperialism.

In other words, a non-racial membership policy, with open and unhindered meetings and elections, would have resulted in much more contested discussions in meetings and in elections to leadership positions, where one's education, skills and experience would obviously be important to consider. This perspective no writer has presented before and engaged with, which is partly why I decided to pursue it in some of my interviews for this book. One gets a sense that so dominant was African nationalism, not only in the ANC but the broad national liberation movement, that to question and criticise the membership policy of the ANC was inherently off-limits, almost as if people from the 'minorities' especially had no right to go there. It was a fait accompli we had to passively live with, as was the seriously mistaken view that the South African revolution necessarily had two stages, which had to be waged in that mechanical sequencing, whether we liked it or not. Both were fatally wrong and their the consequences are written with the blood, sweat and tears of the black working-class majority in post-apartheid SA. I now turn to the performance of the ANC from the 1940s onwards, when it began to grow mass support.

A Brief History of the ANC's Performance since the 1940s

In this section I mainly deal with the policies and activities of the ANC from the 1940s to the release of Mandela in 1990. There is a close and even intimate relationship between the nature of the ANC's aims and the relationships it forged and fostered with people and other organisations from its inception. For example, the relationship between the ANC and white liberals, either businessmen or politicians, was no doubt influenced by the liberalism of both the missionaries and the ANC itself, which was also striking from the early years on. The relationship between the ANC and business then and in subsequent years cannot be seen in isolation from the middle-class liberalism and class nature of the early ANC leaders, who were drawn from the ranks of the clergy, chiefs, lawyers and teachers, the more educated and relatively privileged strata of African society. In other words, the ideas, beliefs and actions of the ANC leadership from the outset spoke largely about their class interests and what *they* wanted, not what the African working masses wanted on the mines, farms and in burgeoning manufacturing industries in the early 20th century.

But who then, given the general conditions of the black masses in SA, could see what was happening and provide a critical analysis of the serious limitations of what these leaders wanted and instead provide a black (even 'African') working-class perspective on the objective situation and the interests and needs of those masses? In 1912 there was no alternative organisation or leadership, except the ANC's various predecessors in all four provinces and the APO. There was no trade union movement for black workers and even manufacturing industry was only beginning to take shape. But from a race–class perspective the total dominance of the mining industry by WMC (local but especially foreign capital) was very clear. Except for Abdurahman's occasional anti-capitalist sentiments in his attacks on Britain's domination of the country, a distinctly socialist or revolutionary voice among the black masses was absent.

But it also, very importantly, shows that the existence of such an African middle class was necessary for British colonialism, only because class divisions among the oppressed served various purposes, which were in its interests in the short, medium and longer term, basically for the same set of reasons why the swelling of the ranks of the black middle class was considered essential by WMC and the NP after Mandela was released in 1990 and during the negotiations process. In fact, the creation of a substantial black middle class and a significant enough elite was central to the strategy of the NP, WMC and their allies abroad, without which the negotiations were dead in the water.

However, I argue that to an increasingly greater extent over the decades the ANC's leadership became not just more middle class but even during the heady days of the struggle in the 1970s and 1980s they did not shift from a non-socialist conception of and approach to the kind of post-apartheid SA they wanted and were fighting for. The ANC and its leaders at no point in the decades after it was formed provided an analysis of what the mineral revolution did to the African people and their livelihoods in both the rural and growing urban areas, and accordingly articulated the needs, demands and aspirations of the growing mining-led African working class.

As earlier indicated, all the ANC wanted was what Marxists refer to as a 'bourgeois democracy' society, though a non-racial one, which did not address and confront capitalism at all. That was essentially the ANC from 1912 until today, which is precisely why they could replace the NP in 1994 without tampering at all with capitalism in SA and in fact made their 'peace' with it, not only because of the global ascendancy of neoliberalism at the time and how that constrained the ANC in the negotiations. No, a study of the ANC from 1912 onwards – notwithstanding the ideological leftward shift when it endorsed the Freedom Charter in 1955 – makes it abundantly clear that the ANC was never at any point in time clearly and unambiguously anti-capitalist.

On the contrary, as I earlier cited Mandela himself, the ANC really wanted not the abolition of capitalism but the right for black people to also be capitalists without any racial restrictions. Whatever radical potential the FC contained for the redistribution of resources and for the wealth of the country to belong to 'the people' was severely compromised by the economic and social-public policies the ANC adopted after 1994. Instead of moving in the direction of public ownership of resources through appropriate legal measures, the ANC went in the opposite direction, with the commercialisation, corporatisation and commodification of even basic public services, such as water, sanitation and electricity, a subject I return to later, and upon which my PhD study was based.

But very significantly the ANC went much further than even the NP to allow and enable some of the giants of white monopoly capital to move offshore and list on the stock exchanges of the US, London and other European capitals, repatriating what must have been a staggering amount of wealth, largely created by the African working class, to overseas destinations. This was an unpardonable betrayal of the black working class in SA, at the hands of the ANC, which not even the racist NP allowed when it ruled from 1948 to 1994. There have been no compelling arguments why such a decision by the ANC and then minister of finance, Trevor Manuel, was necessary. One does not need to be a left-leaning economist to work out and see that such a major move would have been in the interests of these companies and certainly not of the black workers they employed since the mineral revolution of the 19th century.

But much more than a fundamentally false understanding of the main problems facing black people, especially the working class, and eschewing an anti-capitalist analysis, it was the deferential conduct of ANC leaders towards the British which is probably most alienating though a revealing characteristic of themselves and the organisation then. Nothing was more evident of this than what ANC leaders themselves said they aimed for in their struggles. Only later in the 1920s did the ANC under Josiah Gumede lurch briefly closer to the Communist Party of South Africa (CPSA), but not even that shifted it much from its liberal course, until it adopted the African Claims of 1943 and the more radical but ambiguous and contradictory 1955 Freedom Charter. The ANC never wanted anything revolutionary from its inception. They were content to have a fair deal and share in the same capitalist system, but as equals with whites, and even that legal and formal equality could be staggered over time.

All this says a good deal about what the African nationalism of the ANC has amounted to in the liberation struggles that have been fought since the 19th-century mineral revolution, especially those fought by the black working-class majority. The ANC in fact had no orientation to this working class from its birth in 1912, and only through the influence of the CPSA (and later the SACP) did it begin to entertain those interests, but in ways which never once openly confronted the capitalist system in which that mineral revolution was situated and which was responsible for the gross and brutal exploitation of African mine labour. In the years that followed the ANC's birth in 1912 it was generally content to remain the thoroughly liberal and reformist organisation it always was.

The British, without a shred of doubt, tutored the ANC leaders of the early 20th century in their own image, from which the ANC never seriously departed: a liberal and 'non-racial' constitutional democracy within a free enterprise and capitalist economic framework. Nowhere has it made its opposition to capitalism palpably clear and unambiguous. On the contrary, since its inception it has mostly appealed for the franchise, legal equality with whites, and the opportunity and space for the emergence and development of a black capitalist class.

By the 1940s, despite mounting militancy among popular movements, including the 1943–4 Alexandra bus boycott, Dr Xuma and other ANC leaders did not support or channel the political impetus from below.

Noor Nieftagodien indicates something of the class interests at play:

> Notwithstanding his role in rebuilding the ANC in the 1940s, Xuma (then president of the ANC) remained resolutely moderate. He opposed strike action during the war, echoing Jan Smuts's stance that it would undermine the war effort. In Alexandra he and RG Baloyi (treasurer of the ANC) attempted to use the bus boycotts to become bus owners themselves. Growing dissatisfaction among local leaders about the ANC's ineffectiveness led, in the case of Alexandra, to the launch of the ADP, which Peter Walshe interprets as a signal of 'growing radicalism among certain sections of the politically active classes', especially its declared intention to engage in mass mobilisation. It was a sign of the mounting frustrations about the ANC leadership's continued imperviousness to the profound events unfolding around it.

He claims more generally that 'the ANC of the 1940s seemed unwilling and unable to offer itself as a political banner behind which struggle could be coordinated or provided with a degree of political coherence. At the time, the ANC leadership was still largely drawn from the ranks of the educated urban elite, which reflected the character of its primary constituency in the locations'.[71] But what is perhaps even more striking and revealing than not acting decisively to provide leadership during the bus boycott and other mass struggle was the attempt by Xuma to exploit the boycott for business purposes. This is not an anomaly, but instead relates to what the ANC has been about since its inception in 1912. Its leaders all along clearly and unambiguously expressed their interest in conducting business without racial hindrances.

Younger members of the ANC began to express their dissatisfaction with the moderate and ineffective politics of the leadership in what proved to be a far more significant and durable political formation than the African Democratic Party (ADP), the ANC Youth League. Anton Lembede played an important role in calling for a more radical orientation of the ANC in its struggles against the white supremacist state, in the formation of the ANC Youth League, and in combating the very negative image of African people assiduously cultivated by white politicians and their followers. With regard to those goals he played an important and leading role. However, considering the return by the ANC to what I called in 1999 a 'narrow Africanist majoritarian chauvinism', my approach to Lembede's ideas, teachings and legacy is highly critical.

A striking aspect of this resurgent chauvinism is that it can be traced ideologically and politically back to the influence of Lembede's views. These were rooted in an often amorphous, abstract and obscure African nationalism and spiritualism. Gail Gerhart characterised Lembede's Africanism as projecting 'a new and aggressive positive self-image compounded of pride in the past, confident expectations for the future and an emotional, burning love for the African's God-given blackness'.[72] Lembede's message, Martin Meredith summarises, 'was that Africa belonged to Africans'. He cites Lembede: 'Africans are the natives of Africa and they have inhabited Africa, their Motherland, from times immemorial. Africa belongs to them.'[73] This Africanist stance directly influenced the breakaway formation of the PAC and, to some extent, the origins of BC thinking in the late 1960s.

While asserting that Africa belonged to the 'Africans', he never acknowledged that it was not 'African' people – the Bantu-speaking people from central Africa who migrated to southern Africa – who were the original inhabitants of southern Africa but the Khoisan people. The ANC's persistent neglect of the Khoisan and the Coloured people has its roots in the thinking of Lembede. As Meredith notes, his 'Africanism was essentially a philosophy of racial exclusivity.'[74] Bear in mind that apartheid was based on racial exclusivity. This is a strikingly ironical contradiction. Such exclusivity excluded not only white people but Coloureds and Indians too. Here are the roots of the current Africanist majoritarian chauvinism inside and, to some extent, outside the ANC and as a result the alienation of the so-called minorities.

Lembede's chauvinistic Africanism not only failed to link the struggles of African people with those of Indians and Coloureds but was also virulently anti-communist. With bitter irony, this placed the ANCYL in bed with the hysterical anti-communism of the white supremacist state. Lembede's nationalism could also take extreme forms: the ANC historian Francis Meli writes that 'He was so nationalistic in his approach that he was even impressed by the element of nation-building in Hitler's nationalism (national socialism)'.[75] More than any other ANCYL leader, Lembede led a misguided, counterproductive and vituperative campaign against non-racialism and anti-racism.

Jon Soske discusses Lembede's pronounced antipathy towards South African Indians. Arguing that Indians 'are fighting only for their rights to trade and extract as much wealth as possible from Africa', Lembede 'systematically reduced the entire Indian population in South Africa to the figure of the exploitative merchant'.[76] Today there are echoes of Lembede's hostility to Indians within the EFF and elements of the ANC – as discussed in chapter 6 below.

The significance of Lembede and the ANCYL is that after a lacklustre dormancy during the 1930s, the ANC now acquired a dynamism, attracted a cohort of younger members, and increased its membership to 5,500 by the late 1940s. This created a platform for its growth into a mass movement in the early 1950s. The ANCYL also pushed the parent body into a more radical turn, with the adoption of its Programme of Action in 1949. This embraced a strategy of mass action, through the use of boycotts, strikes and civil disobedience. But what distinguished the ANCYL leadership from the ANC was that its radicalism was channelled 'into a fiercely nationalistic framework, hostile both to the class politics of socialism and to liberal individualism'.[77] Their more strident form of African nationalism resembled what is today referred to as 'racial nationalism' or what I call a 'narrow Africanist majoritarian chauvinism'.

But Fine and Davis show that the Programme of Action and the extent of the ANC's shift to the left were limited. The Programme of Action to some extent 'reflected the specific aspirations of the African middle class, notably calling for "the establishment of commercial, industrial, transport and other enterprises" by and for Africans'. The somewhat restricted militancy of the Programme was the subject of a left critique by the Communist Party in January 1950, which charged that 'the radicalisation of African nationalism did not fundamentally change the ANC's middle-class coloration'.[78]

In the 1950s, the ANC adopted a 'multiracial' approach in the form of the Congress Alliance and a more assertive policy approach, demonstrated in the Freedom Charter of 1955 (its limitations and contradictions are analysed in later chapters). Lembede's legacy persisted through the 1950s in the form of 'the growing Africanist faction in the Transvaal and the Eastern Cape [which] rejected the Defiance Campaign on the basis of Lembede's earlier criticism of non-European unity'[79] and subsequently broke away to form the PAC. Bonner points out that 'The shift towards multiracialism and the Congress Alliance was spearheaded by the CPSA/SACP, which itself recruited members on a non-racial basis'. The importance of this point must not be underestimated. The Africanism was so deep inside the ANC from its inception that it was very unlikely that the move to 'multiracialism', as murky as it is, or 'non-racialism', as obscure as it always was, would have come from itself.

Bonner pointed out that 'Until 1950 the ANC remained resolutely African in character, with Mandela leading the anti-alliance, anti-multiracial collaboration camp.' However, this situation was 'transformed radically' in the early 1950s, firstly with the shift towards the politics of the Congress Alliance, and secondly with the new ANC constitution of 1958 which endorsed non-racialism and the Freedom Charter. Even so, Bonner continued, 'the Africanist strand remained an important undercurrent in the ANC ... In other words, non-racialism remained a contentious issue in the ANC in exile – hence only in the Morogoro conference was membership opened and eligibility for the NEC only at Kabwe.'[80]

If one studies the relationship between the SANNC/ANC and all other political forces, such as the APO and later the Indian Congresses, the Coloured People's Congress, the white liberals and its ally, the SACP, it is very evident that they have exploited the simple demographic fact that the African people are the overwhelming majority of the South African population. Not only have they wantonly abused this numerical superiority in a racialist chauvinistic sense, but they have exploited it in their own class interests, and not to advance the interests of the black working class, which has been the chief support base of the ANC since the 1940s onwards. They leant on this mass opportunistically throughout their existence and used and abused it when it suited them, as they did in 1994 in order to win the elections, only to advocate and implement nakedly harmful neoliberal economic, social and public policies after winning the elections.

Fine and Davis show how the ANC leadership manipulated the militancy of the African masses as it suited them from one decade to the next, and pointed out something of profound importance and insight:

> Rather than the electoral strategy of Congress having derailed the working-class movement, the weakness of the working-class movement allowed the electoral strategy of Congress to come to the fore in 1958.

The idealist method of the left critics of Congress led them to see the fall in mass militancy as the effect of leadership but not see the nature of leadership as the effect of the weakness of the masses.[81]

That weakness derived in part from the illiteracy and lack of formal education has been a major factor hindering the development of political and class consciousness in the ANC, to their huge detriment, and to that of the labour movement. This is partly why the ANC's alliance with first SACTU and later Cosatu lasted as long as it did, no matter how many times it has fundamentally contradicted its electoral and other promises, especially its commitment to 'building a better life for all'.

This history of poor education and the lack of a reading culture will have profound implications for present-day SA, meaning, for example, that the transition from a class-in-itself to a class-for-itself among the African working class will be a massive journey which requires an appropriate level of political consciousness and cultural development. Bantu education also did enormous damage to African communities, with long-term implications. It is partly against that historical background that we have also had serious problems in our education results in SA after 1994, especially in schools.

The power of capitalism is undeniable: till today, we have had no single successful socialist overthrow of capitalism, except the Russian Revolution of 1917, which, however, was stricken with congenital weaknesses that disposed it towards its inevitable demise in the early 1990s. Fine and Davis cite many examples of how the left outside the ANC too often projected a militant triumphalism between the 1940s and 1980s, at different times, about the imminence of a successful black working class-led socialist revolution in SA. And as far as the ANC was concerned, according to its own policies, programmes and analyses it was not consciously leading an anti-capitalist revolution. No, it was leading the national democratic revolution (NDR), which it claimed consisted of various classes and whose priority was the abolition of apartheid racism, but decidedly not a declared struggle against capitalism, with which the ANC was overwhelmingly linked for very long.

However, despite this multi-class alliance the ANC and SACP foregrounded the leadership of the black working class in the struggle against apartheid, especially from its 1969 Morogoro conference onwards, but not in order to advance the class interests and needs of black workers. Instead, the ANC used the numerical weight of the African working class to ensure its leadership of the national liberation movement, which was used to ascend to political power in the 1994 elections. But if one studies the literature of the ANC itself since the 1969 conference, not once is that leading role of the black working class, as the 'motor force of the revolution', given the necessary policy, political and organisational expression in the only conceivable direction it should proceed – that is, in an anti-capitalist direction. In fact, it consciously avoided dealing with capitalism, which is arguably the primary root cause of the deepening social crisis in SA today.

Not to have explicitly anti-capitalist policies meant that the putatively leading role of the black working class was little more than a formal shell, lacking any clear and strong class direction, which by then was in objective and programmatic terms urgently required for the kind of socialist transformation imperative to even address the most basic needs of the majority black working class. But search as closely as you wish, you will find nowhere an explicit ANC statement of anti-capitalist policies. This raises very serious questions of the quality of ANC leadership this country has had since 1912 and especially from the 1940s onwards, given the greater mass following it achieved and the more militant mass struggles that were waged by the black working class at various times from the 1940s, and especially during the 1980s. But even following this considerable radicalisation of the ANC, the leadership was not only left wanting but some of the leaders tried to restrain and tame militant black mass struggles.

It is necessary to say a few things about the history of the ANC which are particularly pertinent to present-day SA and its future. What this critical reflection on the history of the ANC has done is to show with abundant clarity that it is far from what its leaders since its inception have made it out to be. The ANC was never at any point in time a revolutionary mass movement, leading the struggle for the fundamental transformation of this society.

I conclude this chapter with a few critically important comments about South African history and the concrete conditions under which capitalism developed in this country, largely because all the major problems of SA after 1994 resonate with its unlearnt lessons. We are today therefore reliving our history, and in that regard, are stuck with the severe limitations under which capitalism developed here: severe repression and the denial of the most basic democratic and human rights. The overwhelming majority of people of this country were denied basic public services, such as water, flush sanitation, electricity, decent and adequate wages, housing, education and health services. What existed was inferior, inadequate, and most often the infrastructure was simply degrading and inhumane.

No fundamental changes have occurred to the South African economy since the mineral revolution of the 19th century. The capitalist system, which for over one and a half centuries grew out of the mineral revolution, is basically the same system we inhabit today, bar the formal abolition of all apartheid laws in 1994. That was at best a genuine political revolution, subverting an avalanche of racist legislation on the statute book. But that is as far as the transition of the 1990s went, without in any way tampering with the capitalist system, which was the economic framework within which all those laws existed.

Removing all those laws formally deracialised society and the capitalist structure, but by so doing it did a major service to WMC and its reform-minded wing, clearing the way for the perpetuation of a system which embodied since the 19th century the brutal exploitation of cheap black labour, key aspects of which remained intact. How this was done, how that system perpetuated itself in ways which hardly raise an eyebrow today, and how, as a result of the fundamental compromises the ANC made, SA was reshaped but in ways which left it virtually intact, wittingly or unwittingly paving the way for all that has happened after 1994.

Once material conditions are structurally embedded in urban areas over a long historical period, it is virtually impossible to change them unless the capitalist social relations which underpin them are confronted and changed. That is why the dismal conditions around water and sanitation in the rest of Africa, for example, have largely remained the same after political independence was won between the 1950s and 1980s and later in 1994 in SA. Similar problems which afflict African townships today in SA can be found throughout Africa. If those fundamentally important causal factors are not pointed out and confronted – which clearly link the struggle for these basic services to the struggles against the capitalist system wherever it might be – there will be no different future for the many millions of people who today languish in such degrading and inhumane conditions.

There is no country in the world where race, class and gender cohere systemically to the same extent as in SA. The present crisis in SA is so deeply structural and so systemically linked to our history that I will boldly claim that the ANC will not be able to adequately provide even the most basic of services in the black townships. This dismal situation must be seen alongside the trade union demands for a 'living wage' and other changes on the shop floor, which capital, still mainly white, will be unable to provide. The biggest constraints are the entrenched racism in every facet of life, the lack of even the most basic democratic rights and services, such as access to water, sanitation, housing, a decent education and much more.

I believe that what has happened after 1994 makes it impossible for such changes to occur on the existing basis of capitalism. The ANC and capital are simply unable to afford to satisfy these basic needs, especially within an explicitly neoliberal macroeconomic framework. Even before the onset of the Covid-19 pandemic, poverty remained a very serious problem. Unemployment and social inequalities are much worse today than they were under apartheid.

Those social realities were not ended but were deepened and widened with the mineral revolution, especially as regards the key requirement for cheap black labour. It is against that deeper historical background that the negotiations of the 1990s took place and the 1994 first-ever non-racial democratic elections ensued. The final point is that this virtually symbiotic history in the relationship between colonialism-racism-apartheid and capitalism in SA – especially in light of the results of the past 25 years of ANC rule – will have enormous implications for the future and what can or cannot be achieved within that historically evolved framework. And as the capitalist crisis remains and perhaps even deepens further, the implications it will have for this perspective will be ever starker.

As for the 'broad church' the ANC always claimed it represents, often when criticised about its policies, its rule in post-apartheid SA has exploded the myth which it always was. But it is a myth linked to other myths in its history, like the mantra of 'blacks in general and Africans in particular'. Firstly, the 'broad church' myth is an insult to even a person with average intelligence, in the light of the palpably clear fact that after 1994, through BEE and AA policies, the ANC and WMC created a small black bourgeoisie and more numerous black middle class, at the evident expense of the interests and needs of the black working-class majority. Secondly, that myth is inextricably linked to the 'blacks in general, Africans in particular' one, because it is as palpably clear that it is only the African elite and middle class who have benefited handsomely from our neoliberal transition, and not the African working class.

One of the major and palpable pitfalls of African nationalism is how it has crumbled before the hurricane of class through the rupturing impact of BEE and AA. But the African people were always divided by social-class factors. Yet the magnitude of such divisions in post-apartheid SA is unprecedented. Never again will SA see the degree of black solidarity achieved in the anti-apartheid struggle – because the ANC emphasised race at the expense of class. As the capitalist crisis deepens, which is inevitable in the light of the further impact of both the deepening global capitalist crisis and the inevitable job losses of the 4IR over the next decade, this intra-black class division will deepen further.

Endnotes

1. Gordon S. Wood, *The Purpose of the Past* (New York: Penguin Press, 2008). p. 7.
2. Philip Bonner, 'Fragmentation and cohesion in the ANC: The first 70 years', in *One Hundred Years of the ANC: Debating Liberation Histories Today*, ed. Arianna Lissoni et al. (Johannesburg: Wits University Press, 2012), pp. 1–2.
3. Norman Etherington, 'Religion and resistance in Natal, 1900–1910', in Lissoni, *One Hundred Years*, pp. 55–76.
4. Andre Odendaal, *The Founders: The Origins of the ANC and the Struggle for Democracy in South Africa* (Johannesburg: Jacana, 2013), pp. 367–8.
5. Odendaal, *The Founders*, p. 364.
6. Odendaal, *The Founders*, pp. 241, 249.
7. Odendaal, *The Founders*, p. 259.
8. Odendaal, *The Founders*, p. 260.
9. Odendaal, *The Founders*, p. 241.
10. Odendaal, *The Founders*, p. 242.
11. Odendaal, *The Founders*, p. 247.
12. Natal Society Foundation, 'The early African press in Natal', *Inkanyiso Yase Natal*, April 1889 – June 1896', *Natalia*, 16 (2010), pp. 6–11.
13. Odendaal, *The Founders*, pp. 162–3.
14. Etherington, 'Religion and resistance', p. 56.
15. Etherington, 'Religion and resistance', p. 56.
16. Odendaal, *The Founders*, p. 250.

17 Odendaal, *The Founders*, pp. 253–4.
18 Odendaal, *The Founders*, p. 255.
19 Odendaal, *The Founders*, pp. 287, 290.
20 Odendaal, *The Founders*, p. 287.
21 Luli Callinicos interview, 22 January 2018, Johannesburg.
22 Interview with Luli Callinicos, 22 January 2017, Johannesburg. This was the view of Callinicos, the biographer of Oliver Tambo. I firmly believe that it is a lopsided account of African nationalism, which I have already alluded to and much of which lies ahead in this work. A critical socialist analysis must necessarily combine an anti-racist or anti-apartheid discourse with questions of political economy and issues of social justice.
23 Michael MacDonald, *Why Race Matters in South Africa* (Cambridge, MA and London: Harvard University Press, 2006), pp. 96, 101.
24 See https://camissapeople.wordpress.com/2018/06/27/the-national-question-non-racialism-or-ethnicism.
25 MacDonald, *Why Race Matters*, pp. 99–100.
26 Ebrahim Harvey, 'ANC policies divisive in the Western Cape', *The Sowetan*, 16 July 1999.
27 MacDonald, *Why Race Matters*, pp. 103, 105, 103.
28 MacDonald, *Why Race Matters*, p. 105.
29 https://camissapeople.wordpress.com.
30 https://camissapeople.wordpress.com.
31 https://camissapeople.wordpress.com.
32 https://camissapeople.wordpress.com.
33 Cited in Crain Soudien, 'Robben Island University revisited' in Lissoni et al., *One Hundred Years*, pp. 221–2.
34 Odendaal, *The Founders*, p. 294.
35 See https://www.sahistory.org.za/article/anc-org-origins-and-background.
36 Odendaal, *The Founders*, p. 395.
37 Callinicos interview.
38 Email reply by Eddie Webster, 26 October 2017.
39 Email reply by Webster.
40 Timothy Keegan, *Colonial South Africa and the Origins of the Racial Order* (Cape Town and Johannesburg: David Philip, 2006), p. 93.
41 Callinicos interview.
42 Cited in Fine and Davis, *Beyond Apartheid: Labour and Liberation in South Africa*, p. 195.
43 Robert Fine and Dennis Davis, *Beyond Apartheid: Labour and Liberation in South Africa* (Johannesburg: Ravan Press, 1990), p. 195.
44 Fine and Davis, *Beyond Apartheid*, p. 193.
45 Enver Motala and Salim Vally, 'Neville Alexander and the National Question', in *The Unanswered National Question: Left Thoughts under Apartheid*, eds. Edward Webster and Karin Pampallis (Johannesburg: Wits University Press, 2017), p. 131.
46 Neville Alexander, *One Azania, One Nation: The National Question in South Africa* (London: Zed Press, 1979), p. 49.
47 Fine and Davis, *Beyond Apartheid*, p.193.
48 Quoted in MacDonald, *Why Race Matters*, p. 130.
49 Cited in Fine and Davis, *Beyond Apartheid*, pp. 3–4.
50 Fine and Davis, *Beyond Apartheid*, p. 17.

51 MacDonald, *Why Race Matters*, pp. 100–1.
52 Cited in MacDonald, *Why Race Matters* p. 100.
53 Odendaal, *The Founders*, p. 368.
54 Odendaal, *The Founders*, p. 118.
55 All quotations in this paragraph from Jack and Ray Simons, *Class and Colour in South Africa, 1850–1950* (London: Penguin, 1969), pp. 119–20.
56 Simons and Simons, *Class and Colour*, p. 120.
57 Simons and Simons, *Class and Colour*, p. 124.
58 Simons and Simons, *Class and Colour*, p. 126.
59 Simons and Simons, *Class and Colour*, p. 127.
60 Simons and Simons, *Class and Colour*, p. 118.
61 Odendaal, *The Founders*, p. 391.
62 Ebrahim Harvey, 'Breaking free from the white left', *Mail & Guardian*, 15 December 2000.
63 Interview, Pali Lehohla, 22 October 2017, Pretoria.
64 Interview, Solly Mapaila, 22 February 2018, Johannesburg.
65 Philip Bonner, 'South African society and culture, 1910–1948', in *Cambridge History of South Africa*, Vol. 2, ed. Robert Ross, Anne Mager and Bill Nasson (Cambridge: Cambridge University Press, 2011), pp. 260, 274.
66 Bonner, 'South African society and culture', p. 257.
67 Bonner, 'South African society and culture', p. 305.
68 Simon Clark, ed., *Nelson Mandela Speaks: Forging a Democratic Non-Racial South Africa* (Johannesburg; David Philip, 1993), p. 123. This is cited from a speech Mandela made in Cuba on 26 July 1991.
69 See Anthony Sampson, *Mandela: The Authorised Biography* (London: HarperCollins Publishers, 1999), p. 95.
70 Bonner, 'South African society and culture', pp. 286–93.
71 Noor Nieftagodien, 'Popular movements, contentious spaces and the ANC, 1943–1956', in Lissoni et al., eds, *One Hundred Years*, p. 149.
72 Gail Gerhart, *Black Power in South Africa: The Evolution of an Ideology* (Berkeley: University of California Press, 1978), p. 58.
73 Martin Meredith, *Nelson Mandela: A Biography* (London: Penguin Books, 1997), p. 46.
74 Meredith, *Nelson Mandela*, p. 66.
75 Francis Meli, 'South Africa and the rise of African nationalism', in M. van Diepen, ed., *The National Question in South Africa* (London and New Jersey: Zed Books, 1988), p. 72.
76 Jon Soske, 'Unravelling the 1947 "Doctors' Pact": Race, metonymy and the evasions of nationalist history', in Lissoni et al., *One Hundred Years*, p. 182.
77 Fine and Davis, *Beyond Apartheid*, p. 74.
78 Fine and Davis, *Beyond Apartheid*, pp. 109–10, 111–12.
79 Soske, 'Unravelling', p. 185.
80 Bonner, 'Fragmentation and cohesion', p. 10.
81 Fine and Davis, *Beyond Apartheid*, p. 187.

FIVE

Mandela, negotiations and the rise to power of the ANC

> Our people's expectations are about acquiring basic essentials, like housing, electrification, water, sanitation, decent education and jobs. These are the very issues which are set out in our Bill of Rights and in the Freedom Charter. One of the threads that run through all our policy documents is the unshakeable commitment of the ANC to direct resources towards precisely those ends.
>
> Nelson Mandela (1994)[1]

Mandela's Release: Brief Observations on the National and Global Situation

THIS CHAPTER IDENTIFIES some key considerations at the time of Mandela's release from prison in 1990 and what transpired in the negotiations and elections which followed over the next few years. Several major developments had already occurred in SA to make that historic event possible, desirable and indeed inevitable. Mandela's release and the multiple processes which rapidly unfolded had a particular genealogy, which began in earnest after the 1976 black student uprisings. In December of that year, Anglo American formed the Urban Foundation (UF).[2] The dominant intention was to seek liberal-reformist solutions to the gathering crisis within the framework of the capitalist economic system from which AAC and Oppenheimer had profited in the midst of appalling levels of poverty, unemployment and social inequalities.[3] It was Gavin Relly, of the economically dominant AAC, who with other business leaders held talks with the ANC in Lusaka in 1985, aiming to ward off the growing threats to their interests posed by domestic militancy. WMC and the AAC moved ahead and independent of the NP in approaching the ANC for talks, but to varying degrees capital, the *verligte* sections of the NP and the ANC in exile were already considering the possibility of a negotiated political settlement after the cataclysmic 1976 student uprisings and especially after the very serious mid-1980s economic and financial crisis in SA.

Alongside the designs of WMC and the NP – moving towards seeking a negotiated settlement of the deepening and perilous crisis of the 1980s – the ANC's entire history predisposed it towards wanting a similar resolution to the crisis. No single individual played as important a role in steering the country towards this outcome as Mandela himself. His engagement with NP leaders in the second half of the 1980s, and especially from 1988, at times tested the loyalty of the handful of his comrades in Pollsmoor Prison.

By the time Mandela was released on 11 February 1990, major global changes had already occurred, notably the collapse of the Soviet bloc, without which it is unlikely that he and other senior leaders would have been released and negotiations with the NP begun. These circumstances are important to understand, whatever criticisms of the ANC may be made about its major compromises on economic and social policy during and after the negotiations. Debate continues about whether those compromises were avoidable and whether the ANC gave too much away, for example on the policy on nationalisation of major sectors of the economy, which was a provision in the 1955 Freedom Charter (FC).

But we must also bear in mind what Mandela himself said about the provisions of the FC before the ANC took office in 1994: 'It was the ANC that initiated the current peace process that we hope will lead to a negotiated transfer of power to the people. Our goals remain the achievement of the demands of the Freedom Charter and we will settle for nothing less than that.'[4] However, the FC's ambiguity and contradictions were identified by Mandela's authorised biographer, Anthony Sampson. Although 'It was frequently condemned as a Marxist document, with its bold promise: "The mineral wealth beneath the soil, the banks and monopoly industry shall be transferred to the ownership of the people as a whole" ... in fact it was carefully designed to be all things to all men.'[5]

Indeed, Mandela himself, in a 1956 article, demonstrated the flexibility of interpretations of the FC. While on the one hand he stated that 'The Charter strikes a fatal blow at the financial and gold-mining monopolies that have for centuries plundered the country and condemned its people to servitude', he also wrote that this would 'open up fresh fields for the development of a prosperous non-European bourgeois class. For the first time in the history of this country the non-European bourgeoisie will have the opportunity to own in their own name and right mills and factories, and trade and private enterprise will boom and flourish as never before.'[6]

Ambiguity is also evident in his 'I am prepared to die' speech during the Rivonia Trial. 'The Freedom Charter calls for redistribution of land; but not nationalisation of land; it provides for nationalisation of mines, banks and monopoly industry because big monopolies are owned by one race only, and without such nationalisation racial domination would be perpetuated despite the spread of political power.' But, as MacDonald points out,

> read carefully, Mandela called for nationalisation as a means to the goal of achieving racial, not economic equality. Mandela called for nationalisation because mines, banks and monopoly industries were the exclusive property of whites. But Mandela's logic implied a subtext. Implicitly, he allowed for the possibility that mines, banks and monopolies could escape nationalisation provided they shed their racial character, that they ceased to be the preserve of whites.[7]

MacDonald's is a profoundly insightful observation: this is exactly what happened in SA under ANC rule. Not only has the ANC emasculated the more radical interpretation of the FC in this fundamental respect, it went in the opposite direction where it mattered most in the lives of the black working-class majority: it commercialised, corporatised and commodified basic services, such as water, sanitation and electricity. As a result of these processes arm's-length companies, such as Johannesburg Water and City Power, were formed in 2000–1 to administer these services, after the relevant departments in the city were shut down.

In the case of water, sanitation and electricity the widespread installation of prepaid meters meant that once the small 'lifelines' provided to indigent families were exhausted and they lacked money to recharge the meters, they had to do without these services. The manner in which these processes unfolded in the targeted black townships in Johannesburg was nothing less than brutal. In the case of Phiri, in Soweto, the police and army were called in to enable prepaid water meters to be forcefully installed at the homes of residents, after they damaged and, in some cases, destroyed the meter infrastructure. The consequences, my research revealed, were devastating.[8]

Although upon his release in 1990 Mandela recommitted the ANC to nationalisation, when he returned from the WEF in Davos in 1992 he asserted that the ANC was no longer wedded to it, without any mandate from the ANC to say so. Neither did anyone in the ANC contradict him. Once again, the iconic stature of Mandela allowed him to escape opprobrium inside the ANC alliance. It was a measure of the saintly, but highly problematic, stature of Mandela at that time. Nobody in the ANC alliance dared to question or contradict him, which spurred a critique of his presidency which I wrote in 2000.[9]

I pointed out that in fact it was under Mandela's presidency that neoliberal economic and social policies were adopted and implemented – including the Growth, Employment and Redistribution (Gear) strategy of 1996. Mandela was thus substantially responsible for the social crisis which followed, between 1996 and 1999. Yet his leadership was virtually unquestioned, inside the ANC and beyond, I argued: 'There can be no doubt that the revered stature of Mandela during his presidency had served to absorb, prevent, diminish or deflect criticism of his own weaknesses and failures. Seldom, if at all, did the media treat him with anything near the robust criticism they regularly dished out to President Thabo Mbeki.'

With the benefit of hindsight we now know how the ANC in office fundamentally deviated from the provisions of the FC on nationalisation and 'redistribution' – a deviation which once appeared inconceivable. Yet while the ANC reneged on nationalisation and the transfer of the wealth 'to the people', it proceeded after 1994 to facilitate the creation of a black bourgeoisie, for which purpose BEE legislation was passed. Instead of the enormous wealth of SA being 'transferred' to the people, the poverty, joblessness and related social miseries of the black working-class majority were perpetuated after 1994 and social inequality increased.[10]

In the early 1990s, under the influence of WMC and its allies abroad, on the one hand, and the weaknesses, exhaustion and contradictions of the 'mass democratic movement' (MDM), on the other, radical interpretations of the FC were deliberately marginalised in the run-up to and following the 1994 elections.

During negotiations, the unstated and unwritten code was 'Whatever else may be fine, don't touch the economy'. While WMC had no representatives at Kempton Park, its preferred policies prevailed by virtue of the uncontested fact that no threat to its interests was made during three years of negotiations. Quite apart from Mandela's backtracking on nationalisation, the ANC's economics team 'turned their backs with undue haste on alternative progressive policy ideas and advice from their own research think tanks'.[11]

Mandela was a key player in the negotiated settlement of 1993, which left the black working-class majority of this country in some respects worse off than they were under NP rule, particularly in so far as basic municipal services are concerned. This is probably the most important indication of the failures of the ANC and its betrayal of the basic needs and aspirations of that class of people. Given our history, for any government to fail in regard to basic services, upon which people rely daily in order to live, makes a powerful and compelling case against Mandela and the ANC.

And if there are any doubts that Mandela had by 1994 – having had meetings with the leaders of Western countries and the global corporate world – changed his thinking it was when he referred to the free market as a 'magic elixir' in a speech he made to a joint sitting of the Houses of Congress in Washington in that year. Mandela, says Bond, 'came to accept a firmly capitalist South Africa in just such a "commonsensical" manner'.[12] Given his global stature, nobody in the ANC said one critical word about it, even when it flagrantly contradicted his own earlier views about the Freedom Charter. By 1994, Mandela's and the ANC's thinking had undergone a sea change.

However, it was a combination of the local and global conditions which made Mandela's release and the subsequent negotiations possible. WMC, led by Harry Oppenheimer's AAC, had since the 1970s, especially after the 1976 student uprisings, called for the release of Mandela.

WMC had by far the most to lose if SA had a revolution. To protect the staggering wealth it owned and controlled, the AAC called for Mandela's release and a negotiated settlement with the ANC. These moves were all calculated to ward off revolution and keep SA safe for capitalism, albeit a deracialised version.

There can, however, be no doubt that the mass struggles and militancy of the 1980s – arguably the most important and militant period ever for the liberation movement in SA – finally pushed the NP towards negotiations. But this would not have happened without the demise of the Stalinist regimes in Russia and other East European countries and the ascendancy of neoliberalism globally. The NP leadership carefully and strategically considered various factors, while De Klerk not only grasped the opportunities in that global situation but capitalised on it, moving swiftly to release Mandela and making negotiations possible.

Many, especially black radicals, still fail to understand and appreciate the key role played by De Klerk, which remains indelibly grafted into history. His historic role is clear, especially since the ANC's MK was little more than a nuisance and would never have come anywhere close to being able militarily to defeat the most powerful state in Africa. Negotiations averted intense conflict between the contending parties, and the prospect of a bloody and combustible civil war between whites and blacks. But, above all else, the NP and WMC desperately needed to secure a negotiated political settlement which would guarantee their economic, financial and material interests over the long term.

Many tend also to forget that in fact it was the former president, P.W. Botha, who was the first white president of SA to institute various reform measures. The Wiehahn (labour legislation) and Riekert (influx control) Commissions, which respectively led to significant trade union and urban rights for black workers, occurred during his presidency, also serving the objective interests of employers who were shifting to a more skilled and permanently settled workforce. He was also the first president to meet with Mandela before he was released. By the mid-1980s the NP was preparing itself and white SA for significant shifts in political and constitutional terms; for benefits to urban black 'insiders' while still excluding unskilled, unemployed and rural people.

The NP, as was the case with WMC, was willing to make whatever political and legislative reforms were necessary for capitalism to survive in SA. The NP and WMC knew in advance that given the demographics of the country it was a foregone conclusion that in a constitutional democracy the ANC would govern after an election. But after 1976 they had tentatively travelled far down the road leading to black majority rule. That was no longer their primary fear. In fact, they came to welcome it, as long as it did not in any way subvert the capitalist economy. That was the key interest of both the NP and WMC, with the release of Mandela. And indeed, they got more than they bargained for.

There is, however, a big gap in the understanding and analysis of what alternatives the independent left could have presented in 1994.[13] While many books deal with this problem, none of them explores the deeper 'race' and cultural issues which have throughout the many decades of struggle against both Dutch and British colonialism and later apartheid been a formidable, if not virtually insuperable, problem in SA, given our historical racial and ethnic demographics, especially after the mineral revolution, which led to a massive influx of African people into the cities. This demographic reality is simply that the African people, with all their traditional, cultural and linguistic properties, are the overwhelming majority of the population. That numerical fact has been the seedbed of African nationalism and the Africanist majoritarian chauvinism we have seen so much of over the past decade in SA, inside and outside the ANC.

The leadership of the 'independent left' outside of the ANC alliance has largely come from so-called 'minorities' – whites, Coloureds and Indians. This is an unalterable fact of the long struggle in SA. An educational system that was highly racialised in the 20th century, including the fact that African languages were deliberately not taught at those schools, had negative consequences for building a revolutionary consciousness and organisation, especially among the Coloured and Indian working classes and activists. These socio-linguistic-cultural separations and divisions seriously affected the capacity of political activists from those communities to work with and among the majority African masses. From my own experience, even when they entered the trade unions and other political organisations, language and cultural barriers were serious problems.

This has meant that while this left leadership broadly had an incomparably better knowledge of our history and analysis of our society – precisely because they had relatively better education and resources than activists in African communities – they seriously lacked a mass movement in which they could build a revolutionary socialist politics. No doubt, their 'minority' status, the language and traditional-cultural differences with African people and, very importantly, the segregation and apartheid periods – which geographically divided the black working class – together made it virtually impossible for them to build substantial African support the ANC enjoyed for several decades.

In the past those realities were exploited, especially by African nationalist activists and leaders, particularly when they had ideological and political differences with those 'minority' activists and their organisations, even when these were non-racial and anti-racist, such as the Cape-based Non-European Unity Movement (NEUM). The NEUM, consisting largely of Coloured middle-class intellectuals, had probably the clearest and strongest anti-racist stance in the broad national liberation movement in the 1940s and 1950s, but their biggest weakness was that they lacked mass support, including even among the Coloured working class. Among the African masses they had very little support. Like the SANNC of 1912, they consisted of teachers, lawyers and other professionals, unable to penetrate the ranks of the masses with any significance. In terms of a historical understanding of the situation in SA, NEUM leaders like Isaac Tabata were more advanced than leaders of the ANC. Mandela himself implied this in conversation with Richard Stengel: 'It was difficult to cope with his arguments ... I didn't want to continue arguing with the fellow [Tabata] because he was demolishing me just like that.'[14]

It was difficult for the racial 'minorities' to collaborate with African organisations like the ANC because the Africanists in the ANC actively discouraged unity with them. They favoured the existence of separate racial organisations, even though this stance had serious debilitating consequences for the struggle in several respects. The ANC's membership policy and its advocacy of separate organisations were essentially defensive measures, springing from a leadership not very confident of themselves. They felt that their knowledge, understanding and skills might be deficient and, in an open, non-racial, anti-racist and united organisation, would count against them in the election of leaders.

The Africanists of the ANC and ANCYL did not want unity with Coloureds and Indians, let alone whites. John Soske has analysed the contrasting positions of the NEUM and ANC in the 1940s with respect to relations with other 'non-European' political organisations. The NEUM sought 'unity', the ANC 'co-operation'. The cautious position of ANC President A.B. Xuma, which I argue was generally the attitude of the African nationalists towards Coloureds and Indians, is described by Soske as expressing 'the conservative outlook of a middle class nationalist, insistent on the subordination of mass struggle ... and working-class organisations to a "responsible" leadership and committed to political mobilisation along racial lines'. This perspective favoured 'co-operation at an organisational level' between the elites of racial groups, rather than a fusion of groups.[15] I have no doubt that it was not only the ideological and political differences the ANC then had with the NEUM that was in question, but their Coloured 'minority' status too.

Decades later it was reported that Vishwas Satgar, the former provincial secretary of the SACP in Gauteng, was reminded in some argument he had in the party in the early 2000s that he was 'not even African'.[16] That this came from within the SACP, which since its inception had a totally non-racial policy, indicated how strongly the current of majoritarian Africanist chauvinism flowed inside and outside the ANC. There can be nothing in political life generally, and especially in a supposedly non-racial constitutional democracy, that is as alienating and unhealthy as such a racial or ethnic demographic majoritarianism which rests entirely on the sheer weight of numbers. Such conduct is especially destructive given our deeply racialist and racist history. But it is much more so when it comes from the thinking of African people who have not only been the most oppressed and exploited people in SA for long but who suffered most the effects of white racism. The longer this persists the greater will be the obstacles to the ongoing struggle for the total emancipation of SA.

African nationalism, especially of the chauvinistic majoritarian type, uses homogeneous appeals to race and ethnicity to obscure from the African working class its own class interests, which run contrary to its own, as has been so nakedly and sadly seen in post-apartheid SA, especially from what has come out of the Zondo Commission of Enquiry (ZCI).[17]

But the really negative and destructive results of such self-serving petit bourgeois nationalism were not conspicuous until the ANC came to power after the 1994 elections. It required power in order for its 'true colours' (no pun intended) to be seen, and that is the power that comes from access to state-public resources, notably the state-owned enterprises (SOEs). Other than through BEE and AA legislation, and with the exception of companies such as Bosasa, the ANC could not loot the resources of the white-dominated private sector much. It could instead use and abuse the resources of the state, which has been overwhelmingly the source of the corruption which the ZCI has unearthed. Such looting is theft of resources the ANC-controlled state should have consciously directed towards dealing with the social devastation wrought by centuries-long oppression, racism and exploitation.

There is probably no other country where all the issues of race, class and gender coalesced and are congealed as much as in South Africa, especially given its virulent racist history and the symbiotic relationship of racism and capitalism. That history has come to haunt in different ways both the ANC and WMC in post-apartheid SA. The explicitly racist and violent claws of that history were sunk deep into our economics and politics from the 19th century onwards, and therefore after 1994 trying to release their grip has proven to be virtually impossible. The intertwined dominance of that history was the material basis from which to approach not only how highly developed capitalism was in SA but the implications it had for the nature and degree of revolutionary 'transformation' in order to secure even the most basic rights to which citizens are entitled by the constitution's Bill of Rights. Hence, a central argument of this book is that there is simply no way whatsoever to achieve the fulfilment of those rights within a system whose very existence was historically shaped to deny them to black people.

I need to dwell a bit further on this point. The 'highly developed capitalism' I refer to was achieved because of the abundance of rightless, cheap and super-exploitable black labour. South African capitalism, in other words, was baptised in the systemic confluence of racism, in varying forms, and capitalist exploitation. And therein lie the roots of the serious limitations of liberal reforms before, but especially after 1994, when it was time for the ANC in power to 'deliver' to the black masses whose labour built the economy and many of whom supported it loyally over several decades. The black middle-class liberalism of the ANC merged with neoliberalism, which was in the ascendancy globally at the time of the negotiations.

Two important factors were in play at the time of Mandela's release. Firstly, there were powerful forces at work behind his release, both local and global. No organisation inside or outside this country could stop processes whose genesis lay in the 1970s. Secondly, it was not only the NP and WMC that wanted a political settlement. Given the stalemate with the NP, the unprecedented state repression of the 1980s, the fact that the ANC was banned in SA, the weakness of MK, and the serious problems it was experiencing in exile, the ANC wanted it desperately too.

In regard to its problems in exile, it is instructive to recall the charges made by Ben Turok, Chris Hani and others about the exiled leadership before its 1969 Morogoro conference. Turok lamented a 'deep-going malaise', officials who have 'come to adopt authoritarian attitudes towards comrades in lower positions', 'evidence of maladministration ... embezzlement ... and drunkeness'. Hani and his co-signatories identified 'very disturbing and dispiriting' symptoms of malaise, including 'secret trials and secret executions', the 'fossilization of the leadership' – and more.[18]

It is even more significant – seen against what has transpired after 1994 – that in the *Strategy and Tactics* document adopted at Morogoro, the ANC asserted:

> The struggle is also happening in a new South Africa in which there is a large and well-developed working class whose class consciousness and in which the independent expressions of the working class – the political organs and trade unions – are very much part of the liberation front. Thus, our nationalism must not be confused with a chauvinism or narrow nationalism of a previous epoch. It must not be confused with the classical drive by an elitist group among the oppressed to gain ascendancy so that they can replace the oppressor in the exploitation of the masses.[19]

This is probably the most important statement by the ANC while in exile, against which the ANC since 1994 must be judged.

There can also be no doubt that the NP had taken a conscious and strategic decision to prepare the conditions for the eventual release of Mandela, a process which began with his transfer from Pollsmoor to Victor Verster prison in December 1988. I have little doubt that the trajectory of important decisions and developments regarding his release and what would happen thereafter, including the initial steps of the negotiations process, was agreed within the NP in the year before his release and that the release of Sisulu and other senior ANC figures was meant to test the waters of public reaction. In this regard the visits the NP allowed Mandela to have with leaders of the Mass Democratic Movement at Victor Verster prison were meant to facilitate the entire process of both his release and how that would pave the way towards negotiations.

After his separation from Winnie, Mandela moved into a house in Houghton. By making Houghton his home, the contrast between his life and that of the African masses became stark and his leadership more questionable in that light. But it was what happened after 1994, largely the result of the policies he presided over between 1994 and 1999, which has led to increasing criticism of him since his passing, including from his former wife. The policies he presided over after 1994 would ensure not only that poverty, joblessness and related social miseries would continue in places like Soweto but that the stark social inequalities between it and places like Houghton would increase in the years ahead. Moreover, the move showed not only how successful the NP and WMC strategy for his release was, but that he played to their script.

In this regard it was very significant that his ex-wife, Winnie, strongly criticised him. Though she later denied it, she bravely told Nadira Naipaul of the *Evening Standard*: 'Mandela let us down. He agreed to a bad deal for the blacks. Economically, we are still on the outside. The economy is very much white. It has a few token blacks, but so many who gave their lives in the struggle have died unrewarded.'[20]

So vividly evident was this cohabitation between racism and capitalism in our history that it was revealing that neither the ANC nor Cosatu, the SACP nor Sanco insisted that those issues of economic policy and control be on the negotiations agenda. There is no record of any attempts to do so at all in the literature. It is also important to recognise how the ANC actively sought to marginalise civil society before and after the 1994 elections. Instead, the only programme, produced by Cosatu in 1993, the Reconstruction and Development Programme (RDP), which dealt with the provision of basic services after the elections and which could be described as mildly social democratic in nature, with minimal decommodified provisions, was dumped just two years after the 1994 elections. In its place the explicitly neoliberal

Gear was introduced in June 1996,[21] just three months after the RDP office was closed.

The closure of the RDP office was especially problematic and suspicious, given Mandela's emphasis on the programme: 'We have emerged as the majority party on the basis of the programme which is contained in the Reconstruction and Development book. That is going to be the cornerstone, the foundation upon which the Government of National Unity is going to be based. I appeal to all leaders who are going to serve in this government to honour this programme.'[22] But it was not long after this strong ANC commitment to the RDP that it fell by the wayside.

Mbeki's fierce denial that Gear had replaced the RDP, arguing that the RDP Base Document drew attention to fiscal constraints, was not convincing. Bond's rebuttal was that 'the charge by the Left that the ANC had abandoned the RDP was indeed true in most crucial areas of social policy'. He went on to list concrete examples in terms of wages, land redistribution, housing standards, basic services, transport and so on.[23]

A distinctly neoliberal emasculation of the RDP had taken place in the RDP White Paper, which had won Jay Naidoo praise as a 'hard-nosed ANC pragmatist' in *The Economist* and was lauded in the *Business Day*: 'Minister Jay Naidoo's technocrats want to foster new, business-like attitudes towards the management of government- and state-backed projects …The central government has realised that a business-like approach is needed at all levels of the RDP if the private sector is to play its willing part.' So stark was this emasculation that Cosatu argued: 'The RDP White Paper will reduce the RDP to no more than a social net to cushion the impact of job losses and poverty.' And the National Economic Institute for Economic Policy worried that, as a result of the White Paper, the original RDP had become 'fairly worthless'.[24]

But it is what happened after Gear was adopted that settled the matter. Job losses in the public sector and severe deficit reductions had a devastating effect on basic services and job creation. There were many strikes at the time by Cosatu's public sector affiliates, resisting retrenchments. Teachers and nurses were particularly affected. Civil society mobilised against Gear's effects but were not strong enough to beat it. Bond captured the central problem well: 'Notwithstanding wildly overoptimistic claims about job creation, post-apartheid economic policies have generated job losses at unprecedented levels, which in turn are the basis for many urban ecological and health problems associated with lack of affordability of water, sanitation and electricity.'25 These circumstances gave rise to militant social movements in black townships around the country, but particularly in Gauteng.

This programmatic switch indicated how eagerly the ANC was going to be true to form: occupying the state not in the interests of the black working class but serving instead the interests of the same WMC which advocated its unbanning in the 1980s and supported the non-racial political democratisation of SA before and after Mandela's release. It is the agenda of WMC which triumphantly prevailed in post-apartheid SA. The economic and social policies the ANC adopted after 1994 were the clearest manifestation of this fact, to the extent that in Mbeki's last State of the Nation address in 2008 he stated that the ANC government had been kind to big business.

Important too is the fact that neither the ANC nor the SACP supported the request by Cosatu to be independently represented in the negotiations. Nor did Cosatu fight for such inclusion, especially since by then it was clear that what was in the making was an ANC–NP elite pact, supported by the Western powers, and a top-down and highly bureaucratic process. But there can be little doubt that both the ANC and especially the SACP prevailed upon Cosatu to relent on the matter. Why? Because the SACP was officially regarded by both the ANC and itself as the party of the working class, meaning that they were best placed to represent their interests at the negotiations, dubbed the Convention for a Democratic SA (Codesa).

Events in SA after Mandela's release and the unbanning of the ANC, SACP and PAC must be seen against the backdrop of the cataclysmic demise of the Stalinist states of Eastern Europe in the late 1980s and early 1990s, especially the Soviet Union, which collapsed in December 1991, after the downfall of Mikhail Gorbachev and the emergence of Boris Yeltsin, who favoured market reforms in Russia. In fact, it was the beginning of those events in late 1989 which paved the way for the release of Mandela. There can be no doubt that those huge events had a dampening effect on the ANC and SACP, especially since they had been supported for decades by the Soviet Union, politically, financially and militarily.

But the effect of those developments strengthened those forces in the

ANC which wanted a deracialised capitalism, especially since the defeats in the Soviet Union were interpreted as the death of 'communism' and triumph of capitalism globally, or rather its neoliberal version.

The mood among the broad left in SA was very sombre after the collapse of the Berlin Wall and the Soviet Union. As Stalinist as the Soviet Union had been for decades, events there were incalculable blows to the cause of socialism, globally. A decade later I wrote: 'Something big, historic and numbing has happened to socialists and activists the world over. Since the dramatic collapse of the Soviet empire and other Eastern European Stalinist regimes in 1989, many have turned away from political and community involvement and towards themselves, friends and families.'[26] So deep and devastating was that crisis that the left has wobbled along since and never quite recovered, certainly not as a force to be reckoned with in South African politics.

Left critics of the compromised settlement the ANC reached with the NP need to consider the international context and its negative impact on the ANC and SACP during negotiations. There can be little doubt that the global ascendancy and power of neoliberalism – which the NP and WMC were well aware of – would have made a more radical programme much more difficult to fight for and win during negotiations between 1991 and 1993. We need to combine the destructive legacy of Stalinism with the ascendancy of neoliberalism at the time, and the global weaknesses of the Marxist left, to fully appreciate the extent of the adverse balance of forces at that juncture inside and outside SA.

But that adverse balance of forces was also opportunistically used by the more conservative forces in both the ANC and the SACP to push for a negotiated settlement which did not threaten the capitalist system. It could be argued that the ANC in the first place never really wanted a socialist society, meaning that such an adverse global situation did not seriously affect the outcome of the negotiations. But it did, in the sense that it considerably weakened left voices in the ANC alliance and in the actual negotiations to fight for more radical solutions, such as for nationalisation of key sectors of the economy.

However, there was more to it than global neoliberal ascendancy. It was quite simply that only a settlement within the framework of capitalism could create some space for the emergence of a significant black bourgeoisie and more numerous black middle class, without which no settlement could be reached. The NP, WMC and the ANC leadership knew this, and reached the negotiated settlement on that basis. Furthermore, there was no organisation of the left in the country, outside the ANC alliance, which could even try to stop this process, in which the global capitalist interests were also heavily involved and invested.

This situation was compounded by the fact that by the late 1980s the militant mass movement led by the UDF had waned considerably, because of a combination of severe state repression and sheer exhaustion. This was an important consideration of De Klerk and the NP when they decided to release Mandela in February 1990. In terms of both local and global factors Mandela was released at the 'right' time. The Berlin Wall came down on 9 November 1989, just two months before his release: De Klerk's timing could not have been more propitiously calculated.

But whether that situation would have also justified the collapse of the RDP office two years later and the overtly neoliberal Gear strategy adopted in 1996 is doubtful. The RDP might have appeared as the start of a leftist fight-back. But the jettisoning of the social democratic *Making Democracy Work*, an economic policy document which the Macroeconomic Research Group (Merg) had produced, made it very clear that a neoliberal paradigm had become the prevailing orthodoxy in the ANC, pushed in that direction by the economists of WMC, the NP, and the IMF and World Bank. The ANC's rejection of the Merg policy document – which was firmly opposed to the independence of the Reserve Bank – set the tone for Gear in 1996.[27]

By then the writing was very clearly on the wall about what had happened and how it had laid an ominous basis for later further lurches to the right in economic and social policy. To place these developments in perspective, it is vitally important to point out that the ANC is a black majority government which has ruled the state since 1994. Their 1994 electoral victory enabled them to replace a white racist regime that went further than any previous government in using the legislature to secure the total oppression, subjugation and exploitation of black people by the use of violence, torture, and the gruesome ways in which some black detainees were murdered.

Against this brutal background, one can just imagine what the 1994 elections meant to black voters. The media carried pictures of voters, especially the aged, crying at the prospect of casting their votes for the first time ever. There was a general sense of elation and euphoria among black people all over the country. Legitimately, against that long history of dispossession, oppression and exploitation, ordinary black people were imbued with a sense of optimism and indeed a new dawn in their lives.

Except for the left outside of the ANC alliance, which pointed out the likely consequences of the compromises the ANC made during the negotiations, virtually everyone seemed to be put to sleep by the euphoria of the occasion. Within the ANC alliance itself, including Cosatu, nobody really asked the tough questions about what exactly the much-vaunted 'transition' and 'transformation' were going to mean for the majority black working class. Sanco too hardly objected to what was happening, especially the neoliberal policies and processes which were beginning to unfold at local government level.

Cosatu, more than any other mass organisation in SA, was the most disappointing, especially given its size, influence and leading role after its formation in 1985. Yet Cosatu leader Jay Naidoo was sucked into the bureaucratic networks of top-down negotiations, basically echoing whatever came out of the negotiations at Kempton Park. There were no warnings and no critical analysis by Cosatu about the already very worrying trends in the negotiations. Cosatu just could not withstand the pressure from Mandela and the rest of the ANC top leadership and that of the SACP, the supposed party of the working class, led by Slovo, who championed the 'sunset clauses' in the negotiations, which agreed that white civil servants would remain in their jobs for five years. Similarly, Cosatu failed to defend its own programme – the RDP – when Naidoo engineered the shift from base document to White Paper.

Scholars have also not paid adequate attention to why Cosatu had no independent representation at the negotiations, allowing its voice and role to be subsumed under and subordinated to that of the ANC–SACP leadership. We only need to look at the serious and continuous conflict between Cosatu and the ANC after 1994 and the often fundamental differences between them to realise that it was a big mistake for Cosatu to have allowed their independent voice during the negotiations to be marginalised by the unilateral dominance of the ANC leaders.

However, let me turn to the 'Faustian Pact' between the ANC and capital, which former minister Ronnie Kasrils now criticises and blames for the serious problems we have today.

> What I call our Faustian moment came when we took an IMF loan on the eve of our first democratic election. That loan, with strings attached that precluded a radical economic agenda, was considered a necessary evil, as were concessions to keep the negotiations on track and take delivery of the promised land for our people. Doubt had come to reign supreme: we believed, wrongly, there was no other option ... Inexcusably, we had lost faith in the ability of our own revolutionary masses to overcome all obstacles ... The ANC leadership needed to remain determined, united and free of corruption – and, above all, to hold onto its revolutionary will. Instead, we chickened out.[28]

Kasrils deals with a complex combination of objective and subjective conditions in the 1990s in a mistaken and superficial manner. Aside from the very adverse global situation, following the collapse of the Soviet Union and the subsequent spread and strengthening of neoliberalism, there was a definite and palpable decline in the mass militancy of the 1980s. Not only Cosatu but the rest of civil society was exhausted and weakened by a decade of fierce suppression. Kasrils does not deal with this major factor which informed the balance of forces between the NP, the ANC and the MDM in 1990.

It was those factors which created the ANC's lack of 'revolutionary will' and explains why the ANC had 'chickened out'. The masses were exhausted by then, which is precisely why the ANC itself did not face much mass pressure during the negotiations, in terms of specific demands which it might have neglected. The ANC encountered no serious and sustained criticism or opposition by any of the forces in the MDM, which was really an ANC-UDF-aligned movement. Rather than the ANC not being vigilant about what was transpiring at the negotiations, it was the virtual silence of the MDM which was the biggest problem, alongside the fact that broad civil society also did not directly, strongly and consistently protest against the ANC during the negotiations.

John Saul responded at some length to Kasrils's admission of error. Saul finds Kasrils's explanation of why the ANC failed to hold its nerve unconvincing. He argues that Kasrils 'tends to see the ANC elite ... as having been just too busy to notice that a handful of "young ANC intellectuals schooled in Western economics" and working hand-in-glove with Harry Oppenheimer had managed to steal the game away from the masses while the ANC brass was not looking!'[29] Kasrils conceded that the ANC accepted responsibility for apartheid-era debt instead of calling for its cancellation; dropped a wealth tax on the super-rich to fund development projects; and absolved domestic and international capital of any financial reparations. 'Extremely tight budgetary obligations to implement a free-trade policy and abolish all forms of tariff protection in keeping with neoliberal free trade fundamentals were accepted.'[30]

These belated admissions are quite remarkable. From the time the negotiations started in 1991 until 2008, when he resigned, Kasrils never once spoke of this pact with capital and its impact on the ANC's ability to deal with the devastating socioeconomic consequences of apartheid. Yet after his resignation Kasrils suddenly had his moment of revolutionary epiphany and found his voice.

Saul is equally critical of the 'fatuous argument' presented by Jeremy Cronin. In a 2013 speech titled 'How we misread the situation in the 1990s', Cronin said: 'In particular, we vastly overestimated the patriotic credentials of South African monopoly capitalism (and its soon to emerge narrow BEE hangers-on); these advised us "to open all doors and windows to attract inward investment flows".' Given that almost the opposite had occurred – surpluses generated in the country had been repatriated and between a fifth and a quarter of GDP disinvested since 1994 – Cronin asked, 'Why had it taken us nearly 19 years to appreciate the need for a second, radical phase of our democratic transition?' 'But,' responded Saul, 'he really gives no answer to his own question nor makes any attempt to explain two decades of extraordinary naïvety as to the progressive propensities of South African monopoly capitalism.'[31] Cronin's question is nonsensical, dishonest and misleading, all at once.

I don't agree with any suggestion that ANC leaders at the negotiations inadvertently omitted questions about economic power and control. How could they, when the FC makes demands, though ambiguous, in that regard? I believe that the most senior leaders of the negotiating teams of De Klerk and Mandela had a tacit agreement that such questions would not be raised at that crucial stage because if the parties were far apart on economic policy – which they could not but be, according to the FC – it would scupper the negotiations and end in failure.

Both sides of this elite deal-making sought a settlement within the existing capitalist framework of the most powerful economy in Africa.

Why? Without retaining that economy – as history had made it – there would be no elite settlement between the NP and ANC, which would also contradict the whole motive of the NP's decision to release Mandela and all other ANC leaders, allow the return of the exiles, and unban all the organisations. Politically, those were all major steps which would not only be in vain, had the talks collapsed, but could trigger chaos in the country. It was on this basis that the negotiations proceeded.

Many authors misread the dynamics of the negotiations. For example, Hlumelo Biko, after much speculation, argued that 'The ANC's economic thinkers lost sight of the need to actively restructure the economy upfront as a precondition of long-term stability.'[32] Not only is Biko misguided about why economics was consciously put on the back burner during the 1991-3 negotiations, but if you read his book you quickly begin to see that he had no interest in any anti-capitalism discourse. Instead, he is consumed with removing any remaining obstacles to a thriving big black business class that are a legacy of apartheid policies.

However, Biko made a crucial point about the debilitating extent of the compromises made by the ANC. The NP had recently implemented a fully funded pension scheme for public sector employees which 'led directly to a dramatic increase in national debt ... By 1996 it had grown phenomenally to R308 billion, of which R297 billion was domestic and R11 billion was foreign debt. The servicing costs for these debts rose from about R12 billion in 1989 to more than R30 billion per annum in 1996'.[33] By accepting this, the ANC severely affected in advance the post-apartheid fiscus, especially in addressing the enormous social deficits inherited from apartheid. If one adds the agreement by the ANC to settle the foreign debt of the apartheid state, the magnitude of this betrayal is staggering. Yet there was little focus by the media on the severely negative implications this would have for a new ANC government and especially for attending to the vast needs of the black working-class majority. The ANC itself has hardly provided a clear and convincing explanation for all this, and neither did the ANC's alliance partners, Cosatu and the SACP, say much about these matters at the time or subsequently.

In 2000, six years after the 1994 Uhuru election, which was supposedly the implementation of the NDR, as the first stage, I wrote: 'With the second post-apartheid election having passed, when do we enter the second socialist stage?' I continued:

Is there something sinister and cynical about this sophistry (first the nonsensical 'two stages' and now 'consolidation of the democratic revolution') when, even were we to grant theoretical and strategic credence to the two-stage approach, are we clearly supposed to be in the second stage? But is the party (SACP) now leading the working class and the alliance on a clear socialist programme? No, it is not. Why? Here is the answer: nowhere has the application of the two-stage theory approach led to socialism in the 'second stage', simply because there is no such stage.[34]

Nowhere does the SACP offer any reappraisal of the two-stage approach, to accommodate any different perspectives after 1994, except very interestingly to state that it had abandoned that approach in the 1990s. And if it has been abandoned, what then? We don't know and neither does the SACP. All these questions are shrouded in the quandary in which the SACP finds itself, no closer today to genuinely leading a socialist second-stage revolution, simply because it is diversionary nonsense.

It was Trotsky who first coherently explained why the basic democratic task in any revolution is inseparably intertwined with the socialist or anti-capitalist tasks, in what became known as the Permanent Revolution theory.[35] I have provided enough evidence to support such an approach to a country in which race and racism were for most of our history not only inseparably intertwined with capitalist development but were tools in its rapid development. Nowhere was this more evident than in the super-exploitable and abundant cheap African labour on the diamond and gold mines and the migrant labour system which took root then. Today both cheap black labour and many of the institutional mechanisms of the migrant labour system remain intact despite the 'miraculous' political transition.

Saul briefly considers explanations offered by Naomi Klein, William Gumede and Vishnu Padayachee for the failures of the ANC in the negotiations of the early 1990s. These included short-sightedness and naïvety; that the ANC negotiators were simply outmanoeuvred; and that too many in the ANC dismissed economic issues as technical – so much so, Gumede lamented, that 'We missed it! We missed the real story.' Saul asks rhetorically whether Padayachee, Gumede and Klein had read Fanon: 'For it is impossible to think that the ANC leadership, having sought assiduously to will just such an outcome, such a "false decolonization", from at least the mid-1980s, could have "missed it" – missed, that is, the main point as to what was happening in SA'.[36] My own attempt at an answer to this painful confusion is that the ANC never was a revolutionary socialist movement or organisation.

The key to the answer about the negotiations period is not that the initiative was in the hands of the NP nor the global environment of neoliberal ascendancy. Those were undoubtedly important contextual factors in which the settlement deal was hammered out between the contending parties. But the key lies instead in Saul's point: that the ANC leadership had 'sought assiduously to will such an outcome'.

Indeed, since its inception the leaders of the ANC were members of the better-educated African middle class, most of whom attended missionary schools. But they not only wanted the bourgeois democratic rights to be extended to all black people – they wanted, above all, to better themselves. If in any doubt, just look at the ANC in office in post-apartheid SA: unbridled corruption by ANC officials in government; the theft and wanton abuse of public resources on a massive scale; self-enrichment while the vast majority of black people remain trapped in poverty.

This is the depressing lot of poor black adults and children at the hands of a black majority government. This is post-apartheid South Africa. The last thing on first-time black voters' minds in 1994 was that this sorrowful tragedy lay ahead of them. But these conditions were inevitable in SA, based on what the ANC agreed to during negotiations and their subsequent neoliberal policy choices.

These were justified by virtue of the programmatic distinction the ANC and SACP drew between the NDR, as the first stage of the revolution, and thereafter (but when, nobody knew or said anything about) the second anti-capitalist stage. But there is no document in which the ANC and SACP spelled out and periodised these stages and processes. How can a programmatic perspective of a revolution not be clarified and explained, even if only to its own members? Simply because it is in fact impossible to do so.

Life under apartheid or 'racial capitalism' was carried out daily in concrete ways which combined politics and economics in an inextricable and dynamic relationship. Nowhere is that dialectical reality more evident than in that very same race–class nexus, which is why it is black workers who bore the brunt of the apartheid system and who after 1994 have borne the brunt of the ANC's neoliberalism. When we identify today who are the poor, the unemployed, the homeless and those most afflicted by the worst class inequalities in South African history, it is the majority black working class.

The two-stage theory is nothing less than bizarrely impossible and unreal. It is tantamount to implying that under apartheid in the morning black people suffered from racist politics, such as the denial of the right to vote and a host of other racist laws, and in the afternoon and evening suffered the pangs of poverty, joblessness, hunger, homelessness, malnutrition and so on. Since the inception of such thinking, in the 1920s, this was, to put it bluntly, a whole lot of nonsense, with which the ANC and SACP leaders over the decades hoodwinked its members and supporters. Apartheid and capitalism were tied by countless threads in real life, not in the diversionary petit bourgeois minds of the ANC and SACP leaders, aided and abetted by the leadership of both Sactu and Cosatu, who were supposed to know much better, drawn from the actual lives of black workers, in which racism and capitalism were overwhelmingly intertwined.

The 1994 Elections, the Coloured Question and Culture

At the very outset it is necessary to say there is a Coloured Question that inherently lies at the heart of the unresolved National Question (NQ). I disagree with those who argue against identifying such a question, as it opens a slew of other ethnic questions, such as an Indian Question etc.[37] If there were any doubts about the existence in real life of a Coloured Question, what has happened after 1994 in SA has imposed this particular question, as an organic constituent of the wider NQ. My approach does not pander to ethnicity but deals with the realities on the ground.

In this regard, an unfortunate development after the unbanning of the ANC in 1990 was the decision of the mass-based United Democratic Front (UDF) in March 1991 to disband itself. I have argued elsewhere that the pressure to disband the UDF must have come from the ANC leaders, especially those who were in exile, such as Mbeki, and others who wanted a clean slate from which to proceed with the negotiations. Given the contentious and sensitive nature of some of the demands which were likely to surface at some stage during the negotiations, such as the policy of nationalisation, the ANC probably assessed that the UDF would present possible problems, the pressures of which could scupper the negotiations.

But it was the political consequences of the premature disbanding of the UDF that were most significant, especially in the 1994 election results in the Western Cape. This was arguably the most important overall development in the national results of those elections, the consequences of which the ANC is still faced with today. The most serious electoral consequence of this decision came when the NP won the Western Cape decisively. The ANC only received 24.6% of the Coloured vote in 1994, a significant outcome especially since it set the tone for Coloured voter sympathies in subsequent elections. Never afterwards did the ANC enjoy an outright win in Cape Town and the Western Cape. Several leading activists in Cape Town said that I had over-estimated the level of support for the UDF in the Coloured townships of the Western Cape. As a result, the electoral defeat of the ANC in 1994 did not really surprise them. However, I believe that the level of support was substantial enough to make the 1994 result somewhat surprising. The decision to disband the UDF was premature and a political mistake because it created a vacuum in the Coloured townships which the NP assiduously exploited in the run-up to the 1994 elections.

The UDF was born in the Cape's biggest Coloured working-class township, Mitchells Plain, and it had a strong militant and socialist current within it, which was not so much the case with the ANC in the Cape. It organised boycotts of African and Coloured local elections in 1983–4, suggesting the basis of a non-racial mass movement – even though this was not really established in the Western Cape. Successive states of emergency and waves of detention drastically weakened the UDF after 1986 and it never really recovered in Coloured areas. No previous political organisation in the Western Cape had achieved as much mass support as the UDF between 1983 and 1986, especially given the long divide-and-rule policy of the NP in order to prevent organised unity between Coloured, African and Indian people, especially of their working classes. Had the UDF not disbanded itself in 1991, it might have brought greater pressure to bear upon the kind of society post-apartheid SA needed to be, and influenced the outcome of the negotiations, particularly regarding economic and public policy.

Mandela himself acknowledged in March 1992 that the ANC had neglected Coloured people because of its focus on Africans; and he made a series of overtures – not very successfully – to the Coloured population in subsequent years. Mandela attempted to persuade the late Richard Dudley, a renowned Unity Movement intellectual and activist, to help secure the 'Coloured vote' for the ANC in 1999 but this request was spurned after he and his wife were invited by Mandela for lunch in 1998. Clive Kirkwood reported that Dudley responded: 'I am not a coloured person ... I am not a coloured leader ... (I have) for the past fifty years been associated with a political movement that does not accept these classifications ... I will never want people to vote as coloured persons.'[38]

The hard fact is that Mandela and other ANC leaders not only betrayed the revolutionary provisions of the FC, despite its ambiguity and contradictions, but their approach towards and understanding of the closely related NQ were nothing less than racialist and backward, if we must speak plainly and not succumb to political correctness, especially that of the African nationalist type, which is embedded in the convenient populism of an undivided Africanism, phrased nowhere more aptly than this or that conduct being 'unAfrican'. The term 'unAfrican' is a crudely populist and unthinking term. The term has often been used by members of the African middle class, though it is less a consequence of any class aspirations but entirely born out of the womb of a seriously discredited and maimed African nationalist populism and culturalism. Its backward pandering to race and ethnicity is flagrant.

Besides, it is such a nebulous term that it begs definitional clarity and is rendered meaningless in discourse. The accompanying absurdity, which also carries obscure cultural connotations, is that it serves to promote a racial and ethnic chauvinism and is an expression of that same narrow Africanist majoritarian nationalism I have railed against throughout this book. It bears not an ounce of scientific thinking. On the contrary, it suggests that there is a homogenised African identity which automatically and immutably means certain values and conduct ontologically etched into one's cultural and social DNA. It is my considered view that it is mostly among the African majority that we have a debilitating culturalist baggage which is often at odds not only with a capitalist modernity but with the very notion of progressive emancipation from cultural taboos and rituals which are oppressive, patriarchal and sometimes downright reactionary.

While there are many examples of an Africanist cultural chauvinism in SA today, probably nothing showed this more than the bizarre reaction of many African people, especially Xhosa-speaking, to the movie *The Wound*, in 2017. The screening of this movie – a critical appraisal of African tradition, sexuality, masculinity and the practice of circumcision, which has claimed the lives of numerous young African men over many years, as a result of incompetence and unhygienic procedures – had to be temporarily halted because of violent threats which were made when it was first released. An intersectional story of three Xhosa men, it was a deeply moving and educational film and, indeed, controversial. But that is precisely the reason why people should watch it and collectively engage in public discussions and debates about its merits and demerits.

The film was thought-provoking about the various problems facing African men who circumcise under dangerous circumstances. The film calls for attention not to circumcision per se but to the steps which must be taken to prevent more lives being lost in the process. That is a noble cause, regardless of the vociferous condemnation and violent threats the film received from African and specifically Xhosa traditionalists, a hideous form of cultural autarky and backwardness.

To threaten violence if the film was screened is reprehensible, illegal and unconstitutional. That the screening of the film was negatively affected by these threats is a sinister instance of Africanist culturalist chauvinism, setting a bad precedent not only for the movie industry but for our cultural, social and political development as a country. This country will have no future if we are going to allow any form of Africanist nationalist and cultural chauvinism to determine and dominate our lives, as the white Afrikaner nationalists before them attempted. It must be fiercely resisted.

If civil society submits to these threats, they do so against the progressive interests not only of the present generation but of future ones too. The ANC should have been in the forefront of condemning and combating this thuggery, which masqueraded as a defence of Xhosa culture. In fact, the ANC itself has never again seriously spoken about the NQ after it won the 1994 elections. Nothing. You will find no document authored by the ANC on the NQ in post-apartheid SA, for a simple reason. The ANC's attitude towards 'minorities', in terms of its own bankrupt, erroneous and unscientific 'four-nation thesis', is starkly clear, which is precisely why the majority 'Coloured vote' has eluded them since 1994.

The problem is not the circumcision of men, but the botched and dangerous circumstances under which many young men have tragically died. But when the media raise these important matters, it is often construed as opposition to the cultural practice of circumcision. However, in this and many other African cultural practices, the approach to 'culture' is highly problematic within African communities. Keyan Tomaselli, a cultural theorist, criticised the assumption that 'culture' is 'God' and the Congress of Traditional Leaders of SA for assuming that culture is 'immutably fixed' for all time, arguing that all cultures are 'constantly changing'. He cited the treatment of HIV/Aids by 'voodoo medicine' thanks to a minister of health who 'fell for the garlic and olive oil theory of HIV cures during the era of denialism', which a Harvard University study found left '330,000 prematurely deceased'. He concluded that culture 'must be critically debated'.[39] Writing at the same time, William Gumede pointed out how African leaders use 'black "traditions", "culture" and "customs" to entrench their despotic powers' and was scathingly critical that 25 initiates had died from botched circumcisions in the Eastern Cape.[40] It is the ordinary African people who allow this situation to continue, because of ignorance and lack of power which the requisite knowledge would give them.

I need to state upfront that 'culture' is an elephant in the room in SA. Because many are afraid to stray away from or contradict 'political correctness', they keep their mouths shut, something I could never easily do, thankfully. We have too much ignorance in this country – a major problem in our society. On social media utter ignorance of matters at hand is displayed with an air of profundity. Well-grounded and rounded knowledge imparts finesse and sophistication in approaching complex matters. When that is lacking, we have all manner of vulgar, emotional and often racialist displays. We have not even begun to seriously debate the complexity and vicissitudes of culture in SA, or to discuss culture openly and honestly and, most importantly, to deracialise it and be bold enough to call things by their proper names.

If the bold truth be told – and it should be – African people have many very conservative cultural beliefs which present serious problems for any truly meaningful emancipatory discourse, precisely because they are the vast majority of the population. But not many want to talk openly about such matters for fear of probably being labelled racist or an enemy of African people or culture. Let me give another very important example. When the Department of Education introduced the Comprehensive Sexuality Education (CSE) curriculum in schools, newspaper reports pointed *largely* to African parents strongly objecting to CSE on grounds that it is inappropriate for girls and boys to be exposed to explicit sexual education. Basically, the view is that the school should not get involved in providing such education to their children – yet parents do not do so at home. I am not suggesting that there are no cultural challenges among other groups. There are many, including among Jewish and Muslim people. But it is the *nature* of the cultural problems among African people and the fact that they constitute the overwhelming majority of the population which is my biggest concern.

To clarify an important matter: I am convinced that the roots of this stubborn conservatism with many or most African people – who developed under different conditions from white, Coloured and Indian people – lie in two interrelated themes: education and development. And in this pivotal regard there must be no doubt that in every sphere of knowledge and the sciences African people, generally speaking, were right at the bottom of the epistemological hierarchy in SA, with whites at the top and Indians and Coloureds, as in everything else, in between. Look closely at what has happened with governance under ANC rule since 1994, in every SOE and every level of the state. If truth be told, ignorance, incompetence and corruption have largely characterised ANC rule since 1994, unpalatable as that fact might be for the ANC and its supporters.

When it comes to certain very serious problems in our society, such as the widespread prevalence of rape and patriarchal abuse in African townships, there is no doubt that the same factors of education and development, or the lack thereof, have been at play both before and especially after 1994. Another glaring example is the attitude and conduct of African taxi drivers. What African taxi drivers are allowed to get away with on South African roads is an appalling disgrace. Try to imagine what would happen if they did what they regularly do on the streets of London or New York.

But it took me many years to realise an important truth about the significant socio-cultural differences among black (African, Coloured and Indian) people, and the many traditional beliefs Africans have, which are not shared by Coloureds and Indians. I never thought much about this until my interview with Ayanda Nabe in Cape Town. She is a traditional medicinal healer. Coming from the Transkei, she spoke about her experiences in dealing with the Coloured people of Cape Town since she moved there some years ago. She pointed out that during the anti-apartheid struggle in earlier decades, the political unity of black people against the NP seriously obscured these intra-black differences and divisions. With the benefit of hindsight, cultural differences within the broad black population were never seriously discussed during the anti-apartheid struggles. Given the protracted and complex history of enforced divisions among black people, especially since 1948, we were clearly short-sighted.

The negative attitude of the ANC towards Coloured people, and its failure to realise that they are probably the most alienated, demoralised and brutalised group of people in this country, by virtue of both their history and their treatment under an ANC government, are most disturbing. As I wrote in 2017: 'And like the rest of the black population the stepchildren of South African history have suffered increased poverty, unemployment, social misery and crime since 1994.'[41] In fact, they have been, ironically, relatively worse off after 1994 than they were under NP rule, especially in the Cape, where the Coloured Labour Preference Policy prevailed for a few decades before 1994.

What the ANC appears to have done was to use AA policies to reverse the labour situation in the Western Cape, prioritising African labour as a result of that past and in the process marginalising Coloured workers, and earning the wrath of Coloured people, reflected in every election since 1994. As a result, the situation in Cape Town and the wider Western Cape is probably the most unfortunate reality afflicting the black working class in SA, which might take many years to resolve, but there is little or no doubt that the ANC is utterly incapable, under an Africanist leadership, of constructively dealing with and resolving that black internecine strife. Factionalism within the ANC in the Cape has made the already combustible situation there much worse, especially since much of it appears to be ethnically driven. As a result, there has not only been competition for municipal resources and infrastructure between Coloured and African communities but a competition too between Coloured and African leaders of the ANC for government posts.

But there are further reasons why the 1994 election results were an anomaly. As I wrote in 1999, never, anywhere, in the colonial world did an oppressed and exploited people vote for their oppressors and exploiters in the Uhuru elections. 'As a result, no place in the country projected this great paradox more than Cape Town, where it is not going to be easy reversing these losses. Though history has its momentous bursts, which rupture prevailing relations, it otherwise moves slowly and can take decades to undo damage as deep as exists in this city.'[42]

Shortly after the 1999 election, when the ANC again lost the Western Cape, I attributed the defeat to 'The emergence of an arrogant majoritarian African chauvinism which is conspicuously present in government, the middle class and the corporate world. While the ANC is quick to point out and condemn instances of alleged white racism, it continues itself to use the very same divisive and denigrating designations invented by slavery and apartheid.'[43] This refers to the ANC's retention of the apartheid racialist and racist classification system.

Given the history of the Coloured people – an impoverished, oppressed and exploited mainly working-class people since the mid-19th century – and given all the claims the ANC has made about being the 'sole representative' of the struggles of black people, what happened in the Cape in 1994 was in political terms indeed 'earth-shattering', but has been inadequately discussed. The relevance of this matter is heightened by the fact that African and Coloured workers have been the heart of the black working class in SA and its most exploited and oppressed, dating back to the days of the Cape Colony. It was the divide-and-rule strategy of the NP, especially the Coloured Labour Preference Policy, which most damaged relations between those workers and their respective communities. The damage done by the policies of the NP and later the DA in Coloured communities across the country might take decades to heal, if it ever will. Today, relations between these communities are probably worse than they were under apartheid, and I doubt that given Africanist majoritarian chauvinism it will get better any time soon.

Competition for jobs, housing and basic services has divided these communities and today constitutes the basis of ongoing conflict. What has deepened the enmity is that Coloured working-class communities, even often adjacent to African townships, have been sorely neglected at local government level. The contrast in urban infrastructure, shopping centres and amenities is stark if you compare, for example, Eldorado Park and Soweto in Johannesburg and Mitchells Plain and Khayelitsha in the Cape.[44] So obvious has been the neglect of Coloured townships in Gauteng that both the MEC for education, Panyaza Lesufi,[45] and the Gauteng premier, David Makhura, have conceded that those communities have been sorely neglected.[46] Lesufi was direct: 'There is no doubt serious problems in those schools and communities: lack of development, infrastructure, schools, housing and so on.'[47] Makhura was equally forthright: 'I have come across indisputable evidence of serious neglect by our government and under-investment in the coloured communities of our province. This neglect has far-reaching consequences.'[48]

These are the painful observations ordinary Coloured people in those areas have been making for many years. The alienation of Coloured people from the ANC is serious, complex and multi-faceted, and will probably not be resolved for a long time to come. But because it has mostly to do with the neoliberal policies of the ANC, of which both the African and Coloured working class are to varying degrees victims, if those matters are dealt with more fairly and evenly it will go a long way to healing these caustic divisions.

These divisions are exacerbated by the history of the ANC and how it has racially perceived 'minority' populations, not only of Coloureds and Indians, but whites too. The racialised notion of 'minorities' is a central demographic and political problem. In 1999 I wrote: 'People who are called minorities are ineluctably pushed into small corners and tend to isolate themselves. The more Coloureds and Indians are regarded as minorities, the more their alienation from the transformation will grow.' An entirely different and new politics is required by the ANC, which is very unlikely to happen. The problems run deep and long, as I stated: 'For decades the ANC treated coloured people at various times as either a racial, ethnic or national minority group – all of which they are not – and for which there exists no scientific validity whatsoever.'[49]

My experience is that this majoritarian Africanist chauvinism runs right across the South African political spectrum, irrespective of political identity, ideology, ethnic group or even class, but plays out largely subtly.

It exists to a lesser or greater degree across the political, economic and social spectrum, but it is undoubtedly there all the time. In fact, ironically, it has become the biggest problem and threat to growing a culture of non-racialism and anti-racism in SA today. This is not a 'white' problem. No, it may have its roots in white racism and the appalling treatment of Africans over the centuries, but it is not only a historical legacy.

I am convinced from my own experiences over more than four decades that two other endogenous factors have contributed to these problems. These are cultural traditions and the lack of education, which includes a perception by many that a mere demographic majority entitles one to make decisions, and to enjoy the power and the largesse that follow. I believe this is in turn a product of the accumulated impacts over three centuries of slavery and colonialism which have defined the SA of today.

But even more than the exhilaration at voting for the very first time in an open, democratic and non-racial basis was the yearning for social justice after many decades of deliberate neglect of the most basic needs of black people. Having come themselves mostly from poor black townships, ANC politicians understood what those conditions were like and how much the satisfaction of those needs was the highest priority for the black working-class majority. It is important to bear in mind that the black majority, especially Africans, had no prior practical experience of the most basic tenets of democracy and because of the dire lack of education and skills most black people were both ignorant and naïve about many things they had not experienced before. But that things would generally be much better than the conditions under apartheid was a natural expectation black people had, especially since Mandela was elected the first black president of SA.

The very powerful forces of capitalist modernity and liberalism, which have informed and shaped ANC politics since 1912 and until today in post-apartheid SA, serve to reinforce the power of class and capitalism. A study of what happened to Afrikaner capitalism reflects similar class patterns. After 1948 Afrikaner business grew closer to English WMC as a result of business mergers and acquisitions and further away from the Afrikaner working class, exactly as the ANC did after 1994.[50] AAC led the way in these processes. In fact, given that SA was the economic giant of Africa, those class processes have been far sharper here than elsewhere in Africa.

A study of revolutionary nationalisms around the world and the class changes which activists undergo when they ascend to power in the state is stark. Whether we like it or not, the fact is that nationalist political movements – including African nationalism – in many respects paved the way for the compromises and betrayals at critical stages of the struggle. The main reason for this is that such movements conceive of and prosecute their struggles for political independence or for the attainment of political freedoms without linking those demands with the struggles against capitalism as an economic system, within which those oppressions and denials are often rooted. In other words, African nationalism and many other nationalisms congenitally contain the seeds of their own woes.

Karl Marx and other Marxist thinkers opened our minds to the key importance of political economy in any struggle for freedom from oppression and exploitation. Nationalism tends often, if not always, to subordinate questions of class and capitalism to those of 'race' and the 'nation', at the helm of which often stood a petit bourgeois leadership. The neglect of political economy and its class dimension lies at the heart of all nationalisms globally and historically.

What has happened to the ANC since 1994 played itself out in different conditions and countries in Africa in previous decades. The pattern is unambiguously clear: colonial powers largely bought off the leadership of the nationalist liberation movements in post-colonial Africa. Nobody spells out these facts better than Frantz Fanon. African national liberation movements have a dismal record in power, partly due to the devastation wrought by slavery and colonialism, the middle-class nature of the leadership, their reformist policies, and the compromises inherent in the political independence granted by the colonial powers, especially regarding the economy.

The native bourgeoisie certainly looked after its own economic and class interests. Fanon describes this bourgeoisie well: 'It waves aloft the notion of the nationalization and Africanization of the ruling classes. The fact is that such action will become more and more tinged with racism, until the bourgeoisie bluntly puts the problem to the government by saying, "We must have those posts". They will not stop their snarling until they have taken every one of them.' In this acquisitive drive by the native bourgeoisie in post-independence Africa, Fanon says that they have passed from nationalism 'to ultra-nationalism, to chauvinism and finally to racism'.[51] This trend is manifest in SA over the past decade, under the guise of BEE and AA, which have been heavily tinged by race, ethnicity and a crude racial demography: that African people are numerically the vast majority of the population.

But in a vigorous constitutional democracy with a world-renowned Bill of Rights, that statistical fact should be treated as nothing more than that. It cannot empower any African person or people to make claims on resources or special dispensations merely because they are African. To do so would be similar to what white privilege was under apartheid. Social justice rights apply equally to the broader working class, especially Coloured, Indian and white working class. Their social demands and rights should be as fully observed as those of African people, but proportionately.

Neo-colonialism is essentially economic in nature, enabling the continued domination and exploitation of the economies of the African countries following the grant of political independence. The granting of such independence was the crucial strategic device used by colonial and imperial powers in perpetuating their continued domination of ex-colonies, in the guise of allowing them to determine their own destinies, when in fact neo-colonialism structurally determined it. This is essentially what happened in SA in 1994. The elections of 1994 were tantamount to the granting of our political independence, particularly the right for all citizens to vote in a non-racial and anti-racist constitutional democracy.

My interviews with leading African figures, such as Pali Lehohla and Solly Mapaila, opened my eyes further about cultural differences and deepened an awareness of their importance. The hard fact, socio-culturally, is that there always were many differences not only among and between 'black' people (Africans, Coloureds and Indians) but very much within the 'African' people themselves, as we have seen after 1994, in the form of tribal conflicts in particular townships.

It helps nobody and certainly not the impoverished black masses to deny these palpable divisions, the manifestations of which also distract attention from solutions to the terrible conditions of their lives. Such material plight, which cuts across ethnic and linguistic divisions, is what we need to turn our attention to with renewed vigour, as we did during the anti-apartheid struggles in the 1970s and 1980s. The commonality of material interests across these divides must become the focus of renewed mass struggles in the years ahead, armed with the lessons of earlier struggles on the National Question, at the heart of which the biggest problem we face is a narrow Africanist majoritarian chauvinism.

The ANC has a dismal history in its attitude towards Coloured people and had scant knowledge of the history of these people. These problems run deep inside the ANC, as this statement by Dr A.B. Xuma, who later became ANC president, makes clear way back in 1930: 'As we intend to build bridges between White and Black, we can dismiss the case of the Coloured man by stating that the missionaries fought and secured some of the rights for the Hottentots until the Coloured man of today is, in principle, accepted as a White man politically, industrially, economically and educationally.'[52] Anybody with even limited knowledge of the Cape Colony in the 18th and 19th centuries will know that statement reflects a very flawed understanding of Coloured people and their origins. Although a wide range of people came to constitute 'Coloured' people in the Cape Colony, Xuma's statement appears to restrict the term 'Coloured' to Khoikhoi ancestry, by using 'Hottentot', the pejorative term coined by the Dutch.

Even left-wing Africans tend to revert to a narrow Africanist majoritarian chauvinism in relation to these 'minority' groups. Irvin Jim, the leader of the National Union of Metalworkers of South Africa (Numsa) and the Socialist Workers Revolutionary Party (SWRP), is one of them. Often Numsa makes public statements which refer to 'African' workers, even though they have many Coloured members. Jim's usage of the term 'African' also feeds off what I believe was an opportunistic retention by the ANC after 1994 of the apartheid-era classification which separated whites, Indians, Coloureds and Africans.

Dig deeper into their literature and you will find conspicuous or subtle African nationalism in all organisations with an African leadership, including those that profess an adherence to socialism, such as the EFF, Saftu, Numsa, SWRP and Azapo. It is deep, prevalent and tenacious. They appear unable to do without it. Go and look at who the top leaders are of all these organisations today. Under the influence of the rise of Africanist majoritarian chauvinism over the past decade, even the top leadership of the SACP is now all African, which the deputy general secretary of the party, Solly Mapaila, conceded in an interview was a worrying problem. In addition, in recent congresses of the SACP television coverage shows such an overwhelming African presence that you have to search the audience to find any white, Coloured or Indian people.

Among multiple problems is the problematic usage of the 'minorities' identity. A massive educational programme around race is required in order to deal comprehensively with the fallacy of 'minorities', as a racial-demographic term, and debunk it once and for all. It is in fact a crude racialisation of the population of the country, arrived at by virtue of the demographic fact that Africans are the majority of the population. And it would appear that in SA it is opportunistically wielded for business and class purposes, as are BEE and tenders in government. There can be absolutely no doubt that in various ways race is being used for utterly opportunistic reasons: blackness, Africanness and the bogeyman invoking of 'minorities', to gain financial and material advantages, have been conspicuously present over the past decade.

These trends have challenged us to redefine anew both non-racialism and anti-racism in ways which spell out clearly a vehement opposition to artificially divisive and counterproductive terms. But it is vitally important to recognise that the 'minorities' discourse is derived from the racialist and racist thinking of the ANC. The fingerprints of this crude and ugly Africanist chauvinism are also evident on social media platforms, in different guises.

I now turn to the Khoisan revivalist movement and the rise of a 'Coloured nationalism'. I mainly attribute this recent phenomenon, which has gained momentum over the past three years, to a narrow Africanist majoritarian chauvinism inside SA, especially inside the ruling ANC. I have identified this as probably the biggest danger yet to the National Question in post-apartheid SA and the growth of a genuinely non-racial or anti-racist consciousness and practice. There has been rising conflict between African and Coloured people, especially working-class people in recent years, in Coloured working-class townships of Cape Town and in places like Eldorado Park in Johannesburg. This conflict is largely to do with fierce competition for municipal services and resources between two sections of the same black working class, which is the essence of the tragedy.

It is critically important to trace the roots of this surge of 'Coloured nationalism' after 1994, especially over the past decade. Gangsterism, drugs and alcohol abuse have been rampant in Coloured working-class townships: problems that were significant during apartheid grew worse after 1994. There is no doubt that this is due to the social and political alienation of these communities from the ANC and the wider political fabric of post-apartheid SA. There has been a lack of a clear, visible and strong leadership to guide the struggles that have spontaneously arisen in those communities, especially in areas such as Eldorado Park in Gauteng and the Cape Flats townships. It was in the absence of such leadership that the Coloured nationalist group, Gatvol Capetonian,[53] emerged in Cape Town, including an element which wanted Cape Town to secede from the rest of the country, such was the degree of social and political alienation of these communities.

Coloured people are fed up with what the ANC has done to this country since 1994. How they have been ill-treated and marginalised in many ways is an unmitigated disgrace. In this regard it is the Coloured working class, in places like the Cape Flats, Westbury and Eldorado Park, which has suffered from what is nothing less than callous, conscious, criminal and in fact racist neglect. However, the central problem of these developments is that any sectionalist and nationalistic ethnic-based oppositional currents, cut adrift from mainstream politics in SA, are not going to succeed in resolving the social and political crisis within these communities. Only movements which remain true to the non-racialist and anti-racist tradition of struggle and which are linked to the numerous and often intense and combustible struggles for basic services in all black townships, as sometimes occurred during the UDF anti-apartheid days, are going to stand a chance of changing the material conditions of poverty, joblessness and related social scourges.

Bear in mind that the Gauteng premier, David Makhura, and Gauteng MEC for education, Lesufi, conceded that Coloured communities have been seriously neglected over the years.[54] This was after they had visited some of these townships. These two ANC leaders must be commended for acknowledging this problem, especially in a highly racialised conflict-ridden situation, but it does not appear that much has changed since then, except that during 2019 there were fewer disturbances reported in Eldorado Park.

However, it is this situation of wanton neglect over a long period which elicited this comment by Patrick Maglua:

> With the Boere we knew that they oppressed everybody who is not white but what have the Coloureds got to show for the many years of solidarity that they had with the Africans? Today they are instead being deserted by the ANC. We are not even recognised for the role we played in the struggle. We can articulate our objections without being racist but the man in the street does not have those tools of consciousness and education.[55]

Maglua helps explain the occasional angry outbursts of racism by ordinary people in Eldorado Park, when faced with many years of conscious neglect. This has been seen in all facets of township life, from housing to refuse collection and to schools. Maglua also remarked, following the social unrest that gripped Eldorado Park and Kliptown in 2017: 'During the social unrest minister Lindiwe Sisulu (then minister of housing in Zuma's cabinet) asked, "Who do Coloured people think they are and what makes them so special?" She was invited to Eldorado Park during the unrest. She was not just against the unrest but went on to racialise it. This is on record. The Coloured people were angry.'[56] The irony of Sisulu's words did not escape me. One good look at her and her siblings and you can readily see the white blood of the grandfather, Walter's father. How rich it is for her to be calling Coloured protesters into question when she was born of mixed racial ancestry.

Ultimately, Sisulu's reactionary and arguably racist remarks about Coloureds in Eldorado Park are linked to the provocative, bizarre, insulting and also overtly racist comments by Jimmy Manyi, then spokesman for the ANC government, in March 2010, that there was an 'oversupply of Coloureds in the Western Cape'.[57] This comment triggered a massive public reaction in the media, including an open letter from former finance minister, Trevor Manuel, who said Manyi was a 'racist of the worst order'.[58] But Sisulu's very specific chastising of 'Coloureds' in Eldorado Park can similarly be construed as racist, especially as Makhura and Lesufi have stated that those people had been seriously neglected for many years in Gauteng.

Besides, in the light of such treatment of Coloured people it is a stark contradiction of the facts for her to have told parliament during a State of the Nation debate that 'wherever the DA governs there is misery for black people'.[59] She also failed to realise that it is the constitutional and legal right of people to protest, especially if Coloured communities were protesting against the ANC government's neglect of them. However, it must be now abundantly clear that there exists an intolerant, authoritarian, dangerous and in fact backward African nationalist politics in the ruling ANC. It is deep, stubborn and ugly.

In Eldorado Park, in the Gauteng province, probably the worst dissatisfaction in these communities concerned schooling. What has unfolded here is perhaps best illustrative of the history that lies beneath the hostilities. For almost a decade there have been palpable racial tensions around the appointment of staff at schools. Coloured pupils and parents allege that there is a departmental bias against Coloured applicants for posts and that African candidates have been favoured for posts, unfairly so.

On the other hand, the South African Democratic Teachers' Union (SADTU) claims that the Coloured parents and pupils are racist towards African teachers and officials and averse to their appointment to posts, often at predominantly Coloured schools. The first thing to be said is that both sides to this conflict are black working class, whether Coloured or African, and their needs are similar. In the struggles under apartheid they were also often working together in protests. Given that background, at first glance this conflict would not make sense but there is an underlying factor causing it. After several interviews, including with a former teacher, a principal and Panyaza Lesufi, the Gauteng MEC for education, I conclude that Africanist majoritarian chauvinism is the biggest political problem facing public schools under the ANC-controlled department of education.

Some commentators, like the late Leonard Martin,[60] are convinced that SADTU is a racist organisation, bent on excluding and marginalising Coloured people, especially as regards staffing appointments at public schools. This, he insists, is his experience in various Coloured communities, especially in Eldorado Park, where he resides. He adamantly rejects the very notion of 'Coloured nationalism':

> The notion of Coloured nationalism is a non-starter. It's just loaded with fear. It is social denialism because you have to explain to me how nationalism would suddenly have a basis. Where is the institutional

architecture? It becomes a means of explaining away the hegemony of black Africanism and that these people should not awaken and instead say 'yes' to our new masters, 'we accept your black African hegemony'. I mean, really, where has that happened anywhere in the world. I reject the notion of Coloured nationalism; what would be its premise? Besides, the ANC manufactures a 'Coloured vote' and then they accuse those people who resist their politics of racialisation of Coloured nationalism. Bear in mind that the NP itself earlier talked of and targeted the 'Coloured vote'.[61]

In an interview the late Mudney Halim was scathing about the decision by SADTU to withdraw all its teachers from Klipspruit West Secondary School, a predominantly Coloured school in Eldorado Park, where there was conflict over the appointment of a African principal. He felt that such action, aside from its disruption of classes and teaching, was racist in that SADTU specifically called on its members to stay away from a predominantly Coloured school in a predominantly Coloured area in favour of the appointment of a African principal, notwithstanding administrative irregularities. In the conflict over the appointment the pupils and teachers were divided along racial lines. What has lent itself to the distinct racialisation of the matter is the fact that there existed a close political relationship between SADTU, the ANC and the Gauteng Department of Education (GDE).

They are all members and supporters of the ANC. In fact, they were more often than not seen as a collective, acting in unison against the Coloured community, whereas, had proper procedures been followed in the appointment of the principal, none of this racial acrimony would have occurred. While SADTU's call for the stay-away was not necessarily racist, the overwhelming dominance in the country of an Africanist chauvinism in the entire public-state sectors gives rise, wittingly or unwittingly, to racialised perceptions, especially when it concerns material issues, such as jobs in a country with a high rate of unemployment. It is important, however, to bear in mind that these are internecine conflicts within predominantly working-class townships, in which the learners, teachers and parents are from working-class homes. That is the real tragedy for me.

In an interview a school principal, Michael Davey, related a story about SADTU's actions at his school that left me both shocked and sad, not only about what had happened but that the story never got into the newspapers.[62] When Davey objected to SADTU members holding a meeting during exams the teachers began to walk out of the school. He then summoned them to a disciplinary meeting, but they refused. Suspecting that there might be trouble he sent the teachers home. Not long thereafter two busses, reportedly hired by SADTU, arrived at the school. Not long thereafter he heard some girl pupils screaming and running into the toilets. The buses had arrived, and the passengers (African men, who Davey heard were picked up from Orange Farm) descended on the school with sjamboks, hitting the pupils and telling them to 'fuck-off' from the school. 'The girls were clinging to me and the deputy principal. The majority of the pupils were African, and they were telling them, "You cannot protect that white man" and "why are you hanging onto him?"'

But how on earth could these brutal assaults on pupils at their own school have been carried out in broad daylight by SADTU and with such impunity? Davey reported the matter to the GDE, but nothing was done about it. Now try to imagine if SADTU and the GDE were Coloured-dominated in their leadership, what would have happened under those circumstances under an ANC government. This matter would have been all over the news and SADTU would have been accused of racism towards African pupils and teachers. The fact is that nothing at all was done by the GDE, which not only had all the legal authority to intervene on behalf of the students who were assaulted, but by doing nothing violated the relevant laws and in fact the constitution.

It is also important to take note that for many years SADTU has been accused of corruption at schools, especially in the appointment of staff at all levels. So heavily tainted has SADTU been with corruption that in 2019 the new MEC for education in KZN, Kwazi Mshengu, urged the union to 'rid itself of the corruption and teachers' absenteeism stigma that has followed it for years'. And that, furthermore, 'there is a public perception that the union has a hand in everything that is wrong in the education sector.'[63] In fact, SADTU is regarded as the most corrupt union in SA: 'No trade union in the democratic history of South Africa has attracted as much criticism as SADTU.'[64]

Davey went on to argue that the 'Colouredism' I have objected to many times has been a reality in his life as a teacher.

> It is a kind of elephant in the room, which intellectuals like you seem to eschew the very notion and thought that there could exist some sort of coloured consciousness, narrowly coloured I mean. It seems like there is that in fact. I also feel that the ANC is part of it, out of expediency perhaps or something else. There is a prevailing sense that coloured people have been marginalised. Ninety percent of the time I work with and among Coloured people. They feel extremely marginalised and it is a deliberate thing, especially by the ANC. SADTU dominates the appointments of staff, including principals. Let me give you an example. Two years ago, I had five head of department posts to fill. SADTU came to me and they said there must be no question about the fact that they want five Africans for all those posts. They said to me that I should know that they will get their way with those posts.[65]

What Davey identified as the ANC's partial responsibility for this racialist manipulation is precisely rooted in Africanist majoritarian chauvinism. He also hotly denied that at Klipspruit West the Coloured pupils and parents were insisting that they wanted only a Coloured principal. Coloured pupils and teachers were not objecting per se to the appointment of an African principal but rather that proper procedures and processes were not followed. Davey was emphatic: 'I have been in touch with all the role players in Klipspruit West and at none of those meetings was it said that we want a Coloured principal. Instead, they expressed their concerns with the process and procedure followed with appointments. In fact, Lesufi first agreed that it was not a racial thing; then he changed his mind and said it is!'[66]

There has been a disturbing pattern at play in schools in several Coloured areas in Johannesburg for a few years. In 2015 it was the Roodepoort Primary School, where mainly Coloured pupils and parents refused to accept the appointment of a new African principal. Once again, the appointment process followed was in dispute. My own castigation of some parents for angrily using the 'k-word' at a very tense moment of confrontation, I think with hindsight, underestimated the extent to which Coloured pupils and parents were justifiably aggrieved at the apparent violation of procedure in that appointment. What served to reinforce a sense that this violation had indeed occurred was when the GDE failed or refused to respond to attempts by me to get answers to a few questions about the procedure in 2015.[67]

However, Mercia Andrews hit the nail on the head when she argued that

> The big problem is that the NQ has never been a deeply rooted thing in the ranks of the ANC and other movements. Those of us in the independent left who denounced from the beginning the four-nation thesis of the ANC are reaping terrible consequences today. The other big mistake we made was to get caught up in a single narrative of the ANC and hardly any other movements. As a result, we even have today youth who believe that we Coloureds did not contribute to the liberation movement of SA. Even today, we still have a ruling party that is completely narrowly nationalistic.[68]

Until this regressive and reactionary African nationalism is confronted and dealt with, the ANC is going nowhere with this country.

Andrews also takes issue with the untrammelled dominance by the ANC of the national liberation movement, certainly from the 1950s onwards, as if there were no other credible alternatives:

> There are various factors at play about what happened in 1994 and afterwards but for me the single biggest narrative is that of the ANC who came to liberate us, Mandela went to the Island and it is the Africans who liberated us. This single narrative is what shaped our consciousness, regrettably. There was a hundred years of war here in the Cape, who were those people who were the first fighters against slavery and Dutch colonialism and where are their forebears today? It is the people of this province, they were the first people, it's true. We must know where we come from.[69]

She was also at pains to object to indiscriminately lumping Coloured people together with Khoisan people: 'The Coloured community is not only from the Khoisan community. Its origins are from slaves, the Khoisan, Xhosa, white and other peoples.'

Leonard Martin also made some important points about race in SA today: 'The people of this country do not search for the correct answers to racism; it's very dangerous; they feed off racism itself, this white–

black thing. In any case I don't believe people are indeed separated by race. It's instead ideology and politics which has enforced this division and I find that intellectuals are too relaxed about both the dangers of racism and this black Africanism.'[70] This regressive racialist thinking has got nothing in common with either non-racialism or anti-racism. Besides, it is thoroughly opportunistic in its pursuit of class and business interests and self-enrichment. The African working-class majority itself has nothing in common with this nationalism. On the contrary, they also suffer gross exploitation in the BEE companies they are employed in.

But it is how Martin captures the historical relationship between white liberalism and African nationalism, which has been a dominant theme in ANC politics since its inception, which struck me as most pertinent:

> The liberalist penetration of African nationalism was meant to replace, monitor, control and manage the development of knowledge. Who was doing the research then? It was white liberals. The ANC was formed on that basis. This was not a nationalism that tore apart the status quo. Instead, it reinforced it. We are left with that epistemological gap which is like a festering sore. There has been a related slide into a hegemonic blackness which is meant to suppress everything else around it. And because you are the majority, you have the power to interdict the expression of difference.[71]

This is a compelling insight. A different, important point was raised by Maglua: that in 1979 the ANC leaders in exile invited Chief Gatsha Buthelezi to London for talks.

> They said at that time that the face of Buthelezi was the face of the ANC inside the country. But it blew up in their faces in the 1980s when Buthelezi's *impis* ran amok inside the country. The problem is that the ANC is intrinsically racialistic. The chiefs, Contralesa, etc, are all driven by a desire to see the country being ruled in that fashion, which has caused them to openly undermine democratic processes.[72]

The accuracy of this statement must be seen in relation to all the concessions the ANC has made to traditional leaders since 1994, though as monarchs they have never enjoyed any constitutional and electoral legitimacy.

But not even that history could have foreseen how Ramaphosa

went, cap in hand, to King Goodwill Zwelithini in 2019 and agreed to withdraw the recommendation of the parliament-appointed High Level Panel inquiry into land reform that the Ingonyama Trust be dissolved or its powers cut. He made this concession to the Zulu king despite the fact that the recommendation followed a thorough process of research and public consultation. The panel, appointed by Ramaphosa in 2016, recommended that the Ingonyama Trust be dissolved on the grounds that the constitutional rights of the people living on that land were being violated in several respects.

Ramaphosa halted the parliamentary process, so that the panel's report was not discussed. In an indictment of our constitutional democracy, Ramaphosa basically aborted the important report of a parliamentary-appointed investigation into land reform and the ANC did nothing about it. Ramaphosa was not called to account for his actions. But I was not at all surprised that Ramaphosa went cap in hand to King Zwelithini given the historical relations between the ANC and the Zulu monarchy I alluded to earlier. I am also convinced that this unconstitutional move by Ramaphosa and the ANC paved the way for the draconian Traditional and Khoisan Leadership Act he signed into law in 2019.

That Act bears upon the Khoisan revivalist movement. Because of the historical fact that the heart of the industrial black working class of SA has always comprised both African and Coloured workers, it is clear to me that this revivalist movement and the alleged Coloured nationalist current within it, the centre of which is in the Western Cape, are an inevitable reaction against the Africanist majoritarian chauvinism, arguably the biggest threat to a just resolution of the NQ in SA.

However, the Khoisan movement faces serious political and organisational problems. If they are not addressed, it faces a bleak future in which even its more positive features will be dissipated. What has been unfolding over the past few years reminds me of what has happened to the ANC and all other nationalist organisations in our history: race and ethnicity, the elemental features of all hues of nationalism, ultimately reveal distinct material and financial – not necessarily in consciously class terms – interests within its leadership. No doubt, this trend will be influenced by the general climate of self-seeking acquisitiveness and corruption that has become endemic in SA, particularly within the ANC over the past decade.

Martin, himself a vigorous campaigner for the constitutional rights of Khoisan people, has been at the forefront of warning about a creeping authoritarianism at the top of the Khoisan movement: 'The Khoisan/Coloured people are at a crisis-ridden crossroads.'[73] He warns that Coloured people must be aware of the 'cultural traders of fake purity', including those in the leadership. The 'real crisis', he believes, is 'manifested in the fragmentation and absence of appropriate leadership of the Khoesan/'Coloured' people'. He attributes this grave danger to the movement as a result of what he calls a 'culturalist bloodline tribal ancestral ideology'[74] within its leadership.

Finally, he argues that 'education is vitally needed because "bloodline" is actually stating a case for genetic uniqueness, which is however cloaked as cultural uniqueness'. He goes on to argue that the leadership has produced 'fake queens and kings and plastic chiefs' and that they have now become 'ultra-Khoen'.[75] It is this 'ultra-Khoen' which carries the seeds of a Khoisan/Coloured nationalism in the making. But the most interesting developments for me are twofold. Firstly, the pecuniary interests that have increasingly grown among the Khoisan leadership and which I believe were partly why the demand to have representation in parliament was made. This is unsurprising because it has consistently been a central feature of the middle-class leadership of nationalist movements, as is the case with the ANC too.

Secondly, there is a striking similarity between how racism mutated from biology and physiology to culture in the 19th century and how the Khoisan movement mutated from racial to cultural issues in the forefront of its struggles in the early 21st century. That the crisis in the movement which Martin identifies is shifting, ironically, to cultural issues is most revealing. And the more ethnic origins and 'bloodline' and cultural traits move to the forefront of the movement the greater will its political linkages with Coloured people, especially activists, recede to the margins. That Martin has himself moved from a critical embrace of the movement to outright condemnation of these latest trends in the leadership is very significant because it shows an awakening to the class dimensions emerging within the leadership.

There has undoubtedly been an increased interest shown by Khoisan leaders in representational politics, particularly in parliament, as a result, no doubt, of the financial and material benefits it would bring them. The

Traditional and Khoisan Leadership Act, which was characterised as 'robbing millions of people living in rural areas of fundamental rights and shoring up the power of unelected and predominantly male traditional leaders against women in particular',[76] became law on 20 November 2019. In exchange for obtaining a degree of political recognition and power in parliament for some Khoisan leaders, this law will, most regrettably, erode further the constitutional rights of ordinary African people who live in rural areas. Mine companies and traditional leaders would be most happy with what the ANC has done.

A most worrying trend of the Khoisan revivalist movement, besides the increasingly ethnic-nationalistic ethos, is an accompanying inward-looking preoccupation, in which Martin himself appears to be trapped. This movement cannot detach itself from the political mainstream of SA, and if they don't link up organically with the black working-class movement and consciously see their struggles as a part and extension of it, they won't go far. These dangers will multiply once the new legislation takes effect and they secure parliamentary representation. My suspicion is that they will get sucked into the elitist politics which characterises parliament. They appear to have little interest in matters outside their parochial representational politics and it is very unlikely that the fully legitimate Khoisan cause will be advanced by their presence in parliament. Neither will the legitimate concerns of the Coloured working-class majority be advanced by such a presence.

Finally, two points must be made. Firstly, the ongoing debate about who is Coloured and who is Khoisan and the difference between the two identities is a time-wasting, peripheral, insignificant and in fact futile exercise. There are too many serious social problems common to all Khoisan/Coloured people, especially the working class, to be detained any further by such esoteric trivialities and diversionary preoccupations. Their emergence also complicates the National Question. Secondly, Martin and all the other leading figures of this movement have been validly criticised for their absorption in nationalistic politics, which seriously neglects working-class concerns and needs.

Khoisan leaders are mainly concerned with their representational political rights and how African nationalism, especially of the African chauvinist type, frustrates those aspirations. This was exactly what constituted the motive for the formation of the ANC in 1912. The concrete demands, which for example feature in black township struggles around basic services, hardly feature in the literature of this movement, as was the case too when the ANC was formed. The tortuous politics and ideology of race and identity, especially vis-à-vis the ruling ANC, are what dominates, almost exclusively, the approach of this movement and Martin in particular. No doubt, race and identity politics continue to have a resonance in SA, given our history, but it is their relationship with political economy and social justice issues which render them meaningful, not as isolated phenomena. To be totally consumed by this theme, day in and day out, wittingly or unwittingly, itself stridently nationalist in both content and tone, is not helpful, and serves to fan the flames of other competing nationalisms.

Finally, Mohamed Adhikari makes a few important points about a disparaging culturalist and (I would argue) racist attitude many African people have long had towards Coloured people, as a result of their particular historical formation, indicative of just how complex and difficult the development of anti-racist politics is in SA. Adhikari draws attention to the disparaging racialist and even arguably racist remarks many African people make about the cultural heritage of Coloured people, a 'racial hybridity' which he says is virtually inherent in the concept of Colouredness in the popular mind. He notes the widespread usage of terms such as 'mixed race', 'half-caste', 'bastard' and 'illegitimate' in reference to Coloured people and the claim that they have no culture. In this regard he cites a Coloured academic, Roy du Pre: 'Africans despise Coloured people in general. They look upon them as "mixed-breeds" with no nationhood, no identity, no culture. The African, on the other hand, is a proud, full-blooded "pure-breed" with a history, culture and identity going back centuries.'[77]

This is remarkably and ominously similar to the racialist and racist thinking of the white Dutch and British colonisers and in fact of 'scientific racism' of the 18th and 19th centuries. Adhikari invokes the term *malau*, which is a pejorative Xhosa reference to Coloured people, 'signifying a supposed lack of cultural or racial integrity and thus suggesting they are rootless and uncouth...'[78] Having worked among African people in the student and labour movement in the 1970s and 1980s, I have seen a lot of what was always to my mind simply reflective of ignorance of the history of Coloured people and a painful backwardness in relation to it.

It is still widespread a quarter of a century into our purportedly new democracy. Look for leadership by the ANC around these issues, and you will find little or nothing. They either don't know that history or look at it through the jaundiced eyes of a decayed and ultimately reactionary petit bourgeois African nationalism.

What this and much else tells us is that the NQ lies in tatters today, arguably in a worse state than it was in 1994. It is the deleterious effects of the worsening socioeconomic crisis which has both radicalised the NQ and given rise to a generalised race-ridden atmosphere, very evident on social and mainstream media. I believe that the Coloured Question, especially as it has played itself out on the Cape Flats over the past few years, has made a resolution of the broader NQ more difficult and more intractable than ever before.

The ANC Takes Office in 1994

But what really happened in SA after 1994? There will be many narratives about life in SA after apartheid, influenced by various factors of race, class, culture and gender. But it is only an approach which cogently integrates these aspects into a comprehensive and coherent analysis that can fruitfully answer this key and critical question. It is primarily the intersecting factors of race, class and gender which have determined the nature of the problems we today have in SA, namely poverty, black mass unemployment and a wide variety of class-related social injustices. The majority of people in this country continued to be oppressed and exploited after 1994. The big difference from the apartheid period is that it is now a joint white and black political and economic elite which holds power, based on the economic dominance of WMP and the political dominance of African nationalism via the ANC.

The generalised euphoric excitement which accompanied the 1994 Uhuru elections was somewhat contagious, except for the left outside the ANC alliance, who were sceptical and critical of the negotiations.[79] But the stark lack of mass support reduced their opposition to words, documents and papers largely, though various attempts were made to organise mass opposition to the elite deal-making then in progress. In this regard the Trotskyist-inclined Workers Organisation for Socialist Action (Wosa), led then by Neville Alexander, tried hard to build an opposition but with negligible results. Wosa entered the election under the Workers List Party (WLP) but failed to win one seat. Azapo won just one seat and the PAC three seats. Today Azapo has none and the PAC has been reduced to one. That pretty much sums up the paltry state of the left outside the ANC alliance inside and outside parliament.

Despite their defensive protestations to the contrary, the hard though unpalatable fact is that the BC movement has dismally failed to provide an opposition and alternative to the ANC or to win significant mass support in elections. If one studies both the BC movement and the PAC, they have been characterised by factional splits since the 1990s, which squandered whatever potential they might have had to build a mass opposition to the ANC, especially Azapo, which has had a clearer grasp of the situation in SA and the tasks facing us than the PAC. It is one of the major reasons why its virtual demise has been so unfortunate.

There are a few leaders who were part of the negotiations and its results, but much later found their voice to speak critically of its outcomes, such as Phillip Dexter, Jay Naidoo, and others. But none were as vocal as Kasrils, who was also minister of water affairs during Mbeki's first term. He presided over the neoliberal commercialisation, corporatisation and commodification of water and sanitation services, which severely affected black working-class communities who could not afford to pay for these services. Naidoo presided not only over the partial privatisation of Telkom in the late 1990s but when he was RDP minister he accepted the October 1995 draft Urban Development Strategy (UDS),[80] the first blatantly neoliberal class-based differential provision of municipal services, such as water, sanitation and electricity, strictly according to income and affordability.

Dependent on income, the UDS had three different levels of service, meaning a distribution of 55:25:20 between full, intermediate and basic levels of service in municipal areas: 'Full services' meant house-connected water supplies, full water-borne sanitation, paved roads with kerbs and pipes drain, and 60 amps electricity provision. 'Intermediate services' meant yard taps and paved roads with no kerbs, open drains and 30 amps electricity with prepaid meters for households. And 'basic services' meant communal water standpipes, on-site sanitation, graded roads with gravel and open stormwater drains. Bond described this system as 'class-based services segregation'.[81] It is important to see that this distinctly neoliberal class-based municipality services regime began to be designed as early as 1995.

It is necessary to pause here for a while, so shocking was this monetised regime so soon after the April 1994 Uhuru election, especially when applied to a majority black working class which for well over a century were the 'niggers' of SA. But at the very moment that they expected that at least their most basic needs would be met, they were told by the ANC that they would only get the level of service they could afford to pay for. This remains the case. The ANC government has been crudely and in fact cruelly based on the neoliberal commodification of basic services. Not even the long history of the racist denial of such services by various white regimes or the long struggles by black people for those services and rights persuaded the ANC to exempt at least water, sanitation and electricity from arbitrary and inexcusable monetisation.

Bear in mind that this is a black majority ANC government, which is what they wanted all along. The black or, more specifically, African leaders of the ANC rule this country and have the political power to determine policy in every area of our society, as they have with BEE and AA, though we know that these policies did not originate in the ANC, but were a big part of the strategy of the NP and WMC in the late 1990s. Today it is crystal clear that the redress of BEE and AA policies has benefited the black middle class and elite and certainly not the working-class majority, whose conditions and standards have instead deteriorated.

But back to the belated epiphany of Kasrils. What is most startling and somewhat incredible is that so many truths only dawned on him after he resigned following Mbeki's own forced resignation in September 2008. For a seasoned politician it is highly improbable that he sincerely only realised this after 2008, 16 years after the negotiations started. No, I find this retreat by Kasrils contrived, probably because the collaborationist agenda of the ANC and SACP had come full circle after Mbeki was recalled. Their own compromised and contradictory politics had exploded under their feet. He needed, for posterity's sake, a new script for himself, one he had not been able to craft when the neoliberal regime was established between 1994 and 2000.

There is an even more compelling argument to be made why his conversion to the position roughly of the independent left is belatedly contrived: in order to save face before the judgement of history. But Kasrils was minister of water affairs and forestry when the Municipal

Systems Act (MSA) was implemented and prepaid water meters began to be installed in some black working-class townships. Besides, as a result of Gear, Bond points out that there was a '85% real decline in central-to-local operating and maintenance subsidies during the 1990s'.[82] He also points out that in contrast to the RDP's 50–60 litres per person per day 'it was inexplicable that after so many years in government Kasrils and his staff still worked on an RDP short-term target of 25l for large families. Moreover, in late 1998, Dwaf bureaucrats had attempted to revise the target figure for low-density areas downwards to 7 litres.'[83] Incredible.

Nobody has done more splendid work on post-apartheid water and sanitation under ANC rule than Patrick Bond and Greg Ruiters.[84] The argument about what had happened under neoliberal policies went way beyond whether taps were indoors or communal. Bond argued that a 'third of all municipalities suffered major spills from sewerage into their water supplies.' He also pointed out that the very limited 'free water' to households from 2000 was not due to some magnanimous gesture from the ANC government, but as a result of the massive cholera outbreak in KZN in that year and the 'growing alienation and apathy in townships, along with declining activity in ANC branches, leading to fears that substantial vote abstention would lower the ruling party's overall vote and cost it control in key municipalities'.[85]

However, it is when the meagre free water consumption in black townships is compared with that consumed by hedonistic consumers in white upper-class suburbia and the nearly 90% of water used by South Africa's non-household consumers – commercial farmers, forestry companies, mines, industries and commercial enterprises – that the tragic magnitude of stark inequality is manifest. Tragic too when one considers what Bond argued: 'The struggle against apartheid was both a struggle against the politico-juridical system of racism and for improved quality of life. Improved residential infrastructure and service delivery are among the most crucial objectives of public policy by all accounts.'[86] But the ANC was well aware that it was basic services in townships which were of burning (no pun intended) importance during the struggle, especially in the 1980s. Yet, it was precisely in this crucial area that the jackboot of monetisation, despite the widespread and deep poverty of black working-class townships, first imposed itself.

In fact, well before the October 1995 UDS, the ANC government issued the Housing White Paper and the Water Supply and Sanitation White Paper of November 1994, both of which departed from the relevant provisions of the RDP, which made explicit provision for adequate subsidisation of basic services. Instead of cross-subsidisation from big users of water to poor consumers, the Water Supply and Sanitation White Paper stated that the 'lifeline price of water to retail consumers should be at least equal to the "operating and maintenance" expenses (i.e. full marginal costs), instead of being "free"'. This, Bond argued, was a 'startling indication that neoliberal pricing principles would prevail in the water sector, instead of the mandate adopted in the RDP'.[87]

Dealing with post-apartheid SA, and given our history, David Smith approaches social justice in the only way in which the daily needs of the majority black working class can be secured: 'While social justice is a very broad concept, attention is usually focussed on the unequal distribution of income and other sources of need satisfaction on which the material conditions of the population depend.' He importantly points out that 'The emphasis is on who gets what and where and how this might be changed for the better. This approach is encouraged by the conspicuous inequality in people's material living conditions.'[88] It is hard to think of a country with a history such as ours where this kind of social justice is more appropriate.

Today, in post-apartheid SA, the ANC leaders have their children in top private schools, while the masses of poor African children attend run-down and grossly neglected public schools. Bear in mind that this is the lot of African children 25 years since the 1994 elections. There have been regular reports in the media about the depressing and deplorable conditions black, especially African, pupils from primary to high schools have faced since 1994. The ruling ANC and its leading officials in government have not had the kind of knowledge, skills and development which would have enabled them to realise a very basic truth about this situation: the lack of basic infrastructure in so many respects will severely affect academic results because such an environment is not conducive to learning. But it does more damage than that: it also affects the longer-term development of those black pupils and severely disadvantages them in planning for the future, especially one that will be dominated by the technical knowledge and skills which the 4IR is going to demand over the coming decade.

Here lie the real roots of the palpable failures of the much-vaunted NDR and its related two-stage theory of revolution, which the ANC and SACP had adhered to for decades before the 1994 elections, and continue to do, despite the SACP's unconvincing claim in 2016 that it no longer subscribed to a mechanical two-stages approach and went on to deny that the NDR was the first stage.[89] The most effective way to show that this denial is false is the indisputable fact that there is no evidence that the SACP has seriously and resolutely waged an explicit second-stage socialist revolution since 1994. On the contrary, instead of asserting itself in order to meaningfully play that leading role in an explicit socialist programme, it has continued to play second fiddle to the ANC.

They do so notwithstanding the negative and often horrific results of this false programmatic distinction between a first (anti-apartheid) stage and a second and later anti-capitalist socialist stage. Some black people today, as well as the ANC leadership, still tell us that things have changed a lot and that much has been achieved in post-apartheid SA, for which we should be grateful. These are the sentiments of the black elite and middle classes, especially the upper layer whose children are either in former Model C schools or in private schools, who earn enough to take an annual holiday and who generally live in formerly white suburbia.

This is not the lot of the overwhelming majority of black households who still live in black townships and who languish in the doldrums of joblessness, poor housing and inadequate services, and whose children are forced to go to severely under-resourced public schools. The lot of these black adults and children has taught us of the severe limitations of the non-socialist and in fact essentially pro-capitalist NDR, via BEE and AA. It is very important to see that these policies and conditions did not just happen carelessly. It was instead conscious and deliberate, as Bond explains: 'In November 1994 and March 1995, the World Bank had deployed deputy resident representative Ahmed to coordinate work on the Urban Infrastructure Investment Framework. He persuaded Pretoria's chief infrastructure bureaucrat, Chippy Olver, that the post-apartheid government should provide only minimal standards and service levels to low-income South Africans.'[90]

This 'transition' or 'transformation' in SA was clearly orchestrated by the ANC along neoliberal lines. Local and global forces were at play to ensure that the outcome of the negotiations did not disturb or disrupt the white-dominated capitalist economy. What has happened in post-apartheid SA has dramatically exposed the inherent limitations of the NDR as the first stage of the moribund two-stage theory of revolution that the SACP and ANC have for decades advocated. The results over the past 25 years have been an abysmal record of mass poverty, unemployment, homelessness and class inequalities.

But it is this fact which perhaps more than anything else depicts the serious, systemic and strategic limitations of both the notion of the NDR and the compromised deal it was linked to in the negotiations between the ANC and the NP struck in the 1990s. Instead of leaning on the masses at critical moments in the negotiations in their own interests, the ANC used the threat of mass action to strengthen the hand of the leadership. But the ANC has always had an instrumentalist approach to the black masses of this country, including when the organisation was banned and many of its leaders in exile, especially as regards MK.

The NDR, by all accounts, has failed dismally, even after 25 years, to provide decent basic services to black townships. Not even the stark deprivation and degradation in black townships which ANC leaders see with their own eyes at election times have been enough to muster the resolve to deal satisfactorily with those pervasive problems. And not even the fact that ordinary black residents have repeatedly pointed out that it is only at election time that ANC leaders visit those townships to make empty promises, has been enough for them to decisively secure those basic municipal services which working-class households are especially reliant upon. It has gone on ritualistically, from one election to the next.

Bond argues that, notwithstanding official rhetoric to the contrary,

> SA suffered a durable replacement of racial apartheid with what can be considered 'class apartheid': systemic underdevelopment and segregation of the oppressed majority, through structured economic, political and environmental, legal, medical and cultural practices largely codified by Pretoria politicians and bureaucrats. Patriarchy and racism remained largely intact in many areas of daily life, even if a small elite of women and black people were incorporated into state management and the accumulation of capital.[91]

And if I have not made the links between the African elite and African nationalism clear enough, Bond refers to 'how forcefully African nationalism triumphed as the philosophy of South Africa's new petit bourgeois political elite'.[92]

Probably in no other African country has such rapid class formation played such a huge role following the granting of political independence, than SA, as a direct result of its enormous wealth, built up since the mineral revolution of the 19th century. But this class formation (a small black capitalist class and more numerous middle class without racial restrictions) was what the ANC in any case always wanted. By the political settlement of 1993 the NP and WMC finally acceded to the decades-old demand of the ANC for a non-racial democracy, which under the conditions that capitalism developed in SA could only mean a 'bourgeois democracy'. And where better to experiment with it than in the richest and most industrially developed country in Africa? But the results since 1994 speak volumes about the catastrophic failure of 'bourgeois democracy' to provide and satisfy even the most basic services and 'human rights' to the poor working-class majority.

The central problem, however, is that this 'bourgeois democracy' has been very good for the black elite and middle class, but decidedly not for the black working-class majority. There can be no getting away from the fact that the staggering wealth of the black elite (Patrice Motsepe, Cyril Ramaphosa, Tokyo Sexwale and others) was obtained and persists at the expense of the impoverished black majority. These are two sides of the same coin: staggering black wealth and staggering black poverty; without one side the other could not exist. That was the inevitable essence of the compromise deal of 1993 and in it lies the primary reason for our shocking statistics on poverty, unemployment and inequalities currently.

In other words, the NP and WMC could not afford a democracy in which there was no poverty, unemployment and inequality, not that such a democracy exists anywhere in the capitalist world. While the black and white capitalist elite probably wish it were different, the historical conditions under which capitalism developed did not permit a state-welfarist democracy, such as in the Scandinavian countries. What has happened historically cannot be changed. That is precisely where we are stuck in SA at this moment and it largely determines and defines the intractable nature of the social crisis, which gathers steam endlessly, as the continuation of many structural features of the colonial-apartheid period after 1994.

If one studies the constitution, which is reputed to be the most progressive in the world, it has in fact serious limitations in so far as the realisation of the social justice rights in the Bill of Rights is concerned. The most debilitating caveat in it is criticised by Themba Sono: 'To claim, as our silly subsection 26(2) does, that the government shall deliver only when it has the material means to do so is to hoodwink the populace. What if the state never has enough funds to fulfil these rights? Does it mean these rights are held in permanent abeyance? Could such a right be a right then?'[93] If the fulfilment of those rights depends on the availability of resources, within a neoliberal budgetary framework the results of such a provision is a foregone conclusion or a self-fulfilling prophecy. In other words, the hallmark of neoliberalism is severe budgetary constraints by the state, under relentless pressure by capital to curb public spending.

But this severe budgetary limitation is not because the ANC does not want to resolve those problems. No, it is directly because of the neoliberal fiscal constraints which the NP and WMC demanded were necessary during the period of the negotiations, from 1991 to 1993. The ANC, if it was going take office after the elections, was compelled to comply.

It is vitally important to recognise that tapped water inside homes and flush sanitation were for very long considered the hallmarks of civilisation, culture and modernity in the West. As we know, not many black homes in townships had such facilities under apartheid. It was therefore taken for granted that those services would be provided for by the ANC government. But given the severe neoliberal budgetary constraints, millions of black people are still without piped water inside their homes and water-borne sanitation. Flush sanitation the white working class enjoyed from 1908, in Johannesburg, which was 22 years after gold was discovered in 1886. Today, 119 years later and millions of black people still lack it in their homes under the ANC government. A similar story for electricity exists. By far most white homes had electricity during apartheid, while by far most black homes never had it.

It is with these basic municipal services that the socio-material effects of white ruling-class racism were most devastating. From this perspective the effects of the avalanche of overtly racist legislation on the statute book, such as the Group Areas Act, the Immorality Act and many more such racist restrictions, were relatively mild by comparison with the daily material deficits, such as low wages, poor working conditions, and inadequate housing and services. It is with regard to these matters that the black working class bore the brunt of apartheid and not the better-educated and trained blacks living in middle-class areas, such as Dube and Diepkloof in Soweto. This dynamic of class and race under apartheid did not receive the attention it should have in the past.

The ANC and its writers and thinkers never seriously explored those intra-black class issues because their emphasis for decades was on race and colour and their main goal therefore was to end racial discrimination and establish a non-racial democracy, as we have had since 1994. Our democracy, especially during the present social crisis – the worst since 1994 – which has battered the majority black working class, has suffered immensely. Poverty has persisted with a vengeance; unemployment is at its highest ever; and class inequalities are at their worst ever.

That the black elite and middle class benefited from it and the majority black working class were disadvantaged by it must now be abundantly clear. In other words, it is the majority black working class who in the final analysis paid for the emergence of a black elite and middle class after 1994.

Had the ANC's politics before it was banned paid serious attention to class, its cadres would have been more conscious of and sensitised to its workings after Mandela was released and the ANC unbanned. In fact, even after the ANC took office in 1994 its leaders did not explain, even to its own members, what had really happened in SA since then, to account for the perpetuation of mass poverty, joblessness and the unprecedented intra-black class inequalities. The last-mentioned is especially important because that is the story of the chasmic class divide between the leaders and mass membership of the ANC for many years now.

Endnotes

1 Steve Clark, ed., *Nelson Mandela Speaks: Forging a Democratic Non-Racial South Africa* (Cape Town: David Philip, 1995), p. 171.
2 The Urban Foundation was the first serious initiative of WMC, of which the AAC was the undisputed leader in SA. They had utterly dominated the South African economy for several decades and had a stranglehold over every major industry in addition to mining.
3 Two books that stand out most in this regard are Duncan Innes, *Anglo American and the Rise of Modern South Africa* (Johannesburg: Ravan Press, 1984) and Geoffrey Wheatcroft, *The Randlords: The Men Who Made South Africa* (London: Weidenfeld, 1985).

4 Clark, *Nelson Mandela Speaks*, p. 124.
5 Anthony Sampson, *Mandela: The Authorised Biography* (London: HarperCollins Publishers, 1999), p. 92.
6 Sampson, *Mandela*, p. 95.
7 Michael MacDonald, *Why Race Matters in South Africa* (Cambridge MA: Harvard University Press, 2006), pp. 127–8.
8 Ebrahim Harvey, 'The commodification of water in Soweto and its implications for social justice', (PhD thesis, University of the Witwatersrand, 2008).
9 Ebrahim Harvey, 'Mbeki inherited his problems from Mandela', *Mail & Guardian*, 23 March 2000.
10 Economic and social inequality has risen in post-apartheid SA, from a Gini co-efficient in 1993 of 6.6 to a measure of 7.0 by 2018. Within this overall rise, inequality *between* racial groups has diminished, while inequality within the African population has risen very sharply. It provides an important demonstration of the hollowness of 'democracy' without meaningful social justice.
11 Vishnu Padayachee and Robert van Niekerk, *Shadow of Liberation* (Johannesburg: Wits University Press, 2019), p. 228.
12 See John Saul, 'The apartheid endgame, 1990–1994' in John Saul and Patrick Bond, *South Africa: The Present as History* (Woodbridge: James Currey, 2014), p.129.
13 Called the 'independent left', several small groups outside and critical of the ANC alliance have had a long history in SA, but on the margins of the black and specifically African mass movement.
14 Sampson, *Mandela*, p. 50.
15 Jon Soske, 'Unravelling the 1947 "Doctors' Pact": Race, metonymy and the evasions of nationalist history', in Arianna Lissoni et al., eds, *One Hundred Years* (Johannesburg: Wits University Press, 2012), pp. 171, 172.
16 Ebrahim Harvey, 'ANC still paying for earlier blunder', *Cape Times*, 17 May 2007.
17 The Judicial Commission of Enquiry into Allegations against State Capture, also known as the Zondo Commission of Enquiry, was established by Ramaphosa in August 2018.
18 See 'Memorandum by Ben Turok before the ANC's Morogoro Conference' and a 'Reply by Joe Matthews', 5 April 1969, at http://www.anc.org.za/content/memorandum-ben-turok-ancs-morogoro-and-reply-joe-mathews and Hugh Macmillan, 'The "Hani Memorandum" – introduced and annotated', *Transformation* 69 (2009), pp. 106–29.
19 Thomas Karis and Gail Gerhart, *From Protest to Challenge: A Documentary History of African Politics in South Africa, Vol. 5, Nadir and Resurgence, 1964–1979* (Bloomington: Indiana University Press, 1997), 'Strategy and Tactics', pp. 387–92.
20 Ebrahim Harvey, 'Winnie will be remembered for sticking her neck out', *Sunday Independent*, 22 April 2018.
21 Patrick Bond, *Elite Transition: From Apartheid to Neoliberalism in South Africa* (Pietermaritzburg: UKZN Press, 2000).
22 Bond, *Elite Transition*, p. 197.
23 Bond, *Elite Transition*, pp. 11–17.
24 Bond, *Elite Transition*, p. 99.
25 Patrick Bond, *Unsustainable South Africa: Environment, Development and Social Protest* (Pietermaritzburg: UKZN Press, 2002), p. 44.
26 Ebrahim Harvey, 'Time for the left to end its hibernation', *Mail & Guardian*, 22 May 2000.

27 Bond, *Elite Transition*, pp. 74–6.
28 Cited in Saul, 'Apartheid endgame', pp. 125–6.
29 Saul, 'Apartheid endgame', p. 126.
30 Cited in Saul, 'Apartheid endgame', p. 126.
31 Saul, 'Apartheid endgame', p. 128.
32 Hlumelo Biko, *The Great African Society: A Plan for a Nation Gone Astray* (Johannesburg: Jonathan Ball, 2013), p. 51.
33 Biko, *Great African Society*, p. 52.
34 Ebrahim Harvey, 'It's time for the SACP to step out of the ANC's shadow', *Mail & Guardian*, 22 October 1999.
35 See Leo Trotsky, *The History of the Russian Revolution* (London: Pluto Press, 1977). See Appendix 1 and 2 for a theoretical grasp of the Permanent Revolution, pp. 1195–257.
36 Saul, 'Apartheid endgame', p. 127.
37 Interview with Jonathan Jansen, 22 July 2017, Cape Town.
38 See 'The Papers of Richard Dudley and anti-apartheid liberation movements, at https://digitalcollections.lib.uct.ac.za.
39 Keyan Tomaselli, 'Culture must be critically debated – it should nurture rather than kill', *Sunday Times*, 5 January 2020.
40 William Gumede, 'Black poverty appropriated for self-enrichment', *Sunday Times*, 5 January 2020.
41 Ebrahim Harvey, 'Cry, our beloved stepchildren', *Saturday Star*, 20 May 2017.
42 Ebrahim Harvey, 'Tragic tale of two cities divided by inequalities', *Cape Times*, 19 June 2007.
43 Ebrahim Harvey, 'ANC policies divisive in W Cape', *Sowetan*, 16 July 1999.
44 Interview with Martin Jansen, 31 July 2017, Cape Town.
45 Panyaza Lesufi interview, Johannesburg, 22 March 2017.
46 'Makhura admits ANC has neglected Coloured communities in Gauteng', *TimesLive*, 20 July 2018.
47 Lesufi interview.
48 *TimesLive*, 20 July 2018.
49 Harvey, 'ANC policies divisive'.
50 Edwin S. Munger, *Afrikaner and African Nationalism* (London: Oxford University Press, 1967). See Chapter 2, 'Class and Nationalism among Afrikaners, pp. 24–43.
51 Franz Fanon, *The Wretched of the Earth* (London: Penguin Books, 1990), p.125.
52 Cited in Neville Alexander, *One Azania, One Nation: The National Question in South Africa*, (London: Zed Press, 1979), p.47.
53 'Gatvol Capetonian sets its sight on 2019 elections', *Mail & Guardian*, 9 November 2018.
54 'Makhura admits ANC has neglected coloured communities in Gauteng', *TimesLive*, at www.timeslive.co.za, 20 July 2018. Interview with Panyaza Lesufi, Johannesburg, 23 October 2018.
55 Interview with Patrick Maglua, 23 August 2017, Johannesburg.
56 Maglua interview.
57 This comment Manyi had made on a show in March 2010.
58 See 'Manuel's letter to Manyi leaves ANCYL fuming', *Mail & Guardian*, 2 March 2011
59 See 'Where the DA governs there is misery for black people', at www.politicsweb. co.za, 18 June 2014.
60 The late Leonard Martin was the convenor of the Khoisan Leadership Conference and was probably the leading Khoisan activist, who constantly agonised over the ANC's descent into a crude Africanist majoritarian chauvinism, under which, he

argued, the Khoisan and Coloured people have suffered.
61. Interview with Leonard Martin, 12 March 2017, Johannesburg.
62. Interview with Mike Davey, 23 September 2017, Johannesburg.
63. 'Sadtu urged to rid itself of corruption stigma', *Daily News*, 24 June 2019.
64. Rebecca Davis, 'SADTU: SA's most controversial union faces human rights probe', *Daily Maverick*, 11 May 2017, at www.dailymaverick.co.za.
65. Davey interview.
66. Davey interview.
67. Ebrahim Harvey, 'So many questions in Roodepoort school race row', *City Press*, 30 August 2015.
68. Interview with Mercia Andrews, 23 July 2017, Cape Town.
69. Andrews interview.
70. Martin interview.
71. Martin interview.
72. Magluai interview.
73. Leonard Martin, WhatsApp message, 23 October 2019.
74. Leonard Martin, WhatsApp message, 16 October 2019.
75. Leonard Martin, WhatsApp message, 28 September 2019. 'Khoi' and 'Khoen' have been used interchangeably in the literature.
76. Martin Heywood, 'The Traditional and Khoisan Leadership Bill: President signs away rural people's rights', *Daily Maverick*, 29 November 2019.
77. Mohamed Adhikari, *Not White Enough, Not Black Enough* (Athens: Ohio University Press and Cape Town: Double Story Books, 2005), pp. 21, 24.
78. Adhikari, *Not White Enough*, p. 24.
79. This 'independent left' were generally correct about their criticisms of the ANC, its alliance partners, and the nature of the elite deal-making negotiations in progress between 1991–1993. But they had very little support among the African masses, whose support for the ANC dominated political life from the 1940s.
80. The Urban Development Strategy was released by Jay Naidoo's Ministry for Reconstruction and Development in October 1995.
81. Bond, *Unsustainable South Africa*, p. 203.
82. Bond, *Unsustainable South Africa*, p. 227.
83. Bond, *Unsustainable South Africa*, pp. 237, 239.
84. See Bond, *Unsustainable South Africa*, and Greg Ruiters, 'Commodified water, race and social justice in South Africa', PhD dissertation, University of Johns Hopkins, 2002.
85. Bond, *Unsustainable South Africa*, pp. 227, 233.
86. Bond, *Unsustainable South Africa*, p. 242.
87. Bond, *Unsustainable South Africa*, p. 196.
88. David Smith, 'Redistribution and social justice after apartheid', in *The Geography of Change in South Africa*, ed. Anthony Lemon (Chichester: John Wiley & Sons, 1995), pp. 45–64, 59.
89. 'Now more than ever the SACP has a leadership duty in the NDR', *African Communist*, 193, 3rd quarter, 2016, p. 21.
90. Bond, *Unsustainable South Africa*, p. 202.
91. Bond, *Unsustainable South Africa*, p. 253.
92. Bond, *Elite Transition*, p. 6.
93. Sono, cited in Ebrahim Harvey, 'Popular control over decision-makers', in *In the Balance: Debating the State of Democracy in South Africa*, ed. Paul Graham and Alice Coetzee (Cape Town: Idasa, 2000), pp. 39–40.

SIX

Some notes on the National Question

Placing the National Question in Perspective

THIS CHAPTER BRIEFLY discusses the NQ and attempts a strategic approach. Gerhard Maré warns that 'The National Question is an ideological notion, resting as it does on the constructed notion of "the nation" – an "imagined community of inhabitants of nation states", of "building the nation"; of what can be justified in the name of "the nation". Here it differs from the structurally located origin and existence of terms such as class, sex and gender.'[1]

However, the NQ is only partly about who constitutes the 'nation', which is primarily a geographical matter, as is the question of who is an 'African'. Over twenty years ago I argued: 'If a true African identity means more than just geography and country of birth, then let us spell out what these criteria are – whether it be cultural, social, ideological or historical aspects, which distinguish "real" Africans from others who have lived on this continent for more than 300 years.'[2] This means that all people born in South Africa, from whichever part of the world their ancestors originally came from, are Africans. We are all South *Africans*, meaning simply that we are all born in the South of Africa.

But because of the long racist history of SA, which systematically denied black people the most basic democratic rights, including citizenship (membership of 'the nation'), the NQ was highly political from the outset. Brutal racism, national oppression and the lack of the most basic democratic rights imparted an explosive character to the NQ. The resolution of the NQ in SA has in real terms nothing to do with geography and its related history. Instead, at the heart of the NQ are questions about the kind and quality of life of people who constitute the nation: the material conditions of life and social justice. In a country such as SA, where race and class were inextricably intertwined over centuries, these questions assume an acute and urgent character along racial lines. My approach in this chapter is similar to that proposed by Maria van Diepen: there is a need 'for both politics and science to search for an adequate conceptualization of the dynamics of race and class; that is, the conceptualization of the socio-economic inequalities in the national reality of South Africa.'[3]

Under colonialism and apartheid it was assumed that only white people constituted the nation. In this sense the anti-apartheid struggle which the ANC led was meant to include black people as part of the nation, with the same democratic rights as white people. This required doing away with all the laws on the statute books which discriminated against blacks and allowing them to live side by side with white people in a common democracy, which is arguably what we have today in SA. But this rearrangement and new democratic status quo which gave the right to vote and other democratic rights to black people left untouched the capitalist economic architecture which had been built from the mid-19th century, largely by an abundant supply of cheap black labour. Right here lies the quandary of present-day SA and the massive social crises of unemployment, poverty and raging social inequalities which the 'rainbow nation' created by negotiations.

As has been explained previously, it is the black working-class majority who bore the brunt of colonialism and apartheid, especially when racism and capitalism jointly took their toll on them. The excruciating irony therefore of this devastating crisis is that it is the same black working class who built this country that today bears the brunt of the current crisis. This is the heart of the tragic betrayal of the needs, wishes and aspirations of this black majority, who have been the 'niggers' of this country since the 19th century. But this was as a result of the African nationalism of the ANC, which was all about race in terms of the political transformation it fought for, but without linking that NQ approach (race or the nation) to the key and cardinal questions of the kind of economy that would frame those new democratic rights. That was the result of the two-stage approach to the struggle, which birthed the NDR, as I earlier explained.

However, because the anti-apartheid struggle was tied by many threads to struggles against the capitalist system itself, not abstractly, but in very concrete, everyday terms, such as wages, municipal services, housing, health, education and so on, the serious limits of the NDR and two-stage approach resulted in the resumption of those same struggles after 1994, but this time fought far more fiercely than they were under apartheid, as can be seen by the unstoppable township protests since 2004, which have made SA the protest capital of the world. I am reminded of what Mandela told a Cosatu congress in 1997: basically, if the ANC treated black people poorly, they must do to the ANC what they did to the apartheid regime. This could only have meant black resistance to the social effects of the neoliberal policies the ANC adopted after 1994. It could have no other meaning.

However, there were numerous times in fact when the ANC itself spoke of the simultaneity of the struggle against apartheid the struggle against capitalism, as Martin Legassick points out: 'The ANC Commission meeting in Lusaka at the time concluded, like us, that capitalist exploitation and racial oppression operate together and reinforce one another.'[4] The ANC, while in exile, frequently linked the anti-apartheid and anti-capitalist struggles, as is the case too with the NDR. In this regard, Roger Southall argues that 'The principal dynamic of the NDR is said to be the liberation of Africans in particular and blacks in general from political and socioeconomic bondage.'[5]

While I critically review the racialist mantra of 'blacks in general and Africans in particular' in the next section, it is important to note that Southall states that its task was not only the political liberation of blacks but their emancipation from socioeconomic bondage too. What is clear from the literature is that while the ANC almost inseparably linked talk of the NDR with the anti-apartheid struggle, and as much as it wanted to separate the anti-apartheid struggle from the anti-capitalist struggle, so linked were the conditions of oppression and exploitation in real life that they were compelled to refer at times to the social conditions of poverty, unemployment, homelessness and so on.

But the ANC failed to develop a revolutionary theory which inseparably linked these struggles together, analytically or in a programme of action. Hence I propose that the conscious function of the NDR was to prevent a joint and indivisible struggle, and instead confine it to a struggle that was not anti-capitalist. The result of this NDR, combined with the neoliberal policies introduced after 1994, resulted in the fact that 'the ANC's constituency has remained extremely poor and has been denied the opportunity for material improvements in their standards of living which liberation was expected to bring.'[6] There are many more deleterious consequences which this completely artificial, unnecessary and in fact counterproductive approach had after 1994, which I discuss in the next two chapters.

In fact, so entrenched was the thinking of the NDR as the first anti-apartheid stage – to be followed at an indeterminate future stage by a struggle for socialism[7] – that it was along precisely these lines that ANC leaders on Robben Island debated these matters. Kgalema Motlanthe recalled that on Robben Island there were fierce 'debates for years about whether the struggle was for a NDR or a socialist revolution'.[8] This served to confirm that the understanding was that the NDR was not waging a fight against capitalism, even though it has been for decades palpably clear that such an approach was highly problematic and in fact inherently implausible, because of the sheer impossibility of separating these struggles, especially when in theoretical, practical and concrete terms they were at virtually all times inseparable.

I have already dealt with the inherent limitations of the contingency theory and don't agree with Patrick Bond, who asserts that the term "contingency" means that it cannot be theorised: 'The whole point of 'contingency' is that it is not theorisable ... that's what distinguishes race-class relations from other relations.'[9] How on earth can any social phenomenon be untheorisable? Theory is simply the ability to think through and determine the nature of society, what is happening in real life, the ability to provide a coherent explanation of objective conditions and to point to solutions, but which is always dependent on organising the social forces to carry through those struggles. The central problem, however, that Bond fails to realise is that this view of his is itself a theory he has about the relationship between race and class or racism and capitalism: that it is indeterminable. But I have argued that it is determinable.

Capitalism does not need to have a relationship with racism which is absolutely mutually dependent, determinate and beneficial at every moment in order to recognise the nature of that relationship. This is even more critically important for the struggles of the masses simply because it might appear that this contingency thesis undermines opposition to the two-stage revolution of the SACP, since it argues that the relationship between racism and capitalism is not a necessary one, but relative, meaning that since they are not always coterminous, the theory of permanent revolution is not always a valid one. In other words, I believe the thesis of contingency can be seen as a counterrevolutionary *theoretical* device.

I argue, relying on empirical evidence during the apartheid period and on the relevant literature which points overwhelmingly to a symbiotic relationship between racism and capitalism, that we must oppose this thesis. Race and apartheid were overwhelmingly tools with which to increase the rate of the super-exploitation of black, especially migrant, labour. Contrary to the theoreticist ethos of many academics, more often than not white, we must not be detained and derailed by the contingency thesis. Had the objective of the ANC's struggles been not only against racial oppression and apartheid but also against the capitalist system, and had the ANC upheld that view in the 1990s, we would not have the appalling poverty, unemployment and numerous social injustices that exists today in SA. Instead, there is no doubt that the settlement prevented critical engagement with questions of the economy.

What this approach to the NQ conclusively means is that it is imperative today, more than ever before, to link it at all times to the wide range of questions of social justice I earlier dealt with. In other words, I argue that any discussion about race and colour today in SA must necessarily engage with its capitalist political economy, which historically was very clearly linked to the apartheid edifice, with compelling empirical indicators to attest to that nexus. To do this is in fact quite simple: forgetting for the moment who had the right to vote and who did not, ask who had access to piped water indoors, and flush sanitation, decent housing and education, jobs, good wages and so on. It is in this regard that the essence of 'white privilege' resides. Now, move forward to life in SA after 1994 and you will not only find that this race–class situation continued to prevail but that, regarding basic services, it got much worse, as I have demonstrated. Incredibly, black people in the townships had easier access to basic services under apartheid than they did in post-apartheid SA. I discussed this earlier in reference to the Municipal Systems Act.

It is unhelpful, historically or at present, to pose the question: did race matter more than class? What came first, race or class? It is similar to the chicken and egg analogy in many ways. I have concluded that the left who favoured a socialist outcome to the struggles were wrong also to place a greater emphasis on class than on race. The lesson seems abundantly clear now upon reflection: it was mistaken to place an emphasis on either race or class in theory, organisation and agitation, so intertwined historically were both factors in terms of how the system worked. This is probably best expressed in the term 'racial capitalism', which captures the race–class nexus in South African history.

However, it is these facts of our history which both white liberals and black liberals in the ANC could never come to terms with. In the case of the latter it was understandable, since they wanted reforms for black people but within a capitalist economy. For all intents and purposes, that too is what the ANC wanted since its inception. But because it was the leader of black struggles in SA, faced with that history, which still stubbornly persists, it referred to and called for changes to social conditions and the economy here and there. This, however, was always in a reformist manner which never unambiguously called and stood for a struggle against capitalism itself or asserted that the struggles against apartheid could not be consummated without a simultaneous struggle against capitalism, for which purpose it was convenient for the ANC to argue that it was always a multi-class organisation.

The point of the leadership emphasising the multi-class nature of this movement was to pave the way for it at any time in the future to become integrated into the capitalist economy. With regard to the latter, Mandela spoke very clearly of what the ANC's interests were, as I noted earlier. They were explicitly in favour of disenfranchised black people becoming part of that system. Nowhere does the ANC seek to even analyse what the implications of its pro-capitalist stance would be in a future democracy in SA, especially whether that arrangement will resolve the deep and wide-ranging socioeconomic deprivations of the black working-class majority. We have had for over a quarter of a century a sham 'democracy' which in fact has left those people worse off than they were under apartheid. I have shown what a dismal situation exists in black townships across SA. Hence, the unstoppable township protests.

The generally poor and often degrading living conditions in townships have created the dismal situation we still have there after the 'miracle' democracy the world praised in the 1990s, without any understanding or realisation of the dreadful future that the nature of the 1993 settlement and the related neoliberal policies the ANC adopted after 1994 made both regrettable and inevitable. What this has done is to highlight race as never before, which alters the race–class dynamic in much more concrete and in fact potentially radical forms. It is post-apartheid SA which provided the best lessons retrospectively about the race–class dynamic under apartheid. And it is the negotiated settlement which unleashed class forces which never obtained under apartheid: the considerable expansion of the black middle class and the programmed emergence of a small black capitalist class. But it is quite clear that the ANC, NP and WMC did not comprehend what that new status quo, amidst an ocean of black mass poverty, joblessness and related social miseries, would do to the country in the years ahead.

After two decades a chasmic gulf, which steadily increases, separates those class forces from the majority of black people, the bulk of whom are either unemployed or are low-paid workers or what is referred to as the 'working poor'. It is these developments which imparted a contentious and explosive character to the unresolved NQ, because the race–class matrix, of which it is the axis, was now much more embedded and intractable than it was under apartheid. The interesting thing is that this has happened as a consequence of the negotiated settlement, meaning ironically that increasingly in the years ahead the race–class nexus, in so far as its relationship to poverty, unemployment and inequalities is concerned, will sharpen much more, but in ways which are going to urgently demand answers. Given the deepening global economic crisis, which is likely to worsen, according to all indicators, we are heading for very choppy waters into the future.

There can be no doubt, especially given a long history of militancy, that SA faces a combustible future, and given the neoliberal policy regime of the ANC there seems no way out of that crisis and its probable trajectory. In the absence of a unified and coherent left organisational alternative and presence across the political spectrum, this crisis is going to erode further the already very fragile fabric of our society. We just don't quite realise that the convergence of several crises at this conjuncture can catapult us into a protracted civil war of increasingly racial proportions. Those who dismiss this possibility are dangerously naïve. The war against and numerous killings of white farmers over the past decade in particular and the vitriolic reaction of white right forces in the US, Australia and elsewhere are a rough indication of how quickly we can end up in a cataclysmic international crisis which includes the possibility of this racial conflict escalating into armed combat.

Given what is at stake for white South Africans anything is possible, and let there be no doubt that should this happen, there is the likelihood that we will have a very bloody conflict on our streets, the outcome of which is far from certain, either way. But what is certain is that we will be plunged into a crisis which will make the worst of the apartheid nightmare look mild by comparison. This country is a tinder box of various racial animosities, either overtly or covertly, which only needs a spark to ignite a long fuse of historical baggage laden with extensive deprivation and unresolved demands. This country and all its people must exercise the utmost caution not to provoke a racial conflagration, which, were it to happen, would cause us all to suffer immensely and whose bloody effects and related trauma would last for many years.

In fact, as much as the race–class nexus is bound to become more combustible in the coming period, especially if the economic crisis worsens, we must try to deal with race in ways which prevent matters escalating to open conflict. To do this will be immensely difficult, given the material conditions to which race is strongly tied. That is going to be our greatest challenge because of the solidified race–class nexus. The only way to address this is through the resurrection of the NQ from the dustbin the ANC has relegated it to after 1994. The key question is how to contain the potentially combustible elements within that nexus, since the social crisis is likely to deepen and its effects on poor black people worsen to the point where violence might beckon. The ANC has not only been totally incapable of providing leadership on these matters but has not even identified these problems in the first place.

It is almost as if the ANC naïvely believed the NQ had resolved itself after the first non-racial democratic elections in 1994. Instead, by all accounts what has happened after 1994 has reinstated and reinforced the NQ. The massive resurgence of race since has in fact made the NQ more combustible than ever before in the history of SA. Nowhere can this be seen more than on social media, a space which has both immense benefits and vices. Benefits, because they are very important social platforms where ordinary people can express their thoughts and feelings on a wide range of issues of national concern, and as a result are major sites where learning and development of people can occur. The main vice is the vitriolic explosion, especially around race, of voices which have been suppressed for long, but are often bereft of the nuance and sophistication in understanding which only often studied knowledge can impart. That is precisely why I decided on a study of race which goes back deep into history, to tap both its roots and evolution.

The main reason why the NQ has imposed itself on our consciousness after 1994 is simply because the tragic lack of social justice is directly and indirectly related to the ongoing salience of race. Race always stood at the heart of the NQ but more as a signifier of class than standing on its own as a factor in our history and politics. The fact is that the ANC has never explained what happened to the NQ after 1994. Yet, in previous decades the NQ was at the top of its agenda in its anti-apartheid struggles. 'The national question is one of the most important topics of concern to the South African liberation movement,' stated ANC historian Francis Meli.[10] How then could the NQ virtually disappear after 1994? This question assumes even much greater importance in the light of the fact that 'At the root of national oppression lay the stripping of the dignity of black people'.[11] The latter view by another historian, Martin Legassick, places into perspective why Meli would regard the NQ so highly. But as we know, the conditions of black poverty and squalor in townships across SA reek today of gross indignity and, worst of all, with regard to the most basic services any human community depends on daily to survive, let alone live a much better life.

The ANC's 'Blacks in General, Africans in Particular' Mantra: A Critical Appraisal

Nobody in the literature has confronted this mantra of the ANC in terms of both the NQ and the host of social questions inherently related to it. Why is this so? The probable answer lies in the unfortunate untrammelled dominance of the narrow African nationalism of the ANC. The ANC itself has never once subjected this racialist and divisive approach to a critical review in relation to both the liberation struggles and the related NQ. In a country which has for centuries been polarised by race and ethnicity as SA has been, it is not only completely inappropriate but provocative in terms of the NQ and especially about who has historically constituted the ranks of the oppressed and exploited of this country.

In this regard it is the class dynamics of the NQ that have not been addressed by the ANC or other components of the national liberation movement. The reason, I argue, is that all the various versions of African or black nationalism have conspicuously neglected the class dynamics both within the liberation struggles more generally and specifically within the NQ. The fundamental problem with this approach, and its biggest weakness, is that it ignores, conveniently I argue, the notion of class and its implications within both the struggles waged and the future of SA. This is particularly problematic as it is class dynamics which are today ultimately the dominant theme in the world, despite the outward manifestation of the resurgence of various nationalistic currents, both right and left. It is the unprecedented crisis in global capitalism which has given rise to these currents, as it has always done over centuries. Economics has universally and historically determined in the final analysis what happens in both politics and culture.[12] This historical fact is indelibly inscribed in the formative fabric of South African society.

But scan the literature on the ANC and SACP and you will hardly find these matters of this mantra being addressed, as if it is politically and discursively off limits. I have little doubt that nowhere more does the notion of political correctness apply with a sense of trepidation than to this mantra of the ANC. But we need to interrogate it on its own terms to see what it has delivered to 'Africans in particular'. For the moment I will leave aside the 'blacks in general', which are the Coloureds and Indians whom the ANC regards as 'minorities', and only focus on Africans. In this regard, the greatest and in fact cruel irony of this racialist mantra is that it is African people who are still at the very bottom of the hierarchical race-class-gender structure of our society, but who are mostly worse off than they were under apartheid, especially as regards jobs and basic municipal services. I have spoken enough of the pathetic mess that the African townships are for years.

So, what was this preferential treatment of Africans supposed to mean in a post-apartheid SA? If, in regard to basic services, it is the unpardonable and unmitigated mess in African townships and the fact in every social indicator African people and women in particular are still the worst off in our society, it is unambiguously clear that this mantra was itself an African nationalistic hoax. Now if we combine that with the fact that, instead of genuinely preferential treatment, the wanton corruption of ANC officials has stolen a huge amount of money from all levels of the state and all the SOEs, then the picture we see is nothing less than a very conscious and intentional betrayal of the repeated promises the ANC made since 1994 to selflessly serve the interests and needs of these people who loyally supported them for so many years, both before and after 1994. Forget for the moment about colonialism, white supremacy and apartheid's effects over centuries on black people; the unambiguous and unmitigated fact is that the ANC has betrayed the poorest African masses.

While it claimed to be multi-class, its policies were distinctly class-based in the sense of not really favouring the African working class but the middle class and elite. I have conclusively shown that this is the creature the ANC has been since its birth. That is furthermore why the repeated emphasis by the ANC, while it was banned and in exile, that it had a bias to the working class was false then and has in post-apartheid SA proven so with the blood, sweat and tears of the poorest African masses themselves. Go and travel through African townships to see with your own eyes this lie of the ANC. I have stated it many times in my columns and articles: the African masses have been since 1994 little more than electoral cannon fodder. But voting results since 2004 have shown that the African electorate has begun to wake up from its slumber with regard to its loyalty to the ANC. That has been such has a political awakening occurred among the voters that the ANC was voted out of office in 2016 in arguably the two most important areas of the country: Johannesburg and Tshwane, the financial and political capitals of SA.

The class betrayals of the ANC are vividly evident all over the African townships and in places such as public schools and hospitals, for example. It has been a generally dismal situation for many years: sewage running down streets where children play, children dying in pit latrines, the lack of the most basic school facilities, such as toilets and water, classrooms, furniture and facilities. The list is much longer in the wider sphere of university accommodation for African students and in hospitals. But the worst conditions are in our public schools and hospitals across the country. The media have painted a terrible picture of neglect in all these vitally important areas of public and social policy. What makes the betrayals of the African masses – forget for the moment about conditions in Coloured and Indian areas – so much more tragic is that its victims are often children, pupils and students. The basic interests of the people with whom the future of the country resides have been most severely compromised.

Within the clutches of the ANC's neoliberal policies, the theft of resources through wanton corruption ensured that those communities which should have received the lion's share of state resources to address the devastating apartheid legacy, suffered further irreparable harm. Communities suffering terrible poverty, joblessness and a wide range of social miseries are the result of the ANC's African cadre deployment policy. That is why we will find both administrative incompetence and bungling occurring alongside wanton corruption by the same ANC officials. The ANC's decision to introduce qualification criteria for cadre deployment is good, but far too late.[13] The damage done is enormous and the consequences will last for many years.

The African nationalism which produced this mantra was never going to be kind to the African working class, let alone the broader black working class. The late Neville Alexander, in his book *One Azania, One Nation: The National Question in South Africa*,[14] best captures the relationship between the African nationalism of the ANC and the class-capitalist interests of many in its leadership. He argued that if African nationalism was under the control of a middle-class leadership and not a revolutionary proletarian leadership, it would become much more susceptible to going the capitalist route in post-apartheid SA. For example, never were any of the ANC's top leaders since 1912 unambiguously socialist or Marxist. But it would have been surprising if they were, since all the leaders of the ANC were from the African elite of those times, and most had been to missionary schools, whose job was to prevent revolution by some reforms.

The fact is that the ANC since its inception was never in the hands of a revolutionary leadership. It was always a distinctly middle-class leadership, but whether you can use African nationalism as it has been expressed and understood in the struggle would still have presented not only theoretical problems, particularly in terms of two-stage theory, but especially in programmatic terms. The inherent problems with the NDR are the clearest expression of this point. But because Alexander believed that racism and capitalism were inextricably tied and that therefore you could not get rid of the former without getting rid of the latter, he seemed to think that in the case of SA African nationalism had more revolutionary potential to overthrow the entire system. In the end the African nationalism 'which aims at no more than the integration of the oppressed black people into the existing capitalist structure'[15] triumphed in 1994.

He overestimated the potential of African nationalism because he was wedded to the notion that viewed the relationship between racism and capitalism as inseparable and failed to see that the ANC was never fit for revolutionary anti-capitalist purposes since its inception. On the contrary, it fought strongly against anti-capitalist currents in its midst. There are other examples of this, but the expulsion of the Marxist Workers Tendency group from the ANC in 1979 is the best example.[16] Whether racism has been eliminated in SA is a hugely important and debatable question, both theoretically and practically, which I return to in the final chapter. But the point is that African nationalism, in one form or another, has been overwhelmingly dominant in SA since the ANC was formed in 1912. In fact, the PAC and the BC movement are essentially, disregarding their occasional radical phraseology, different forms of African or black nationalism, I argue.

I indicated earlier that many Numsa media statements refer to the 'African' working class rather than the more inclusive term 'black'. Why persist in doing so into the third decade of a post-apartheid SA? What would workers who are Coloured and Indian assume? They would know immediately that it does not refer to or include them. There, once again, a non-racial and anti-racist approach to the NQ is abdicated, in favour of an African nationalist one, which also flatly contradicts the non-racial constitution and labour relations regime of SA. As I said, an Africanist nationalist chauvinism unfortunately cuts very deep into our political and social history. This is a burdensome menace to a non-racial and anti-racist resolution of the NQ, which this country, including the anti-capitalist left, cannot afford.

The mantra itself is the epitome of this chauvinism, which sets up Coloured and Indian 'minorities' as inferior to this majoritarian African nationalism and deserving of only secondary attention. This is a resounding echo of apartheid racialist ideology, as is the way in which AA has been structured in SA by the ANC. But it has done far more damage because the eagerly aspiring African bourgeoisie exploited this mantra in order to benefit most from the opportunities for capitalist formation and accumulation. The result was the business empires of Patrice Motsepe, Cyril Rampahosa, Tokyo Sexwale and so many more, whose staggering wealth is separated from the devastating material conditions of the African masses in ways which are too appalling for words to describe.

But this situation was the inevitable result of the class dynamics of the negotiated deal they struck formally with the NP and informally with WMC. The legal instruments for this rapid black embourgeoisement were BEE and AA. It is therefore no accident that aside from WMC, these African beneficiaries are the wealthiest people in SA. This fact alone tells us clearly and boldly that African people, even those who were yesterday poor and ordinary, have no abstract principled objection to wealth accumulation, but took to capitalism almost like a duck to water. The only way this could have happened was the convergence of the strategy of the NP and WMC and the historical fact that the ANC wanted black majority rule, but never declared, before, during or after negotiations, that this achievement had to be accompanied by abolishing capitalist social relations in SA. This, and the contradictions and inconsistency of the ANC in relation to the radical demands of the FC, paved the way for the 1993 settlement.

We need, however, to question the critique of a sell-out negotiated settlement which the left outside the ANC alliance has made repeatedly.[17] The point of the review of this thesis is that if this left holds onto both the thesis that the ANC was never since its birth a socialist organisation, that it was in fact a liberal multi-class movement and therefore was most likely to betray the black working class if it assumed power in SA, then the very notion of both a sell-out and fundamental compromises it was alleged to have made is vulnerable to attack. In fact, the whole thesis of a compromised sell-out might need to be abandoned. But it is because the ANC itself also often spoke of the need for social justice in a post-apartheid SA and for the economy to be nationalised in order to ensure equitable redistribution, even if Mandela himself contradicted himself on the question of the provisions of the FC, there are many statements by the ANC while it was banned and in exile about the importance of the socioeconomic aspects of the NDR.

However, my main point about pointing to this mantra of the ANC – besides its explicit racialisation and its implicit discriminatory and biased ethnic indications – is to show that it is a complete falsity to suggest that while it neglected the interests and needs of Coloured and Indian people, it genuinely prioritised those of African people. All present statistical indicators point to the fact that black people on the whole and African people in particular are in all respects still by far the worst off in SA. I argue that there cannot be a bigger and more treacherous hypocrisy of ANC rule than this fact. The political, social and ideological implications of this fact are enormous, and they have far-reaching implications for race and colour. It tells us unambiguously, as does the fact that it is African men who are today the biggest corruption culprits, that post-apartheid SA has once and for all dramatically ended the equation of race or whiteness with wealth, power and corruption.

The combined wealth of just the richest six black billionaires is far greater than that of many thousands of white people combined, let alone that the wealth gap between them and black workers would be even starker. Nothing shows us more glaringly that money and class have trumped race as factors in the demography of wealth in SA, but the tiny black elite was artificially constructed in order to stabilise the capitalist economy in the 1990s. However, the rapid speed at which this occurred was clearly contrived by the convergence of various forces, local and global, whose singular agenda was the creation of a small super-rich black elite and more numerous black middle class with which to provide a buffer between the forces of the old apartheid order and WMC, on the one hand, and the black working-class majority on the other hand. Post-apartheid SA has been consciously and deliberately structured along those lines. It therefore meant from the outset that the majority could not and would not be beneficiaries of the settlement. Instead they were made to pay the price of what Kasrils called the Faustian pact of the 1990s.

This situation, I argue, has huge implications for our understanding of race in post-apartheid SA under ANC rule. The ruling ANC overwhelmingly consists of Africans. There is just a sprinkling of 'minorities' – whites, Coloureds and Indians – in the cabinet and in all levels of the state and in SOEs. What this means for race is that it is under an African leadership that the black and especially African masses have suffered the perpetuation, and in some respects worsening, of poverty, unemployment and social inequalities. The full weight of the relevant statistics today is a staggering indictment of ANC rule. Since 1994 the ANC promised major changes to conditions in the townships, under the electoral slogan of a 'Better Life for All'. Instead, conditions often got worse, while ANC officials at local level were stealing funds meant precisely for building a better life. There cannot be a bigger tragic betrayal than that.

But it is in fact much worse when we realise that the elderly black people who died between 1994 and today did so without realising and enjoying even the basic provisions in the Bill of Rights in the Constitution, which they were denied throughout their lives under various white racist regimes, and especially the worst one of NP rule between 1948 and 1994. No writer on post-apartheid SA has dealt with what is arguably the most critically important question about it. It is in fact probably the most painful and condemnable of the social realities which the black working-class majority endured under ANC rule after 1994. I have spoken enough of the atrociously poor living conditions in townships across SA. I argue that the ANC cannot even begin to explain this post-apartheid legacy without looking at its own history, what it stood for and its policies, both before and especially after 1994. But this assessment must be seen in relation to the tragic legacy of African nationalist rule across Africa since Ghana in 1957 became the first African country to gain independence. It has been nothing less than catastrophic. In this regard we must throw political correctness to the dogs and call things by their proper names: African nationalism across Africa has been a catastrophic failure.

In fact, this racialist mantra of the ANC has been totally discredited by the elitist nature of BEE and AA and the devastating impact of the neoliberal policies the ANC adopted after 1995, whose effects were also to rip apart and destroy the more homogeneous multi-class blackness which apartheid made possible. Instead of the needs of the African working class and the poor taking precedence after 1994, it was the African elite and middle class who benefited in the most palpable and grotesquely unfair manner, the social consequences of which are nakedly visible in townships where the 'Africans in particular' live. Even a rudimentary class analysis will unmistakably conclude that what the ANC has done is not only a betrayal, but a very conscious one. The leadership of the ANC, from the time of Mandela's leadership in the 1990s, knew exactly what they were doing and what the probable outcome would be.

That is why Neville Alexander was so scathing about how the ANC somersaulted during and after the 1990–3 negotiations. Motala and Vally quote his criticism of the leaders of the post-apartheid state for their '180 degree ideological and political turn ... coming to terms with the most barbaric consequences of capitalist or free-market dogma'.[18] But is this criticism justified from the point of view of the historical fact that the ANC was not opposed to capitalism per se, but to the racial restrictions it imposed in SA as it manifested itself after the negotiated settlement? I have come to the conclusion that whenever the ANC is criticised for a major U-turn during negotiations, we need to interrogate it against this fact.

This policy ambiguity of the ANC, which has existed from the 1950s onwards, must be seen against what was both possible and necessary to achieve in SA. I want to very briefly repeat: SA never needed an artificial and inherently contradictory two-stage approach to the struggle, as the ANC adhered to for over fifty years. And it is an indisputable fact that it was the middle-class African leadership of the ANC, with the help of the SACP, which placed SA on a trajectory which landed us in the mess we are in today. However, to argue in that way is incomplete and unsatisfactory until we can answer this key question: what were the alternatives in the 1990s when the Faustian pact between the ANC and NP was hatched and sealed? There was unfortunately no serious mass alternative.

However, this racialist mantra must be seen for what it turned out to be after 1994, when in office the ANC began to quickly look 'white' and to pursue its petit bourgeois class interests nakedly. In an interview Jeff Rudin[19] recalled how the African leaders of the ANC were in the forefront of arguing for an increase in the salaries of MPs. In other words, they fought to be paid higher salaries than the previous white MPs, believe it or not. But revealingly, according to Rudin, leading white members of the SACP, especially Brian Bunting, argued against this. However, they lost the battle. When Rudin protested to ANC MP Jannie Momberg about how that demand could be justified, he received the reply that if it did not happen, MPs would 'open themselves up to corruption.'[20] The objections were in vain. The ANC MPs got a salary increase when they assumed office. But how rich was that objection and how viciously ironical that thereafter we had an avalanche of corruption committed by ANC officials after 1994.

However, the earlier discussion about what Kasrils had to say about that period must be considered. My view is that the Faustian pact was not a foregone conclusion after Mandela was released and that it was a mistake for any organisation to look to the ANC for the appropriate or necessary policy choices or revolutionary leadership, especially given its own history and policies and the global balance of forces in the 1990. But it was Cosatu and the MDM which should shoulder the biggest responsibility for the compromises the ANC was allowed to make during the negotiations, especially on economic policies. In this regard, given its own interests and the immense power it held in the 1980s, it is Cosatu which must be held responsible and in particular its most senior leaders, especially Jay Naidoo, its then general secretary, who did not lift a finger to fight for Cosatu's independent representation at Codesa or utter one word about the dangers of its exclusion or just once publicly express disquiet with the clearly emerging neoliberal policy architecture in the mid-1990s, including Mandela's retreat from nationalisation in 1992, despite the fact that Cosatu was strongly pro-nationalisation in the 1990s.

But one can extend that analysis to ask why the members of Cosatu allowed its own leadership to close their eyes to what was going on and did not put mass pressure on the ANC to, at least, not compromise on the RDP and the FC. Had that been done, the outcomes of the negotiations might possibly have been quite different. But Cosatu did not put up a big fight during that critical period. That period, what happened and did not happen, is now history and cannot be reversed. Cosatu, the most powerful trade union federation in the history of this country, which led the struggles of civil society in the 1980s, should have played a direct role in the negotiations, on an independent platform and with its own mandate.

But unfortunately, Cosatu fell passively into the ANC alliance, alongside the Stalinist SACP, which was never expected in any case to play any other role than the subservient one it had played in relation to the ANC since the 1920s. The history of those relations dictated that the power lay with African nationalism and the ANC, notwithstanding a history replete with ignorance, inconsistency and confusion on policy matters. This point is crystal clear thus far in this book. How could the ANC claim that it was ready to govern SA when it did not even understand its history and when its analysis and understanding of it left much to be desired, especially for an impending ruling party? Till today, any study of the ANC in office will reflect its crass ignorance of broad policy matters, such as education, the economy, the political economy of public and basic services, social justice issues and so on.

Non-Racialism: A Critical Appraisal

Webster and Mawbey asserted that they did 'not see non-racialism as a distinct political project. Instead, it underpins to a greater or lesser extent virtually all of the political discourse'. They cite Jon Soske's analysis of the ambiguous and contested nature of the term non-racialism: it is not possible to 'reduce non-racialism to a single, definite idea (as) ... there are Marxist, liberal and African nationalist versions of (non-racialism)'.[21] While this widespread ideological architecture of non-racialism is true, it is more important to look at its political and organisational expression in SA. In this regard the approach of the ANC to non-racialism has been framed within an amorphous middle-class liberal discourse, as Mazibuko Jara argues: 'The ANC's nation building project, whether in its "rainbow nation" or "home for all" or "liberation of Africans in particular" versions, has not been based on a conscious political strategy which understands and addresses the structural socioeconomic base of national oppression. Where critical structural interventions could have been made, we saw equivocation and even retreat to racialised strategies.'[22]

Jara makes an important point about the ANC's superficial ideological characterisation of non-racialism, but we need to take this argument further. We must not detach the ANC's understanding of non-racialism from its petit bourgeois class aspirations and objectives, especially its post-1994 embrace of capitalist ideology. The two are inseparable, as is the racialisation Jara refers to. The same argument must be made about why therefore it was perfectly convenient for the ANC to retain the apartheid-racialised, four-population classification identities, namely white, Coloured, Indian and African, without seriously thinking about and engaging with civil society and academic think tanks about alternative approaches to redress. Several writers, including Neville Alexander and Jonathan Jansen, believe that there were alternative approaches.

But the ANC was not sincerely interested in alternatives because it was wedded, conveniently I believe, to the four-nation thesis approach, which then paved the way for its elitist BEE and AA policies, essential for the formation of a black elite and a considerable expansion of the ranks of the African middle class. I found my interview with Jeff Rudin insightful and revealing. He was an ANC researcher at the time and was in parliament at the time that the Employment Equity Act was being processed: 'I can now speak from direct knowledge and experience. There was a debate about whether or not to retain the apartheid categories and ... [objections were] unanimously dismissed. I'm talking about the ANC in parliament.' This is a severe indictment of the parliamentary party, as it rejected the principled opposition to the apartheid categories put forward by a Labour Study Group and the Labour Portfolio Committee. The question arises: why did the ANC leadership and members of parliament reject the recommendations of the Portfolio Committee?

The ANC's incredible and dangerous decision to retain the apartheid classification system exactly as it was in the past was a big blow to the building of any progressive notion of non-racialism. As a result, as Webster and Mawbey point out, 'twenty-three years beyond the demise of formal apartheid, we still continue to use four racially defined categories as central descriptors in our statistics and seek to deal with issues of redress using these statistics as a proxy for "advantaged" and "disadvantaged" because of a lack of alternative socioeconomic indicators.'[23]

However, I'm not sure what is meant here because there are alternatives on which redress could have been based, other than overtly racialist criteria. A useful book on this key question is by Adam Habib and Katrina Bentley, *Racial Redress and Citizenship in South Africa*. They make an intriguing assertion that 'deracialising this upper echelon of the class hierarchy is as important a moral and strategic imperative as is eroding the correlation between race and poverty in South Africa.'[24] The authors point this out as one of the problems of a class-based approach to AA. They say such an approach, given the racial profile of poverty, could deracialise the lower echelons of the class hierarchy, but not the upper ones. And therefore no redress programme founded on either race or class is likely to succeed, but one based on both is necessary: 'Only an initiative on more nuanced terms, incorporating both race and class, is capable of addressing South Africa's complex needs.'[25] Their book points to how complex redress is, whether we pursue a race or class approach to it. Filled with empirical data which captures this painful complexity, including AA approaches which marry race to class, the book is essential reading.

The main thing is that the book points out very clearly that there were various alternatives to pursue after 1994, and not only the ANC's race-based AA approach, even if they are very complex combinations. If we had gone that route, much would have been learnt by now about how such a redress programme could have been improved and strengthened. This is so precisely because, according to Mcebisi Ndletyana, AA 'suffers from a class bias. It benefits the educated black elite, not the entire black community. What of the grievance felt by the black working and under classes? Are they not deserving of a similar measure of social redress? Actually, the post-apartheid state, according to most literature, has opted for a policy regime which hardly addresses itself to the specific needs of the poor and unemployed.'[26] While I agree, Ndletyana puts the systemic, and in fact criminal and deliberate neglect of the needs of the black working class rather mildly. Besides, the fact that he bemoans the lack of 'similar measure of social redress' tells us unmistakably of his own liberal and multi-class approach to redress after 1994.

No, it is not that the basic needs of this class, which constitutes the majority of the population, should *also* have received much greater attention. Instead, it is that given the role of that class in South African history, that they bore the brunt of white racism for very long, were in the forefront of the struggle over many decades, and constituted the chief support base of the ANC , they therefore deserved to be the foremost priority of the ANC government. Instead, the unemployed, rural poor and marginalised urban residents still live in poverty and experience various forms of social deprivation. All forms of the media have been saturated with reports which graphically reflect appalling living conditions in black townships across SA. By all accounts it is incredibly sad, revealing and revolting what life under ANC rule has come to, 26 years later. Not even the most pessimistic predictions of life under a future ANC by more conservative and right-wing forces in SA could have envisaged the depth of the degeneration, a very debilitating, undignified and worsening social crisis afflicting the black working-class majority and the avalanche of corruption cases tumbling out of the Zondo Commission of Enquiry.

However, as for the ANC's decision to retain the apartheid population classification system, Webster and Mawbey don't really pursue what likely implications this would have for equitable redress and social justice. Perhaps more importantly, they don't interrogate why this decision was taken when there were feasible alternatives which could have been pursued, using socioeconomic indicators and existing statistics at the time to fashion a redress programme which would have in any case largely reflected existing race-based patterns of advantage and disadvantage. Instead, the ANC racialised redress in the worst imaginable racialist and indeed racist form. Besides, whereas post-apartheid society should have worked at dismantling apartheid racial identities, this decision served instead to reinforce them. And yet wealth and class are still largely reflected along racial lines.

However, what is most disturbing about this retention is that it has created a viciously competitive racial hierarchy of comparison of the possession of material objects, such as housing, cars, jobs, clothing, children's education and so on, especially among the black middle and elite classes. Social media are awash with such status symbols among its primarily middle-class audience. But it is not only the black middle classes. The black working class, especially its upper and more skilled and educated strata, have become as materialistic as the middle class. This must be seen as a result of the combination of various factors, such as the serious decline of trade unions over the past decade, the corruption in the ranks of its leadership, especially those in the investment arms, and the moribund state of the ANC alliance, of which Cosatu is still a part. In fact, the split in Cosatu is undoubtedly attributable to the concerted pressure it has faced from the ANC to toe the neoliberal line.

However, non-racialism has become a tortuously ill-defined conceptual terrain across our society, including in broad civil society. This confusion mainly stems from attempting a definition of the concept which abstracts and separates it from class and gender. This approach is impossible to do, especially in SA, given our historically embedded and combined race–class complexities. Both the white and black liberals and the ANC have failed to locate race and whiteness, especially when defined in more subjective and non-economic terms, within the historical framework of capitalism in SA. Ultimately, it is not helpful to be detained at the level of a scholarly definition of non-racialism that is not related to the structural components of capitalism, with which race has been intertwined since the mineral revolution. The primary reason why a study of race in SA must focus on that period is that it fashioned racist labour and community-controlling legislation as the decades unfolded. The mine compounds and hostels and black townships are all part of the infrastructural logic on which industrial capitalism was founded and built.

This more Marxist materialist bent in theoretical analysis of the race–class dynamic is useful not only to understand the role of race and racism in mining and industrial capitalism but in understanding the roots of all kinds of racism in SA, including the more subjective interpersonal racism, which we have seen so much of in SA over the past decade. While the numerous incidents of the latter type have exploded in the media over this period, there has been little or no analysis of the connections between the two. But if we go back in history and see how the towns, cities and urban areas developed in SA, white people – workers, supervisors and owners of capital – were all conditioned personally and subjectively by the colonial roots of race and racism.

White racism in SA, in all its different forms, is ultimately rooted in those historical processes beginning with Dutch slavery and colonialism in the latter half of the 17th century. That is why I devoted quite a lot of time and space to trace that history and show how it is organically linked to contemporary SA by many threads, perceptible and imperceptible. In fact, the birth of the concept of non-racialism lies with the British missionaries, in their struggles against the Dutch and their virulent racism against the Khoisan, Coloured and African people in the Cape Colony. The concept of non-racialism has white liberal roots in the Cape.

Unless we link non-racialism to the struggle for social justice and against capitalism, which systematically denies it, it can be and has been used and hijacked for various purposes, even for counterrevolutionary purposes. And it is precisely for this reason that the organisations and individuals who aim to fundamentally transform our society so that everyone can live good, comfortable and healthy lives must acknowledge and articulate the race–class linkages, not only in theory, but more importantly in programmatic terms. If not, the social crisis of black poverty, unemployment and related social indignities will persist, regardless of how polished, progressive, clear and attractive the concept of non-racialism is made to become. It is our intertwined history of race and class which itself imposes such a definition of non-racialism.

Any definition which deliberately defines it in ways which do not reckon with capitalism is looking at reforms not to fundamentally change the capitalist system but to deracialise it and make it more appealing – with all the usual claptrap about equal opportunities, hard work and trickle-down bourgeois economics. It is worth noting that the World Bank itself rejected trickle-down economics and acknowledged that huge inequalities are a major challenge.[27] What is happening globally with the current unprecedented economic crisis is that while politically it is manifested by the explosion of nationalistic and racial currents, especially of a right-wing kind, at its roots are pretty straightforward economic, social and material interests. People are fighting around the world, caught in the clutches of this devastating crisis, to either defend what they've got or to win some material gains against the storms it has unleashed, which have eroded the value of whatever money and resources they had, a truly dog-eat-dog and catch-as-catch-can situation, signs of which are all over the world, included in the West. Capitalism faces a mortal crisis in fact, which is evident in so many ways. Just reading newspapers makes this fact clear.

Therefore, this crisis will not be dealt with and resolved by refining definitions of non-racialism or opposing non-racialism in favour of an anti-racism approach, which suggests a more systemic approach to it. This is why I would only cautiously welcome the view of Motala and Vally that 'unless the use of "non-racial" is attached to the struggle against all forms of racism, all talk of non-racialism would remain vacuous. Making the distinction between non-racialists who are in reality no more than multi-racialists and those who are steadfastly "anti-racists, remains the critical thinking factor"'.[28] But there are serious problems with this approach to non-racialism, even if it is hooked onto a broader and more systemic approach located in the term 'anti-racism'. I am, however, not impressed with a semantic squabble – because that is what it amounts to – if the debate is simply about whether it is a non-racial or anti-racist struggle. In fact, what has transpired in post-apartheid SA helps to clarify what is really at stake in this terminological debate. It is the political economy that underpins it. What this means is that we cannot resolve the matter as Motala and Vally suggest without simultaneously raising the central problem of capitalism in SA.

That is why to remain steadfastly 'anti-racist' rather than 'non-racialist' is not the critical factor, as it still leaves the political economy which frames anti-racism as the real critical factor undefined and unresolved. In fact, this contention arises directly from the race–class nexus. The 'class', with which race is linked, is nothing other than dealing with the questions of political economy and social justice which arise from the material conditions of racism. That is why one of the big theoretical and political weaknesses of the BCM is the neglect of class issues, even after the shift by Azapo to 'scientific socialism' at its founding conference in 1978. Neville Alexander was himself acutely aware of this limitation when he criticised the failure of the BC movement to 'understand clearly the relationship between colour-caste and class' because of its preoccupation with racial prejudice.[29]

In fact, it is the organisational and political fate of Azapo and the National Forum, of which it was a leading member, which serves to reinforce the point. Azapo was strongly critical of non-racialism and instead proposed an anti-racism approach which included an anti-capitalist stance, but they declined into virtual oblivion after the 1994 elections. I have concluded that it is an academic and political mistake to emphasise or prefer either the non-racial or anti-racist concept, notwithstanding the liberal origins of non-racialism. It makes little difference whether we talk of either non-racialism or anti-racism, notwithstanding the history of the debate in SA between the non-racialism of the multi-class UDF and the socialist anti-racism of Azapo. It cuts no ice, especially as regards grassroots communities, which are instead preoccupied with daily needs and related struggles which have intensified today. And notwithstanding the liberal origins of non-racialism and anti-capitalist connotation of anti-racism, it appears of little more than academic interest whether we talk of or promote either non-racialism or anti-racism, especially since the non-racial concept does not preclude a socialist or anti-capitalist orientation.

But it is only by linking the question of non-racialism to political economy that the pervasive absence of social justice is sorely evident after 1994. In other words, the question of non-racialism must always be linked to political economy. It is those depressing pictures of poverty, squalor, raw sewage running down township streets, pit latrines, chemical toilets, prepaid meters, jobless despair and so many more debilitating social realities which we have seen so much on our television screens. It is that set of conditions which even an identified anti-racist struggle will have to deal with and resolve. But contrary to what they have tried to say from time to time, the ANC has fundamentally failed to understand the South African society we have had since the mineral revolution, the consequences of which reshaped it decisively and irrevocably.

Very briefly, this permanent revolutionary approach[30] had already suggested by the turn of the 20th century that the lot of black people was so inseparably tied to those consequences that even the most basic changes to those conditions required a struggle against capitalism itself. In other words, the race–class nexus already began to take root then. This was not on the agenda of the ANC when it was founded in 1912. Its focus was that Africans should be included as citizens in the Union of South Africa, with rights such as the vote. And when they were snubbed by Afrikaans and English-speaking white politicians, the SANNC still excluded the Coloureds and Indians by a conscious decision. In other words, the ANC was formed on a completely racialist and even arguably racist basis, which was the complete antithesis to non-racialism.

Besides, by the time the ANC was formed in 1912 the capitalist thrust of our society and those race–class links were already firmly in place. But at its birth and subsequently, the ANC failed to understand the meaning of those processes for any struggle against the new order ushered in by the Union of South Africa in 1910. It is only with the FC in 1955 that the ANC began to appreciate the race–class links more, which resulted in the economic clauses of the FC that deal with the mineral wealth of the country, nationalisation and so on. But this radical turn, as we have seen so many times since then, was not decisively a fundamental reorientation from the earlier more reformist middle-class ANC.

Its reformism continued after 1955 but now armed with radical phraseology which it utilised when it was opportunistically suitable. The equivocation and opportunism of the ANC of today are rooted in the 1950s. Study the ANC in office from 1994 and you will find the very same haphazard policy fluctuations, as we have seen again on the question of land reform and redistribution and the role of the Reserve Bank over the past few years. Writing about the approach of the ANC since 1994 regarding questions of race, national identity and the NQ, Motala and Vally argue that 'This confusion is partly attributable to the unfamiliarity of those who engage in these issues with the historical development of the present state of affairs in South Africa.'[31] They are referring to the failure to link questions of race and identity to political economy, and how these were inextricably linked to capitalist development in SA.

We can say the very same thing basically about the ANC regarding just about every major policy question after 1994, when the fundamental policy weakness and confusion played itself out. But it is its Africanist majoritarian chauvinism which is absolutely the biggest threat to a more progressive definition of non-racialism, especially one in which the better life for all that the ANC repeatedly promised but failed to deliver becomes a reality. In this regard, there will be no better life for the impoverished black masses until the ANC adequately satisfies the most basic needs of water, sanitation and electricity, without termination of these services because of non-payment, especially in a situation of high unemployment, which has been aggravated by the impact of Covid-19.

But it is by tying non-racialism, by definition, to the conditions of people's lives that it becomes more meaningful, especially given the race–class dynamics of our history. Only by concretising this definition can we distinguish the chaff from the wheat about the kind of society we need to build in the future, which abolishes poverty, unemployment and multiple social scourges. If the ANC does not realise that they have to put their money where their mouths are and prioritise the provisions in the Bill of Rights in our constitution and eliminate the caveat which links the realisation of those rights to the availability of resources within a neoliberal economy which in advance imposes budgetary limitations, they might as well abolish the constitution.

What this approach to non-racialism really means is that any definition must stand or fall by what it offers to deal with and combat poverty and inequalities and the crass commercialisation and commodification of basic human needs. Michael Morris of the Institute of Race Relations (IRR) recently usefully cited Colin Bundy on non-racialism in his column: 'As long as Khayelitsha or Alexandra exist, how do we achieve nonracialism?'[32] As liberal as the IRR is, that is a very important point, but the irony of it, which Morris appears completely to fail to realise, is that taken to its logical conclusion, given the way in which capitalism developed in SA, to fundamentally transform those and all the other poor black townships into anything even approximating the standards of living and infrastructure in today's black middle-class areas has proven impossible after 1994.

In conclusion two things must be pointed out about the politics and ideology of non-racialism and the kind of populist humanism it appears to artificially generate and to which even Marxist writers such as Alexander at times succumbed. The prominence of the discourse of non-racialism and its contentious nature, especially after 1994, has grown in inverse proportion to the dominance of race and racism in our history and is also generally linked not only to liberation from political oppression and white racism but also to the social aspirations of black people during apartheid.

Alexander uncritically refers to the promotion of an amorphous 'social cohesion'.[33] But just what exactly is it? In fact, however it is defined, social cohesion is a pretty useless concept, contrary to what people want to make of it, unless it is intrinsically linked to notions of social justice. Only in this way can we root social cohesion talk in more concrete ways which deliver the social justice the black majority yearns for. But once you relate such vague terms to questions of social justice you not only concretise it in knowing what we are talking about but are also able to measure how effective it is in terms of securing the rights, for example, in the Bill of Rights in the constitution. When definitions, especially of a transformative and redress nature, are very clear, we are able to measure the steps taken to change things more easily. I find social cohesion a very unhelpful concept because it is far too vague and tells us nothing about what exactly in society is cohesive and what and whose specific interests it serves.

However, when Crain Soudien asserts that the 'politics of non-racialism' has served us well into post-apartheid SA,[34] I'm not too sure if that is true. I'm reminded now of the fierce ideological battle between the UDF and the NF in the 1980s, between the UDF's notion of 'non-racialism' and the NF's 'anti-racism'. Then it was very clear in the relevant literature that the NF position of anti-racism was, unlike that of the UDF, explicitly anti-capitalist. So much was the UDF an internal expression in SA of the banned and exiled ANC that the UDF basically continued the ANC line in our politics, including the ideological battles between aiming for a non-racial post-apartheid democracy, which leaves the capitalist system intact, or an anti-racist socialist Azania as the NF put it.

With the benefit of hindsight, the NF was right and the UDF-ANC wrong. However, this difference flowed from the fundamental analytical and programmatic differences between these organisations, which basically revolved around the permanent revolutionary approach to the struggle in SA, which regarded the anti-racist and anti-capitalist struggles as one inseparable struggle, and the UDF-ANC-SACP approach, which placed a disproportionate emphasis on race, racism and apartheid at the expense of the social and class interests of the black working-class majority. The results are tragically woven into the post-apartheid social fabric, as we have seen many times thus far in this work. The biggest problem with Azapo and the NF was the lack of a mass base.

But I often sense a reliance on vague and celebratory language in Soudien's otherwise useful and insightful work on race and racism. In some of his work, especially around concepts of race and non-racialism, he basically flogs the definition to such an extent as to create subjective and abstract slices of conceptual meaning. Trotsky writes about this abstractionist danger. In other words, it becomes in a sense a case of intellectual masturbation, which does not get you anywhere closer to a more precise definitional clarity about non-racialism, especially for purposes of social transformation. Instead, you end up with a supposedly disaggregating analysis which leaves you no wiser about a more precise and concretised definition than before, one that would help realise the social changes it calls for and envisages.

With all due respect to Soudien, I believe that his work on race suffers from the emphasis on an appealing but abstract 'humanism'. If we are to take the fight for non-racialism or anti-racism seriously in ways that are meaningful for social transformation and social justice, that strategic focus tends to be lost in a somewhat abstract, too generalist and even esoteric approach. In any case, I find the language of humanism very vague and obscure in the field of critical analysis. It is because the history of non-racialism has been decked in so many colours, languages and political idioms that I desire greater clarity and less humanist obfuscation and distraction. This tendency by Soudien to lapse into abstraction and subjectivism can be illustrated by just a few examples of language he uses in the discourse of non-racialism, which for me beg precise definitional clarity. There is too much of a personalised subjectivity in 'the compulsion to live a fully ethical life', 'the restoration of African cosmology, in all its multiplicity and complexity, to its fully human and global place' and 'knowing oneself in deeply ethical ways, scrutiny, self-scrutiny of all one's conceits, pretensions, prejudices and biases'.[35]

The main point is that the debate about non-racialism has been around for about a century in SA. Hence, the question is this: should the worst social crisis in post-apartheid SA not enable a more rooted and concrete definition of non-racialism which helps us to get to grips with the race–class or racism–capitalism nexus and its destructive social consequences, which have been overwhelmingly dominant in our history?

I also think we should drop the debate about whether it is a struggle for non-racialism or anti-racism that we should rally behind. The debate may be of academic interest but is less relevant to developing a programme of action which unites mass organisations to confront and change the material conditions of poverty, unemployment and inequalities that the majority black working class has faced under apartheid and continues to face under ANC rule.

Still on the question of language and discourses, I have often asked myself if the amorphous nature of many of the ANC's policies, its history and understandings has influenced to some degree the discourses and debates in SA, including those of academics. For example, just what do Webster and Pampallis mean when they state that 'The goal of one *united nation* living *prosperously* under a constitutional democracy remains elusive.'[36] How on earth can 'one nation' even be contemplated when South African society is today arguably more fragmented, especially by the impacts of the race–class social engineering which neoliberalism has wrought since 1994, which massively extended the ranks of the black middle class and gave birth to an immensely rich but tiny black elite? We are in fact further away from such a unified nation than we even were under apartheid.

The ANC has historically been riddled with policy and terminological ambiguity and inconsistency, as I have shown thus far, especially in relation to the FC. Today, I argue that any fight for non-racialism, even within the tradition of the FC, has been largely betrayed, even its limited social democratic provisions, especially in relation to the fulfilment of basic needs and the right to jobs, education and culture. But probably more than anything else, the unstoppable and increasingly more combustible black township protests since June 2004 have exposed that fact. The aspirations and dreams of the black working-class majority have gone up with the flames that are so often a searing sight in those townships.

On the contrary, I believe that as the social and political crisis in the ANC deepens, as it will probably happen, the ANC will be so torn asunder by it that it will not have the capacity and resources to deal with it and instead SA will descend into a worsening crisis, whose resolution will require a totally new government consisting of the best representatives of the trade unions, community organisations and other organs of civil society and political formations to the left of the ANC alliance, such as the Numsa-led Socialist Workers Revolutionary Party (SWRP). It is only from these forces, after the nightmare of ANC rule for the black working class, that a genuinely non-racial or anti-racist mass-based anti-capitalist party will arise to deal with such grave problems which only an explicitly socialist party will be resolutely able to do.

I want to refer to some interesting and useful research by Fiona Anciano on the problems and prospects of non-racialism in four ANC branches in Johannesburg. The research paints a seriously unhealthy picture of 'non-racialism' within these branches, especially in the biggest Coloured township of Eldorado Park. Gross alienation, particularly of Coloured members, and a deep sense that they have been neglected and marginalised by the untrammelled dominance of African members are vividly evident in the article.

Anciano noted that while respondents acknowledged that the ANC supported non-racialism in theory, 'it was clear, almost across the board that members feel there are significant problems with race relations within the ANC, at all levels. The strongest concerns about race relations came from Eldorado Park, followed by Sandton, Lenasia and to a much lesser extent Soweto.' It is among the 'minority' Coloureds and Indians that the alienation is greatest. She identifies a general unease 'that the party disproportionately supports and promotes Africans'. Many Coloured, Indian and white members feel that 'there is no space for them in the ANC and their views and skills are not valued in the party'. Quotes from her respondents included such sentiments as 'there is definitely racism taking place there'; 'they don't regard Coloured people as important'; 'we are cannon fodder for getting votes'; 'it feels like we are sitting in a PAC meeting'; 'in the ANC racism is very strong and it can be proven any day anywhere', and 'the ANC is perpetuating what the NP did'.[37]

This alienation of Coloured members in ANC branches occurs in the same township where the ANC has repeatedly over the past two decades lost to the DA in elections. I have little or no doubt that there is a degree of common ground between the alienation of Coloured members of the ANC and Coloureds who vote for the DA. Having grown up in Coloured communities and having lived for over a decade in Cape Town, I have experienced growing alienation from the ANC since 1994 among Coloured people across classes. A combination of aggrievement with basic services in townships and the ongoing and deep problems with the ANC's Africanist slant in the application of its AA policies has taken its toll on both the working and middle classes.

To reinforce beyond doubt that a new African racism is at work in the ANC, Jessie Duarte, its deputy secretary-general, in a speech in Soweto accused the party of being 'tribalistic and racist'. 'We are racist in the ANC because we marginalise people who are not black African people; keep them out of the ANC at all costs. And put one or two of them as tokens...'.[38] She added: 'We won't accept the fact that non-racialism is a core value of the ANC.' She went on to say that some members of the ANC argued that Coloured people benefited from apartheid, to which she responded by asking if they have been to Coloured working-class townships, such as Newclare or Riverlea Extension. Why would such a senior leader make such serious accusations of the ANC, unless it is true?

It is also very interesting to take note of the fact that Ramaphosa himself has commented on the declining value of non-racialism in the ANC. He told an election rally of the ANC in Pretoria early in 2019, made up of mainly white Afrikaners, that there were problems: 'Yes, there was a time when we weakened on this (non-racialism) and where coloured people in our movement told us they feel unwelcomed ... we were also told this by our Indian and white colleagues ... the ANC must be non-racial.'[39] I have spent much of this book providing a contextual history of the origins of these problems, which will persist as long as the debilitating resource constraints of the neoliberal policies of the ANC continue.

As argued, the extensive and ongoing debates about a definition of non-racialism have serious limitations. This endless academic exercise must also relate to the fact that the social realities which have historically accompanied race and racism, out of which the concept and struggle for non-racialism emerge, have in fact worsened in neoliberal post-apartheid SA. One important example for now will suffice. A news story in the *Mail & Guardian* in January 2020 concluded that water services in black townships were worse than in 1994.[40] And a news report in the same paper a week later showed that there are still 12,000 bucket toilets in SA.[41]

My PhD research conclusively confirmed not only that poor sanitation has in fact been an even bigger problem in SA since 1994 than lack of water supply, but that regarding human indignities it ranks higher than lack of water. Nothing, not even a lack of water, distressed residents as much as lack of decent sanitation or its total absence when households ran out of water and could not flush the toilets and therefore had to defecate somewhere outside the house.

This section closes with an important insight by David Everatt, which flows directly from the central problem of Africanist majoritarian chauvinism I have identified in this work. Critiquing the progressive white left of the 1950s, he argues that 'few, if any, managed to move beyond the general notion of equality under African leadership – exactly the approach of all post-1994 governments. That remains a partial, under-developed and ham-fisted interpretation of what non-racialism could and should be.'[42] If only more scholars and activists within the African community could acknowledge this serious problem, we would be much better off, with a more effective definition and practice of non-racialism in so far as the NQ is concerned, and a healthier understanding of the much more important social justice issues to which it is ultimately deeply linked.

An important point on non-racialism was made by Amanda Alexander and Andile Mngxitama: 'The ANC's idea of non-racialism has proven particularly well-suited to legitimising a neoliberal market-based project.' Who could even begin to attempt to deny one of the most palpably clear and irrefutable realities of SA since 1994 under ANC rule? They aptly conclude: 'The ANC mobilises race to get access to capital. The BEE programme mobilises the common historical experience of oppression and exclusion of black South Africans to carve for itself a slice of white-owned wealth.'⁴³ Contrast that picture with the massive squalor, poverty and unemployment and related social miseries of the majority of black people in the townships of SA.

Last, but certainly not least, I wish to pose arguably one of the most explosive questions in relation to the unresolved notions of non-racialism and anti-racism: how do we even begin to attempt to reconcile, however we define these terms, without addressing the raging xenophobia that has stalked SA for the past decade in particular? I proceed from the premise that xenophobia is the other side of the coin of racism. For as long as xenophobia persists in SA, all attempts to iron out the meaning of non-racialism will be hamstrung by a fundamental contradiction. There can be no doubt at all that the rise of xenophobia in SA has bedevilled and complicated the struggles for a non-racial and anti-racist world.

The savage violence in black townships against people (I don't like the term 'foreigner') from other parts of Africa has muddied the waters of the struggles for non-racialism and in fact severely compromised it. It is not just an unpalatable but horrific contradiction confronting the struggles of black people in the townships, no matter what the issues are, because unless every demand and right they struggle for applies equally to people from other countries in Africa, there will be both no peace and no social justice. Today the struggle for social justice in SA will mean little or nothing unless anti-xenophobia lies at its heart. Xenophobic violence, including by elements in the black working-class majority, is as bad as, if not worse than, what the former white racist regime did against black people.

But I have written at length on how the impact of the neoliberal policies of the ANC – which has resulted in increasing black poverty, joblessness, homelessness and related social miseries – has in fact created the material conditions for a destructive xenophobia and therefore been a major contributor to it in SA: 'Ultimately – and this is the heart of the tragedy – it is poor and working-class people at each other's throats, while those whose policies are responsible for this situation watch on.'⁴⁴ What has made that objective situation much worse is the indisputably xenophobic public comments that various leading figures in SA, including several ANC leaders too, have made. The late King Zwelithini went as far as to urge foreigners to 'please go back to their countries'.⁴⁵ Premier of Gaunteng, David Makhura, was also accused of xenophobia when he stated: 'In some specific crimes, specific nationalities are involved in some specific crimes, (such as) drugs, violent crimes and murders including cash in transit heists.'[46]

This is not the kind of statement one expects of Makhura, especially in a province which has by far the most African immigrants. He also said that 'There are countries that must pay for their citizens to use our health services. Those countries must pay ... their citizens get almost everything from South Africa.'[47] Quite clearly, the pressure of neoliberal budgetary constraints is reflected in these statements, but instead of dealing with it he turns to very sensitive matters which could worsen xenophobic sentiments among black South Africans in the townships and indeed worsen the violence against people from other countries in Africa. These budgetary constraints which affect social relations between people in the townships are evident across SA and are largely the reason for the xenophobic attacks. But the ANC has never once directed attention to these problems. African migrants are an easier target, which in turn feeds into xenophobia.

Dali Mpofu's Intervention

In 2017 a very significant event occurred in parliament. Floyd Shivambu, deputy leader of the Economic Freedom Fighters (EFF), waged an angry attack on Ismail Momoniat, deputy director-general of the Treasury, for his alleged dominance of the standing committee on finance and marginalisation of Africans in the Treasury. But what further racialised the matter was a subsequent tweet by Shivambu about a 1990 report which investigated allegations that Indians and whites in the MDM were responsible for a lack of unity. There was no explicit finding in the report that the allegations were verifiable and indisputable facts. But as often happens with matters of race, he opportunistically used that report. A flurry of reactions occurred on social media and it quickly became a major topic of discussion across society.

We have seen race used for thoroughly opportunistic and in fact self-seeking reasons in this debacle. The question that logically arises is this: if indeed Momoniat was too domineering and therefore a problem that required attention, why could Shivambu not have drawn attention to it and requested an investigation into the matter without racialising it by specific reference to Indians? Malema and the EFF did the same thing when they had problems with Pravin Gordhan when he was commissioner of the SARS some years back. They alleged he was part of an 'Indian cabal' which was targeting Malema and the EFF. But the crux of the issues Malema had with SARS concerned tax and money matters. Malema's attempts at tax evasion and news that he owed SARS many millions of rands have been widely reported. Every time there are financial interests involved, the EFF and Malema particularly are very quick to resort to race, in one form or another.

Why? Because in a country with our demography and serious problems of a lack of education and the debillitating legacy of illiteracy, this tactic could 'work' at the level of public propaganda. It is the same set of reasons why the African masses continue to vote the ANC back into power, despite an abundance of evidence of it having failed dismally and repeatedly to 'build a better life for all', its earlier electoral slogan. The same set of reasons ultimately lies behind the former president Kgalema Motlanthe's repeated complaints about the lack of political education and understanding among the ordinary membership of the ANC. He spoke often about this in interviews for his biography.[48] This is for me one of the most neglected questions about SA and ANC rule after 1994, probably because to air those undeniable facts would be one of the no-go areas of political correctness.

Neville Alexander once spoke to me at length about this major problem and also wrote about it. He used the words 'herd mentality' to describe this problem and, whether we like to admit it or not, it resides primarily among the African masses, mainly in the rural areas. There are millions of people there who are poor, unemployed, illiterate or with minimal formal education, trying to eke out a living from the little fertile land they might have access to. This is the main reason why the ANC is returned to power after each election, though the tide began turning seriously against it since the 2016 local government elections, when it lost both Johannesburg and Tshwane to a coalition of the DA and the EFF. But it is also returned to power because the 17 million recipients of social grants are expected to support the ANC in elections. Moeletsi Mbeki has written quite a bit about this phenomenon, arguing that this factor is largely why the ANC remains in power.[49]

I do not believe that the ANC would still have been in power were it not for these combined reasons: lack of knowledge, inadequate education, the absence of class consciousness, in the Marxian sense of a class-for-itself, among the majority African masses, and the social grants they receive. But whether the ANC would lose power if those circumstances did not obtain, and in the absence of an alternative mass party of the working class, is also not a foregone conclusion.

However, responding to the news about Shivambu's clash with Momoniat in parliament and how it was racialised by Shivambu's tweet, I wrote:

> I get a profound sense that contrary to its official affinity with and pretensions to 'Marxism-Leninism' and the leftist rhetoric it so often rants about in order to secure a mass base among the African youth – the EFF is deep down a narrow African nationalist organisation ... But more than that if you conduct a study of the EFF you'll find a naked and narrow Africanist majoritarian chauvinism rampant in it, the fierce but brutal logic of which is that since the African people are the overwhelming majority they can say and do anything they wish to and basically to hell with the rest of society.[50]

The media was generally scathing about this arguably racist attack by Shivambu and rightly so, including the newspapers with black editors. This was important since it graphically showed, especially the stories carried in the *Mail & Guardian* and *Daily Maverick*, how race is often used for ulterior motives which have in fact little or nothing to do with it. In other words, given a race-saturated history, race can be a big and effective diversionary tactic to use against opponents and it is indeed done so ruthlessly. That is exactly what Shivambu did.

The NQ is right now arguably in the worst intellectual and political space after 1994, thanks to the narrowly Africanised and elitist BEE. It was reported in 2017 that these African nationalist reactionaries – bent on using race to secure the utmost riches for themselves and not for the African masses – declared war on Indian and Coloured businesses in KZN because of the competitive edge and market share they might have.[51] Significantly, it was reported that it was 'radical economic transformation', that give-away opportunistic BEE business rhetoric, which drove this unconstitutional attempt to alter regional legislation in KZN to its advantage. But so much was it at odds with the constitution that Treasury declined the request.

However, it is an article by Dali Mpofu, then chairperson of the EFF, which revealed far more than what took place in parliament and Shivambu's tweet. The article by Mpofu in the *Daily Maverick*, very interestingly, was titled 'On the Indian Question in SA: A Response to Mob Psychologists'. The object of his attack was several journalists and commentators, including myself, whom he refers to as 'quasi-intellectuals', in contrast to 'the EFF's political and ideological telescope which is one of the most dynamic and superior forms of insight, one which sees into the future.' As if that was not a grotesque manifestation of intellectual arrogance and conceit from a EFF leader who really does not know what he is talking about, Mpofu promised us to 'stand firm on principle and take time to *enlighten* society on the National Question'[52] (emphasis added).

In my 47 years of political activism, in one form or another, and many years of intense study and in related debates, I have never come across a more vain, pretentious and obtuse display of intellectual vacuity, masquerading as great and inspiring wisdom. Not only that, his and the EFF's wisdom has a further clairvoyant bonus which it has to offer us: it can see into the future! But the confusion is immense and pitiable. This should not be surprising because across Africa the forays of African nationalism into socialist ideology were often half-baked or opportunistic. The problem is that all nationalisms have a built-in vulnerability to being manipulated for ulterior material and class interests, but under the rubric of the 'nation', of 'us' and 'we'. That's what we have learnt from the reign of African nationalist rule in Africa for decades. The result was in almost every country a self-serving elite which got rich from the coffers of the state.

Mpofu's tirade recalls the cheap psychology Malema and the EFF began with a few years back. In several places they began to invoke a deliberate discursive and political tactic to elicit sympathy from the public and mainly from other African people. Suddenly we were lectured about the 'pain' of the black or African child in this or that matter. The idea of using an analogy of a 'child' and especially an 'African child' and linking it to the emotion of 'pain' was calculated to secure maximum sympathy and support for whatever the main point was. Hence, Mpofu claims: 'In the realm of the mob, an African child cannot criticise *overly dominant minorities* unless they are running away from corruption or some sort of wrongdoing' (emphasis added). This racialist language reminded me of the overtly racist comments made by Jimmy Manyi about Cape Town Coloureds. However, the image of a pained African child has become a give-away sentimental ruse of the EFF, hoping to tug at our heartstrings.

In an interview with Bobby Godsell, he had an interesting take on how race has been constructed after 1994 when the ANC came to power:

> Now race plays a different role; race is a useful propagandising or communicating vehicle because you can quite often gain command over a situation by giving it a race label. It is funny, but the higher the elite climbed up the social or corporate ladder the more they spoke of race. Right now, at the bottom of society people don't talk about race. In the middle there is this contestation, am I securely in the middle class, am I inside and on top; on the top there is this constant desire to play the race card, to some degree for understandable functional reasons, but often also for self-serving opportunistic ones.[53]

That race is not a big matter among ordinary black people in townships was also recognised by Moeletsi Mbeki when I interviewed him. He was emphatic that race and racism discourses were dominated by the aspiring black middle class.

But on the question of race, what has been happening in Cape Town is horrendous. The unprecedented gang warfare on the Cape Flats has claimed the lives of several thousand Coloured people over the past three years, including that of children. What has been allowed by this ANC state to happen on the Cape Flats has never happened anywhere else in the entire history of SA. It is nothing less than criminal neglect of those areas. The ANC, which has control of the army and police, would never have allowed such levels of death to occur in African townships, because there are votes to be lost were that to happen. However, on the Cape Flats, which has helped put the DA in power in the Western Cape and keep it there, the loss of lives appeared not serious enough to warrant decisive state intervention. So, when Mpofu and the EFF talk about the pain of an African child, they appear oblivious to the protracted and savage war Coloured children have been exposed to daily for very long on the Cape Flats and in other Coloured townships, such as Westbury,

Newclare, Eldorado Park and Reiger Park. His 'African child', it appears, resides only in African townships.

Mpofu then strays into a long lecture on the EFF Manifesto and Indian people, which is seriously reflective of a lack of knowledge of their origins and history in SA and of their social composition. But the most intriguing and alarming part was his attempt to explain the stance of the EFF in the clash against Momoniat in parliament by invoking the NQ. Mpofu's knowledge of the NQ, I discovered, is worse than his lack of knowledge and understanding of Indian people in SA. In fact, his attempt to denigrate the knowledge of others on the NQ and 'enlighten' us is shot through with an abysmal lack of knowledge of the NQ in general and particularly in SA. I have argued that we cannot seriously and authoritatively talk about race and the NQ without having gained an incisive knowledge of South African history and how that history has shaped the state we live in.

However, it is how Mpofu latched onto the ANCYL of old to legitimise his and the EFF's shallow African nationalism approach to the NQ which is the biggest bone of contention I have. Here he is at one with rabid African nationalism, but of the most backward kind, which argues for the affirmation of African leadership, regardless of its policies, ideology, programme and capacity, but simply because Africans happen to be in the numerical majority. In this day and age such chauvinistic African nationalism, left unchecked, is going to destroy SA. But it is deeply ingrained in the political psyche of just about every African political organisation in our history. The problem lies, however, not only in a democracy based on sheer demographic weight but in the policies African nationalism in power has pursued: liberal or neoliberal policies, at the behest of the former colonial power, Britain, the US, the IMF and the World Bank.

Mpofu's article deliberately laid a disproportionate emphasis on Africanism ('Africa for the Africans', old ANCYL and PAC talk). He went on to cite Sobukwe and Lembede on the central importance of African leadership, almost for its own sake and regardless of anything else. He also ignored the fact that to insist on African leadership in advance, especially in a supposed constitutional non-racial democracy, was itself arguably racialist and racist: 'On African leadership this generation (the ANCYL of the 1940s) emphatically said … that "the Africans are nationally oppressed and that they can win freedom through a national liberation movement led by the Africans themselves". This marked the qualified acceptance by Mandela and others of Indian participation in the struggle "as long as they do not impede our liberation struggle".'[54]

So damnable is Mpofu's line of racialist thought, and the attempt to secure historical legitimacy for it by invoking past leaders of the ANCYL, that one has to pause to enable its full implications to settle in. And that this happened in 2018 and was led by the EEF gives serious food for thought. Bear in mind too that this nationalist and racialist ethos comes from a purportedly 'Marxist-Leninist' party. But 'Marxism-Leninism' today is not what it was in the days of Lenin and Trotsky. Besides, it has no truck whatsoever with African nationalism, though the SACP tried to marry the two since the 1920s. However, it never 'worked'. All strands of nationalist politics which undermine, neglect and obscure class exploitation and contradictions in society, which is exactly what the role of the ANCYL and ANC was, are anathema to revolutionary Marxism. That much must be very clear.

What has happened to the interests and needs of the black working-class majority under ANC rule shows unmistakably what the politics and ideology of African nationalism have done. It is a petit bourgeois politics which is far more interested in securing state power and its immense resources for the top leaders and their families, friends and related networks of patronage. That is exactly what the ANC has done with the power the black masses who voted for it has given them. In fact, where this decadent nationalist politics is most crassly and conspicuously seen is in the sharp and deplorable contrast between the material conditions of the African masses and the top elite leadership of the ANC and the SACP and all levels of the state and the SOEs.

Now compare that picture of the ANC in power with the record of the EFF leadership itself since it won seats in parliament in the 2014 elections. Space limits prevent me listing all the many instances in which the media have reported allegations of corruption involving the EFF leadership, especially Malema and Shivambu. In fact, Mpofu's article is one of the crassest manifestations of how African nationalism, in all its guises, has both overtly and covertly used the African masses as little more than electoral cannon fodder to secure and maintain political and state power in its own class interests. This, alongside what has happened with the creation of a black economic elite, is very instructive about African nationalism at work in power.

Mpofu and the EFF – forget completely about all the 'Marxist-Leninist' rhetoric they often spew – are using African nationalism to secure and extend their power at the expense of the interests of the same African masses who put them in office. What separates the ANC from the EFF is little other than the leftist rhetoric of the latter, which is an orchestrated cover for their material class interests. Like the ANC, the EFF has learnt that the representative power of politics and parliament enables access to huge state resources with which to line their pockets. Political power in the various arms and levels of the state enables access to a staggering fiscus, which can in fact enable access to the proceeds of corruption, which are incomparably greater than anything they would have earned in top jobs in the corporate sector. Look at the colossal amounts looted in SA by the ANC in office to get a sense of this point, all under the cover of representational politics and a constitutional democracy. Until you get caught and apprehended, it is an unbeatable scheme for dizzying self-enrichment in the name of democracy.

On the other hand, the key players of RET, which emerged in the latter part of Zuma's presidency, appear to be yet another get-rich scheme using radical rhetoric, as the EFF has done, to access state resources. The extensive and protracted networks of self-enrichment involving factions in the ANC and EFF run so deep that only forensic and journalistic investigations can unearth them, which is precisely why the EFF hates the probing and prying eyes of the media so much. That is why, with all its warts, the media are a fundamentally important asset in SA in exposing and combating state-centred corruption. Here too we have seen how the EFF has used race to hit out at the exposures by white journalists working for *Daily Maverick*. The opportunistic utility of the race discourse for ulterior motives, which ultimately has nothing to do with race and is as often related to one or other material interests, is legendary.

The increasing racism of the EFF towards Gordhan and Indian people is illustrated in an excellent article by Ashwin Desai about the EFF's recent continuous reference to Gordhan by his middle name, Jamnadas. Desai points out that it is similar to 'jananda', a derogatory slang word for 'Indian' among the prisoner population in SA, and is a clear-cut case of racism towards Gordhan and Indian people. He argues that 'the EFF, of course, does not idly yell Jamnadas. They shout it into a well of racial chauvinism growing in the lower middle class. It's an eclectic constituency of clawing male youth, frustrated clerks, ambitious tenderpreneurs, desperate graduates, political adventurists and a small but vocal suckling of racial nationalists bravely manufacturing outrage on Twitter.'[55]

Desai concludes his critique with an important observation: 'Africans are the dominant victims of apartheid. That is a socio-political fact. But I sometimes wonder whether that cloak has prevented a thoroughgoing honest (self)-evaluation of the ugly parts of an emerging black social and political culture.'[56] I would add that it is not so much an 'emerging black social and political culture' in which such racism is rooted. Instead, I trace it to that more explicit Africanist majoritarian chauvinism which has grown out of the womb of a narrow and racially conceived African nationalism when the ANC was born in 1912.

Endnotes

1 Gerhard Maré, 'The National Question confronts the Ethnic Question', in *The Unresolved National Question: Left Thought under Apartheid and Beyond*, ed. Edward Webster and Karin Pampallis (Johannesburg: Wits University Press, 2017), pp. 164–5.
2 Ebrahim Harvey, 'Dispel the myth of a black African identity', *Mail Guardian*, 22 September 1999.
3 Maria van Diepen, 'Introduction', in *The National Question in South Africa*, ed. Maria van Diepen (London: Zed Books, 1988), p. 6.
4 Martin Leggasick, 'The Marxist Workers Tendency of the African National Congress' in Webster and Pampallis, *Unresolved National Question*, p. 161, n. 4.
5 Roger Southall, 'The ANC: Party vanguard of the black middle class', in *One Hundred Years of the ANC: Debating Liberation Histories Today*, eds. Arianna Lissoni et al. (Johannesburg: Wits University Press, 2012), p. 325.
6 Southall, 'The ANC', p. 334.
7 Ebrahim Harvey, 'It's time for the SACP to step out of the ANC's shadow', *Mail & Guardian*, 16 October 1999.
8 Interview with Kgalema Motlanthe, 22 September 2011, Johannesburg.
9 Email from Patrick Bond, 11 January 2020.
10 See Francis Meli, 'South Africa and the rise of African nationalism', in *The National Question in South Africa*', ed. Maria van Diepen (London: Zed Books, 1988), pp. 66–76.
11 Legassick, 'The Marxist Workers Tendency', p. 157.
12 Leo Trotsky, *Problems of Everyday Life* (London: Pathfinder, 1973).
13 See 'ANC to introduce qualifications criteria for cadre deployments', at www.Sowetanlive.co.za, 20 January 2020.
14 See N. Alexander, *One Azania, One Nation: The National Question in South Africa* (London: Zed Press, 1979).

15 Alexander, *One Azania*, p. 108.
16 See M. Leggasick, *Socialist Democracy* (Pietermaritzburg: UKZN Press, 2017). As one of the leading figures of the group expelled, Leggasick provides a coherent account of MWT and why and how it was expelled. There is, however, a big problem with his account because it omits the fact that many of the black comrades of MWT insisted that they not only with the ANC but with left elements of the PAC and the BC movement, which the white leadership of MWT resisted.
17 There are many books which deal with this allegation, notably P. Bond, *Elite Transition: From Apartheid to Neoliberalism in South Africa* (2000) and P. Bond, *Against Global Apartheid: South Africa Meets the World Bank, IMF and International Finance* (2003) and N. Alexander, *Ordinary Country: Issues in the Transition from Apartheid to Democracy* (2002).
18 See Enver Motala and Salim Vally, 'Neville Alexander and the National Question', in Webster and Pampallis, *Unresolved National Question*, p. 142.
19 Interview with Jeff Rudin, 26 July 2017, Cape Town.
20 Rudin interview.
21 Edward Webster and John Mawbey, 'Revisiting the National Question', in Webster and Pampallis, *Unresolved National Question*, p. 15, n. 3.
22 Quoted by Webster and Mawbey, 'Revisiting', p. 3.
23 Webster and Mawbey, 'Revisiting', p. 3.
24 Adam Habib and Kristina Bentley, *Racial Redress and Citizenship in South Africa* (Cape Town: HSRC Press, 2008), p. 347.
25 Habib and Bentley, *Racial Redress*, p.347.
26 See Mcebisi Ndletyana, 'Affirmative action in the public service', in Habib and Bentley, *Racial Redress*, p. 93.
27 See 'Oxfam applauds World Bank's rejection of trickle-down economics, and recognition of huge inequality challenge', at www.oxfam.org, 1 October 2015.
28 Motala and Vally, 'Neville Alexander', p. 138. The final phrase quoted is by Derek Swart in an address in 2010.
29 Motala and Vally, 'Neville Alexander', p. 139.
30 The theory of Permanent Revolution, I argue, is Trotsky's biggest theoretical, conceptual, political and programmatic contribution. I have explained earlier why the deep and systemically formative racism–capitalism nexus in South African history makes it an ideal candidate for this revolutionary theory, which was developed by Trotsky in the Russian Revolution in the first two decades of the 20th century.
31 Motala and Vally, 'Neville Alexander', p. 142.
32 Michael Morris, 'New identity crisis abused like old ones', *Business Day*, 27 January 2020.
33 Motala and Valley, 'Neville Alexander', p. 142.
34 See Crain Soudien, 'Non-racialism's politics: Reading being human through the life of Neville Alexander', in *Non-Racialism in South Africa: The Life and Times of Neville Alexander*, ed. Allan Zinn (Stellenbosch: Sun Media, 2016), p. 131.
35 Soudien, 'Non-racialism's politics', p. 133.
36 Webster and Pampallis, 'Preface', in Webster and Pampallis, *Unresolved National Question*, p. xi.
37 Fiona Anciano, 'Non-racialism and the African National Congress: Views from the branches', *Journal of Contemporary African Studies*, 32, 1, pp. 35–44, DOI: 10.1080/02589001.2014.900308.
38 'The ANC is racist and tribalistic, says gatvol Jessie Duarte', *The Star*, 23 November 2019.

39 'Ramaphosa acknowledges ANC's drift on non-racialism', https://www.news24.com.elections/voices/ramaphosa-acknowledges-ancs-rift-on-non-racialism.
40 'Water services worse than in 1994', *Mail & Guardian*, 31 January 2020.
41 'Sisulu and the bucket toilet stink', *Mail & Guardian*, 7 February 2020.
42 David Everatt, *The Origins of Non-Racialism: White Opposition to Apartheid in the 1950s* (Johannesburg: Wits University Press, 2009), p. 6.
43 Amanda Alexander and Andile Mngxitama, 'Race and resistance in post-apartheid South Africa', in *Searching for South Africa: The New Calculus of Dignity*, eds. Shireen Essof and Daniel Moshenberg (Pretoria: UNISA Press, 2011), p. 52.
44 Ebrahim Harvey, 'Scramble for jobs, housing ignites violence', *Cape Times*, 22 April 2008.
45 'Zulu king's comment on foreigners "hurtful and harmful, but not hate speech"', SAHRC, at www.sahrc.org.za.
46 'Makhura blames foreigners for crime, denies xenophobia', 6 March 2019, at www.enca.com. See also 'Makhura's attacks on foreign nationals is abhorrent and shocking says Eusebius – 702', at www.702.co.za.articles/makhura-s-remarks-on-foreigners.
47 Mpho Sibanyoni, 'Gauteng premier talks tough on foreigners', 2019, at www.sowetanlive.co.za.
48 Ebrahim Harvey, *Kgalema Motlanthe: A Political Biography* (Johannesburg: Jacana Media, 2012).
49 Moeletsi Mbeki, *Architects of Poverty: Why African Capitalism Needs Changing* (Johannesburg: Pan Macmillan, 2009).
50 Ebrahim Harvey, 'Abhorrent racism in EFF has deep connotation', *Sunday Independent*, 9 June 2018.
51 'Indians not black enough for BEE', 15 October 2017, at https://www.timeslive.co.za.
52 Dali Mpofu, 'On the Indian Question in SA: A response to mob psychologists', *Daily Maverick*, 21 June 2018.
53 Interview with Bobby Godsell, 22 November 2017, Johannesburg.
54 Mpofu, 'On the Indian Question'.
55 Ashwin Desai, 'Slurs, slander and slang: The red overalls' insults need to be called out for what they are', *Daily Maverick*, 27 February 2020.
56 Desai, 'Slurs, slander and slang'.

SEVEN

The 'New South Africa' unravels: Race, class and gender struggles

Introduction

FOR THIS AND THE NEXT chapter I need to make a few preliminary remarks. I argue that there is no country in post-independence Africa in which a liberation movement after winning state power compromised as much as the ANC did in SA, certainly not one which held so much promise to fundamentally change the social conditions inherited from apartheid and in fact pledged to do so. The racism–capitalism nexus did not alter significantly in post-apartheid SA to create the space for such changes and improvements to the lives of the black working-class majority. This was so even though various provisions in the FC, the RDP and the 1996 constitution made significant changes to the material conditions of the black working-class majority both possible and necessary, even within its own limitations from a revolutionary Marxist standpoint.

Remember that the black working class was in the ANC's own words the 'motor force' of the revolution in SA and, since the 1950s, its main support base. The ANC recognised that they were the most exploited and oppressed people in SA, who had built it to be the most economically developed and industrialised country in Africa. It is vitally important for this work that such a context be stated and appreciated. The themes I deal with in this chapter and the next are arguably the most important developments in post-apartheid SA, which have unmistakably shown the betrayal of the ANC in stark terms.

Significant improvements in the daily lives of black workers were possible even within the framework of South African neoliberal capitalism, had we not suffered the ravages of destructive corruption. SA had the resources to afford the black working-class majority at least significant changes to the social conditions of their lives. Instead, in several respects, like basic municipal services, conditions got worse and access to water, sanitation and electricity more difficult. Much of the massive amounts of money which was transferred by Treasury to local governments to be spent on the provision of housing and various municipal services was stolen by ANC officials through corruption, some of which surfaced at the Zondo Commission of Enquiry (ZCE). The same applies to funds provided to provincial and national government and the various government departments and to state-owned enterprises (SOEs). Furthermore, just look at the enormous sums of public resources the ANC has spent on bailing out corrupt SOEs, as a result of actions of its own 'cadres'.[1]

Virtually every SOE has been run into the ground with a plethora of stories in the media of corruption by ANC cadres deployed to top posts. Eskom and South African Airways are the worst examples. I firmly believe that the corrupt actions by those ANC 'cadres' were driven to some extent by the belief that so vitally important were those services to society, especially in the case of electricity and Eskom, that this realisation in fact stoked much of the corruption, based on expectations that the ANC state would come to their rescue and bail them out. That is exactly what has happened. Even ordinary people have awakened to this cynical corruption, seen in many letters to the press in recent years, especially around Eskom. Besides, not even schools, public hospitals and basic municipal services have escaped the claws of ANC corruption.[2] I cannot think of any country – especially in Africa – with so much economic power and therefore the immense potential to transform the lives of the black majority, but which instead became the source of massive looting of state coffers. The Eskom crisis must be located within the context of the devastation wrought by ANC corruption on the one hand and neoliberalism on the other hand. It is the poorest black people who suffer most from load shedding, while the black elite and wealthier black middle class can afford to buy expensive generators.

It is with the Eskom crisis that the most devastating consequences of both inappropriate ANC cadre deployment and an elitist BBE/AA can be most conspicuously and tragically seen. But we can only get a more complete picture of this tragedy when we combine it with the huge salaries paid to Eskom executives, increasingly unaffordable tariff hikes over the years for working-class residents already facing soaring cost-of-living increases, and the chronic corruption that is now a regular news item in SA. The point of this is that the ANC was in power. But when since 1994 have they ever accorded the 'motor force of the revolution' the respect and dignity one would have expected of a liberation movement once in power? On the contrary, the lives of the black working class got harder after 1994. But the lives of ANC leaders, both in government and those who went into big business, went from virtual rags to riches, living lives of opulence, glamour and glitter, while the African masses who supported them over decades were being crushed by poverty, unemployment and related social miseries in black townships.

I argue that not even the most pessimistic forecasts under apartheid of future ANC rule in SA could have foreseen the depth of the degeneration, decay and corruption we have seen since 1994. As the richest and most powerful economy in Africa, no country held so much promise to realise a much better life for black people than SA did. Instead, that wealth was redistributed to a tiny black elite and more numerous black middle class, leaving the working-class majority empty-handed and in some respects worse off than under apartheid.

The HIV/Aids crisis under the Mbeki regime (1999–2004)

Not enough work has been done on the implications of the devastation the HIV/Aids crisis wreaked on the black working class under an African-centred ANC rule. Too much emphasis was placed on Mbeki's Aids denialism as the cause of the crisis and too little on the fact that the ANC as the ruling party allowed it and its devastating consequences.[3] The unmitigated tragedy of the HIV/Aids crisis in the late 1990s and early

2000s was the fact that the preventable deaths of mainly African women and their babies took place among the poorest of the African masses.

This was the essence of the tragedy, and it was mostly preventable had the antiretrovirals been rolled out when they were required, rather than the role of Mbeki and the then minister of health, Manto Tshabalala-Msimang, and her bizarre garlic and beetroot panacea for the treatment of HIV. As I argued in my biography of Motlanthe, the key question was what had happened to the ANC itself and its members to have allowed this human tragedy to unfold when it could have been prevented had they taken a stand on the matter. But the fact of the matter is that not the ANC or in fact Cosatu and the SACP took a strong enough stand to make a difference when it was most needed. After all, what was at issue was such a huge public interest matter that it required decisive intervention.

Instead it was the tireless and dedicated work of the Treatment Action Campaign (TAC), which was specifically formed to fight for antiretroviral treatment for HIV patients, that piled enough pressure on the ANC to secure ARV treatment. But this only occurred after a staggering cost to human life. Few authors deal with the utter devastation wrought by ANC Aids denialism better than Hein Marais. Citing figures from Statistics SA, he found that 'The annual number of recorded deaths increased by 100% between 1997 and 2005, when it reached 634 100.'[4] But Marais also found what is probably even more shocking: the death rates for women aged 20–39 years more than tripled in that same period and for males aged 30–44 they more than doubled.[5] During that period SA had the fastest-growing rate of HIV infections in the world.

Although Marais draws attention to the racialised pattern of HIV/Aids, in which the overwhelming number of victims were poor and young African women, he does not analyse its implications for ANC rule, what the struggles in SA over a very long period were about, or how the meaning of race in our history was altered by those tragic events. In this regard, the unalterable fact is that this avoidable, devastating human tragedy of staggering proportions happened under ANC rule or more specifically an African-centred government. The first question that arises in our race-ridden history is how this was possible, given the ANC's own mantra of 'blacks in general and Africans in particular'? But the real answer to this apparent contradiction is the resource constraints imposed by the ANC's neoliberal policies in dealing with the HIV/Aids crisis.

In this regard Marais cites Helen Schneider and her colleagues: 'GEAR and its operational presence in the Public Finance Management Act have had an enduring impact on health services, establishing cost containment as the de facto driver of everyday practice in the health system ... Staying within budget became and remains the key preoccupation of managers, implicitly relegating equity and other dimensions of institutional change to secondary goals.'[6] Marais also found compelling evidence that the most seriously affected by the HIV/Aids crisis were the poorest and most vulnerable African women, who were for decades at the lowest rung of our society. In other words, the HIV/Aids crisis had a devastating impact on those already worst off. Marais shows in detail how such devastation affected everything in the lives of these African women. The direct relationship between HIV/Aids and poverty and inequalities was stark.

The media reported many instances in which both parents were killed by this crisis, with teenagers and even pre-teens having to take responsibility for the remaining household members, who were often unemployed and with little or no money to support themselves. The wide-ranging devastation of the HIV/Aids crisis of late the 1990s and early 2000s was arguably the very worst calamity to strike the black working-class majority and, though both men and women were affected, the overwhelming majority were poor African women. No wonder Patrick Bond could argue that

> The most severe blight on South Africa's post-apartheid record of health leadership was, without question, its HIV/AIDS policy. This could be blamed upon both the personal leadership flaws of presidents Mandela and Mbeki and their health ministers, and also upon features of the socio-political structure of accumulation. With millions of people dying early because of AIDS, and with approximately five million HIV-positive South Africans by 2000, the battle against the disease was one of the most crucial tests of the post-apartheid government.[7]

Not only neoliberal budgetary constraints and poor leadership, but African cultural factors got in the way too, as indicated by Mandela with reference to the 1994 elections: 'I was very careful because in our culture you don't talk about sex, no matter what you do.' And Mandela cited the advice he was given by a school principal after he had asked her if he could add Aids to his speech: 'Please don't, otherwise you'll lose the election.'[8] Any social transformation programme in SA faces severe challenges, not as a result of any white supremacy, but the socio-cultural ignorance and backwardness of many African people, a sad legacy of the precolonial days.

But I am only scratching the surface of these deeply historical and cultural problems. There is just no way these facts can be ignored or evaded to suit some antiquated 'political correctness'. There is just too much at stake in this country for us to succumb to those dark shadows, dressed in whatever traditional or cultural garb. These truths cannot be held hostage to some inviolable traditional authorities, which in our constitutional democracy nobody, certainly not from the 'minorities', dares to question or criticise. Up to the Constitutional Court if necessary, we need to fight these issues and not succumb to either traditional cultural customs or their political manifestation in African chauvinistic nationalism, which has become rampant over the past decade in SA, expecting 'minorities' to quiver in its sight. Those days are up.

However, where I differ with Marais is his attempt, on the one hand, to criticise the Stalinist CST and the two-stage approach of the SACP, but on the other hand to concede that for the purpose of the broad anti-apartheid struggle it had advantages and strengths.[9] But that is the result of a kind of pragmatic short-termism and it is not assessed over a longer period which stretches into present times. It is that longer view which was necessary to hold to, especially if we see how the ANC and its alliance with the SACP and Cosatu have unravelled since 1994 and especially over the past decade. In other words, that short-term view is the seductive pragmatic catch to show a 'balanced' analysis. But this perspective is as false as was the two-stage theory of the ANC and SACP. In fact, an analysis that does not integrate apartheid with post-apartheid SA and treats the two periods separately is playing into the hands of the Stalinist two-stage politics, especially given the inherent problems in the two-stage approach and its results after 1994.

But this view must itself be tempered by the fact that given how compromised Cosatu and the MDM became after Mandela's release, in no small part as a result of the ANC's apprehensions about a vibrant and vigorous civil society, and the notorious weaknesses of the left outside the ANC alliance, there was indeed little or no serious mass alternative to the ANC and the negotiations. However, it is what has happened to the black working-class majority after 1994 and their needs, wishes and expectations under ANC rule which powerfully reinforces and resonates with the correctness of the permanent revolutionary approach. That is why ultimately it is not even the adverse balance of forces of the 1990s, when global neoliberalism was in the ascendancy, which must serve as a barrier to what was possible in SA.

In other words, the ANC never really sought the kind of changes which could have realised a much better life for all. The years since 1994 have demonstrated with absolute certainty two interrelated lessons. First, it is completely impossible to disentangle race and racism from the solidified capitalist-class historical linkages. Secondly, integrally related to that, it has proven as impossible to build a much better life (even if it was not necessarily socialist changes) within the framework of a racial capitalism which was materially and socially structured to exclude black people, especially the working class, from decent basic municipal and public services and facilities in townships.

But even more important is the fact that had it not been for the deep and destructive corruption in the ANC government, the limited potential for some significant redistribution that was possible with the provisions in the Bill of Rights of the constitution, was seriously compromised by the wanton looting of the coffers of the state by ANC 'cadres'. What this did was to compound the already severely limited neoliberal budgets for basic services and infrastructural development in black townships. Obviously, the caveats in the constitution which stated that implementation of socioeconomic rights was dependent on the availability of resources, also had a very negative effect on their realisation and the modest improvements they entailed.

It is against such a background that we need to assess the multifaceted tragedy of the HIV/Aids crisis on black people who were already languishing in the doldrums of mass poverty and unemployment. We are indebted to the meticulous research by Marais on the social impacts of this crisis on black HIV/Aids patients across the country, and for the information and insights he provided. From extensive data it is unmistakably clear that the lives of hundreds of thousands of black adults and babies from HIV-infected mothers could have been saved, had the

ANC government acted decisively at the required time of the outbreak of the epidemic. Though Mbeki continues to this day to deny government complicity in the deaths of so many black people and infected babies, it is abundantly clear that this did happen in SA under his watch. But importantly, Marais correctly concludes that the blame must lie ultimately not with Mbeki, though he was the key figure in government driving ANC policy on HIV/Aids, but on the ANC as the ruling party.[10]

It is on the latter crucially important point that I must dwell for a moment. Given that ours is a country where the African masses are the vast majority of the population and the most exploited and oppressed, which according to the ANC informed its mantra of 'blacks in general and Africans in particular', how are we to assess the ANC government's stance on the HIV/Aids crisis and the staggering numbers of people who died as a result? And what does that say in a country whose entire history has been saturated with white racist rule and supremacy, before the ANC's black majority government came to power? In answering this key question, the most important thing is to recognise that in all the bluster, denials and prevarication of Mbeki and the ANC government around the science of HIV/Aids, there stood stingy and constrained neoliberal budgetary policy, which regarded the costs of ARVs as unaffordable, as then health minister, Nkosazana Dlamini-Zuma, argued.[11] This was despite the high death toll already from this crisis and the bigger tragedy that lay ahead.

In conclusion, to comprehensively grasp the full implications of the social and physical devastation wrought by this epidemic on African people, especially women, babies and children, and the tragic stance of the ANC government, one should read the rich and detailed research of Marais. But perhaps even more important are the political conclusions reached from such research and the brief analysis offered here. For me the single most important lesson from the calamitous and tragic depths of the broader social crisis this health crisis triggered is the fact that it happened under an ANC government which for decades claimed to champion the interests of the African masses above all others in SA. What this did was to demolish any integrity that the Africanist mantra of the ANC might have had before it assumed office in 1994. We have seen many times that when it mattered most to those masses, their hopes and expectations were dashed.

What stands out most conspicuously about the tragic HIV/Aids crisis is that it was the abject failure of our public health services to care for and treat black patients. Given the starkly deficient and appallingly poor hospital services during apartheid and in fact all previous white racist regimes, health policies and outcomes after 1994 were arguably as important as access to water, sanitation and electricity. But treatment assumed an even greater public importance because of the death and devastation which followed if it failed. The ANC and its minister of health were obviously aware of these facts and yet they failed patients and the public health system, with catastrophic results.

Of the different dimensions of this tragedy it was the failure to provide ARVs to pregnant mothers to prevent transmission of HIV to babies which was the biggest blight upon the ANC government since 1994. Therein lies the heart of this human tragedy: the preventable deaths of many thousands of black mothers and babies. And yet Mbeki has continued to defend the stance of the ANC government while he was president and when the loss of life was of staggering proportions.[12] It is almost as if Mbeki believes that the more he repeats the same lame attempt to explain away that unmitigated tragedy, the more credible it will become. Repeatedly, he has declined opportunities to concede that mistakes might have been made, especially in the very costly and lengthy delays in the roll-out of ARVs. But he would not budge. History will not be kind to him in this regard. At the time he was the object of scorn and derision around the world. It remains clear, however, from the record that neoliberal budgetary constraints were probably the biggest failure, even bigger than that of fake science and related Aids denialism.

The Marikana Massacre (2012)

I go from black bodies dying unnecessarily to their being shot unnecessarily. The killing of 34 striking black miners in Marikana on 16 August 2012 is widely recognised as the 'Marikana massacre'. The point about Marikana was not that the material conditions which gave rise to that militant strike were bad. No, it was that while the ANC government had moved steadily to the neoliberal right since 1994, which is why the strike and its demands occurred, the global shock it unleashed was as a result of the preventable cold-blooded killing of striking black miners with scores seriously injured.

That these savage killings and repression occurred in post-apartheid SA was the heart of the public shock, which very quickly became headline news around the world. More specifically, an African-centred ANC government effectively murdered and injured African miners who were demanding a living wage and decent living conditions. Cutting through circumstantial and legal technicalities, that is the bottom line of what happened in Marikana.

Arguably, nowhere was the race–class nexus at play in more tragic and dramatic terms in post-apartheid SA than in those events. But Bond's analysis of Marikana does not really deal with race in the final analysis and tends instead to jump to class factors rather quickly.[13] This approach is indeed tempting because these were miners exploited by Lonmin, a multinational mining company. Bond tends to downplay the criticality of race and colour in the massacre. I argue that race was key to Marikana, no less because these were African miners shot by African police in a state controlled by Africans. Race is not only a factor when white people are in control of the state. Race has perhaps become a more important factor in post-apartheid SA, in spite of the formal deracialisation of all laws. Instead, its salience resides in the fact that the state the ANC inherited still overwhelmingly operates in the interests of WMC and still observes the regulatory institutional structure of the migrant labour system, for example. The systemic perpetuation after 1994 of cheap black labour, historically the most pervasive feature of capitalist development in SA, is notoriously evident.

But it was in the week before the massacre, when Ramaphosa, then a director of Lonmin, urged 'concomitant action' against the strikers that his role became all too clear. The treacherous role played by the founding leader of the NUM, against African miners like those he once led, was most regrettable and revealing of how he had changed. There can also be little doubt that as a director of Lonmin and given his political seniority in ANC circles, the email in which Ramaphosa called for such action contributed to the temperament among police when the massacre occurred a few days later. Bear in mind too that Ramaphosa directed such urging to the management at the mine and to the police minister, Nathi Mthethwa, who conceded that Ramaphosa had put him 'under pressure' about the situation at the mine.[14]

The role played by the ANC state in the massacre was well put by

Bond: 'When a ruling party in any African country sinks to the depths of allowing its police force to serve white-dominated multinational capital by killing dozens of black workers so as to end a brief strike, it represents an inflection point.'[15] It was a crucial turning point – not only because 34 miners were shot dead by the police – but because 34 African miners were shot dead and 78 injured by African police employed by an African-led state with an African minister of police. Therein lies the heart of the human tragedy of Marikana, where race is indelibly woven into its fabric.

Had these been African police acting under white apartheid orders, it would have been different. We expected the apartheid state to kill black strikers and they frequently did. The scale of the tragedy is vastly different in the Marikana massacre because it was meant to be a post-apartheid state controlled by the ANC, rhetorically committed to prioritising the interests of black people, and particularly the black working class. But what makes Marikana particularly explosive and tragic is that the massacre occurred during a strike over something as basic as wages, at a time when drill operators belonging to the Association of Mineworkers and Construction Union (Amcu) were paid as little as just over R4,000 a month. They demanded a salary of R12,500.

The other important aspect of Marikana, which analysts have hardly paid attention to, is this: why were the wages of an important job such as drill operators so low to start with in a purportedly post-apartheid SA and in the richest and most powerful country in Africa? And how does one even begin to reconcile such low wages with the fact that Ramaphosa was not just a director of Lonmin but a past leader of the NUM, aware of the wage level and the related fact that the housing conditions of the miners were also poor and shoddy? There was much evidence to show that the board of Lonmin seriously neglected the housing needs of its African employees.

These important facts strongly suggest that low African wages on the mines were a deeply structural feature of the industry since its inception in the 19th century. From the outset very low wages and terrible working and living conditions of miners were common across all mines. In fact, it was upon those conditions that the mining industry developed and profited as quickly and handsomely as it did. Most unfortunately, the miners in Marikana and the leaders of the NUM, out of which Amcu was born later, failed to deal with the historical low wages and poor working and living conditions on the mines since the political transition of the 1990s. But we should not be surprised, since this lopsided situation was the result of the ANC's separating the anti-apartheid struggle from that against the capitalist system, of which cheap black labour was always a part of. Even with the potentially radical elements of the FC, the ANC failed to explain when they endorsed it how and why they were essential to the social transformation necessary to fundamentally change the lives of the black working-class majority.

But even that is not as striking as the treacherous role played by the ANC government and by Ramaphosa in particular. In this regard it is patent nonsense to suggest that Ramaphosa's urging 'concomitant action' against the strikers did not influence the conduct of the police when the miners were shot dead less than a week after his email. His role as ex-leader of NUM and his leading role in the 1993 settlement and in shaping the constitution would have given the police minister, the commissioner of police and the mine management the confidence they needed to 'deal' with the situation, should it become necessary. But Marikana did more than that. In the most dramatic and tragic terms imaginable, it told us and the world how terribly unfinished the revolution in SA in the 1990s was and, as importantly, the treacherous nature, once again, of African nationalism in power, especially within a neoliberal framework.

Marikana was not only about the poor wages of drill operators but equally the tragic neglect over many years of the housing needs of miners. For example, while Lonmin had undertaken to build 5,500 houses by the time of the killings, only three had been built. This created a situation in which 'large numbers of Lonmin workers lived in squalid informal settlements, creating an environment conducive to the creation of tension, labour unrest, disunity among its employees or other harmful conduct'.[16] Moreover, Ramaphosa, founding leader of the NUM, was on the board of Lonmin. It is rather obvious that both management and the board were hardly concerned with those deplorable conditions for years before the massacre. To make matters worse, and to deepen the indictment of the ANC government, more than four years after the massacre the deplorable housing situation of miners had hardly changed.[17]

However, it is how the ANC government and Ramaphosa in particular treated the widows and children of those murdered by the police after the massacre which provides the finishing touches to its tragic betrayal.

The media was full of anguished stories about the neglect of the families of those killed after the shootings. The affected families were not even given legal support at the Farlam Commission of Enquiry. The lawyers who represented the families also struggled for years to be paid by the government.[18] Long bureaucratic delays in compensation payments and the suffering this caused to affected families, who no longer had the income of those killed, were rife in the media. The callous indifference of government officials also received considerable coverage in the media, as did the fact that the living conditions of the miners changed very little following the massacre.

Marikana also told us how fickle race can be and how the racial or black solidarities of the anti-apartheid period were torn asunder once the ANC took office in 1994. Inevitably, the ANC succumbed to new class forces unleashed by the 1990s 'transition'. Probably, the African striking miners expected that 'their' government would side with them, especially in a matter that challenged historically low wages paid by the white mining companies. But that was not to be. When WMC placed Ramaphosa and other African directors on its board, it knew well what it was doing. It reminds one of how the British dealt with African liberation movements after they gained political independence: placing a few Africans on the board of companies was a stratagem that worked each and every time. Elated to get a break into the world of white corporate privilege, they probably often tried to do an even better job in their new posts than did white board members.

But Ramaphosa's call for 'concomitant action' was true to form. There is no better study of what happened in post-apartheid SA under ANC rule to the black working-class majority than the Marikana massacre. The hard and very painful lessons were etched crystal clear in those bloody events. Race, in a very big sense, was put in its place, so to say, but only when it got separated from class and social interests. Dubbed the 'Marikana Massacre', it was regarded as the single most lethal use of force by South African security forces against civilians since the end of apartheid.[19] However, Peter Alexander and his team who penned a book on the massacre a year after it took place do not adequately place Marikana in a historical perspective. I argue that Marikana was inevitable, as was the killing by the police of Andries Tatane and many other township protesters over the years.

Once we understand the demands made by the miners at Marikana and the township protesters, on the one hand, and the policies the ANC adopted after 1994, on the other hand, then those killings were inevitable. That is how any state – especially one whose policies protect the interests of capital and whose leaders pursue their own class interests – will react when the interests of the Lonmin bosses and 'law and order' at the mine were seriously threatened. The ANC has not departed at all from the typical role of the state vis-à-vis capitalist interests; and Ramaphosa's role in the events that led up to the massacre reinforced the coincidence of the interests of the ANC and Lonmin bosses.

But could he have acted differently when, according to Bond, his company, Shanduka, was incredibly being paid '$360,000 a year for providing "empowerment" consulting, not to mention Ramaphosa's board salary and dividend returns on Lonmin share ownership'.[20] The main point is that the Marikana massacre was ultimately about money and profits and the compromised deal the NP and the ANC struck in the 1990s, which gave birth to a small black bourgeoisie, of which President Ramaphosa is a leading member. All other matters, such as whether the police opened fire prematurely, and other technical aspects of what happened, the details of which have been abundantly aired in the media since 2012 and especially during the Farlam Commission of Enquiry, are not in the final analysis as important as they were made out to be.

No, it is in the killings of those miners that the facts and meaning of the negotiated settlement of the 1990s are to be poignantly found. The state the ANC constructed on the basis of that settlement and with due recognition of the fact that the power of WMC, especially in the mines, was left intact, together with some of the institutional features of the migrant labour system, made those killings possible in the first place. Obviously, very little really changed in terms of wages and working conditions for those miners, but that is what happened too in the black townships under ANC rule after 1994, which is why as a result SA is the protest capital of the world. Marikana and the townships burning unstoppably since 2004 reflect palpable unhappiness with the 1993 settlement. There can be no other conclusion.

So, when Jay Naidoo reacted to the Marikana killings, he behaved as if he did not understand all the policy compromises the ANC made while he was a minister in the ANC government. In fact, when he was minister of telecommunications, posts and broadcasting he presided over the partial privatisation of Telkom, much to the chagrin of the relevant union. Naidoo says: 'I was part of the leadership that led Cosatu into an alliance with the ANC and SACP. It had a clear objective. We were making a commitment to a profound transformation that struck at the heart of Apartheid – the cheap labour system and its attendant diseases of poverty, gender violence and inequality. But these same diseases remain …'[21] But Naidoo did not come out in opposition to the overtly neoliberal Gear policy of 1996 when he was in government, while Cosatu, which he had led since its inception, condemned it because it was responsible for the increased poverty, unemployment and social injustices in the late 1990s and early 2000s.

How much more topsy-turvy can our politics get? This is the same Naidoo who proposed crudely class-based levels of municipal services when he was minister in the RDP office in 1997. Who, furthermore, found his social democratic voice, but only after making many millions in the private sector through the elitist BEE. But that's only possible because he pursues a pro-capitalist social democracy, which is why at the same time he became chairman of the J&J group of companies, in which Old Mutual had a 25% stake, sat on the board of Old Mutual, was chairman of the Development Bank of Southern Africa and was profitably involved in several other business ventures. Yet, in 2019 he called for 'radical transformation',[22] though, not of the kind that's going to take the wealth he acquired since he left government and went into big business. His later move into spiritualism and other esoteric philosophies became an enticing distraction after becoming as rich as he is today.

Naidoo, together with Ramaphosa, Marcel Golding and Johnny Copelyn, is the face of trade union leaders I worked with in the 1980s, whose lives completely changed after they became part of the new elite since 1994. I am certain that none of them will escape the reckoning of a history which does not seek to embellish, distort and misrepresent the facts. 1994 will be the historical cut-off point which separates their earlier laudable role in the development of the trade union movement from what happened thereafter to their lives. Today, the combined wealth of Ramaphosa, Golding and Copelyn probably approaches a staggering R10 billion. Nowhere, probably not only in Africa but in the world, have trade unionists gone from such virtual rags to untold riches as they did.

From representing workers they've become big bosses overnight in major sectors of the economy.

Naidoo's response to the Marikana massacre is contradictory simply because he fails to understand that the conditions the striking miners fought against were the inevitable result of the fundamental compromises he, the ANC and Cosatu made in the 1990s. It is false to separate the conditions of Marikana from the compromised settlement, as they were the direct result of it. The killings of the strikers were an expression of the fierce determination of Ramaphosa and other directors of Lonmin to protect the profitable conditions which gave rise to the strike. Besides, from the evidence at the Farlam Commission of Enquiry it is very clear that the directors of Lonmin knew about both the low wages and the deplorable living conditions of the African miners and did nothing or very little about them.

What difference did the presence of Ramaphosa and other black directors at Lonmin make to the way they operated in the 20th century? Nothing much. In fact, the steady blackening of the faces of company boards after 1994 brought much-needed stability to white companies, which in turn provided the 'non-racial' basis for the bigger profits they made thereafter. As mentioned previously, in his last State of the Nation address in 2008, Thabo Mbeki specifically mentioned that post-apartheid SA had been kind to big business. In fact, in his defence of the miners at the Farlam Commission of Enquiry, Dali Mpofu regarded the events that led to the killing of the miners as a pretty clear-cut case of collusion between capital and the ANC state. He never minced his words and did not need to, so blatantly clear was such collusion, including the treacherous role of the NUM.

We must always keep in mind that the entire mining industry was notoriously neglectful of the living conditions of miners since its inception in the 19th century, which is why Pallo Jordan, in the aftermath of Marikana, could point to the 'manner in which the mining industry is evading its responsibilities to its workforce who live in shanty-towns around the mines'.[23] Bear in mind that what historically informed this blatant and inhumane negligence was that for the white mining industry to provide decent housing for its miners would have eaten into its profit margins. It is not complicated stuff to analyse, especially given the historically evolved racism–capitalism links and the virulently racist and exploitative forms white mining always embodied in SA. What Marikana did was to tell us loud and clear that the race-ridden political economy that incipiently shaped capitalism in SA never really changed much after 1994.

I end this brief review of Marikana with a vitally important consideration: the largely defensive role of the state in capitalist democracies, which is ultimately what we have here and across the world in fact. Behind all the rhetoric about democracy and the will of the people, all democratic states, to a greater or lesser degree, defend capitalist interests, profits and accumulation. Capital is a very powerful force which even the most robust constitutional democracies know to be an undeniable fact. In *Capitalist Democracy on Trial*,[24] David Smith systematically shows how the British ruling class, arguably the most sophisticated ever, have used and manipulated democracy in clever ways to retain power since the Industrial Revolution.

We see such awesome power in countless ways, but especially regarding economic policies and how the state behaves when the interests of capital are threatened. Here race and colour and culture do not really matter at all in the final analysis. The state flexibly adapts to whatever requirements capital makes of it, especially when the construction, life and role of that state are dependent on capital, as happened with the 1993 settlement in SA, via the policies of both BEE and AA. That is precisely why WMC and the NP made certain that the constitution of 1996 provided for the protection of private property, which is a shorthand for capitalism.

WMC is a pervasive and fatal reality and decidedly not the myth many inside and outside the ANC claim it to be, since capitalism has been deracialised after 1994. It is ultimately the power of WMC that Ramaphosa was defending when he urged concomitant action, not merely his own interests as a director of Lonmin. It is this angle to the Marikana massacre which analysts have not probed sufficiently. What WMC and the NP did, together with the active collaboration of the ANC leadership, which was dependent on such an outcome for its own material interests, was to give black people all the trappings of formal democracy and a few of them a significant stake in the capitalist economy in order to secure the political conditions necessary for economic stability. Today political and economic elites have mutual vested interests in defending a stable capitalist economy. That is ultimately what happened in Marikana.

The African police officers who killed the striking African miners at Marikana were compelled to act as instruments of an elite pact between the ANC government and a white-dominated global company, Lonmin. The black police and indeed Ramaphosa were ultimately instruments in the hands of WMC, still dominant in the mining industry, though it is now much more diversified than it was during apartheid. There was no hesitation by African police officers to shoot at the strikers because they were African, nor any hesitation because they were fighting for what the police officers probably themselves would have wanted: a salary increase. No, they did what they were instructed to do against the strikers. They did so because their job, as part of the states' 'special bodies of armed men' – as Lenin called them – demanded it. The police and army have performed this role against strikers and protesters for centuries. Marikana, even under an ANC African government, was no different.

Marikana cannot be deracialised, not even in the slightest degree. In fact, it was not only deeply racial in that it was a bloody and fatal clash of WMC and its representatives, like Ramaphosa, against a black proletariat, but it was a slice of our history replaying itself on the world stage. The historical factors which decisively shaped SA in the 19th century and their socio-material consequences still reside in and shape contemporary SA.

Finally, one of the most striking things about Marikana is the typical historical setting of the mineral revolution during colonial times. The geographical location of the mine, on the outskirts of the nearest city, men working far from their rural homes, poor wages and working and living conditions and the careless attitude of mine owners and management were all features of both the diamond and gold mines in the 19th century. There is much resonance between contemporary SA and that older history of industrial SA. The main difference, which has not, however, altered the capitalist essence of our economy, is an outcome of the deal of the 1990s: the black elitist and middle-class BEE and AA, which have augmented an economy still under the control of WMC.

Marikana, much more than any other crisis since 1994, showed conclusively that the 1993 negotiated settlement contradicted and compromised the yearning over centuries of racism and capitalism for a life free of exploitation and oppression. The power of Marxist analysis is that it shows us why the most vitally important questions of our emancipation reside in being free of economic exploitation and subjugation to the logic of profits and capitalist accumulation. Exploited and oppressed people don't yearn to be rich. They yearn for what should easily be possible if our lives were not subjected to capitalist exploitation and if the wealth produced by labour was shared equally among workers, their families and communities. A good standard of living does not require one to be wealthy but requires a measure of equitable redistribution in society.

The profits Lonmin has generated over the past few decades could easily have allowed a good minimum wage and housing, health and other basic services for workers and their families. But this is not possible because the directors and owners of Lonmin pay workers a fraction of the profits they generate in low wages and poor working conditions. When the Marikana workers demanded R12,500 for drill operators, the bosses screamed that it was impossible and unaffordable, but when they pay themselves hundreds of times more in salaries and perks it becomes affordable. This regime of exploitation, especially of workers whose back-breaking labour produces the wealth that makes their salaries, perks and profits possible, is the real source of the great unhappiness in SA and the world. Marikana showed us yet again the barbarism of capitalism.

The problem, however, is that the balance of class forces in SA, cutting across race, is not in favour of the working class for the foreseeable future, including miners at Marikana, especially against the background of setbacks of the past few years. There are numerous reasons for this situation, chief among which is the decimation of trade unions over the past few decades because of the globalised restructuring of production as a result of technological changes, which will become much worse when the Fourth Industrial Revolution really gets under way in SA. The deepening global economic crisis will make things more difficult. This will make it much more difficult for trade unions, meaning their future will probably become bleaker, especially since it will negatively affect their bargaining power for wages and working conditions.

Navigating such a troubled future is going to be especially hard since the labour movement is already quite weak and fragmented into a few federations. The split in Cosatu considerably worsened the fragmentation which already existed. This has complicated the situation facing workers at Marikana, most of whom became demoralised with the NUM and formed Amcu, which has been for a few years the dominant force there. Capitalism, especially mining, and the trade union movement, including at Marikana, face a difficult future, which might compromise the interests of workers further. Whether a socialist working-class party, such as the Numsa-based Socialist Workers Revolutionary Party (SWRP), can emerge after Marikana to unite workers behind a strong programme that builds the unity of the labour movement is key to the future of the Marikana miners and the community it comes from. But for that purpose, they will require strong trade union leadership, which has not been forthcoming for a long while.

The Nkandla Scandal (2014)

The years of Zuma's presidency were the most momentous in post-apartheid SA. In a series of events, the ANC in office was on trial. It is arguably true that no former liberation movement in Africa descended so steeply from the dizzying euphoric heights of the mid-1990s into the pits of unprecedented malfeasance and corruption at every level of the state, every government department, every SOE and other spheres of the public sector. By the standards of other episodes of corruption and looting of the state, the failure to regulate spending on the security upgrades to Zuma's Nkandla home – and his liability for improvements that had nothing to do with security – was smaller in scale and scope. But Nkandla is extremely important for what it revealed of the ANC's refusal to acknowledge corruption and crime by its own members, and its willingness instead to justify and defend the actions of Zuma and other perpetrators. Because it involved the President himself, Nkandla was also notable for raising public concerns about corruption and state capture. In this respect it cleared a path towards the Zondo Commission and the prosecutions of Ace Magashule and others in 2020.

A major problem, which made Nkandla and other corruption scandals involving ANC officials more possible, if not likely, was the huge distance that opened up between the ANC as an organisation, with its head office in Luthuli House, and the ANC as the ruling party with access to vast resources in hundreds of tenders and contracts in all sectors of the economy. Following the many serious allegations of corruption against Zuma in the arms deal and the 'generally corrupt relationship' Judge Hilary Squires found to have existed between him and Schabir Shaik was strong enough to have compelled the ANC to be much more vigilant about any further allegations of wrongdoing or corruption against him, as to what happened in the Nkandla case. But they were not. Instead, they rallied to his defence.

But the fact that the ANC elected him as its president in 2007 and as the nation's president in 2009 goes to show what the ANC deep down is made of. A learning organisation? And with what kind of membership, especially in a supposedly post-apartheid SA? It is bizarre, but quite frankly that is what the bulk of the ANC membership is like, lacking sufficient political consciousness and education in order to act in their own interests. It in fact is more bizarre when the fate and future of the country are in the hands ultimately of delegates who are drawn mainly from that pool of largely uneducated people. No wonder Neville Alexander spoke of a 'herd mentality' among them. In the main, what else would you find there, given the enormous weight of our history and how its key elements were retained intact after 1994?

It is against such a background that we need to appraise what happened in the Nkandla scandal, warnings of which first appeared in 2009 in media reports of expenditure on Nkandla, Zuma's personal residence. Gwede Mantashe was then the ANC's secretary-general and, like Ramaphosa, a former leader of NUM. We might be forgiven if we expected that former leaders of the most powerful and militant trade union in South African history would be more sensitive to instances of corruption, let alone the countless examples of raging social injustices in the wages and working and living conditions of miners at Marikana and elsewhere. But both Mantashe and Ramaphosa were found wanting with regard to Marikana and Nkandla. They supported the ANC report which found that nothing untoward happened at Nkandla and were equally quick to dispel rumours of corruption there, even spending on upgrades that had swelled, without proper oversight, to nearly R250 million.

In fact, the entire ANC leadership and government rallied to defend Zuma, even when Thuli Madonsela, the Public Protector, reported in 2014. Her report, 'Secure in Comfort', provided material evidence of abuse and corruption in the Nkandla upgrades.[25] But the ANC's failure was not only in its upper reaches: as often before, the branch membership of the ANC failed to lift a finger even when the material evidence of corruption and mismanagement was evident. The ANC branches had become increasingly emasculated over the years, a process that can be traced back to the arms deal in 1998. In all the major crises affecting the ruling ANC not once did the branches, its core organisational structures, take a stand and demand accountability from their leaders.

There was no resistance to whatever decision the leadership took. In fact, their decisions were taken precisely because they did not anticipate any resistance from the branches. Very often the branches merely rubber-stamp the authority of the provincial and national structures, especially decisions of the NEC, whatever the decisions might be about. That is how the ANC dealt with every major crisis it faced since 1994. The ANC has become entirely bureaucratised from top to bottom. The most senior officials control the party, especially those in the top six, ministers, MPs and, most important of all, the NEC.

But it is important to point out that many cases of ANC corruption both preceded and succeeded the Nkandla scandal. It was a shocking shame that the late Jackson Mthembu, minister in the presidency, could in 2019, in relation to some challenging issues facing Ramaphosa's campaign donation controversy, refer to 'our *glorious* movement'[26] (emphasis added), with a ring of cynicism made possible by contemptuously taking people for granted.

Madonsela's report is a litany of violations, both procedural and substantive, in virtually every respect of the security upgrades. Her report revealed gross ignorance by Zuma, the presidential staff, the Department of Public Works and other government departments, about the prescribed regulations, criteria and processes that were flouted. Costs for the work spiralled without proper controls – leaving taxpayers with a hefty bill for the upgrades. The excesses include the unlawful enforced relocating of neighbours elsewhere to make way for the property expansions, which cost the state and taxpayers about R8 million.[27]

The report identified certain features – cattle kraal, visitors' centre, amphitheatre – that were not justified by security considerations, including of course the swimming pool. Zuma's lawyers rationalised it as a fire-pool in case of a fire, because it would take 80 minutes for the fire brigade to get to his home and the experts found that 'an open water source is best for firefighting and nothing could be better than the pool'.[28] This is possibly the most cynically bizarre attempt to cover up an act of corruption in post-apartheid SA.

Like the HIV/Aids crisis of the late 1990s and early 2000s, the Nkandla scandal demanded action by members of the ANC – but predictably there was none. When critical public issues involve the ANC, the party bosses intervene very quickly to stamp out any dissenting voices in the branches. This is only possible because the ANC uses its bureaucracy, not moral authority, to whip disgruntled members into line. At a time of social crisis and rampant unemployment it is easy for local party bosses to impose order among such members, no matter what the issue might be. That is what happened with Nkandla. The most you will find are rumours of dissent in some branches but no discernible organised opposition in the open.

Nobody has expressed in clearer terms the processes of such internal party degeneration than Leon Trotsky, after he witnessed the steady emasculation of the Soviets, especially after Stalin came to power in 1924.[29] Notwithstanding the huge differences between the ANC and the Russian Communist Party, the processes of how the ANC branches steadily lost their power are similar to what happened to the Soviets, and though the signs were there already during Lenin's time, it became much more pronounced after his death in 1924. I argue that this degeneration of ANC branches was inevitable for several reasons, including the low level of education and class consciousness among the majority African membership, the multi-class nature of the ANC, and the impact of its shift to overt neoliberalism after 1994.

After Gear was adopted in 1996, behind the backs of ANC members, major policy decisions were increasingly taken without active rank-and-file participation. No wonder Trevor Manuel could tell me that macroeconomic policy cannot be negotiated by stakeholders, as can be done with wages, because only financial and technical specialists were qualified to do so.[30] The ANC's policy conferences are choreographed in order not to rock the neoliberal boat in which the ANC has sailed since 1994.

Executive decisions without prior agreement at policy conferences have determined the crisis in every area of public and social policy, based on a combination of neoliberal budgetary constraints, incompetence and corruption. In other words, there is an extensive pre-history to Nkandla which determined the stony silences from ANC branches, even when media reports revealed credible evidence of chronic corruption in that so-called security upgrade at Nkandla. But I have spoken to many leading ANC people, including Motlanthe, and it's very clear that few of that membership read newspapers, let alone take up relevant issues which affect the ANC at branch, provincial and national level. In this day and age those circumstances are a recipe for disaster in so far as the conscious control of the ANC by its members is concerned, or for that matter in any other organisation. Such control is arguably the foundation of a democratic organisation, without which it is meaningless. But so pervasive is corruption at all levels that I'm certain that even the most ordinary workers and members of the ANC have been sucked into its networks in one way or another, especially within the processes of local government. This will itself be a big hindrance to grassroots control of the ANC by its members. In fact, the temptations of moneyed corruption might be greater at the lower and poorer levels of the African working class and ANC membership employed within municipalities.

There are countless other municipal tenders involving ANC members who became councillors or held other official positions, who have been involved in one or other form of moneyed corruption. From downtrodden African working-class backgrounds, they've become sucked into patronage and factionalist networks, taking them even further away from the Marxist notion of a class-conscious and a class-for-itself stratum. Perhaps some of them were drawn into the web of corruption spun at Nkandla. The point is that the Marxist notion of a potential revolutionary working class is up against chaotic fragmentation and dispersal in neoliberal post-apartheid SA. No wonder the trade unions have seriously declined.

To conclude: the most unnerving thing about Nkandla is what it says about the ANC as the ruling party, taking its place among many other stories of corruption stretching to every area and level of the state. The alarming thing about the ANC in this mountain of corruption-related activities is how it operated as a protector of the officials involved, even when credible evidence against them existed. For 25 years after 1994 only a handful of senior ANC officials were sanctioned or prosecuted. Only in 2020 – belatedly – was there a significant series of arrests and charges involving over a hundred individuals.

For over two decades Zuma has evaded prosecution for a mountain of fraud and corruption cases, and it remains to be seen what the outcome of the Zondo Commission will be in this respect. It certainly says a lot about the ANC that members could elect Zuma to be the president of both the ANC and SA, knowing full well the hundreds of fraud and corruption charges he faces. They did the same when Ramaphosa was elected president in 2017 despite the multi-faceted horrors of the Marikana massacre hanging over his head. But ANC members apparently don't care much about anything leaders might do, as they also shrugged off Ramaphosa's willingness to bid almost R20 million on a buffalo cow and her calf in the same year as Marikana in 2012, when many millions of black people were steeped in daily poverty and unemployment. The apology he rendered later did little to assuage that social tragedy.

Beginning of Student Uprisings (2015/16)

I have little doubt that the explosive student uprisings from 2015, which have continued unstoppably in one form or another since, were to some extent influenced by the spirit of militancy which characterised Marikana. This is because Marikana itself was the first big explosion of the myth of a 'rainbow nation', a 'miracle transition' and so on, which the white-dominated media raved about during the 1990s. Raved because the 1993 negotiated deal had preserved the capitalist economy and left its social relations intact and all the wealth accumulated since the days of the old Cape Colony.

Looking at the period from 1994 to 2020, one can only wonder at how the trajectory of South African history since 1652 was so kind to white people and their interests, needs and wants. With the most painful irony, perhaps no earlier period in our history was as kind to white people as the 'miracle transition' period from 1994 until now. White people were always astute as to how to preserve their material interests during turbulent periods of our history, but they outdid even that history between 1994 to the present moment. Transition was a 'miracle' because the white economy and all the wealth created there over generations were left untouched by the settlement that Mandela and the ANC reached with the NP in the 1990s.

It is against that historical background that the black student uprisings of 2015/16 took place and shook this country in ways reminiscent of the 1976 uprisings, only this time directed against the ANC government. Just as Marikana was bound to happen, so were these uprisings. In fact, the student uprisings complemented the struggle of workers at Marikana in ways which together told the story of the severe limitations of the 1993 settlement. The question is this: what was that deal worth if it did not include a living wage for workers, especially black, and the ability of black students to study without a constant struggle for the most basic things like fees, books, accommodation, meals and transport costs? But this problem is systemically linked to all the other problems of education in schools, such as basic infrastructure, classrooms, furniture and IT equipment, all related to mass black poverty, unemployment and unprecedented social inequalities in townships where most students come from.

The unalterable fact is that the student uprisings and the issues it gave rise to are directly and indirectly the result of neoliberalism in SA, characterised by the constant struggle by the majority of black working-class students to pay for fees, books, stationery, food, accommodation and transport. The first question that arises in such a situation is what happened to the constitutionally enshrined right to education and the provision in the FC that 'The doors of learning and culture shall be open to all'? They were casualties of the debilitating neoliberal caveat in the constitution that whatever rights exist in it are only realisable to the extent that the government has the resources to implement them.

It is a foregone conclusion that there will be severe budgetary constraints within a neoliberal macroeconomic framework which is evidently not geared to adequately meeting the needs of the black working-class majority. The multi-faceted and worsening social crisis of poverty, unemployment and raging inequalities that we face today is palpable evidence of this fact. The caveat was originally designed to structure the constitution so as to serve two interrelated aims. Firstly, it establishes the right to hold private property. Secondly, it limits, in advance, the amount of funds budgeted to meet acute basic needs. The constitution reflected scant regard for the extent of the social deficits that the apartheid period of rule in particular generated in townships and the ANC inherited in 1994 and the related inability of students and their parents to meet the varied and soaring costs of education.

The general situation in townships of massive poverty and unemployment – which not only continued after 1994 but grew worse in the second decade of the 21st century – would naturally affect the ability of black parents to meet all these soaring costs. Under those circumstances the caveat in the constitution is in fact a fiscal justification for the inability of the state to pay for the costs of higher education to the extent required or for any other rights in the Bill of Rights. It is in fact by virtue of such a miserable caveat that we could have, on the one hand, a constitution said to be among the most progressive in the world and, on the other hand, the most unequal society in the world and a country where in January 2020 over 10 million people are jobless and millions are still without adequate basic services. In both cases – education and municipal services – it is once again, as with the student demands, about the policies the ANC decided on in the 1990s.

This brings me to the important historical background to the student uprisings which was sorely lacking in the commentary and analyses at the time. Adam Habib's book *Rebels and Rage*,[31] which reflects on the Fees Must Fall movement, contains some insightful comments and analysis of its weaknesses, such as its propensity for spontaneous violence which wreaked havoc at Wits and other universities, the ultra-leftist opportunism of some academics who seemed to uncritically support the violence that the students often resorted to, and so on. But a major and unfortunate weakness of this book is that Habib provides no historical background or context at all to the student uprisings. His surprising failure to deal with that background informed his approach towards and response to the dramatic student unrest at Wits which gripped the country during 2016.

Had he started with an appreciation of that history, he would have realised why the uprisings became so inflammatory and quickly spread from where it originally started at UCT in 2015 to other campuses. He also would have understood much better two other very important elements to the conflict at Wits: the radical nature of the demands of students and the extent of student violence during the protests. Habib's strong Marxist background should have made it imperative for him to begin an understanding and analysis of the student uprisings with that history in mind. I was not impressed with his book and believe he missed a big opportunity to place the student uprisings in its historical context and reflect on what lessons it held for education policy and practice in the future. I sent a message to Habib on its lack of historical background, which I think it is useful to cite here:

> You jump from the outset into the dramatic events at Wits but without that history. You become, as a result, too engrossed in empirical details at Wits during those tumultuous times, but without that larger

context which I argue is imperative. There is nothing much about the ANC and its policies both before and after 1994 and how it embraced neoliberalism after 1994 and how that affected education seriously. There is also nothing much about how education has become as a result quite commercialised and commodified after 1994. I argue that you need to look seriously at how all of that affected Wits and other universities.[32]

While the book is rich in important empirical details, related to incidents of unrest and Wits processes to try to address the crisis, had Habib considered their historical context it would have helped his own cause: that government funding was grossly insufficient and therefore he had to increase fees and so on. Though the disruptive and violent tactics of the EFF and other groups made it difficult to constructively address the seething problems of funding and the needs of students for various kinds of assistance, I asked Habib during discussion time at his launch if there was not enough common ground between him and the students to create a joint fight for greater government funding, but he did not confront the question directly and failed to address it adequately. Yet surely there was a lot of common ground regarding broad principles and a commitment to free education, especially for all needy students.

But the biggest problem was what started the crisis: the students' lack of money to pay for fees, accommodation, books and so on. This was the result of reduced funding for universities from national government due to neoliberal budgetary constraints. The student uprisings and the crisis that followed were always about money and resources. How could Habib, who attended many meetings with the minister of education and other government officials meant to address and resolve the crisis, not have provided that causal background in his book? As a leading scholar and someone who was an activist himself against apartheid and a Marxist, this critical deficiency in his analysis of what happened at Wits always intrigued me.

Habib should have been putting the ANC government under far greater pressure to intervene and assist financially. After all, it was the slashing of such funding over the years, while student numbers were climbing, which lay at the root of the raging conflicts between disaffected students and university authorities and the police during that period.

Habib instead took his eye off that critical ball and focused on bringing order to Wits and ending the chaos there. While he had all the statistics of the major discrepancy between student number increases and the funding from government, he failed to use that information more effectively in his liaison with the minister and other government officials.

In his capacity as vice chancellor (VC), he had the executive power to be more assertive in his dealings with government, especially given what was at stake. Even trying to source funding from the private sector to cover the shortfall in government funding should have been the responsibility of the ANC government and not his, but he needed to make that point very clear to the minister. Did he? This important aspect of the crisis Habib does not say much about in his book. Instead, I have read and heard him talk a lot about essentially neoliberal budgetary trade-offs at university, and not once in the book does he identify and critique the neoliberal policies of the ANC government in education and other areas of economic, public and social policy. The media hardly focused on this aspect of the crisis. They seemed much more interested in the violent dramas that unfolded at Wits and other universities and the politics of the warring student factions embroiled in the conflicts.

In an interview Habib complained about the rise of racism among the protesters, which he also wrote about. He was completely correct about that. Racism was directed at him, as an 'Indian', and at whites, Coloureds and Jews at other times. The racism from African student protesters at Wits and at other universities came, from my own understanding, mostly from the EFF, but according to Habib also from 'parts of the ANC, the BLF and parts of other parties.' As VC he should know. But this widespread problem, what Habib calls a 'racially or ethnically chauvinist approach', has deep political roots in SA, which I have traced.

That much of this exclusivist African racism came from the EFF did not surprise me at all. Its historical roots lie in the ANCYL of the 1940s and grew into a major problem, which has seriously bedevilled the NQ. What happened in this regard at Wits and elsewhere, especially where it concerns the EFF, is a repetition of their views on the NQ, which they have turned into a crass Africanist majoritarian chauvinism, especially in relation to the 'minorities' of Coloureds, Indians and whites. It got quite bizarre at certain universities, where students from these racial constituencies were aggressively forbidden to engage in the struggles at universities, which they had every right to. Why? Because these Africanist chauvinists and racists said so! After all, who can tell them anything? They belong to the African majority. This element was vividly present in those struggles.

Such was the ignorance about race and racism of these students that they appeared not to know better. So deep is this problem that, most unfortunately, I think it's still going to be around for a long time to come. Habib correctly linked such backward racism to the failures of the ANC to understand the NQ in SA: 'Had it (ANC) been more astute and intellectually thoughtful on the National Question it would have been capable of confronting the challenges of post-1994 in a much more effective way than it has.'[33] So deep is race in the consciousness of black people, and so limiting the lack of education, culture and development, that even university students are not likely to have a much better intellectual understanding of the problems than someone who has never been to a university.

To demonstrate this point, consider the notion of 'decolonisation' used so glibly by students during those heady days at Wits and other universities. No demand or term during that struggle reflected more ignorance and confusion than 'decolonisation'. At one stage some black UCT students went to the bizarre extent of asserting that science itself must be decolonised and that a new 'African scientific tradition' created in its place. This statement alone is bizarrely unscientific. In a reply Saliem Fakir and I argued that 'Western science is the product of contributions from many different cultures and civilisations. We have a right to claim it as our own and use it to our advantage.'[34]

But the fact that university students could hold such backward views about science in the first place is indicative of the huge and still lingering damage which inferior colonial and later overtly racist Bantu education did to African people. This is an undeniable fact which is starkly evident in fact in ANC rule in many ways. To confirm this some of the students calling for the demise of Western science also argued that there must be a place for superstition and traditional folklore in African science, such that people are able to 'send lightning through witchcraft to strike someone' and that 'we ought to be able to explain this scientifically because it happens'. Our reply was that 'lightning kills, witch or no witch.' We added, importantly: 'Students are getting carried away when they no longer see decolonisation as a political project, instead (of) using a metaphorical hair test to decide what constitutes decolonial knowledge and what does not, without having a proper historical understanding of the evolution of science in human history.'[35] There is a sharp contrast between this backward thinking and the thinking of the Non-European Unity Movement (NEUM) teachers of the Western Cape and their splendid educational work, mainly in Coloured schools.

I don't think there was a better and more progressive school of thought in SA than what came from this movement, though it was predominantly among Coloured schools and communities. They dealt not only with political questions about the struggle against apartheid but inculcated a grasp of scientific approaches to questions of history and culture and the evolution of mankind over many centuries. SA lost a powerful generation of teachers with the decline of the Teachers League of South Africa (TLSA), a Unity Movement affiliate. Their contribution, notwithstanding the organisational and political weaknesses of the NEUM, is demonstrated in the work of Mohamed Adhikari and Crain Soudien.[36]

I remember how I looked forward in the 1970s to reading the TLSA journal. The student uprisings of 2015/16 seriously lacked that kind of solid educational grounding. They sorely lacked any tradition of knowledge, not only about politics, but of history and culture. Instead, a narrow Africanist majoritarian chauvinism was rampant across the country among sections of the student movement, but especially at UCT and Wits.

I also found immense ignorance and confusion among students in an understanding of decolonisation, within the context of what actually happened during the colonisation of SA. In many respects the understanding of decolonisation was often appallingly poor, but journalists did not detect this because they probably did not know much better. Once you begin to call for decolonisation, it is naturally presumed you know what colonisation is. But these students were not using the libraries at their universities to go and read up on both colonisation or the decolonisation they were now demanding. Colonisation in SA was not just racist but imperialist. Economic and financial interests grew soon after the arrival of the settlers in 1652. Trade and agriculture developed under Dutch rule, underpinned by slave labour. Economic activity accelerated under the British in the first half of the 19th century but changed dramatically with the mineral revolution. British colonialism in

SA from that time was rampantly imperialist, especially after gold was discovered in 1886. From then on, colonisation was inextricably bound to the growth of monopoly capitalism in SA. In other words, to talk of decolonisation within that context necessarily contains massive anti-capitalist connotations.

Besides, because colonisation affected everything in SA and defined life in every respect of political, social and economic relations, including its destructive impact on the various cultures of black people, one cannot seriously talk of decolonisation in ways that are limited to race or to white supremacy. Like apartheid, colonisation was a total and comprehensive system of white rule within an explicitly capitalist economic framework. From this perspective those radical students were approaching decolonisation rather conservatively and with limited knowledge about the history and meaning of colonisation in SA. In short, I argue that no student or any other movement can seriously invoke decolonisation as a cause without an adequate knowledge of colonisation in SA from the time of the Dutch up to at least the 1910 Union of SA.

However, the pitfalls of the students' understanding of decolonisation did not escape Habib: 'It's just been a lot of rhetoric from students and a lack of understanding of decolonisation in a broader sense and specifically as it affects higher education. There's an enormous amount of confusion. There's been one or two thoughtful pieces on decolonisation, otherwise it's been rhetorical.'[37] But former deputy VC of Wits University, Tawana Kupe, also made a very important point about this lack of understanding of decolonisation among students: 'We need to be mindful that this problem also reflects adversely on our curriculum and lecturers.'[38] This aspect was hardly identified and pursued in discourses at the time. In other words, the ignorance and confusion among protesting students about decolonisation arguably had its roots partly within the academy itself.

Dinga Sikwebu provided a major insight into the question of decolonisation and how students understood its meaning:

> I am always amazed at these students' lack of knowledge of our history. Because history is not seriously studied, they borrow from America and elsewhere, bell hooks, Black Lives Matter, intersectionality and the decolonial school. But we have a serious problem among students

of intolerance and arrogance. They are also aggressive. It's the same thing in branches of the ANC. Politics in this country is highly intolerant. That is why we need to review what we mean by politics because it's becoming a spectacle often. But there is something else happening. There is a new student politics, I call maximalism. In fact, capitalism is producing it because it's in a deep crisis and cannot grant significant reforms to the working-class or in this case the fees and other demands of students, which tends to create an all-or-nothing reaction of students. While very left-sounding, it is questionable on matters of programme, strategy and tactics.[39]

Two important points are made here. The first is the intolerance, arrogance and aggression of student activists at Wits and at every other university. I think it is causally related to some extent to the frustration as a result of a lack of knowledge and understanding of some of the issues that struggle threw up, which, especially during a crisis, can be very debilitating. Secondly, South African capitalism's virtual symbiosis with racism seriously limited its capacity for what would ordinarily be seen as liberal reforms, which shaped the maximalism of student demands.

Despite all the weaknesses in student politics – inexperience, tactical naïvety, 'maximalism' and intolerance – nothing could diminish the formidable impact their struggles had on the universities, government and SA. In political terms, what they did was revolutionary for its time.

Habib has been consistently clear in his opposition to any form of racism in the student movement and has spoken out against it boldly. However, a position he derived from it is deeply problematic. He said that the struggles of students were fine but had to

> play out in ways that did not undermine the university as a safe and free space for ideas. Moreover, the decisions that university executives make in response to these demands could not compromise universities' long-term sustainability: this would compromise the educational prospects of future generations of poor South Africans. Achieving a strategic balance between allowing this legitimate social movement to evolve and maintaining the free, safe space and the long-term financial sustainability of the university became the principal task of the Wits executive in managing the students protest.[40]

Once again Habib loses sight of the explosive context I earlier referred to, especially how the ANC's neoliberal policies had damaged education and denied black students at Wits and elsewhere the constitutional right to education, knowledge and skills. To approach things in what is essentially a bureaucratic manner was deeply ahistorical and outside the immediate context of the student militancy unleashed during 2015/16 and the explosive issues it gave rise to on campuses. He was not pushing, with the angry students, against institutional boundaries around fees and the costs of education at Wits and exerting the utmost pressure against government to find the funds necessary. No, his focus was on what he called the 'long-term sustainability' of Wits. But it was precisely the long-term sustainability of black students at South African universities which was threatened by those neoliberal policies.

The pressure during that crisis should have been on the ANC government to find the funds to resolve the stand-off between students and university authorities, private security companies and police. Unarmed students were up against all these combined forces, but it seemed that the spirit of the 1976 student rebellion inspired them. This is how I summed up the situation at Wits: 'What we have seen after 1994 is that the cost of education has soared to unaffordable levels for the majority of black students. Probably nowhere does the race–class nexus apply more than when it comes to meeting the costs of education at universities. As part of their privileges, white students would be more than able to meet these costs than would black, Coloured and Indian students.'[41]

Any study of the student uprisings will unmistakably show very compelling race–class linkages, which is the story of post-apartheid SA. Nothing has dominated our social history after 1994 like these enduring links, in every single aspect of our lives and most notoriously in black working-class townships. Research into the social backgrounds of the black student activists in those uprisings will reveal them to be overwhelmingly from the ranks of black working-class families across the country. But so unstable and precarious has the black middle class been, particularly over the past decade of growing economic crisis, that students from its ranks have suffered hardships too.

The reason why 'identity politics' became a major debate throughout the student upsurge was as a result of the dominance of race not only in our history but also in the struggle against unaffordable fees and related demands. The stark reality of our history and the persistence of its social consequences after 1994 ensured that there would be a racial hierarchy of ability to meet all the costs of tertiary studying: whites, Indians, Coloureds and Africans, in that specific order (albeit with class variations within those categories). That is why in all the marches around the country a sea of black faces was evident, sprinkled here and there with Coloureds, Indians and whites. It is the overwhelming demographic superiority of Africans which is the source of a rabid Africanist majoritarian chauvinism, which can sometimes cut across class differences among them.

But that could arguably be the socio-material face of 'identity politics', notwithstanding the strident criticism it has faced and the interesting racial tendency for white leftists to strongly critique it and black students to be more receptive to it in favour of more straightforward class politics. But the main problem of identity politics is that it takes the focus away from the issues at hand – such as fees and other material demands – and instead foregrounds race and colour in abstraction from those struggles. That can have a disintegrating and diffusive effect rather than a unifying one for those practically involved in a struggle. For me it is especially important to avoid fracturing black (African, Coloured and Indian) unity but in ways which never forbids – as some Africanist chauvinists did at some universities – white student involvement, which was not only divisive but racist. Every single student, irrespective of race or colour, must be totally free to join in any struggles waged by predominantly black students.

Students or any other constituency for that matter need to live, embody and exemplify the non-racial and anti-racist ethos they purportedly embrace on the basis and in the manner in which they conduct any struggle. To assert that Jews or Indians or Coloureds are not welcome is nothing less than unmitigated African racism, which no university or any other institution should accept or tolerate. There were several reported attempts to block white students from participating in the Fees Must Fall movement, and other forms of racist language. The genuinely anti-racist forces in the ANC government and in civil society must combine to stamp out this racism, otherwise it will inevitably give rise to violence. Nothing worth fighting for belongs to any 'race' or group but all must be free to join hands to fight for it.

South Africans need to urgently move away from this racialist posturing, in which it is our mere physical appearance and what we happen to look like – dark, brown or 'white' – which determines how others perceive or relate to us. One of the primary reasons why apartheid was revolting is precisely the emphasis it placed on our skin colour or phenotype. The alienating indignities of these experiences are often well captured in the writings of Soudien. From news coverage this racist phenotypical rejection during the student uprisings was carried out by African students who appeared to have imbibed the worst of the Africanist majoritarian chauvinism of the early days of the ANCYL in the 1940s.

In an interview Helena Sheehan made an insightful point about identity politics during the student uprisings in SA. She was not in principle opposed to it, but added that it was 'complicated, fluid and shifting', while 'class was an even more powerful and stable lever to organise and mobilise for any struggle because it structures not only our relations to production, but indeed the possibilities of life itself, such as our physical health and well-being, our psychological well-being too, what conditions we live under, whether we are educated or not or what we are educated about or not'.[42] She pointed out that while Henry Gates Jr usually emphasised race and tended to neglect class, he had also acknowledged that in the final analysis class was a greater factor in people's lives. But I have argued earlier, in SA the race–class nexus has been so dominantly defining in our history that one should not in fact place one before the other, but instead emphasise the *simultaneity* of both factors at play.

In fact, the grave and worsening social crisis of the past decade in SA has served to reinforce the salience of that nexus, which ironically became more palpably evident after all traces of race and racism were expunged from the statute books. Right here is a crucial lesson about the fundamentally *material* relations between race and class or racism and capitalism in SA for well over a century. While a debate could be had about how necessary race and racism was to capitalism under apartheid, its legacy after 1994 has now beyond any doubt made clear, with the benefit of post-apartheid hindsight, what that relationship was really made of since the mineral revolution of the 19th century. The most serious limits to legal and juridical changes, without tackling capitalism, have been palpably laid bare after 1994.

Sheehan stated that one of the biggest problems of identity politics, in SA as in the US, was that 'it becomes crudely racial and even racist, which is why for me and from my experiences and travels around the world it is class that is more important.' She identified the EFF as an example of the dangers of identity politics in SA. However, when black students graduate and become professionals in their different disciplines, their emphasis on race will dissipate as they start earning good salaries and moving up the tertiary or corporate ladders and living typical middle-class lives. That is precisely why in the final analysis class as a determining factor is bigger than race per se, even when in our history as factors they were virtually symbiotic. Class becomes more detached from race as income and status rise. This process often leads to an increasing depoliticisation of even militant students when they leave universities and move into a professional middle-class life.

The problem, however – which will in fact serve to reinforce the greater salience of class in a compelling sense – is that these prospects are not open to the majority African working class. That is why the beneficiaries of BEE and AA have not been from this class but the elite and middle classes, and why Steven Friedman was so right when he argued in an interview that we must not be naïve about BEE because since its inception it was never meant for the black working class.[43] But what makes this class analysis more attractive is not only because it gets to grips with the real issues more squarely than the approach of identity politics. No, it is also because identity politics generally lays a disproportionate emphasis on race and colour, on the 'immediate, visible problem of the concrete personal other, in very visceral ways', as Feroz Cachalia put it in an interview, with far less emphasis today on 'the system': 'it's not the system any longer; it's this white person; blame is allocated; you are the problem.'[44]

Cachalia went on to make a very important point:

> In the past (under apartheid) the main problem was race, colonialism and capitalism. It was not the racial identity of the person but the content of a person's politics, such as in the case of Neil Aggett and so many other radical whites. That is the big, unresolved issue, which is why I'm questioning the logic of identity politics because at the end of the day I don't believe that approach leads to social, societal and systemic transformation.

The problem is interesting, especially among the African youth: just when the social crisis under capitalism has deepened globally, they are reverting to the identity politics of the early BC period, when in fact that same social crisis clearly demands a clearer and stronger class approach, not to diminish race but to place it in a solid and inseparable race–class perspective. Instead, the deeper the social crisis becomes, the more inwardly they are turning. That is the central paradox, it seems.

But back to Habib. In an interview after he announced his sudden resignation from Wits University in February 2020, he spoke much about his defence of public institutions, against the anarchists and fascists among the students, and that if he had to have a similar experience again he would gladly call in the police to deal with violence. In this regard he kept on emphasising the sanctity of 'public institutions'. But Habib is once again mistaken in his analysis. He decontextualises public institutions, such as Wits University. That Wits is a very important public institution that must be defended is rather obvious. No, the problem is that our public institutions, given the devastating apartheid legacy which particularly disadvantaged Africans generally, were meant to serve the interests and defend the right to study and education of those students first and foremost, and every obstacle in the way of fulfilling that objective Wits was bound to resolve in their favour. Then, and only then, can Habib talk about the sanctity of public institutions, and that is all the more reason why his main focus during that crisis should have been on an emphatic insistence that the ANC government had to find the funds to address it.

This, however, was not what determined his approach to the crisis. Instead of a focus on the origins of the funding crisis in 2015/16, which created a political crisis at Wits, he focused instead on the strong reaction of students to the funding crisis because it had profoundly negative effects on their studies. Not once did Habib point out and emphasise the neoliberal fiscal origins of the funding crisis, which in fact his own figures pointed to repeatedly: the relative decline of government funding received as against the huge increase in student enrolment figures. That discrepancy and its origins are what all along both the students and Habib should have focused on, especially in view of the fact of the continuous looting of state coffers by ANC 'cadres' deployed to the state. Appropriate cuts in budgetary allocations to various other departments, like defence, and the huge earnings of executive staff across the state and public sectors should have been made in the interests of securing the funds students and universities needed desperately.

In fact, the later budgetary concessions made by the ANC of free education to needy students showed that pursuing this angle should have been more aggressively done at the outset of the crisis in October 2015. But Habib's emphasis was on taking security measures to deal with the violence, which undoubtedly had to be addressed, but not at the expense of exerting much greater pressure on government to come up with the requisite funding to help and support desperate students. That should have been in fact the emphasis in a strategy to end the violence instead of the emphasis on security measures, especially of the savagely repressive kind that we saw at Wits and other universities, which only served to provoke and alienate militant students further.

But what were the lessons for university authorities and the government during those heady student struggles? The most important question, and the biggest problem the radical student movement faced, was the unbridled violence which often characterised its struggles, especially when its demands were not met to the extent wanted. Student protesters had fashioned the violence they perpetrated at universities upon the pattern of destructive violence in the black townships. Much that could be broken or destroyed by fire suffered that fate. Nothing was spared, as in the townships, where even clinics and libraries were burnt to the ground. But how does one even begin to fathom the burning down of libraries, which house the knowledge students require in their studies?

Similarly, how does one fathom the bestial destruction of historic art works and paintings at UCT and elsewhere? I argue that these very acts speak to a stark lack of education and its related cultural development of the students who burnt down libraries and artworks. Nothing at all and no circumstance can justify that kind of destruction. Burning down a police station because it is seen as a symbol of repression is one thing but burning down a library is an unpardonable and unconscionable act of destruction. This ethos must be instilled in our minds.

But can Wits and other universities be regarded today as 'non-racial' institutions, when race continues to define so much, such as the affordability of fees and many other costs of studying? Or can it be argued that although racism is outlawed, its institutional form is still prevalent at Wits and elsewhere? This is an important question to answer at Wits or any other institution in purportedly post-apartheid society. The American writer Mia Mercado argues that it is inherently false to argue that institutions are no longer racist by virtue of all racist laws having been rescinded. She asks, 'if Equal Employment Opportunity laws make it federally illegal, how can job discrimination based on race persist?'[45] She points out that there was disagreement at the highest level of the US government about the existence or not of institutional racism. We need to ask the same question in SA, where we have not had that debate, not even in the media.

Mercado argues that institutional racism exists in the US, referring to a range of statistical facts in the US. The figures for convictions for crime and drugs, the composition of the prison population, school attendance and pass rates, ongoing unofficial segregation in many schools, unemployment rates for college graduates overall, applications for jobs, home bond approvals, redlining, wealth disparities and many more examples, conclusively show that race is very prevalent despite the formal removal of racism from the statute books. Probably the results of such statistics would be considerably worse in SA, given that the legal changes came much earlier in the US. Such data reveal, once again, powerful and compelling race–class correlations. She argues therefore that 'Institutional racism is real. Systemic bias exists.'[46]

Mercado's argument applies directly to South Africa. One cannot address the question whether racism still exists after 1994 in a legal, formal and constitutional manner. The legal and constitutional outlawing of racism must be separated from the social and material conditions the black working-class majority have lived under since 1994, notably poverty, unemployment and inequality. To define, identify and explain the continuity of racism after 1994 requires an approach which systemically links race with class. It is within an analysis of how South African capitalism developed historically that we must seek answers to how racism has manifested itself in post-apartheid SA although it has been abolished in law. The answer lies in how racism was for many decades embedded within the structures of the economy, such as job reservation, migrant labour, hostels, compounds, and labour-controlling townships with poor and degraded housing, services, and health and education. Much of this has basically remained the same after 1994. The race–class outlines of our society not only remained the same after 1994 but in some respects worsened.

Post-apartheid racism is not a legal provision, but it is instead the devastating socioeconomic effects of racism over a very long historical period. The persistence of racism today enhances, deepens and consolidates its material links with capitalism. It is arguably inconceivable – especially in the light of the unprecedented social crisis unleashed by Covid-19 – to attempt today to separate racism from its congenital association with the structures of capitalism as they evolved historically. Race, that deeply historical reality of this country since the days of the Cape Colony, is bound to be a combustible feature of our lives in the years ahead. I believe that race and racism will not be defeated within the framework of South African capitalism. Only in some post-capitalist dispensation will race and racism stand the best chance of being overcome.

Related to these issues, the former Wits SRC president, Shaeera Kalla, made an important point when I interviewed her which strikes at the heart of the student uprisings. She emphasised the exclusion of poor black students from Wits over many years simply because they were poor and unable to adequately pay for all the expenses.[47] If we pause to digest the cause and implication of such poverty, which would by far mostly affect African students, it represents a stark indictment of the ANC government. We cannot but ask what happened after 1994, in so many respects, to the ANC's decades-long commitment to the needs and interests of black people, captured in their mantra of 'blacks in general and Africans in particular'?

The answer is irrefutably clear: as with basic municipal services, the ANC's adoption of neoliberal policies and budgets, which prioritised macroeconomic stability in the interests of capital, has sacrificed the adequate fulfilment of the demands, needs and rights expressed in the FC, the RDP and the 1996 constitution's Bill of Rights. The policy choices made by the ANC prevented them simultaneously serving two masters, their own historical constituency, the black working class, on the one hand, and WMC and the interests of the small black elite, on the other hand. Roughly, that is what has happened in SA after 1994 and, if in any doubt, take the time to drive around black townships to see with your own eyes. Then go and drive around former white suburbia. Vividly inscribed in that contrast is the stark betrayal of the black masses. With such results of its rule the ANC has never deserved to remain in power in SA, but it has, though increasingly precariously these days.

The most revolting truth is that while the ANC government failed to adequately provide for the basic right to education or to satisfy other basic needs in black townships, the lives of its leaders were a sharp and bitter contrast. To drive to formerly white suburbia and seek out the palatial homes of the ANC's African leaders is to appreciate the point of a betrayal. On the education front, you will not find any ANC leader whose children struggle to pay for fees and other student expenses and are subjected to so much more humiliating adversity. On the contrary, they attend top private schools and live very comfortable lives. The Fees Must Fall movement graphically laid bare the heart of the betrayal: how is it possible that over two decades after the 'miracle transition' of the 1990s black working-class students could not afford to pay for such basic things as tuition fees and accommodation? And where students without accommodation or the ability to pay for it were sleeping in university buildings and when many could not afford to buy food during the day? For all those who argue that race and colour no longer matter, there are stark reminders that institutional racism is still alive and kicking today. Importantly too, at that time we had no offers from capital, white and black, to pull together and help Wits University, for example. Yet, it was the great-grandparents of those students whose labour enriched Johannesburg and WMC in particular over many decades since the mineral revolution of the 19th century. There have been no historical reparations and social justice at all in ANC-ruled post-apartheid SA.

The Esidimeni Health Crisis of 2015

The state of our public hospitals for a long while has been shockingly poor. Many newspaper stories have for years reported this tragic situation, with virtually every aspect of the services rendered by them seriously compromised, due to shortages of doctors, nurses, wards, medicine and infrastructure. Terribly long queues are a daily problem in public hospitals across the country, as is the shabby treatment and often blatant disrespect meted out to patients by nurses.

It is against that background in the crucially important public service of health that the Life Healthcare Esidimeni scandal broke out in October 2015 in Gauteng. A total of 144 people died at psychiatric facilities across the province, in what was regarded as the greatest cause of human rights violations in democratic SA. The Gauteng Department of Health ended its contract with Life Esidimeni (a subsidiary of Life Healthcare, a private hospital operator) in order to cut costs, and moved the patients to various NGOs around the province. At the hearings into the tragedy an advocate acting for the families of the deceased argued that this act by the Department of Health had violated the constitution, domestic laws as well as international conventions.

Another advocate added: 'The sorry state of extreme neglect, insufficient or rotten food, exposure to cold, lack of medication, overcrowding, abuse, death, late notifications of death, picking through bodies stacked upon each other in morgues is best told by the families themselves.'[48]

The most shocking feature of this crisis was that its victims were poor, desperately needy and vulnerable African psychiatric patients. The Department of Health and the Gauteng government did not oppose the action against them by lawyers acting for the families. The advocate acting for the state admitted that the circumstances around the transfer of the patients was regrettable. In his report on the hearings into the deaths, Health Ombud Malegapuru Makgoba found that the actions of the MEC for health, Qedani Mahlangu, who had resigned shortly before his report, were 'chaotic, hurried, in a rush and a total shambles'.[49] One has to pause to allow this shocking information about the treatment of psychiatric patients by the Gauteng Department of Health and the provincial government to sink in.

However, there has to be a deeper question to pose under those circumstances: how is it possible and what does it say in the first place of the ANC government that it allowed this outrageously inhumane treatment to occur? The fact that these were African psychiatric patients in purportedly post-apartheid SA must serve to deepen the magnitude of the tragedy. How could those factors be irrelevant, given our history and what apartheid specifically meant to black people? Any government anywhere in the world would be held responsible for the tragedy and would certainly need to account for it.

But not in SA under ANC rule. Concerted attempts by the families of the victims of Esidimeni, who were justifiably outraged by the criminal negligence and deaths of their loved ones, to bring those responsible to account in a court of law were turned down by the National Prosecuting Authority (NPA) in September 2019, on the incredible grounds that there was not enough evidence. Instead, the NPA recommended a formal inquest. Andrew Petersen, who represented the families, called the decision 'totally ridiculous. What kind of evidence do they want? There should be more than sufficient evidence from the hearings as well as the comprehensive report submitted by the Health ombudsman. We are shocked...' Members of the families expressed visceral outrage at this NPA decision, with a DA councillor, Rashieda Landis, whose son was also transferred to an NGO but survived, not mincing her words: 'Qedani (Mahlangu) and (David) Makhura were the masterminds behind this unprecedented incident.'[50]

The report of the Health Ombud, Professor Makgoba, and its recommendations were a devastating indictment of both the Gauteng Department of Health and the Gauteng provincial government. That report was combined with a 'lengthy arbitration process that culminated in the acknowledgement by government officials of those who died as a result of the move from Life Esidimeni.' In agreement with the Health Ombud report, the 'arbitrator asserted that the public officials behind the project had acted irrationally and had abused their power. He concluded that the project had been characterised by mismanagement, secrecy, a lack of accountability and transparency ... which led to the suffering and death of mental health care users.'[51]

No wonder Petersen had asked what more evidence was required. Landis asserted that there was a government cover-up which led to the NPA decision not to prosecute based on a lack of evidence. This was not the first time that state agencies that were constitutionally required to be independent acted in cahoots with the ANC government. We could not have had a more blatant cover-up since the ANC won power in the 1994 elections. But if that was not enough to indict the ANC-dominated Gauteng provincial government, the Gauteng ANC re-elected Mahlangu to its Provincial Executive Committee in July 2018. Stephen Grootes said that 'South Africa has lost its capacity to be shocked. It is that simple.'[52]

Over the past decade so many utterly outrageous things have happened under ANC rule that it has become hard to believe. Countless other severely compromised politicians of the ANC continue to be in office with an unmitigated sense of arrogant impunity. South Africans, and especially, if truth be told, so-called minorities, talk about these things all the time and with an increasing sense of helpless incredulity. Much of what has happened under ANC rule would absolutely not be tolerated in Britain and other European countries nor even under the presidency of Trump in the US. The reason for this is simple: the African masses, who are the overwhelming majority of the population, will continue regardless to re-elect the parties of African nationalism, such as the ANC and EFF, back into office. This is because there is little or no consciousness there in the first place about these problems and what they mean for a constitution said to be among the most progressive in the world.

But back to the human tragedy of Esidimeni. After the news that the NPA had decided not to prosecute anyone in the government, a brother of one of the survivors called the NPA's decision an insult to the affected families: 'What do they mean when they say "enough evidence"? It's an insult to the family, especially those who lost their loved ones. I still feel in this country justice only favours those with high positions.'[53] The truth of this sentiment has been pervasive in post-apartheid SA.

There has been much in the media about how legal remedies to a wide range of problems that citizens experience daily are out of reach of the poor majority, either because they don't know how to go about getting help or they don't have funds to brief and pay a lawyer. Invariably, these are by far mostly African people, who often too are unable to speak English or are illiterate.

That, however, was not the problem in this case. The affected families had legal support, but they never had the support of a health department which is supposed to be the leader in implementing the National Health Amendment Act of 2013. This Act insists on the provision of public health care, and also on enforcement and compliance with those requirements. The searing irony of the failure by the Gauteng Department of Health, the Gauteng provincial government and the national Department of Health to adhere to that legislation is a very serious abdication of responsibility by all those players, especially in the light of the many patients who died and the unlawful and intolerable conditions under which they did so.

The most senior officials involved in this tragedy and those who had any responsibility for public health should have been fired and possibly faced further charges for the preventable deaths of so many people. Instead, the ANC has for many years not only protected government officials involved in corruption but either kept them in their posts or transferred them to other departments. But none of those officials, including those who appeared before the ZCE and against whom evidence of malfeasance was found, have been prosecuted, and they probably will not be. I don't know of any other African country which after gaining independence fell into such an extent of gross corruption. Given the mountain of evidence uncovered by the health ombudsman, how can there be no cover-up corruption in this case?

In conclusion, the most striking thing about this tragedy is that notwithstanding the facts that emerged and their implications for the government, the ANC closed ranks and denied culpability on the spurious grounds of a lack of evidence. Though the arbitration awards paid significant compensation for the deaths when it concerned seeking justice, which is arguably even more important than the monetary compensation paid to the families, the ANC government closed ranks and denied responsibility. Not even the gross negligence involved in those deaths and the cruel conditions under which it took place – of which the report of the Health Ombudsman provides extensive details– was enough for the government to accept responsibility for them. That alone destroyed the ANC's mantra of 'blacks in general and Africans in particular'. Instead, 'Africans in particular' died under cruel and clearly negligent circumstances.

The VBS Bank Scandal (2018)

Perhaps no corruption and fraud case riveted and depressed this country as much as the VBS Mutual Bank scandal. If you tried to understand the unprecedented magnitude of it all, perpetrated by African officials against the poorest African people, read the 'VBS Bank Scandal Revealed in Explosive Report', by Corruption Watch,[54] or the report it mentioned: 'The Great Bank Heist: Investigator's Report to the Prudential Authority',[55] by Terry Motau of Werksmans Attorneys. Throughout South African history it was white people who did bad things to blacks. Oppression and exploitation were what white people did to black people and were synonymous with white supremacy.

Is it significant that the VBS scandal occurred under ANC rule, given that the ANC itself has been torn apart by corruption? Did the ANC government, the minister of finance and Treasury have no prior clue about the massive fraud and corruption unfolding at VBS for several years, especially since it is registered with and regulated by the South African Reserve Bank? How was it possible that the audits of the previous few years, before the scandal broke in 2018, did not detect anything wrong or arouse suspicions that there were serious problems that required urgent investigation? An avalanche of fraud and corruption was suddenly discovered in 2018, but what was going on for years before? These questions are much more relevant since we are dealing with a major financial institution owned and run by black people. Yet these questions are not even posed, let alone dealt with, by Corruption Watch or Motau's investigation report. It is inconceivable, I suggest, that there were no prior symptoms of serious problems at VBS bank.

There are three defining features of the VBS scandal which stand out from anything that happened under ANC rule since 1994. Firstly, there was the fact of the massive and unprecedented scale of the fraud and corruption perpetrated over several years by the officials employed at VBS. Secondly, the fact that the victims of this fraud and corruption were reportedly poor African people who banked at VBS, either having ordinary savings or small business accounts. Most of the depositors at VBS belonged to those categories. Thirdly, it was conspicuous how defensively the African officials of VBS resorted to race when the scandal broke in the media. I earlier pointed to this embedded practice in SA after 1994: the opportunistic use of race and colour by African political and business leaders in particular.

A study of newspaper stories over the past decade shows that there is a clear-cut relationship between this discursive practice around race and colour and the growth of a narrow Africanist majoritarian chauvinism inside the ANC itself. But what was crass in the VBS case is how its African leaders used the 'race card' to disparage media criticisms when the scandal first broke, going so far as to argue that the media speculation of corruption was due to the fact that it was a black-owned and black-controlled bank – that the reports were motivated by racism. But the most scathing irony is that the author of the Werksmans report was an African, Terry Motau, who referred explicitly and unambiguously to 'bribes', 'pillaging' and 'looting' by VBS officials.[56]

So blatantly evident was widespread fraud and corruption in VBS bank that Motau's report urged that it be wound up since 'there was no prospect of saving VBS. It is corrupt and rotten to the core. Indeed, there is hardly a person in its employ in any position of authority who is not, in some way or other, complicit.' He strongly recommended criminal prosecutions, including lawyers, accountants and even the police who were complicit in the fraud and corruption activities. The report shockingly stated that on average people involved were paid 'nearly a million per entity per month'.[57] But what grossly aggravates the impact of the corruption and its implications is that many municipal funds were illegally invested in VBS and that this directly hampered the delivery of services such as water and electricity. That funds of municipalities were centrally involved in the VBS scandal is very clear from numerous press reports.

This aspect of the scandal is a very disturbing revelation of what African nationalism in power has done across Africa since Ghana first got its political independence from Britain in 1957. Scholars have not dealt enough with this phenomenon in their work, especially since the African masses have been the chief support base of the ANC since the 1950s. Those involved in the ANC's widespread corruption in the state and public sectors do not give a damn and have no sympathy for the needs and interests of the African masses, no matter how much poverty, joblessness and various social miseries they suffer daily from, even when the perpetrators come from that same African working-class background. What this record in office (political or corporate power) does is unambiguously reveal that race and colour, which African nationalism has since its inception emphasised, form very treacherous terrain indeed. That is the history of African nationalism in every single African country: how the African ruling elites, former leaders of national liberation movements, used state resources to enrich themselves while the masses who supported them for decades lived in dreadful poverty.

Not even the fact that municipal funds are meant to provide basic services was enough to discourage this massive looting. Neither did it matter that those funds were primarily for the basic needs of the poorest African masses, who were also the most oppressed and exploited people under apartheid. There are many instructive lessons for a study of race and colour in what has happened in SA since 1994 and especially, as a result, the ongoing salience of class analysis. The method of understanding what the ANC leadership has done in SA is not to be preoccupied with race and colour – especially since we have seen how it has been opportunistically exploited by the African elite after 1994 – but to conduct a rigorous class analysis that cuts through race in order to penetrate to the essence of things done in the name of the African masses and purportedly for their benefit, but in fact against their basic interests.

The ANC's neoliberalism and corruption have in fact exploded the historical and sociological meaning of race since 1994, in the specific sense that its mythology has been laid bare for all to see. Race and colour have shown up the emperor's clothes. We saw it in the 1990s too when many African journalists eschewed criticism of the ANC because it would look bad for them to criticise the first-ever black ANC government. In fact, Mandela rebuked black journalists for criticising the ANC government when he was president. He could understand criticisms from white journalists but not from Africans. But black editors became bolder after the 1990s, as has been evinced by the stories they carried of VBS, Nkandla and the Zondo Commission of Enquiry. But what they have not done is to analyse its implications for the ANC and African nationalist rule.

However, journalist Ivo Vegter hit this problem on the head: 'Black nationalists and socialist radicals defended VBS Bank vigorously against what they claimed were racist attacks by forces that could not tolerate a successful bank owned and operated by and for black people. Their racist rhetoric now lies exposed as a cover for corruption, fraud and theft'.[58] By 'black nationalists' Vegter is referring to members of the ANC or any other outfit involved in that scandal, and by 'socialist radicals' he can only be referring to people in the SACP. I am not in the least surprised by what has happened under ANC rule, if we look at its policy trajectory since 1912, including the amorphous ambiguity of the FC. The ANC's biggest weakness and vulnerability has been its policies since 1912.

It was also reported that the VBS scam ripped off R60 million of workers' money, that the retirement funds of 26,000 municipal workers were at risk, and the losses involve some other countries too, such as Namibia and Zimbabwe.[59] Once more, there was not an ounce of moral consideration in the VBS scam, as was the case with the Nkandla scandal too. It was also reported that Malema and the EFF are implicated in a R5.5 million scam which is linked to the VBS scandal, which paid for a mansion in Sandown in Johannesburg.[60] The story reported evasive messaged replies from Malema to questions about the circumstances under which the house was purchased and bank payments made for it into trust accounts linked to him and the EFF.

But did the ANC's leadership know absolutely nothing about what was going on at VBS, especially between 2014 and 2018? I doubt it. Did Malema and the top EFF leadership also know nothing about the corruption going on at VBS, even though Brian Shivambu, the brother of deputy leader of the party, Floyd Shivambu, received R16,148,569 in payments from VBS?[61] The Motau report also showed that Floyd was paid R10 million of the amount his brother received. Did Floyd Shivambu and Malema not know anything of those payments when it occurred? The report was explicit, not provisional, about the involvement of Brian Shivambu. There were reports that a cousin of Malema was also linked to the VBS scandal.[62] Though there have been strenuous denials all round, news reports point to some compelling evidence of wrongdoing, if not outright corruption, by both Shivambu brothers.

In conclusion, there must be no doubt at all that the ANC's corruption is related to the rampant corruption of a petit bourgeois African nationalism we saw throughout countries in Africa after they gained political independence. 'One of the shameful achievements of the ANC in its 25 years of governing post-apartheid South Africa is that it's living up to the political stereotype of what is wrong with post-colonial Africa – unethical and corrupt leaders who exercise power through patronage', was how Mandisi Majavu characterised the ANC.[63] But what Majavu does not do is to trace the ideological roots of the patronage and corruption. Key in this regard is the historically middle-class nature of the leadership of African nationalism and the fact that because it emphasised race and not class or the race–class dynamics, it used its access to state power not to meaningfully better the lives of the African masses but as an instrument for its own enrichment.

Even the ANC was itself compelled to condemn the VBS looting.[64] And in June 2020 eight people associated with the bank and its auditor were charged with 47 counts of theft, fraud and corruption. The media have been overflowing with stories of ANC corruption across the state over the past decade, much of which the Zondo Commission hearings revealed. I firmly believe that much more is still going to be uncovered in the years ahead. An avalanche of heart-breaking stories of corruption, fraud, nepotism and cronyism committed by ANC officials at every level of the state, especially local government, and in SOEs, is evident in the media. Anybody in the ANC who even attempts to deny this tragic fact would be wasting his or her time, so palpably evident have these scourges been in the media. Local government, which is the provider of basic services to communities, was hit with R1.5 billion in VBS looting.[65] Not even the deposits from municipalities which were already struggling to provide such services to poor black communities were spared by this scandal.

Endnotes

1. This matter of the ANC's, cadres, is very important to consider because the corrupt actions of those members the ANC deployed to various sites of the state are a violent contradiction of even the most elementary meaning of what a revolutionary cadre is meant to represent and the qualities necessary for that purpose. Instead, the ANC's cadres have looted state coffers meant for townships which desperately required basic municipal services and infrastructural development.
2. I think this factor is most revealing of the sinister depth and expanse of the corruption by the ANC in the sense that it failed even to distinguish between that which was done in the private sector and that in the state and public sectors. In the former case, corruption also had very negative consequences, but nowhere near as bad as its consequences in the latter case, where the ANC as the ruling party dominated and where all the contracts and tenders were done and all monies of the public fiscus concentrated.
3. Ebrahim Harvey, *Kgalema Motlanthe: A Political Biography* (Johannesburg: Jacana, 2012), pp. 132–3.
4. Hein Marais, *South Africa Pushed to the Limit: The Political Economy of Change* (Cape Town: UCT Press, 2011), pp. 262–308.
5. Marais, *South Africa*, p. 281.
6. Marais, *South Africa*, p. 322. See Helen Schneider, P. Baron and S. Fonn, 'The promise and the practice of transformation in South Africa's health system', in Sakhela Buhlungu et al, eds, *State of the Nation: South Africa 2007* (Cape Town: HSRC Press, 2007), pp. 289–311.
7. Patrick Bond, 'Contradictions subside then deepen', in John Saul and Patrick Bond, *South Africa, The Present as History: From Mrs Ples to Mandela and Marikana* (Johannesburg: Jacana Media, 2014), p. 163.
8. Bond, 'Contradictions subside', p. 164.
9. Marais, *South Africa*, pp. 436–8.
10. Marais, *South Africa*, pp. 408–11.
11. See http://edition.cnn.com/HEALTH/9905/06/safrica.azt/1.
12. Kerry Cullinan, 'Mbeki still believes his own AIDS propaganda', 7 March 2016, at www.health-e.org.za.
13. Patrick Bond, 'Consolidating the Contradictions: From Mandela to Marikana, 2000–2012', in John Saul and Patrick Bond, South Africa, The Present as History: From Mrs Ples to Mandela and Marikana (Johannesburg: Jacana Media, 2014), pp 176–210.

14 See David Bruce, 'Marikana: The case against Mthetwa', *Mail & Guardian*, 13 November 2014.
15 Bond, 'Contradictions subside', p. 215.
16 Ralph Hamann. 'What caused a massacre?', *Sunday Independent*, 17 September 2019.
17 See 'Marikana: Shame on you, lying Lonmin – houses promised to workers still not a reality', *Mail & Guardian*, 12 August 2016.
18 Don Makatile, 'Marikana legal fees sought', *Sunday Independent*, 25 August 2019.
19 Peter Alexander et al., *Marikana: Voices from South Africa's Mining Massacre, the Mountain and a Case to Answer* (Athens, OH: Ohio University Press, 2013).
20 See Patrick Bond, 'Uneven and combined development', in Saul and Bond, *South Africa*, p. 228.
21 Cited in John Saul, 'Liberating liberation: The struggle against recolonization in South Africa', in Saul and Bond, *South Africa*, p. 259.
22 See Jay Naidoo, 'We have no other choice', *Daily Maverick*, 5 February 2019, at https://www.dailymaverick.co.za.
23 Pallo Jordan, *Letters to my Comrades: Interviews and Excursions* (Johannesburg: Jacana Media, 2017), p. 428.
24 David Smith, *Capitalist Democracy on Trial: The Transatlantic Debate from Tocqueville to the Present* (London and New York: Routledge, 1990).
25 See 'Secure in Comfort', the report produced by the office of Madonsela at www.publicprotector.org.
26 'ANC media briefing to clear up confusion no longer on the cards', 6 August 2019, at https://m.news24.com.
27 'Secure in Comfort' (s 9.2.20), p. 403.
28 'Nkandla has erratic water supply – in defence of Zuma', *RDM News Wire*, 28 May 2015; see 'Nkandla compound fire-pool controversy', at https://en.m.wikipedia.org
29 See Leon Trotsky, *The History of the Russian Revolution* (London: Pluto Press, 1985).
30 Interview with Trevor Manuel, 22 January 2010.
31 Adam Habib, *Rebels and Rage: Reflection on Fees Must Fall* (Johannesburg and Cape Town: Jonathan Ball, 2019).
32 WhatsApp message to Habib, 19 February 2020.
33 Interview with Adam Habib, Johannesburg, 13 June 2017.
34 Ebrahim Harvey and Saliem Fakir, 'Decolonise science at your peril', *Mail & Guardian*, 23 October 2016.
35 Harvey and Fakir, 'Decolonise science'.
36 Mohamed Adhikari, *'Let Us Live for Our Children': The Teachers League of South Africa, 1913–1940* (Cape Town: UCT Press and Buchu Press, 1996) and Crain Soudien, *Cape Radicals: Intellectual and Political Thought of the New Era Fellowship, 1930s–1960s* (Johannesburg: Wits University Press, 2019).
37 Habib interview.
38 Interview with Tawana Kupe, 23 November 2017, Johannesburg.
39 Interview with Dinga Sikwebu, 22 July 2017, Cape Town.
40 Cited in Claudi Mailovich, 'Adam Habib's future was forged in the summer of discontent at Wits', *Business Day*, 21 February 2020.
41 Ebrahim Harvey, 'ANC must intervene to resolve funding crisis', *City Press*, 25 October 2016.
42 Interview with Helena Sheehan, 22 June 2018, Johannesburg.
43 Interview with Steven Friedman, 22 July 2010, Johannesburg.
44 Interview with Feroz Cachalia, 22 January 2018, Johannesburg.

45. Mia Mercado, 'This is proof that institutional racism is still very much alive', 15 March 2017, at https://bustle.com/p/this-is-proof-that-institutioanl-racism-is-still-very-much-a-problem-43610.
46. Mercado, 'This is proof'.
47. Interview with Shaeera Kalla, 10 December 2017, Johannesburg.
48. 'Life Esidimeni: The greatest cause of human rights violations since democracy', *Mail & Guardian*, 9 October 2017.
49. 'Life Esidimeni: The greatest cause of human rights violations'.
50. 'Esidimeni: "Not enough evidence"', *Sunday Independent*, 22 September 2019.
51. 'Contribution of the Health Ombud to accountability: The Life Esidimeni tragedy', *Health and Human Rights Journal*, 11 November 2018.
52. Stephen Grootes, 'Gauteng ANC's shocking, horrifying re-election of Qedani Mahlangu, 144 lost lives later', *Daily Maverick*, 24 July 2018, at www.dailymaverick.co.za.
53. 'Esidimeni: Not enough evidence'.
54. 'VBS scandal revealed in explosive report', *Corruption Watch*, 11 October 2018.
55. Terry Motau, 'VBS Mutual Bank: The great bank heist. Investigator's report to the prudential authority', Werksmans Attorneys, 2018.
56. Motau, 'VBS Mutual Bank'.
57. Motau, 'VBS Mutual Bank', p. 132.
58. Ivo Vegter, 'VBS defenders expose the intellectual poverty of the race card', *Daily Maverick*, 16 October 2018.
59. Sabelo Skiti, 'Worker's R60 million "lost" in banks scam', *Mail & Guardian*, 24 January 2020.
60. Zingisa Mvumu, 'How VBS loot helped Juju get a R5m house', *Sunday Times*, 24 November 2019.
61. 'VBS scandal revealed'.
62. James Richardson, 'VBS heist: Fresh reports link Malema's cousin to scandal', 13 November 2019, at www.thesouthafrican.com.
63. Mandisi Majhavu, 'Corruption in South Africa: Echoes of leaders who plundered their countries', *The Conversation*, 23 January 2020.
64. Jan Gerber, 'A case of the greedy stealing from the poor: The ANC wants swift action against VBS looters', 23 October 2019, at www.https//m.news24.com.
65. Claudi Mailovich, 'What VBS says about South Africa's struggling local government sector', *Financial Mail*, 3 October 2019, at www.businesslive.co.za.

Eight
The vengeance of history?

The Miserly Minimum Wage Debacle

SOUTH AFRICAN CAPITALISM was built on the back of cheap black (Coloured, African and Indian) labour, and from the time of the mineral revolution of the late 19th century, employers relied heavily on African migrant labour. It was in fact on the basis of cheap labour that the mineral revolution developed so rapidly and thereby laid the basis for the broader industrial and specifically manufacturing revolution of the early to mid-20th century. Manufacturing depended not on migrant labour but mainly on an urbanised and settled African working class. Although industrial workers were paid more than migrant mine workers and agricultural workers, their wages were also kept artificially low by policies favouring white workers and by the exclusion of black workers from trade union organisation and action.[1]

It is against that background that we must appraise what has happened to black wages after 1994 in SA and the National Minimum Wage Act introduced in 2018, a lengthy 14 years after the 1994 democratic breakthrough. The fact that it took the ANC government so long to introduce legislation for a minimum wage is a reliable indication of the expected resistance from employers and the dampening effects they probably thought it might have on employment creation. Furthermore, for precisely the same reasons the new national minimum wage of 2018 was set at the miserably low level of R20 an hour, which mainly affected the lowest paid workers in SA, including domestic and farm workers. The minimum wage was set at an hourly rate, instead of a monthly national minimum wage, which is what was sorely needed to combat a historical low-wage regime in SA and soaring costs of living.[2]

Another deeply disappointing thing about the new hourly minimum wage is that it will have no effect on the majority of workers who earn above R20 an hour. This at a time when the soaring costs of living in SA over the past decade have hit black working-class families very hard. But there is another relevant factor in this paltry hourly minimum wage debacle which is as disappointing and saddening. It was signed into law – alongside the arbitrary changes to strike rules which will require that strike ballots be held before workers can go on strike – by Ramaphosa in 2018, the same man who led the NUM in the tumultuous 1980s, helped build the trade union movement in that important decade, and regarded himself as a socialist. At its 1986 Congress the National Union of Mineworkers (NUM), of which Ramaphosa was leader, had emblazoned across a large hall a striking banner, 'Freedom means Socialism.' It is just incredible how much and quickly his fortunes changed after he left NUM. For a country that was built on cheap black labour for well over a century, and for its foremost trade union leader in the 1980s, the Act is a very negative reflection on both the ANC and Ramaphosa, who today is one of the richest men in SA.

Besides, how are we to reconcile the ANC's endorsement of this poor minimum hourly rate with its 1991 January 8 Statement, when it warned against the private sector's attack on living standards and committed itself to addressing this problem: 'The call for a living wage remains among our principled demands and must be pursued.'[3] That was just one of the many commitments the ANC made to working-class demands and interests.[4]

A similar emasculation occurred with the fulfilment of the Bill of Rights in the constitution, with the calculated insertion of the disempowering caveat in it, that the realisation of socio-economic rights is subject to the availability of funds. But who can believe that this caveat was not motivated in the first place by the neoliberal advisors to the constitution? And who can believe that the drafters of the constitution, which centrally involved Ramaphosa, and the rest of the ANC's leaders, did not understand that to have such a caveat, arguably at the heart of the constitution, was not going to be in the interests of the black working-class majority, who lacked decent basic services for many years under apartheid and would therefore yearn for them after 1994? The same question could be asked about what the consequences would be for the interests of that same constituency of closing the RDP office in 1996 and abandoning the demands in the FC.

In both cases larger neoliberal forces were at work to undermine the fulfilment of the needs, rights and demands in the FC, the constitution and the RDP. And it was those same forces behind the ANC's rejection of a more substantial and decent minimum wage and opting instead for an insultingly meagre hourly minimum wage. And it is in defence of those same neoliberal interests that Ramaphosa stated in 1992: 'Macroeconomic populist pitfalls which can have the opposite effect of good intentions in the medium term have to be avoided.'[5] Knowing the history of racism and capitalism in this country and the devastating social consequences it had on the black working class, two years before the 1994 elections, he had decidedly departed from articulating their needs and interests and succumbed to the tentacles of neoliberalism.

In advance of the 1994 elections he was advocating a neoliberal macroeconomic approach to deal with the devastating socioeconomic legacy of apartheid. No wonder his detractors often refer to him as the man of WMC. But is there not some truth in that charge? After all, long before he became leader of the NUM in 1982, he was appointed to the board of the Anglo American-inspired Urban Foundation (UF) in 1977, and warmly welcomed by the late Clive Menell at his first board meeting. Menell, one of the founders of the UF, formed less than a year after the 1976 Soweto student uprisings, was candid about its main purpose: 'We became involved because we were scared. There was concern for the country, of course, but there was also a selfish concern for our assets.'[6] With all due respect to Ramaphosa, with whom I worked in Cosatu in the 1980s, he has moved in those circles since the 1970s.[7]

But back to the minimum wage. Black wages have generally remained low after 1994, while white incomes have risen dramatically. According to Statistics South Africa (SSA), it was estimated in 2019 that whites earned three times more than blacks. The report pointed out that 'on the highly sensitive issue of inequality, research found that the wage gap between South Africa's groups increased between 2011 and 2015.' It also found that the average monthly earning among blacks – who accounted for about 80 per cent of the population – was R6,899, while the figure was R24,646 for whites and that income earnings remained 'heavily racialised'. If that was not bad enough, the jobless figures for Africans made up the vast majority of the total jobless population, over 46 per cent, while it was 10 per cent for whites. Finally, poverty trends showed that Africans and Coloureds were regarded as 'chronically' poor.[8]

This is unsurprising because it has always been Africans and Coloureds who were the most oppressed and exploited people in SA. This is a major reason for the growing alienation of Coloured workers who feel marginalised and discriminated against by the way in which the ANC's AA and BEE policies have been applied. But there are several things about joblessness, earnings and income which few writers have dealt with in post-apartheid SA. It is not only the staggering 10 million people unemployed at the start of 2010, but the low wages paid to those who did have jobs, as a result of which the notion of the 'working poor' was coined some time ago. I argue that of all middle-income countries this problem is most stark in SA because of our racist history, the results of which have disadvantaged blacks in every single socioeconomic respect: wages, poverty, unemployment, standards of living, inequalities, basic services, education and skills.

But the ANC still has a chance to try and rectify matters and align itself with the interests, needs and aspirations of the majority black masses, which have been its chief constituency from the 1950s. I'm deliberately saying 'black' masses, and not 'African' masses. If the ANC wants to reverse the alienation of the Coloured and Indian working class and middle classes, it needs to break free from the raw nativist chauvinism that has starkly penetrated its ranks. However, at the policy level the first thing it must do is to introduce both a wealth and Tobin tax (a tax on international financial transactions). The key argument for these taxes is that without them we are never going to be able to deal with the devastating social legacy of both apartheid and the neoliberalism that followed it after 1994. In fact, the absence of these taxes renders the paltry minimum hourly wage rate even more unfortunate. Besides, countries which don't have our devastating history, like Spain, Norway,

Switzerland and Belgium, have wealth taxes. So why not SA? Our trade unions should be seriously driving the fight for these demands but cannot even mount a strong enough fight to review the miserable and miserly minimum wage of R20 an hour.

The once-powerful Cosatu of the 1980s has become such a damp squib today under ANC rule. The guardian of the labour movement that it once was has been lost to the cause of the working class. Its bite and even bark have gone. This is partly because of changes within the federation. Cosatu's membership base has shifted from unskilled and semi-skilled workers to one biased to skilled and professional workers – so much so that it has been suggested that Cosatu has 'become a home for middle class civil servants rather than a working class federation'.[9] In any case, instead of spearheading a fight against the minimum hourly wage rate it accepted it. Arguably, just as nobody should be denied food, shelter and crucial services because they cannot afford them, so too the realisation must dawn upon the ANC that a decent minimum wage is key to not only making ends meet but to increasing standards of living. But neoliberalism does not work that way. No, it is generally based on the barest minimums, whether these are wages, social grants or the 'free' basic services it provides to indigents in townships.

There are also other, perhaps more compelling grounds for both a higher hourly *and* monthly minimum wage rates: the crucial question of not only social justice and greater equality, but the related matter of human dignity. In this regard, life under capitalism is generally brutal for working-class people, wherever they are. Unless there is a comprehensive state welfare system, as to a large extent exists in the Scandinavian countries, their lives and life chances and that of their children are seriously compromised. That is why the minimum hourly rate of R20 is so tragically repulsive, all the more so for being signed into law by Ramaphosa himself. That is why I argued against it and for the 'dignity and integrity of a much better minimum wage than R20 an hour...'[10]

Human dignity is what black people around the world were historically denied. In this regard, it is necessary to ask Ramaphosa and the ANC: just what can workers and their families, with today's soaring cost of living, do with R20 an hour though this has been increased very slightly this year to R21.69.[11] It is even more reprehensible when Ramaphosa, the ANC and the Department of Labour have craftily emphasised the difference between a *minimum* wage and a *living wage* in order to make this paltry minimum more attractive and acceptable as a kind of progressive stepping-stone towards a higher living wage at some indeterminate future, as is the case with the second socialist stage of the SACPs two-stage revolutionary theory. It was therefore with miserable satisfaction that he urged acceptance of the minimum wage because it 'provides a firm and unassailable foundation from which to advance the struggle for a living wage.'[12]

It was shocking that Cosatu could accept this minimum wage. In 2016 it officially argued that the apartheid wage structure had not fundamentally changed, that there had been a reversal of some wage gains, that the apartheid wage gap remained intact and that many more workers were defined as the working poor. How then could it accept such a poor minimum wage, which sharply contradicted the thinking in its 2016 official document?[13] Yet Ramaphosa was quick to congratulate Cosatu on its acceptance of this minimum.[14]

But this is in fact a pyrrhic victory for both Ramaphosa and Cosatu. It is going to make the struggle for a good national living wage harder, not easier, I believe. There is a relationship between a minimum wage and a living wage in the sense that the lower a minimum wage is the harder it will be over the longer term to secure a good and satisfactory living wage, especially if it is as comprehensively defined as Cosatu did so in 2016. After all, the title referred to both a living wage *and* a restructuring of the economy. But there is absolutely no way Cosatu can secure the fundamental restructuring of the South African economy within the existing capitalist framework. It is inconceivable how they will proceed to do that.

I need to return to the matter of human dignity. In addition to socio-economic rights, the constitution also enshrines the right to human dignity (s.10). In other words, it is an error to approach the minimum wage as a stand-alone demand. The implicit understanding therefore is that the socioeconomic rights in the Bill of Rights are in fact not only human rights but that they are closely, if not inextricably, related to the minimum and living wage. But though the Bill of Rights is regarded as the 'cornerstone of democracy' in South Africa, after nearly 25 years since the constitution's adoption, we have neither a decent minimum nor a living wage. Besides, over 10 million people are unemployed and millions still lack basic services, while schools are in an atrociously poor situation.

In short, it is palpably evident that ours is a neoliberal constitution in the specific sense that the caveat of subsection 26(2), that 'the state must take all reasonable legislative and other measures, within its available resources, to achieve the progressive realisation of this right', is an inherently serious and debilitating limitation. Though this limitation applies to housing in this clause, it will equally apply to any other rights. The omission of the right to work from the constitution is deliberate, though the FC makes provision for it: 'The state shall recognise the right and duty of all to work …' The constitution cannot enshrine the right to work because it is a globally pervasive structural reality of capitalism that it requires a 'reserve army of labour' in order to suppress wage levels.

Arguably, no other middle-income country has a working class that went through the racist hell we endured in SA and therefore deserved so much better than what the ANC has offered since 1994. In fact, in some respects things are incomparably worse today for black workers and their families than it was in 1994, thanks to a combination of the ANC's neoliberalism and the terrible corruption bedevilling the ANC, which has stolen from the fiscus huge amounts of funds that could have gone towards a substantial improvement in conditions and increase in living standards. In an article on this matter at the time I argued: 'Organised black labour needs a decisive struggle now to end this historical low-wage economy white supremacy was built upon. The most important contributor to reducing intolerably huge income inequalities is a much better minimum and later living wage.'[15]

Unemployment and inequality are today greater than ever before; crime and the abuse of women are at record levels. SA is in an unprecedented socioeconomic and political crisis at this moment, with the prospect, as the Budget revealed in February 2020, that things are likely to worsen further before they get any better. Tito Mboweni, minister of finance, argued that in the interests of cutting the huge deficit and the need for macroeconomic stability, the public sector's wage bill of R160.2 billion will be severely cut, together with likely job cuts over the next three years.[16]

But the unions have already given notice that they will not accept these cuts, indicating that relations between the unions and government are going to be very tough over the next few years. Cosatu spokesperson

Sizwe Pamla said that the government was taking a gamble and that the plan on wage cuts could lead to a public sector strike: 'If push comes to shove, we will have to fight.'[17] This is tough talk only because it is inevitable that such severe cutbacks will lead to increases in black unemployment, poverty and inequality levels.

The most unfortunate fact is that the people who have least benefited from the changes since the 1990s are the same people who are now likely to suffer even greater disadvantages if these neoliberal cost-cutting measures are implemented by the ANC government at a moment of the gravest crisis since 1994 we are facing today in SA. It is important to note that already the public sector is severely understaffed, especially in public hospitals and schools. This can only mean that the quality of services rendered by it will decline further if there are any wage and staff cutbacks, arising out of this budget and the plans to slash the wage bill.

But there is an even more important consideration: why are the wage cutbacks targeting workers in the public sector and not senior managers and executives, especially against the background of so much corruption that has occurred at those levels across the state and public sectors? The first serious attacks against public sectors workers occurred in the 1990s, after Gear was adopted in 1996. While there have been ongoing retrenchments in the public sector, from time to time, this will be the second major attack against these workers. In the late 1990s it was also rank-and-file workers who were targeted for retrenchment and not managerial and executive levels.

I conclude this section with the fact that in our capitalist society, in which race itself has been an instrument of exploitation – in the sense that race allowed white-dominated capital to secure a higher rate of exploitation of cheap black labour and therefore of profit – the probable thinking of the average black worker in 1994 was that her or his life would be much better after 1994 because they would get much better pay and standards of living. The point is that it is only through wages that a worker can secure a better life and higher standard of living. Under capitalism there is simply no other way in which standards of living can be raised, other than state expenditure on providing decommodified housing and other basic municipal services to working-class families who are unemployed or too poor to pay for them. Other than that, at the end of the day what workers can do for themselves and their families and how well they can live, including how healthily, depends entirely on the amount of wage income.

But with the minimum hourly rate of R21.67 the argument of Ramaphosa and his government ignored not only the historical black low-wage regime, especially of domestic and farm workers, but how it was perpetuated by them after 1994. I argue that only in the strictest neoliberal minimalist sense can that hourly rate be regarded as incrementally progressive, not to enable people to live a better life, but to reintroduce that same black low-wage regime under the guise of a minimum wage increase. It is an increase but not one to really make a significant difference for workers and their immediate families. Neoliberal minimalism is evident in wages, working conditions and state benefits. We can see that minimalism at play with all the social grants in SA. While over 18 million people receive pensions and grants, consuming a large portion of the budget, the actual amounts of the grants received by individuals are very low in relation to the very high cost of living.

For example, what can a pensioner do with as little as R1,780 a month (2020) when they often have to support other family dependants too who are not on grants or a parent or a caregiver with a child grant of R430 a month? The highest cost of living since 1994 exists today, such that even middle-class people often struggle to make ends meet. Now contrast that situation with the lives, incomes and profits of the white and black corporate elite and ANC politicians. The 2019 Stats SA's Quarterly Employment Survey showed that the average employee in SA earns R20,190 a month or R242,280 a year, whereas in 2018 the remuneration consultancy 21st Century found that CEOs at some companies earned an average basic salary of R5.35 million, which, with short- and long-term incentives taken into account, approached R13 million.[18] ANC ministers, the president and his deputy earn between R2million and R3 million per annum.

If these matters of income are teased out, it is clear is that in the corporate world the astronomical income of top white executives is rooted in the apartheid past. The embedded pattern of race-based salary differentials of apartheid was perpetuated and replicated after 1994. The simple reason for this is that the ANC left the private sector totally untransformed, except for the changes that BEE and AA laws introduced to that regime, which, however, were not of benefit to the black masses but to a small elite and more numerous black middle class who had some education and skills to take advantage of AA.

There were many reports that the big conglomerates made more profit after 1994 than in the decade before, and I earlier mentioned Mbeki's acknowledgement in his last State of the Nation address that the ANC government had been kind to business interests. These are some of the reasons why a minimum rate of a megre R21.67 an hour was so unfair and unjust. But to add insult to injury, the first increase in the rate was just 76 cents![19] This was a 3.8 per cent increase, below the inflation rate of 4–5 per cent.[20] This was a further confirmation of neoliberal minimalism, with scant regard for the present unprecedented unemployment crisis, the hardships and poverty-ravaged black working-class communities and for the fact that the pension of R1,780 was making it increasingly impossible for pensioners to make ends meet. For the fight for a decent minimum wage, especially during such hard times, this is a further serious setback.

In fact, there in a nutshell we have the brutal irony of the story of post-apartheid SA: while WMC were doing so well with superlative profits and living in the lap of luxury, the black working class was being hammered by neoliberalism in every respect, as I have shown in much detail earlier. But nothing was arguably worse than the lousy and miserly R20 an hour and the 76 cents increase as of 1 March 2020. They could not even round off the increase to R1 an hour for the most brutally exploited and oppressed workers since the days of the old slave Cape Colony, namely black farm and domestic workers.

History will record that all this happened under ANC rule in ways which shamelessly abandoned any pretence to even social democratic policies and conditions of life. Instead, how this minimum wage was handled by Ramaphosa and the ANC should have shattered whatever remaining illusions the African working class still had in the leadership of the ANC. The repeal of all racist laws did nothing to curb the appetite of capitalist exploitation of cheap *black* labour. Despite the existence of a 'non-racial' democracy with a constitution purportedly one of the most progressive in the world, capital, now white and black, still employs that same cheap African labour that WMC grew rich from under apartheid.

Finally, the ANC government also failed to realise that low wages for black workers have been a systemic feature in SA for well over a century, and that this history and its social impact, together with the impact of the neoliberal policies adopted since 1994, have contributed to SA having the highest rate of inequality in the world. Therefore, this low minimum wage is likely going to worsen those already existing social inequalities over the coming period, especially under the corrosive impact of the highest cost of living we've had since 1994. It is for these reasons and the poor benchmark it represents for the fight for a good and meaningful living wage that this was a lost opportunity to make a more significant impact on the standards of living of the lowest-paid workers in the country.

White Monopoly Capital: Myth or Still a Reality?

An interesting debate appeared in the media a few years ago: whether in post-apartheid SA WMC, as we understood it under apartheid, still existed. The temptation to pose this question in the first place was as a result of the emergence of a small black capitalist class as part of the purportedly 'non-racial' democracy after 1994. The first thing to do in examining this debate is to look at the present structure of the JSE, which is still overwhelmingly white-owned and white-controlled. In this regard, I do not accept that we need to draw a distinction between capital owned by white South Africans and white foreigners, especially in the light of the fact that foreign capital was from the outset of the mineral revolution a significant factor in both the mining and later manufacturing industries. I also don't find it necessary to draw such a distinction, other than for statistical purposes perhaps, because white racism was historically a big formative part of the global capitalist order.

Besides the de-racialisation of legislation, what specifically happened in SA after 1994 which defined WMC out of existence, especially in so far as the economy is concerned? How can racism and its effects have continued after 1994 but WMC, which overwhelmingly owned and controlled the economy since the mid-19th century, disappeared? There is no compelling and coherent argument I have read anywhere to support the notion that WMC is no longer relevant because it no longer exists. More so, how can the structures upon which it was based – migrant labour, impoverished black townships on the peripheries of major cities, an abundant supply of super-exploitable cheap black labour, a JSE which is still white-dominated, and ongoing white domination of senior management in the private sector – still be in place, while WMC no longer exists and is therefore not relevant? Or is it that the ANC knows full well that it exists but that to continue to entertain that discourse is to undermine its own efforts at deracialising the economy and society?

But surely the current structure of the JSE and the ownership, leadership and management in the corporate world tell a different story. In 2017 Kate Wilkinson reported the findings (in 2013) of Alternative Prosperity, a BEE advisory group, that direct black investment held 10 per cent of the top 100 companies on the JSE and indirect black investment a further 23 per cent. 'White investment' held 13 per cent, foreign investment 39 per cent, with 16 per cent not analysed. This compared with much lower figures cited by Jacob Zuma in his State of the Nation addresses in 2015 and 2017 – 3 per cent and 10 per cent respectively. Zuma used such data as 'pointing to the need to move faster to achieve meaningful economic emancipation. We have called for radical economic transformation.'[21] Note Zuma's use of the terms 'meaningful economic emancipation' and 'radical economic transformation', when in fact it had little to do with that – certainly in so far as addressing the conditions of mass black poverty, unemployment and related social miseries – but more narrowly about black ownership of shares on the JSE. Wilkinson also pointed to the contested meanings of black ownership and black-controlled and managed companies on the JSE, and she concluded: 'Debate on the share of the JSE held, owned, controlled or managed by black people will no doubt continue for years to come. Transparency on the methodologies used to calculate the estimates is vital.'[22]

Whatever the sizeable proportion of shares held by foreign capital, it reflects two interrelated things. Firstly, the lengthy history of the involvement of foreign capital since the onset of the mineral revolution; and secondly, how consistently attractive investments in SA were to foreign capital for all these years, mainly because of this abundance of cheap black labour since the 19th century, which has persisted after 1994. I argue that the ANC since 1994 made sure that African labour remained cheap and plentiful for both foreign and local investment. It is the combined weight of local white and foreign capital which has probably minimised black ownership on the JSE over the past decade.

However, perhaps more importantly, many of the advocates of radical economic transformation (RET) often link it with a critique of WMC, the strategic purpose of which is to create more space and leverage for BEE deals and the growth of black-owned capital. In this regard it is of critical importance to bear in mind that it was the creation of a black capitalist class and a more numerous black middle class which was the strategic heart of the 1993 settlement, without which there would have been no settlement at all. It was WMC which created the concepts of both BEE and AA, and it was AAC which drove those strategies after Mandela was released. WMC was miles ahead of the political negotiations at Codesa, which, aside from this strategy, was so heavily politically and technically loaded that key questions of the economy in a post-apartheid SA never featured at all. Neither was it meant to, thanks to the power of WMC then. At that time five companies controlled over 80 per cent of the JSE. Such a very high concentration and centralisation of economic power was unmatched anywhere else.

The incontrovertibly elitist nature of BEE deals with the support of WMC is starker and more important than the endless debates and confusion about the extent of black ownership on the JSE. When the financial analysts and JSE-based researchers analyse these trends, they understand 'economic transformation' to be about the extent to which blacks have become owners and managers of capital on the JSE. This is a very serious limitation. There is not even a focus on the wages and working conditions of the workers in those companies, let alone what those elitist deals and whatever black ownership exists do to identify and address black poverty, unemployment, homelessness, the atrocious lack of basic services and other social scourges in poor black communities.

The whole notion of 'economic transformation' and the various methodologies used to determine black ownership and control on the JSE are misleading, as is RET. In fact, what shows this beyond doubt is that RET is wielded by those who want a greater share of the white-dominated economy, in which once again race is craftily used to make such advances, especially by those who invoke a specific critique of WMC as blocking the aspiration by black people to become owners and managers of capital. The point about this entire discourse of black capital is just that. It not only has nothing to do with the needs, aspirations and demands of the black working-class majority but will in fact serve to worsen the prospects for dealing with and resolving them. But that has been the logic of BEE deals thus far.

The reason why dealing with BEE and AA is important when discussing WMC is that these were primarily the tools with which the

NP and WMC were planning the reforms to deracialise the economy and the corporate world through the creation of a tiny black bourgeoisie and a larger black middle class which both thrived under ANC rule. ANC rule, black capital and the instruments of BEE and AA in fact all owe their existence to WMC and its willingness to share some of its ill-gotten and enormous gains with them. The ultimate logic of this arrangement was that the ANC was compelled to be favourably disposed to and finally defensive of the interests of white capital. Nowhere did we see this role more than at Marikana. Arguably, it was the role of the ANC minister and commissioner of police in confronting and killing the strikers which brought home the power of WMC, as illustrated by Ramaphosa's intervention.

For a black director, especially of his political stature, to urge 'concomitant action' against the strikers counted incomparably more than had that been done by any white director on the Lonmin board. In return for taking care of the pecuniary interests of Ramaphosa and the black elite which WMC gave space to after 1994, the ANC had to keep a tight rein over the disgruntled African masses. The political elite of the ANC and the BEE elite have often intermingled in government and the corporate sector and reinforced one another, as much as they both intermingled with WMC to sustain all their collective interests. How vitally important those goals were for WMC after 1994, even more than the NP, was well captured by Moeletsi Mbeki:

> The first purpose of BEE was to create a buffer group among the political class that would become an ally of big business in South Africa. This buffer group would use its newfound power as controller of the government to protect the assets of big business. The buffer group would also protect the modus operandi of big business and thereby maintain the status quo in which South African business operates. That was the design of the BEE conglomerates. Sanlam was soon followed by Anglo American. Sanlam established BEE vehicle Nail; Anglo established Real Africa, Johnnic and so forth. The conglomerates took their marginal assets and gave them to politically influential black people, with the purpose, in my view, not to transform the economy but to create a black political class that is in alliance with the conglomerates and therefore wants to maintain the status quo of our economy and the ways it operates.[23]

In other words, WMC and the ANC mutually needed each other more than ever before, especially since the only way they could secure each other's interests was to fulfil the role imposed by the terms of the 1993 settlement, especially after the NP dissolved in 1997. It is important to note that WMC had learnt to live with the NP's Afrikaner nationalism over several decades and now it used that experience to navigate dealing with the ANC's African nationalism after 1994. It is not only that the priority of Mbeki and the ANC was to develop a black capitalist class, as Dominic Brown argues,[24] but that that was in fact the goal of WMC long before the ANC won the 1994 elections. WMC is the father of the idea of black embourgeoisement. WMC, through Oppenheimer, the AAC and the Urban Foundation, played the role British liberals earlier played in calling for an end to colonial rule, and instead absorbing black people into the capitalist system. But the main reason why many insist that WMC continues to be an unwelcome reality today, besides its dominance of the JSE, is the fact that white people generally profited after 1994. There are many reports which found that white incomes increased after 1994, and that they still overwhelmingly dominated large corporations and their management and executive structures.

A major factor in the fortunes of the conglomerates that dominate South African capital was the legal permission the ANC government and former finance minister Trevor Manuel gave WMC to list offshore. This enabled them to open their main listings on the London and New York stock exchanges. This made possible the export of domestic resources and a form of capital flight. WMC, in the form of South African companies listed off-shore, could now move large amounts of capital out of South Africa legally. An enormous amount of wealth created mainly by black labour in SA was no longer available inside the country. In other words, not only local statistics, including white domination of the private sector, but also the internationalisation of South African companies means that the notion of WMC becomes more salient, not less so.

Answers to the question whether WMC exists or not after 1994 depend on whom you pose that question to. For the African-dominated trade unions, such as Cosatu, there was no doubt whatsoever that WMC continues to be a reality in SA. Former Cosatu general secretary, Zwelinzima Vavi, was very adamant, even a bit emotional, when he was asked the question: 'Absolutely! Who can doubt that? Go and look at the JSE. What is wrong with these people who question it? Go and ask the workers and shop stewards that question. They will tell you what a devastating reality WMC continues to be.'[25]

There have been interesting and intriguing debates, inside and outside the ANC alliance, about the validity or not of the notion of WMC. In this regard, besides the African-dominated trade unions which are adamant that WMC continues to exist, the organisations opposed to the ANC, such as the PAC and Azapo, are equally convinced that WMC exists in the South African economy. The EFF and its by-product, the BLF, are no less adamant. All the radical black-led opposition parties to the ANC are of like mind on the question of WMC. It seems that there are ulterior opportunistic reasons why the EFF, the BLF and the RET forces often slam WMC: to a greater or lesser degree, they appear strongly to be motivated by wanting to gain preferential access, via BEE, to the portals of power still controlled by WMC. In other words, the more they attack the continued dominance of WMC in the economy, the greater will the pressure be to gain a bigger foothold in it. That seems to be the logic. Besides, as complex and fluctuating as the ownership and control of JSE-listed companies might be, one thing must be clear: WMC – especially if we don't distinguish white South African capital from foreign capital – continues to dominate the JSE. Yet post-apartheid dynamics in the economy are far from a simple white–black dichotomy, as there are also significant linkages between emergent black capital and WMC.

However, former ANC leader Saki Macozoma was concerned that that 'laying a disproportionate emphasis on *white* monopoly capital and blaming it for all the ills of society might in our minds create an ogre out there under which all kinds of thieves can hide. It can detract from the real issues facing us, let us focus on white people and let us forget about the thieves among us. We should just drop the "white" part and it will be more effective I think'.[26] The fear that WMC, in that sense, could be invoked for ulterior motives is certainly valid. This is exactly what the Zuma-led RET faction seems to have done, and with the ascendancy of black capital and the opportunistic racial posturing it is capable of, this danger is amplified.

A particularly heated debate about WMC involved the economist Chris Malikane, three SACP leaders – Jeremy Cronin, Alex Mashilo and Malesela Maleka – and the independent Marxist Oupa Lehurele.

The exchanges were triggered by Malikane's privately published paper 'Concerning the Current Situation' which called for a united front in support of the 'black capitalist class' in its 'war' against 'white monopoly capital'. The SACP trio accused Malikane of providing intellectual support for Gupta-linked elements of Africanist tender-capitalists. In turn, Lehulere castigated Cronin and his colleagues for distorting Marxist theory and for attacking Malikane in what amounted to nothing less than an intellectual defence of WMC. All the participants in these combative articles agreed on the importance of the question: does WMC exist in today's South Africa? – although they came up with very different answers. There is no space here to reproduce the exchanges in any detail, but for any readers interested, they capture an important clash of ideas.[27]

In conclusion, while undoubtedly WMC has become a dangerous, misleading and opportunistic plaything in the hands of the RET faction in the ANC and their hangers-on in the BEE world, it is without any doubt a serious problem facing the unfinished revolution in SA. In fact, it remains the biggest obstacle to achieving a SA without the mass black poverty, unemployment and raging class inequalities which plague this otherwise most beautiful country. The central problem is that WMC represents the most serious systemic and structural remnants from the apartheid era, which, as we now know, was left untouched by the political settlement of 1993, except for the inroads made by BEE in the South African economy, which, however, has not changed its inherently capitalist nature but in fact served to reinforce and extend it. Every sector and sphere of our economy is still overwhelmingly dominated by WMC.

The big question therefore is this: given how serious and deeply rooted those problems are, just how will WMC's continued dominance be dealt with, especially when it is hardly likely that those structural issues of power can be negotiated, for example, between trade unions and companies? Answers to this critical question become much harder to answer in today's economic, social and political crisis, and that this situation coincides with the biggest capitalist global crisis, triggered by the Covid-19 pandemic, over the past century will only serve to compound those difficulties. How that key question is finally answered we can only see over this third decade of the 21st century.

But it is no longer just WMC that continues to bedevil serious social transformation in SA today. The emergent black bourgeoisie has in some respects become an even bigger problem in that regard. A big part of the reason for this is the political proximity between the ANC state and the black bourgeoisie, especially where leading figures on both sides continued their membership of the ANC and especially where the state has passed specific legislation to facilitate and promote black business. In fact, the thrust of the corruption we have faced is not only in the state itself, but in key institutions, such as the Public Investment Corporation (PIC). The particular problems of the PIC were revealed by the PIC Commission of Enquiry, appointed in 2018. Its report found astounding cases of corruption, irregularities, negligence and incompetence in an institution that handles investments worth over R2 trillion.

In an insightful article Dominic Brown argued that the PIC enquiry is 'critical to revealing corruption and mismanagement at the PIC. Naming and shaming is an important short-term measure that hopefully results in punitive action being taken against the guilty parties. However, greater structural transformation is required in order to mitigate against similar corrupt practices in the future.'[28] Given the staggering sum of money involved, ending the corruption and mismanagement at the PIC is of critical and urgent importance. As important is the fact that such funds could be used to make big advances in building much-needed infrastructure in black townships and raising standards of living there. The colossal amount of funds looted by ANC 'cadres' deployed all over the state over many years could have been used for that same purpose.

In his article, significantly titled 'PIC: The Financing of a Black Capitalist Class', Brown makes a compelling argument about the PIC: '… the development of a black capitalist class and the parallel rise of corruption are closely intertwined. The material basis of the rise in corruption lies in the dilemma of a would-be-capitalist class having no start-up capital but political power that gave them access to state resources.' Related to this is BEE, now seemingly being replaced by a 'transformation', being used to legalise and legitimise the predatory practices of the 'black bourgeoisie.' He recalls that it was Mbeki who said that the ANC government's priority was to develop a black capitalist class in order to 'deracialise the ownership of productive property in our country.'[29]

Denying the existence of WMC – given our history, in which the race–class linkages were pronounced for most of the time – emphasises that race is still a tinder box. It remains an angry reminder of our history: a history of white privilege, even if you were an ordinary worker, and black subordination, even if you were a doctor. The irony of post-apartheid SA is that race has arguably become much more explosive today than it ever was in the past. It is within this context that the white elite are nervous to be identified with WMC, especially at a time when in some respects we have a combustible social crisis in which most black people are engulfed, which once again has racial connotations.

The post-apartheid resistance by WMC and its apologists to the usage of the expression is strange because claiming that it is no longer applicable or relevant does not thereby alter its character, role and place in the economy. What changed between apartheid and now to justify the removal of the term 'white' from monopoly capital, especially as race has exploded over the past decade because of the palpable unhappiness of the black majority with the status quo after 1994? There is also an impudence to this denialism which arrogates to itself the power to control what words and language black people can use to identify the source of their oppression and exploitation.

This takes us back squarely to the ANC's middle-class and bourgeois aspirations, in one way or another, since its inception. It shows that the ANC's maxim that the African working class was the 'motor force of the revolution' and that 'the ANC had a bias towards the working class' was little more than propaganda. In fact we have seen the opposite of this since 1994. Not only has WMC not been dislodged after 1994 but its tentacles spread thereafter onto the global stage, in a sense returning to where it started with the inception of the involvement of foreign capital in the mineral revolution. The racial characteristics of WMC, as it historically and concretely evolved in the South African economy, are still in place. In every single facet of the South African economy its footprints are deeply etched.

'History' will hopefully call things by their proper name: white monopoly capital, which not even the birth of a small black capitalist class can justify altering the terminology to suit some politically correct notion. That stark reality is inscribed in the JSE. Besides, the black capitalist class owes its existence largely to WMC's own designs in the late 1980s when it began talks with the ANC in exile. Without the eager support of WMC, the NP would never have released Mandela, unbanned the ANC and begun the process of negotiations towards the constitutional democracy we have today, in which its power and wealth were left untouched, without which there would have been no settlement in 1993.

But there is yet another substantial reason why the terminology of WMC must be retained, which is sociologically perhaps the most important. As a result of the neoliberal policies the ANC adopted, at the behest of WMC and powerful countries like Britain and the US, SA is today the most unequal country in the world, our black unemployment levels are the highest they have been since 1994, and material conditions in black townships have never been as bad as today. The situation in many, if not most, black townships under ANC rule in a purportedly post-apartheid SA is tragic. On the other hand, WMC remains firmly entrenched in power in SA.

The Guptas, State Capture and ANC Corruption

In 2016, the Public Protector Thuli Madonsela published what was arguably her most important report, 'State of Capture': it investigated allegations of improper behaviour by Zuma and other state officials and the role of the Gupta family in stealthily removing and appointing ministers and directors of SOEs. Very soon the concept of 'state capture' loomed large in South African media and public awareness. State capture was widely understood as a distinct and pernicious form of corruption in which individuals, politicians and companies used state structures to loot public resources – and at the same time emasculated precisely those institutions intended to protect against corruption, such as the police and the National Prosecuting Authority. It marked the worst ANC corruption seen since 1994. While it certainly cannot be argued that there was no corruption before Zuma became president in 2009, there is no doubt that it has exploded since then. There can also be little or no doubt that the web of patronage and corruption surrounding the Guptas coincided with Zuma's ascendancy to the presidency in 2009.

But before considering the process of state capture more closely, there is a particular historical trajectory to the relationship between capitalism and the state that the public discourse and debate in SA has hardly dealt with. Central to this history is that in England and other European countries, industrialisation and economic development coincided with the development of the modern state. There is an abundant literature which shows in great detail how capitalism developed alongside state formation and development, and that the modern state has typically acted to maintain and defend capitalist relations and class structure – famously expressed by Marx and Engels as 'The executive of the modern state is but a committee for managing the common affairs of the whole bourgeoisie'. Historically, then, access to the state was of increasing importance for emergent companies and industries. It is not hard to understand the rationale for this very long history of why capitalists and companies actively sought links with the state. What the state represents to capitalist development has been powerfully captured by Marxists and countless other writers for well over a century. To put it simply, to have the support of the state is what aspiring capitalists have from time immemorial wished for. And within the intertwined histories of the state and capitalism, there obviously lies the potential for corrupt practices. That is where a study of state capture must begin.

SA is no exception to this rule. The parallel development of the colonial state and capitalist production is in fact deeply woven into its entire history, beginning with the DEIC rule of the Cape Colony from the 1650s. Earlier chapters discussed the DEIC as a powerful seafaring monopoly trading company and Holland as a powerful seafaring and colonial power. It was the commercial interests of the DEIC that led to what became the Cape Colony – in which colonisation was particularly brutal, primarily because it was always laced with race and racism. It is important to remember that there were two currents simultaneously at play in the Cape Colony under the Dutch: the construction of a local state on the one hand, and on the other hand its key role in facilitating commercial, economic and trade development. But it was also the racist colonial character of these twin developments which imposed the imperative of a strong state in order to oversee these processes while keeping control of the resistant Khoisan and later black population. The racist authoritarian character of Dutch/Afrikaner nationalist rule was replicated with the formation of the Boer Republics after the Great Trek.

Chapter 3 also described how the colonial state became more powerful under British rule after 1806, and the symbiosis between it and colonial capitalists, both Dutch-Afrikaner and English-speaking. The protection of capitalist interests by the state increased dramatically after the discovery of diamonds and gold raised the imperial stakes. Once the Union of South Africa was formed, an expanding Afrikaner capital sought to enjoy the same level of cooperation with the state as older English-speaking and foreign capital did. The importance of access to the state – a kind of forerunner of state capture – was woven into Afrikaner nationalism from the outset, most evidently after 1948 in the case of the NP and its relations with both Afrikaner and English capital, but especially the former. The main point to be made is that attempts by capitalists to 'capture' the state in SA and have its power wielded in their economic and financial interests did not begin with the shenanigans of the Guptas in the 2000s. Instead, state capture is indelibly woven into the fabric of South African history, and is a much older phenomenon than that associated with the notorious Gupta family and its corrupt relationship with Zuma after he became president in 2009.

Those who date the beginning of state capture to the Guptas forget what happened to the South African state between 1948 and 1994, the period of NP rule. There has arguably been no prior period in our history when a white-dominated state had such close relations with capital, as did the NP with Afrikaner and British capital during that period. As a result, we saw the rapid growth of Afrikaner capital in all sectors of the economy, including in mining. This was only possible because Afrikaner capital received the utmost assistance from the NP in this process, especially in the spheres of agriculture, insurance and finance. There can be no doubt that Afrikaner capital had 'captured' the NP-led state in its own increasingly diversified economic interests. There were many times too that the NP came to the assistance of agriculture during moments of crisis.

Yet there are significant differences between these earlier processes and the Gupta-related state capture and corruption. It occurred during ANC-led black majority rule, unlike all the earlier versions of it under white minority rule. A second major difference was the extent to which state capture now went far beyond having the state serve the interests of capitalism but involved the organised criminal looting of the SOEs and other entities for personal gain to an unprecedented degree. Rampant corruption under ANC rule included countless instances of bribes, kickbacks and tender frauds, large and small. But it was not only or perhaps even mainly the Guptas who captured the ANC state. The corruption cases that came tumbling out of the Zondo Commission of Enquiry and those that surfaced during the commission of enquiry into the PIC in 2018/19 made it very clear that such ANC state-capture corruption was much more extensive and deeper. Think of the video of Bosasa's Gavin Watson counting out bribes to be paid to officials in the ANC government – which Mark Gevisser described, for a British readership, as 'the most dramatic evidence yet of corruption within the ruling African National Congress'.[30] And think too of reports of the extensive corruption that swirled around the late 1990s arms deal.

A big question that nobody really cared to reflect on when the notion of 'state capture' surfaced a few years ago with the corruption allegations involving the Guptas, Zuma and SOEs, especially Eskom, was what had happened in the 1990s, when wide-ranging neoliberal social and public policies were adopted at local government level. It would be easy to argue that WMC had solidly captured the ANC-led state. Gear has been criticised very extensively since then, especially by the broad left in SA, as a pro-capitalist neoliberal macroeconomic framework whose strategic emphasis was on drastically cutting black on public expenditure at the very time when the devastating socioeconomic legacy of apartheid required urgent attention.[31]

Gear caused huge job losses across the public sector and cutbacks in social services and was largely welcome by WMC then. In other words, Gear was the first major manifestation of state capture after 1994. But hardly anywhere was this pointed out when the state capture discourse became a frenzy in the media round about 2015. Importantly, and ironically, that form of neoliberal state capture occurred at the same time as the question of whether or not the concept of WMC could still be saliently applied to SA. In its first major exercise in economic policy, the ANC so early showed signs of the pressure exerted behind the scenes, from WMC, especially since the RDP hardly had a chance to be implemented before it was dropped three months before Gear was adopted in June 1996. That was also during the Government of National Unity, when the NP itself would have played a part in economic policy decisions, especially if it posed a threat to the interests of its still largely white constituency.

But there are also very important lessons to draw for the future from such corruption: it permanently destroys any notion that African leaders will necessarily serve the interests of the black working-class majority better than white rule did, despite a very long history of dispossession, oppression, exploitation and naked racist brutality. With this goes a whole range of questions about African nationalism, about its history, leadership and its understanding of white racism and colonisation – and its programmes for liberation. Linked to those questions is the palpable failure of the ANC's leadership all along to reflect on and answer key questions about what kind of society and future they advocated and envisaged after the ending of apartheid.

In this regard, what will the political changes, a non-racial constitution and even the most finely articulated and calibrated definition of non-racialism do for changing the material and social conditions of black people, especially the black working class? Had the ANC leaders who led the organisation over so many years, and especially those who led the negotiations, dealt with those key questions, we might have had a very different SA today from the nightmare ANC rule has descended into. In this regard, all the objections to and criticisms of its policies, especially its two-stage approach to the South African struggle for liberation, which arguably paved the way for the fundamental compromises it made during the negotiations, are important to consider.

It is the failure to address those questions which in the first place gave rise to the narratives about state capture, WMC, BEE, the black elite and so on. The root cause of those problems, including the sad and depressing state of affairs in SA today, is the ANC's persistent failure to understand the nature of our society and the mineral revolution's impact on society in the Cape Colony and in the Boer Republics. If they had studied that history, even without necessarily a Marxist lens, they would have realised that securing non-racial political rights which do not address questions of the economy and social justice is inherently untenable and in fact would pave the way for the unmitigated mess we are in today in SA.

The focus on the Guptas as the source of state-capture corruption also serves to obscure the many other BEE players who have been involved in corruption, as both the Zondo and PIC commissions of enquiry revealed. It is important to recognise that it also opportunistically serves the interests of African BEE players, in particular the government's SOEs and the private sector, to exploit the anti-Gupta (often anti-Indian) sentiment in order to secure greater market share as a result of such adverse publicity. As the economic crisis deepens, this element will become more prevalent in a viciously competitive environment, in which the temptations to play up race and colour will become greater, especially against a backdrop in which there has been a distinct resurgence of an Africanist majoritarian chauvinism and a related re-racialisation and even re-tribalisation of our politics. What is very interesting and intriguing about post-apartheid SA is how the two processes of heightened race awareness and black wealth accumulation, via BEE, accompanied each other.

What happened to race after 1994 which paved the way for the facility with which it was employed later? In a sense it justified in advance the later pursuit and existence of black wealth, as against the historical existence of white wealth or, to put it in a nutshell, WMC. As Angelo Fick puts the point:

> Under Jacob Zuma's leadership, an active re-ethnicisation of politics ought to have alarmed many of those who had emerged from the liberation movement. It did not help that this was accompanied by a steady 're-racination' of South Africanness by the continued casual and inaccurate use of abolished Population Registration terms to describe people, situations and phenomena engendered after the abolition of that legislation.[32]

But the creation of a black elite was in tandem with the ANC's own stated objectives and not in conflict with it. There is no evidence that the ANC was ever seriously committed to an anti-capitalist programme. Instead, it wanted the 'non-racial' space to be a part of the capitalist system by outlawing racial discrimination and racism in the economy and society.

That's what it got in 1994. The 1994 elections opened that space. Though other factors also contributed to the path the ANC took, such as the collapse of the Soviet Union and the ascendancy of global neoliberalism, 1994 paved the political way for BEE and black wealth acquisition, out of which process emerged the likes of Cyril Ramaphosa, Tokyo Sexwale, Patrice Motsepe and many other wealthy black people on a scale never before seen in SA. But that is precisely what Oppenheimer and the AAC and other top WMC companies wanted to see in a post-apartheid SA because that was the only way in which the capitalist system could be stabilised and perpetuated and, with it, their interests and wealth.

The Raging Land Question

An interesting policy debate has belatedly emerged in post-apartheid SA, and it concerns the land question – specifically, the issue of whether the state can and should expropriate property without compensation. The constitution (section 25) specifies that property may only be confiscated 'for public purpose or in the public interest' and 'subject to compensation'. But public interest 'includes the nation's commitment to land reform' (s. 25. 4(a)) and can be read to suggest that the government can confiscate land without compensation for this purpose.

In March 2017, the EFF ignited the land issue by tabling a motion in parliament criticising the slow progress in land reform, calling for expropriation without compensation (EWC) and the amendment of section 25. The motion was defeated, and the ANC said it did not support expropriation without compensation. But in December of that year, the ANC – anxious not to be outflanked on land issues by the EFF – did a U-turn at its national conference, and approved of EWC, as long as it did not threaten food security or undermine the economy. So in February 2018, when the EFF tabled a similar motion on land and section 25, the ANC's MPs voted for the motion. Gugile Nkwinti, previously minister of rural affairs and land reform, unblushingly announced that 'The ANC unequivocally supports the principle of expropriation without compensation'. Not only that, the ANC also suggested that the Constitutional Committee should review and amend section 25 to make it more explicitly clear that the state could expropriate land for public purposes. But I have shown why such an amendment was superfluous. The ANC was doing it best to steal the thunder and the high moral ground from the EFF by demonstrating that it was feverishly determined to amend the constitution, in order to make it seem that it was driving land reform in SA, when it in fact had paid little attention to this crucial matter since 1996. In the three major areas of land policy – restitution (return of land confiscated after 1913), reform (redistribution from white to black ownership) and tenure arrangements – progress moved at a very tardy pace, held back by bureaucratic red tape and lack of political will. And the ANC government had certainly chosen not to use the constitution's section 25 property clause to carry out EWC under certain circumstances. There can be very little doubt that given the compromises that had been made by the ANC around nationalisation, the government did not want to rock the boat by using the constitution to implement major land reform.

In other words, what we had was a spectacular failure of governance by the ruling party regarding a most burning issue, which, since the Natives' Land Act, lay at the heart of the national liberation struggle: the struggle to reverse the massive land dispossession that the Act enshrined in law. The first fact that strikes one under those circumstances is why the ANC government did nothing since 1996 – 83 years after that most notorious piece of legislation was passed – to implement the implicit right which section 25(2) allowed for. Bear in mind in this regard that the constitution was adopted in the same year (1996) that the conservative neoliberal Gear was also adopted. I have no doubt that the failure or refusal to act of the ANC government was related to Gear, whose heavy restraints on government and public sector spending ran against the fulfilment of section 25 (2 and 3), which relates to compensation for expropriation.

But in 2018 the ANC followed the EFF in agreeing to amend section 25 of the constitution ('the property clause'). Was this actually necessary? The former president, Kgalema Motlanthe, argued that the amendment to section 25, to 'make it more explicit', as Ramaphosa put it, was unnecessary, precisely because 25(2), in fact, provides that clarity.[33] The 2017 high-level panel report chaired by Motlanthe proposed that instead of amending the constitution, the government should use its expropriation powers more boldly in ways that test the provisions in section 25(3). Besides, the panel also found that lack of leadership and policy direction, corruption and an inadequate budget were to blame for the country's failed land reform and that the budget was less than 0.4 per cent of the national budget, with less than 0.1 per cent set aside for land redistribution. In fact, the Helen Suzman Foundation, Patricia de Lille's Good Party and several other small parties also argued that there was no need to amend the constitution.

Professor Ruth Hall of the University of the Western Cape's Institute for Poverty, Land and Agrarian Studies told the Constitutional Review Committee (CRC) that the country was 'asking the wrong question – instead of asking government why it had not implemented section 25, it asked ordinary South Africans if the Constitution should be changed'. She was explicit about the deeper problem: 'There is no need to change the Constitution in terms of law', adding that 'there seems to be a political need.' She said, 'it was very clear that section 25 of the Constitution had not been used properly, which was ironic as the ANC fought hard in the 1990s to have a transformative clause included in the Constitution.'[34] How much more explicitly clear can an academic expert be about how redundant the amendment was?

The 'political need' that Hall identified was the subterfuge of the ANC, under the guise of hearing the voice of 'the people', to steal the thunder of the EFF, in order to make it appear that it was the ANC which drove a resolution of the long-delayed implementation of section 25. But it is to the EFF, not the ANC at all, that credit must be given for resurrecting the land question from the dustbin of history to which the ANC, by omission, seemed to have consigned it for 22 years.

Appearing before the CRC in 2018, Hall was emphatic: 'We do need to rethink the whole process and that simply changing the Constitution by itself is not going to be an answer because government could (have been) expropriating land for the past 20 years but chose not to do so.'[35] The problem in the media, however, is that journalists never probed these matters to understand why that was the case for so many years, especially since the question of land lay at the heart of the South African liberation movement for the entire 20th century. This was, I argue, the most damning neglect and in fact contradiction of the ANC government since 1994, but as with Gear and many distinctly anti-working class policies and laws, the members and supporters of the ANC did nothing to question, let alone seriously oppose, the decisions which the NEC of the ANC and its leadership in government, especially the cabinet, took on many issues.

Such evidence makes it very clear that the constitutional amendment was therefore unnecessary, superfluous and redundant. Given that fact, why did Ramaphosa and the ANC insist that the amendment was necessary? They did so to forestall the EFF, which first raised the land issue seriously in parliament.[36] Worried that the EFF would champion the combustible land matter, the ANC suddenly became obsessed with amending section 25 to make it 'explicitly' clear. Not only that, Ramaphosa himself appeared to want to take credit as the leader of the ANC who called for the constitutional amendment when in fact it was unnecessary. That is the kind of parliamentary abuse the ANC has many times since 1994 perpetrated because it held the majority of seats in parliament. But it had the audacity to delay implementation of section 25 further by pretending that it needed to engage in a very lengthy public participation process before the amendment could occur, which he and the ANC in any case had already decided on.

However, there are many more concerns regarding the land question, which hardly anyone, inside or outside the ANC, has entertained. In a very insightful article, Mmatshilo Motsei, hit another big problem on the head with stunning accuracy and simplicity, a combination which is not always easy to attain:

> In its role as our guardian, land gave use shelter from our mother's womb to our ancestor's tombs. We relied on land not only for our food for the body. Land was our first school, first factory, our first church and hospital. Writing about land is writing about history. We continue to define sustainable living in capitalist terms. We call for a return of the land within a violent economy. Does our definition of economic growth mean generating the highest profits for the benefit of the few at the expense of many? How do we return the land within an economy that kills people? How do we talk about economic growth in a country in which the basic human rights of the poor are trampled upon without conscience?[37]

Hence, how can we even begin to talk about the land question when the black working-class majority often struggle for access to adequate water and electricity in their homes? Much of the problem of the land debate begins with the artificial distinction between rural and urban land and the fact that lack of housing is a crisis in the urban areas, where poor black people who can no longer eke out a living from the land in rural areas end up as job-seekers, which daily adds to the list of those without housing. It is in urban areas, the big cities and neighbouring towns, where the most expensive and resourceful prime land exists, which any land question has to deal with. For too long we have had a narrow and mechanical restriction of the land question to rural and agricultural areas of the country, without serious regard to the infrastructure-rich and expansive land held overwhelmingly by the wealthy white elite in the cities. Land redistribution and the housing of the homeless must be dealt with in the urban areas. Any approach to the land question which only focuses on land in the rural areas is limited and short-sighted. Questions of land and livelihoods in rural areas are inextricably tied to the well-being of people in the urban areas. Any resolution of the land question is inherently false if it is not inextricably linked to the notion and prerequisites of social justice in its fullest meaning in both rural and urban areas.

There have been many reports of successful land restitution cases in which the beneficiaries lacked the equipment, resources and skills to farm. Given the history of this country and particularly the poverty and lack of literacy, education and skills in rural areas, this outcome is not surprising at all, which further confirms that the land question cannot ever be resolved in isolation from the rest of society and is in fact linked by many threads to other interests and needs of the black working-class majority. Too often the question of EWC is discussed in isolation from this important wider context, without which it is seriously limited, no matter what final juridical wording it consists of. In other words, it is the political economy of land reform and EWC within this wider context that requires further elaboration.

It was therefore apt for Tembeka Ngcukaitobi to argue that

> the true political dynamic of the 'transition' resulted in an unhappy truce. Property relations were not upended at once. The design was that property relations would change over time, guided by a supreme Constitution interpretation and applied by an independent judiciary. So, if you were white and a property owner on April 26, 1994 you remained the owner on April 27, 1994, despite the 'revolution' of 1994. That remains the case largely to date. Hence, the criticism that rather than reversing colonialism, the Constitution has cemented it.

The political importance of this point cannot be sufficiently emphasised. He went on to correctly argue that 'The Constitution is the wrong target. Post-liberation politics have failed the Constitution'.[38]

But what Ngcukaitobi failed to do is to show that these major constraints were due to Gear and the neoliberal policies it set in motion in the same year in which the constitution was adopted, which served to stymie the practical fulfilment of section 25 in the years ahead. Neither does he point to the resources caveat which stipulates that socio-economic rights can only be fulfilled if available resources permit. This neoliberal statutory provision was in fact a self-fulfilling prophecy of the constant inevitability of a perpetual lack of resources within the neoliberal budgetary framework of Gear and the macroeconomic policies of the ANC. Why otherwise would we have in SA today the dreadful situation of poverty, unemployment and inequality?

Although they did not make it explicit, to protect and propagate capitalism in post-apartheid SA was key to the drafters of the constitution. They knew, including Ramaphosa, how much anti-capitalist sentiment there was in the mass movement during the heady days of the 1980s especially. But to protect and defend capitalism they simply needed to insert the right to hold property in the constitution, regardless of how much was owned, where it was held and how it was obtained. Once the right to private property is sanctified in law, the basis and framework are created for the capitalist system to take root and thrive. There is nothing else that is required thereafter, other than land, labour and markets which together produce the profits the system thrives upon.

Although the constitution begins by acknowledging that SA was historically shaped by racism, colonial dispossession of land and capitalism, this remains in contention with the credibility of the property clause in it. But that contradiction was not enough for the ANC to test the limits of section 25 after the constitution was adopted in 1996. The brutal irony of this conscious neglect of the land question was made more reprehensible by the fact that the Natives' Land Act and its devastating impact on black people in the rural areas were foisted upon the ANC just a year after it was formed in 1912, with the result that in its early years it focused a lot of its time and effort in condemning it and trying to mobilise and organise against it. This remained the case for all the years that followed, which resulted in the 1955 FC enshrining the demand that 'The Land Shall be Shared among Those Who Work it'. In fact, if one looks at the entire clause of that demand, the effective abandonment of it by the ANC state is palpably clear.

The FC specifically states that 'Restrictions of land ownership on a racial basis shall be ended and all the land re-divided among those who work it, to banish famine and land hunger; The state shall help the peasants with implements, seed, tractors and dams to save the soil and assist the tillers.'[39] The ANC government failed to honour that demand even where land restitution was blighted by the failure of black people to farm on land they had won back because of the lack of the requisite resources, management and skills. If we read that demand alongside the demand that 'The People Shall Share in the Country's Wealth', the betrayal is even more stark.

But back to section 25. Since 1996 the ANC failed dismally to implement probably the most important legal opportunity to make substantial progress in addressing the land question. But this conservative treatment of the property clause set the neoliberal tone early on for what followed in 2000 with the Municipal Systems Act and basic municipal services. Except for the very limited and meagre free basic services, the ANC completely assimilated neoliberalism, as a result of concerted pressure from the IMF and the World Bank, which is why they initially adopted the 'willing buyer, willing seller' notion in relation to land acquisition. Only in 2015, 21 years after the 1994 elections, did the ANC begin to question this explicitly neoliberal principle which had dominated their approach to land matters until then.[40]

That was in 2015, but nothing much happened until Malema and the EFF threw down the parliamentary gauntlet in 2017. But a most striking thing about the renewed land debate – which lay dormant for two decades – was how it suddenly brought Thabo Mbeki, Pallo Jordan and other ANC intellectuals into it, after Mbeki had stated that the ANC was departing from the non-racial approach to the land question and instead polarising it along racial lines,[41] following extensive publicity of the land issues in 2018 and 2019, largely along white–black lines. Msimang had jumped to Mbeki's defence, supporting his claim that the ANC had not favoured land expropriation without compensation.

But how is it possible that only in 2018 did leading figures of the ANC suddenly become animated with the land question and the interpretation of it in the FC and in the later constitution? Besides the lacklustre pace of land restitution, none of the former presidents of the ANC, including Mandela and Mbeki, said or did much about implementing section 25. The answer is rather simple. Several things happened simultaneously after 1996: the media's attention shifted to land restitution cases and not on section 25 and its implications for land reform; the ANC in government, as the evidence will overwhelmingly show, reflected little or no real interest in section 25; neither did civil society, surprisingly, including the trade unions, show much interest in building a national campaign for the implementation of section 25.

It appeared that the generalised apathy and rapidly declining power of broad civil society after 1994 had taken its toll. The vigorous and vibrant activism of the 1980s had begun to seriously erode after 1994. The land question, alongside other key areas of struggle, like municipal services, suffered, especially with the drastic decline of the social movements after the ANC's Polokwane conference in 2007, when it appeared that the apparent radicalism that swept Zuma to victory there over Mbeki had provided a beacon of transient attraction to them. However, there can be no doubt that aside from the ANC government's own failures, broad civil society had miserably failed to organise and mobilise around the huge potential for land transformation which section 25 provided after 1996.

That is why it was refreshing when John Lamola raised the problem of landless black people who languish in informal settlements on the periphery of the cities and suburbs. He hit out at Mbeki's purportedly 'progressive African nationalism' while he was in power and the fact that 'the ANC did not implement the demands of the Freedom Charter. This he (Mbeki) does not deal with; they deviated from and abandoned those demands'. None of the leading ANC figures who entered the land debate – Mbeki, Jordan or Msimang – said anything about these flagrant contradictions after 1994 or even tried to explain why this was the case, both as regards the FC and section 25 of the constitution, which is why Lamola could conclude: 'The ANC has had twenty years to pilot these principles and the results are there for all to see.'[42]

The biggest and most dangerous compromise the ANC made was arguably on the land question. I conclude this section by visiting two different aspects of land policy, illuminated by two white journalists who penned articles strikingly relevant to the heated land debate since 2018. It is not race and colour that matters when it comes to critical thinking in any area of the ongoing struggles in post-apartheid SA but the ability to raise the things that truly matter in order to advance debates and to serve social objectives. In fact, there is no discourse or debate in which either white or black people are the authoritative custodians. Those South Africans whose thinking is still hampered by racial strictures urgently need to disabuse themselves of them.

Mary de Haas acutely raised the very serious problems the African community of Xolobeni in the Eastern Cape faced as a result of the collusion between the ANC government and an Australian mining company, Transworld Energy and Mineral Resources (TEMR), regarding a licence to mine in the area.⁴³ No land-related matter in post-apartheid SA has more nakedly revealed the duplicity of the ANC government than how it has handled a very sensitive matter for the Xolobeni community. The community has been fiercely opposed to titanium mining in a beautiful coastal region in the Eastern Cape: so fierce that there were reports that leading activists opposed to the proposed mine were killed and others harassed and threatened.⁴⁴ As De Haas stated: '... the anti-mining sector continues to stand firm despite the murder of an activist, attacks and threats.'⁴⁵

So palpably evident was the collusion between the ANC government and the interests of TEMR that the Pretoria High Court ruled in favour of the community which refused to accept the licence which the Department of Mineral Resources and Energy had granted TEMR to mine in Xolobeni.⁴⁶ As a reflection of just how distant the ANC had grown from black communities, the relevant minister, Gwede Mantashe, who was ironically the former leader of the NUM, bemoaned and criticised the high court judgment. I argued in a piece at the time: 'Mantashe forgets that the Xolobeni community's opposition is born out of the experiences black miners and communities have had with the mining companies whose interests were often overwhelmingly exploitative.' In fact, Mantashe and the ANC government ran roughshod over the radical objections of the community. And besides the killing of an activist in the community and many reports of threats that activists faced, Richard Spoor, the lawyer representing the community, was assaulted by the police, arrested and charged in Xolobeni.⁴⁷

The other journalist who struck a deep chord in the land debate was Kathleen Wootton, who explored the implications for land reform of the Ingonyama Trust (IT). She drew attention to the upcoming court case involving 5.2 million Africans who reside within the KwaZulu-Natal jurisdiction controlled by King Zwelithini's IT. Residents who took the matter to court are contesting the unilateral decision of the IT to 'convert their Permission to Occupy or informal land rights to long-term lease agreements, which require them to pay rent, which never existed before.'⁴⁸ She points out that these residents who have worked the land for generations and who built their homes and lives on it are now being forced to pay rent. But the legal gist of this case, which will set a precedent for such cases around the country, is that, as Wootton puts it, 'Broadly speaking, community members also have the right to participate in decision-making processes with respect to the land. This is very unlike the new lease agreements that the trust is imposing top-down on community members. Residents received no information about the consequences of signing these leases; they were not informed that they were in effect watering down their existing land rights ...'[49] As a logical extension of a key point made often in this book, of what 'Africans' do to other 'Africans', here we have a similar point at ethnic or 'tribal' level: what Zulu-speaking IT leaders have done to Zulu-speaking residents. KZN is where they all collectively grew up and still live. But all that similar ethnic history has failed to prevent this blatant assault not only on other Zulu speakers but on the poorest ones.

Finally, a penetrating analyst of land reform in SA is the academic Aninka Claassens. She is unmatched regarding critical insights into the Traditional Courts Bill and the Traditional and Khoisan Leadership Bill, which she calls 'Bantustan Bills'. Poignantly, she asserts that 'The two bills default to the colonial and apartheid denial of the property rights of people who have inherited their homes and land over generations.'[50] What this means is that the ANC's lacklustre performance with section 25 of the constitution must be seen alongside these related legislative measures it has forced through parliament because of the majority it still has there. Seen together, they are an unmitigated betrayal of the prospects which both the FC and section 25 held for land reform for African people in rural areas.

It is vitally important to realise that traditional rulers did not even have all the powers which these bills impose under apartheid. Referring to the Traditional Courts Bill, she argues: 'The current bill compels the 18 million South Africans living in the boundaries of the former homelands to subject themselves to a legal system where traditional leaders are accorded coercive powers that surpass any that chiefs had during colonial times and apartheid.' She also points out that objections to both these bills have been confirmed by a series of 'damning court judgments, reports by the public protector and Human Rights Commission, by the report of Kgalema Motlanthe's High Level Panel on Land Reform and by the Baloyi Commission of Enquiry'.[51]

The ANC's failures on the land question are simply incredible, and they link, crucially, to the earlier section on state capture. Claassens asserts:

> State capture is not just about corruption. It is quintessentially about the state adopting laws and policies that reward its benefactors at the expense of the public good. These laws do just that. They reward traditional leaders and big business at the expense of black people and citizenship rights. They blatantly deepen poverty and inequality at a time when South Africa is already in crisis. People who remain complicit in the abuses that have now been extensively documented are beneficiaries, rather than opponents of state capture.[52]

However, the question to pose and answer is this: how is it that regarding the most damning pieces of legislation against black people in rural areas, it is white journalists and academics who have provided the most insightful analyses in the media? I provided an answer to this question in earlier chapters. And why is it that the best journalism in this country after 1994 is in publications like the *Mail & Guardian* and the *Daily Maverick*? The same answer applies to the fact that you will find in every academic discipline and scientific field of study that the same white people – who though a tiny minority of the population – overwhelmingly dominate. The answers lie in our history, the history of the world and a history of vast epistemic disparities, which shadow all other social inequalities. It is a disparity which is probably going to widen when the floodgates of the 4IR are really unleashed upon SA. The conditions of life for white and black people in SA and the world have been so vastly different that the disparities are sharply and deeply reflected also in knowledge, education, development and all the sciences.

In his recent book, *The Lie of 1652: A Decolonised History of Land*,[53] Patric Tariq Mellet omits arguably the most important period in the history of SA from his analysis of the still unresolved and raging land question in SA. Instead of moving into the period of the mineral revolution, which in fact decisively shaped the contours of the land question, he fails to advance from the useful earlier historical chapters to explaining the real roots of the explosion of the land question in SA over the past decade. That is the nub of this serious limitation of a book which is otherwise in many respects well-researched.

Mellet does not clearly critique capitalism in SA and the strong links between a resolution of the land question and an anti-capitalist agenda. He also fails to deal with the palpable and prolonged failures of the ANC government to implement the provisions for land expropriation in the 1996 constitution. If 'social and economic liberation' is unpacked in the South African context, an anti-capitalist ethos is necessary, especially given our history which inseparably linked race and land to labour and capitalist development. Even the 'restorative justice' Mellet advocates[54] is impossible on a capitalist basis.

Climate Change and its Implications for Race, Class and Gender

The first fact to make patently clear is that global capitalism is primarily responsible for the current climate crisis around the world. This is such an obvious and compelling fact that there is no real need to explain and elaborate on its origins in the Industrial Revolution that began in 18th-century Britain and spread thereafter across the globe. It is fundamentally important that this irrefutable fact be recognised and acknowledged because we are not going to be able to develop policies and strategies to combat climate change without that realisation.

A second key point, which overlaps with the first, is that race and racism have been integral globally to the processes of capitalist industrialisation. Every single country which followed Britain to a greater or lesser extent developed racist laws and practices which discriminated against, oppressed and exploited black people, especially the working class. Arguably these processes were more nakedly evident in SA than in any other country in the world. Here a comprehensive and extensive statutory racist framework was established in the Cape Colony and intensified from the time of the mineral revolution.

The gender dimension comes into the picture as a result of the fact, equally compelling and irrefutable, that African and Coloured women were the most oppressed and exploited of the black people in SA. This point proceeds from the premise, equally incontestable, that African women, even more than Coloured working-class women, were right at the bottom of the social hierarchical ladder in SA, certainly from the time of the mineral revolution. In this regard mention must be made of the fact that the patriarchal oppression these women faced from their own families contributed in no small measure to their overall oppression and exploitation. In other words, not everything that African women have suffered for so long can be attributed to what the white racist regimes did to them. Much of the oppression and exploitation was endogenous.

This must be seen alongside the fact that the nationalist policies of the ANC have left those women worse off in post-apartheid SA, especially in the crucially important domain of basic municipal services. The neoliberalism of post-apartheid SA and the devastating consequences of climate change on women must be foregrounded so as to get a clearer idea of what will be required to deal with its effects over the next decade or two. In this regard, race and its historical effects on black women form a crucial factor in confronting and working through the compounding effects of climate change on them.

Before turning to the implications of climate change, it is important that we appreciate the wider context of those who are ultimately going to suffer most from its fury in the coming years. As I wrote in 2005:

> This is a striking and unsettling contradiction of stunted transformation since 1994. Though there is much that has changed for the better for these women ... they are trapped in growing poverty, fuelled by unemployment, on the one hand, and the commercialisation of basic services on the other, which often places adequate supplies beyond their reach. Elsewhere millions lack sanitation and electricity and often have to walk long distances for water.

I added: 'The absence of skills and education, or low levels of them, has entrenched the marginalisation of these women.'[55]

The horrendous levels of violence against and the rape of black working-class women over the past decade have worsened their lot. It is against this background that we need to discuss climate change in SA. The view of Barbara Creecy, minister of environmental affairs, forestry and fisheries, is compelling: 'Our country's vulnerability to climate change is exacerbated by our economic inequality, poverty and our current dependency on coal-fired power generation.' She added: 'No matter how we look at it, climate change poses significant risks to our country's current and future socioeconomic development.'[56] But Creecy fails to address the fact that our neoliberal policies, and the serious challenges it poses to black working-class women particularly, are going to contribute to and compound the difficulties for them. Neoliberalism is itself a major impediment to tackling climate change and will undermine efforts to do so and worsen the lot of the black working class in general and African people particularly. This is in fact the global situation, in which working-class people will undoubtedly be most negatively affected by climate change.

In SA, African townships situated close to coal-fired power stations have already been negatively affected by their proximity. Many media reports have shown that the health of such communities has been seriously compromised. This historicises and politicises the effects of climate change and the ability or not to respond to its challenges. It is reminiscent of the siting of sewerage works when Johannesburg was formed, deliberately placed far away from white suburbia and close to black townships. In other words, most of the greenhouse gases emitted by the coal-fired power stations in the Limpopo and Mpumalanga provinces affect black townships in the vicinity. SA is the world's 16th-largest emitter of greenhouse gases and the largest in Africa.[57] But the ANC has not done much to factor in the effects of climate change in its planning, or to avoid the construction of fossil-fuel power stations.

Instead, it gave the go-ahead to build the massive Medupi and Kusile coal-fired power stations in Limpopo and Mpumalanga respectively, which have been seriously delayed as a result partly of corruption.[58] Incredibly, a staggering R139 billion theft is being investigated by the Special Investigating Unit. Just as local government funds meant for development and the provision of basic services in African townships were stolen at local government level, so this alleged theft has occurred, notwithstanding the fact that these power stations were built in order to create urgently needed, electricity-generation capacity for SA.

It is a sad reflection on the leadership of the ANC that they could or did not anticipate climate change, already evident in the late 1980s. It's important to note that the most senior leaders of the ANC were based in London and elsewhere in Europe at that time. By then they were virtually a government-in-waiting. But there can be little doubt that the neoliberal policies of the ANC, their lack of prior experience of government, and their inadequate knowledge and understanding of our history and the financial aspects of modern-day SA, had very negative effects. They appear to have had little knowledge of climate change sciences, which took root in the late 1980s in Europe and the USA.

There are no statements by the ANC as the ruling party since 1994 in which they even attempt to educate the public about global warming, the resultant climate crisis and the steps we needed to take to reduce carbon emissions. But it got even worse as global warming increased over the past decade. Extinction Rebellion South Africa was terse about the ANC's performance: 'The state has committed to increasing emissions (Eskom) for another five years and reducing them only in 15 years' time. South Africa and southern Africa are forecast to warm at 1.5 to 2 times the global average.'[59] Edmunds concludes: 'It seems – against the advice of global scientists and the next generation's calls to act – our collective political leadership has ended the decade with another failure.'[60] It is no exaggeration to conclude that ANC rule in SA has been nothing less than disastrous in just about every major area of life.

On top of the wanton corruption and mismanagement that have occurred at Eskom over the past decade and the load shedding which adversely affected lives and businesses, how could the ruling party have even entertained the SOE's applications for exemption from emission targets? This was despite findings of the health threats of emissions, and the estimated death of 2,000 people a year, and the fact that environmentalists had already taken the ANC government to court for failing to rein in emissions.[61] This reveals a pronounced insensitivity to the health of communities which have already been affected by the emissions. How does one even begin to make sense of such a situation involving the lives of many people?

The figures of people who would be affected by requests for exemptions were shocking: 'The exemptions sought by Eskom for just these two power plants would cause an estimated 6,000 to 12,000 premature deaths over the remaining life of the plants, a health burden and economic burden that far exceeds the costs of the equipment required to comply with the standards,'[62] said a lead activist for the Centre for Research on Energy and Clean Air. The serious problem these matters raise in fact goes way beyond Eskom, Ramaphosa or the responsible minister. It raises questions for our whole society about what has happened after 1994 and specifically what the Department of Health has said about these matters and what they have done to prevail upon Eskom, the minister and the ANC government. There is something seriously wrong in SA. If only 100 people died in the USA or any European country as a result of pollution from a coal-fired plant, it would be treated as an emergency. We ourselves give validation to the notion that black lives don't really matter.

But the plan to reduce Eskom's emissions was rejected by the international organisation Climate Action Tracker, which labelled it 'highly insufficient'. So out of step was SA that Sipho Kings, one of the best journalists dealing with climate issues, put it pointedly: 'South Africa's plan – and the national energy plan – doesn't follow what science says is needed.'[63] The thrust of the criticism is not merely government's failure to heed the degree of emission targets recommended by scientists, but the consequences that will have on both the health of people and the environment, especially poor African people who live in the areas where the coal-fired power stations are based.

But there are three major interrelated areas of the climate crisis debate which require serious attention. Firstly, it is abundantly clear that its effects on black working-class communities in SA, especially those who are already in the doldrums of poverty and unemployment, are going to be nothing less than devastating. Once again, we will have a convergence between race and class, in which those who are going to be the worst affected are poor black people. It will again be black women who will bear the brunt of it, alongside the escalation of gender violence and rapes.

The same communities will be worst affected with natural disasters, such as the flash floods in KZN in 2018. Around the world it is the poorest (often black) communities who are the worst affected by climate change-related disasters. In their report 'Global Warming of 1.5°', UN climate scientists pointed out that 'Poverty levels increase to a very large degree and incidents of starvation increase very significantly'. The report came out in late 2018, in the middle of the 'hottest period in recorded history'. In SA we've had 'unseasonal flooding, record temperatures have been set across the highveld and drought crippled large swathes of the country.' Ramaphosa himself warned: 'our region is likely to become drier and drastically warmer' and that it all points to 'major climate change impacts occurring in the region over the next several decades.'[64]

Secondly, there is a clear disjuncture between those acknowledgements by Ramaphosa and the troubling and dangerous government plan 'which allows emissions to grow by more than 20% until 2025, stay there for a decade and then drop from 2035 – but still not to levels scientists say are needed.'⁶⁵ At the centre of the plan's problem lie the coal-fired plants of Eskom, which will grossly retard meeting emission targets recommended by scientists. Enough has been said of the pivotal importance of race in tackling this ecological crisis to appreciate the irrefutable fact that the white-dominated 'just transition' movement in SA and globally has evidently played down its importance.⁶⁶

Thirdly, I have argued that there is a link between the generalised underestimation of race among the white left, and of their own socio-class position, in the ongoing salience in post-apartheid SA of the race–class nexus. It is precisely because those material links persisted after 1994 due to the fundamental compromises made by the ANC that white privilege, of which the white left is structurally and organically a part, also persisted. This is not a sentimental question but a socio-material legacy of the apartheid period and indeed of the colonial era. A long-term view of white privilege is imperative in order to understand both its deep roots and its persistence after 1994, when despite the repeal of racist laws, systemic racism remained intact.

Around the world there are similar race–class links, even within revolutionary left movements. The progressive and even revolutionary Marxist white left, with its access to resources, often plays a leading role in these movements, which are based in universities and other institutions in the West and in SA. But that by itself is not the problem. For any genuinely anti-racist organisation or movement, such a historically rooted reality has consequences for how the relevant struggles are conceptualised and the respective weights allocated to each factor which shapes the issues in them. From this materialist perspective it is patently clear that race is neglected in the 'just transition' movements, whose leadership is overwhelmingly dominated by the white left around the globe.

This is a fatal weakness of 'just transition' theory because the issues thrown up by global warming and the ecological crisis are patently of a race–class nature, but one in which an equal emphasis, rather than promoting class at the expense of race and colour, is required. This is essential, even if ultimately class is the factor which predominates most in shaping the nature of our society and its social relations. I earlier dealt with this conceptual and strategic duality of race and class and the theoretical and strategic tensions it creates, which will be a permanent problem requiring constant attention, analysis and review, a perpetual work in progress, so deep are the roots of both race and class in SA especially.

Not enough attention is paid to race and colour in this movement. I looked closely at who the writers and theorists of climate change are in SA, but they infrequently mention and deal with the consequences of race and racism in SA's environmental and ecological crises. I have raised this question with Patrick Bond and others active in this movement often, but nobody really gets to grips with the issue. Most white activists are evasive on this issue. It is often the same people, both academics and activists, who are strongly opposed to 'identity politics' that also neglect race in their work. A knee-jerk rejection of identity politics is very unhelpful, precisely because it instinctively refutes the validity of race, irrespective of conditions and circumstances.

Earlier I argued that, given our history, race and colour continue to lie at the heart of the NQ, but equally that an approach to the NQ must be at all times linked to class and gender. From that perspective – which I believe is solidly grounded in our history – Vishwas Satgar lost a good opportunity to plug the gaps in the literature. Bizarrely, he instead argued for 'replacing the national question with the ecocide question, in the context of the existential threat posed by the climate crisis to human and non-human life.' There is no space to provide an elaborate answer to this shocking and poorly conceived argument against the existence of the NQ. But what captures best his evident confusion about the NQ is his argument that the 'eco-cide question is central to a post-national liberation, post-neoliberal and renewed left politics, as the basis for radical, non-racial nation-building to sustain life'.[67]

Firstly, it is inherently inconceivable to argue on the one hand for the collapse of the NQ but on the other hand to replace it with a project for an amorphous 'radical, *non-racial* nation-building' (emphasis added) alternative. How can he avoid issues of race and racism inherent in the NQ but continue the pursuit of the 'non-racial' ideal? In both theoretical and practical terms it is hard to fathom what Satgar really has in mind with which to replace the NQ, especially upon such spurious grounds, and with which to build his alternative 'non-racial' and 'nation-building' approach.

He has landed himself in a conceptual mess, especially as he immediately thereafter critiques the ANC's commitment to a 'post-apartheid nation-building nationalism in which non-racialism has been a crucial ideological element', but which is 'part of a project to rule a capitalist South Africa'.[68] Satgar takes a lengthy excursion into the history of non-racialism in order to rehabilitate and deploy the concept in his alternative socialist eco-cide narrative. I argue that the NQ is conceptually flexible enough to accommodate the arguments Satgar is presenting, but instead of changing our approach to the NQ, his premise is to liquidate the NQ itself! But as long as race and especially the race–class nexus operate, so long will the NQ be relevant.

It's also important to realise that the 'just transition' movement's origins lie largely within the ecological crisis we've faced, but it is inseparably linked to the economic crisis within capitalism, the heart of which is largely structural. In other words, we need to link the clearly socialist-inspired 'just transition' to the theory of permanent revolution: to realise that every major struggle today is inseparably bound up with anti-capitalist struggles. It is an illusion to even entertain the possibility that the 'just transition' can occur within the framework of existing capitalism in SA and globally. In fact, as the economic crisis has deepened, so has the necessity to link the 'just transition' to an anti-capitalist agenda.

The reason for this approach relates to the fact that the economic, social and ecological crises of global capitalism have simultaneously converged in SA and elsewhere in the recent period, to the extent that it demands a response in which these converging crises are integrated in an oppositional theory, analysis and programme. This perspective is not sufficiently clear in the literature on SA. For that same set of reasons there will not be a 'fair transition for everyone', as Ahmed Mokgopo was hoping for.[69] It might sound hackneyed but all the most serious social problems of today ineluctably converge in an all-embracing crisis within global capitalism. The irony of this is that though that is the correct systemic conclusion to draw, it might be harder today to defeat capitalism than it ever was before. It is such a global situation – capitalism in a mortal crisis on the one hand and the prospects of an alternative socialist order uninspiring – that we inhabit today. As a result, a prolonged and ever-deepening global capitalist crisis might be what we are going to have for the next five or ten years.

Some may argue that the outpouring of militant struggles in many parts of the world over the past two years might open up a renewed global struggle against capitalism, which is probably true, but until and unless political organisation emerges to unite and cohere all those national struggles with a clear and unifying programme of action and a visible and strong leadership, those struggles, as has been the trend in SA and globally, will probably peter out. The current global conjuncture is terribly complex and fluid. I argue that matters will become even harder for the South African left once the 4IR really gets under way here over the next five years. Its impact is going to weaken the trade unions and wider civil society further, especially with a trade union leadership today that is a sad shadow of its past. There has been no coordinated campaign against or critical engagement by trade unions with the 4IR to date.[70] After the split in its ranks, Cosatu, which was once the spearhead of the labour movement, has considerably weakened.

The split, which saw several affiliates hive off to form the rival South African Federation of Trade Unions (Saftu), led by Zwelinzima Vavi, the former Cosatu general secretary, was the biggest setback in the history of the trade union movement, one from which a recovery is unlikely, especially within the context of the general decline of trade unions since the 1980s and the devastating effects the 4IR is bound to have over the next five or ten years. The hard fact is that the socialist left in SA is so fragmented and weak that unless the Numsa-inspired SWRP makes significant gains and becomes a formidable electoral force to be reckoned with, the systemic problems of poverty, joblessness and inequalities which have devastated black townships across the country will probably worsen further.

Cosatu, especially after its formation in 1985, was the backbone of civil society, but it has seriously declined over the past decade. Unless Saftu and the SWRP can provide a powerful counterweight to the neoliberalism of the ANC and, in the process, give a strong lead to combating the climate crisis, as part of a wider programme of action, the policies and politics of climate change will remain what they have largely been in SA thus far: a leftist middle-class preoccupation. The fact is that the trade unions, including both Cosatu and Saftu, have paid inadequate attention to both the 4IR and to the climate crisis. The other fact is equally clear: because it is the black working-class majority which will suffer most from the climate crisis, it is imperative that the trade unions take the lead in these matters and provide the required leadership to the entire working class.

The magnitude of the current multidimensional crisis should make the trade unions – still the only mass formations we have which can make a big difference – realise that time is of the essence in these matters. An even more devastating ecological crisis awaits us if they do not – even across the existing organisational divisions and differences – take the climate crisis much more seriously. In this regard, the biggest endogenous challenge they face is to deal with both the devastating consequences of coal-fired power stations – where many of their members work – and prevent job losses if they were shut down amidst the universal move towards renewable energy. It is these tough challenges which make the earlier split in Cosatu so much more regrettable.

But a study of socialist parties and movements globally will also show how often when the objective conditions of a deep crisis cried out for unity, they were unable to exploit opportunities to organise and mobilise workers, precisely because of the lack of unity as a result of a combination of the historical weaknesses of sectarianism, ultra-leftism, propagandism and the resultant inability to build a mass base in the working class. Such appears to be the situation in SA today and at the current global conjuncture. Besides, globalisation and now the 4IR are throwing up new problems and complexities which will only worsen the prospects of building a powerful left opposition in SA, unless, of course, there is an electoral coalition of the SWRP, the EFF and militant social movements.

The EFF and the SWRP should look towards such coalitions in the future. There must be no doubt that given its clear causal links to global capitalism, the climate crisis is going to assume an increasingly anti-capitalist character of necessity in the future. The left, however one defines it, is too weak on its own to challenge South African capitalism. Such electoral coalitions could very well open the prospect of a parliamentary route to socialism. Only the most obdurate 'Marxists' in SA will oppose such a prospect. In fact, I think that is the most probable future of the left in SA for at least the next decade or two, whether they like it or not. The only way the parliamentary route could be avoided is with a powerful mass socialist party basis outside of it, which has in fact never existed in SA, either under apartheid or after 1994. The less said of the moribund and counterrevolutionary SACP the better.

Whither South Africa?

Living in SA is going to be very much of a struggle through the 2020s, by all indicators. We face a huge economic, social and political crisis, arguably the worst in the history of this country. That we have this crisis *in post-apartheid* SA is an accurate indication of its magnitude, because it was not supposed to have happened. The mass resistance in so many ongoing township explosions speaks to the disjuncture between the expectations of black people after 1994 and the neoliberal policy regime the ANC imposed, which still dominates the economy a quarter of a century later.

The gravity of this crisis, which is largely the result of major economic, social and public policy compromises the ANC made in the 1990s, is manifest virtually everywhere in SA at this moment. Poverty, unemployment and social inequalities, which mainly affect the majority black working class, are in fact starker today than they were under apartheid. Right there is a recipe for a prolonged and deepening crisis in the decade ahead. Unless the global crisis recedes and conditions improve, and the ANC makes some major changes which significantly and palpably improve conditions for this class, we are in for escalating trouble and instability over the next decade.

A big, if not the biggest, problem we've had since 1994 is that white people, in general terms, have not really had any major adjustments to make in their lives. Yes, many were probably affected by AA and BEE policies, but overall it is estimated that in material terms white people are better off than they were under apartheid. I pointed out earlier that in his last State of the Nation address in 2008 former president Thabo Mbeki pointed out that the ANC had been kind to big business after 1994, understood primarily as WMC. He would know well. The point is that in economic and socio-material terms, not much has changed since 1994. In fact, as I've shown at length, in some respects things have worsened. Largely, the wealthy are still white and the poor black. In just about every social indicator the same pattern exists across SA. Even the cheap RDP houses and the places where they were built for black people reinforced the apartheid spatial and residential race–class divide.

Jonny Steinberg usefully pointed out that the prospect of building cheaper black housing after 1994 in or close to white suburbia was edged out by white suburbanites: 'The white middle-classes of the late 1990s would simply not have allowed it', he argues, pointing out that acquiring land for public transport which crossed white suburbia was hard enough, so imagine 'the outcry if the purpose had been to house the poor.' There was resistance from the white elite of Sandton, too, when they resisted the redistribution of city resources to the townships in 1995–6 before losing a related constitutional case.[71] But it's much worse today than under apartheid as a result of the increased power the ANC has given businesses in places such as Rosebank and Sandton in Johannesburg, following the neoliberal iGoli 2002 Plan which the ANC imposed, as it did with Gear, in Johannesburg in 1999. Imported from the US, Johannesburg now has city improvement districts (CIDs), drawn from the American business improvement districts (BIDs) model, which have substantially increased the power of big business in the major cities.[72]

This points to the fact that SA has in fact regressed in certain respects. I earlier showed what a devastating impact prepaid technology has had on black townships across SA as a result of policies the ANC adopted in the Municipal Systems Act of 2000. Not enough attention is paid to many areas of life in the 'New South Africa' which have in fact made things more difficult for the poor black majority, who are further away today from the 'right to the city' which Henri Lefebvre and other sociologists advocated in the 1970s and 1980s.[73] Given what apartheid represented for black people, the right to the city held even more relevance here than in Europe or the US. In fact, purportedly 'post-apartheid' RDP houses often accentuated the inherited racist segregation of housing, in which black townships were built on the barren periphery of the city, because instead of locating them closer to the city, they were extending outwards and further away from the cities.

In brief, for the poor black majority 'post-apartheid' SA has seemed a cruel joke. I can hardly remember raw sewage running down township streets under apartheid, but it is a common sight under ANC rule. In this regard ANC rule has also totally messed up the Vaal River system. Corruption vied with blatant incompetence in the steady degradation of a place once a favourite for people from Johannesburg to visit and enjoy, picnicking and relaxing with families. That is no more. Almost everything the ANC has touched in its rule – schools, health, municipal services and much more – has been run into the ground. The most powerful and richest city in Africa, Johannesburg, is a sad and depressing shadow of its past, with dirt strewn all over in certain parts of the city, including the

CBD. Walk today into places like Hillbrow, a favourite of mine during the apartheid days, at your peril, especially at night. It has become dirty, dangerous and crime-infested, like so many other parts of the country.

In conclusion, it must be said that many or most people, especially from the 'minorities', and not only from the middle classes, regularly these days quietly condemn the atrocious decay of our cities over the past decade and the countless problems with the delivery of basic municipal services. What is less well known is that the unmitigated mess that ANC rule has led to, especially when seen alongside the load shedding SA has suffered – at great cost to big and small businesses and particularly to poor households who don't have generators – has served to create a searing and fully justifiable cynicism about the capacity of African people to govern the country. I firmly believe that the history of African people generally in SA and the specific history of the ANC to a large extent explain the mess SA has been reduced to under ANC rule.

When things like the unemployment crisis and the wanton corruption across the state and public sectors are factored in, there is currently a generalised and pronounced negativity about both the present and the future sweeping across SA, much of which the media have captured. The stream of immigrants from elsewhere in Africa and the flood of unemployed black people from rural areas into our cities have dramatically shot up over the past few years and will continue with negative consequences for not only the economy but for the ability of the state to continue providing the social grants on which many millions of the poorest people rely.

I often argue that so disastrous, and even tragic, has ANC rule been that one does not require detailed research to see it. Just keeping abreast with the newspapers should be enough to appreciate the calamitous magnitude of the current crisis. And as cruel fate would have it, the recent pandemic outbreak of the coronavirus has considerably worsened the already existing multiple crises we face. As with the climate crisis, it is the black working-class majority who are going to suffer most from Covid-19. In South Africa as elsewhere, Covid-19 has acted to widen existing social disparities and inequities, to deepen poverty and joblessness, and to sharpen the effects of hunger, malnutrition, anxiety, depression and domestic violence.

The preventive measures the ANC government recommended to stem the tide of the pandemic – such as using hand sanitisers, facial masks and disinfectant wipes – were welcome, but who could afford these where they were needed most, in the townships and informal settlements? Even the price controls the ANC government imposed for these and other products – as welcome as they were too – will be of minimal benefit to black people living under conditions of rampant unemployment and poverty and struggling to put food on their tables. Besides, given the conditions in black townships and informal settlements, it is clearly not possible to operate a lockdown there and observe the stringent requirements imposed by the ANC government.[74]

Hence, it clearly appears that the Covid-19 crisis has unleashed that old race–class nexus and its related variables. These factors are determining the differential capacity of white and black people to respond to the pandemic, including that it was mainly white people using their spending power selfishly to ransack the shelves of grocery shops when there first was talk of a lockdown. The Covid-19 virus cannot be successfully combated without addressing the deeply systemic issues of which is an expression and symptom. The virus has dramatically disrupted a capitalist global order which has for long been breaking at the seams. The 2008/9 global financial meltdown, the worst of the climate crisis that followed it, and the decimating impact of the unfolding 4IR are all systemic facets of that order.

However, an interesting and revealing development is clear on social media over the past few years, especially on Facebook and in letters to editors of newspapers: ordinary people expressing their disgust with the orgy of corruption oozing out of the pores of the ANC. That feeling is today widespread in the black townships, including in strongholds of the ANC from the 1950s, such as Alexandra and Soweto and in a place where the FC was born, Kliptown. Given the enormous wealth of SA there is probably no other post-independence party in Africa which has so wasted the enormous potential the country had to adequately meet at least the basic daily needs of people who were terribly oppressed and exploited for so long. Instead, the ANC, through mistaken and inappropriate policies and an orgy of unconscionable corruption and fraud, squandered the dreams and aspirations of black people, especially the majority working class.

The way to approach this tragedy is rather simple: we need to imagine how many more houses (of better quality than the cheap RDP ones) could have been built; how many more water and electricity connections could have been made; how many more schools could have had basic facilities, such as classrooms, furniture, toilets and water; and how many more public hospitals could have been built. And so on. It is impossible to say just how many billions of rands South Africa has lost to corruption since 1994 – a frequently cited estimate of about R700 billion may overstate the amount, but it is still staggeringly high.[75] Though research does not provide information about the people or political parties involved, it is reasonable to assume that the vast majority of cases would involve people the ANC 'deployed' to various levels and sites of the state, especially to the SOEs and local governments.

But no matter how bad any situation is, hope is an eternal human quality needed in order to still have the will to strive for a different and changed world. In this regard I must be clear in these concluding words of this book: this three-year study has made very clear two interrelated things. Firstly, SA and the world will have no future worth speaking about and pursuing unless we realise that there will be no resolution of the multiple crises we face unless we break with and oppose the capitalist system, which has lived cheek by jowl with racism and gender oppression for at least 150 years. Secondly, unless the EFF sheds its racialist and often racist posturing and unites with other socialist forces, no matter how much smaller they might be, such as the Marxist Workers Party, or the SWRP grows into a powerful mass-based party of the majority working class – in order to win an election and replace the beleaguered ANC – our future will be imperilled, probably much more than it is already today.

A great deal could be written about the disaster capitalism has been for centuries around the world. This book has made it palpably clear that white supremacy – upon which apartheid domination was based – would not have had the tenacious power it had and the longevity it enjoyed had racism not been historically intertwined with capitalism in SA. And the super-exploitable cheap black labour regime imposed by apartheid and all preceding forms of white racist rule – whose laws were consciously designed to buttress and enforce it – would not have occurred and survived had there not been a system developed which was largely of mutual interest to both Dutch and later white Afrikaner rule and mainly English WMC.

To varying degrees these protagonists benefited from what was called under apartheid 'racial capitalism', the legacy of which post-apartheid SA has conclusively shown is still embedded in our society, not by virtue of racist laws, as under apartheid, but as a result of the devastating social consequences that were carried over into post-apartheid neoliberal SA under ANC rule. The dismal results are evident in the statistics of this country. Even when the ANC acted for the benefit of poorer citizens, such steps were undercut by their overall neoliberal approach. It was similar to the ANC giving, for example, R100 a day to an unemployed black person, while the effects of the neoliberal policies took back R120 a day. The result was that such people, especially of the black working class, actually grew poorer.

The problem is that time is not on our side, and depending which way we go, there is a sense – a constant reminder of which is the unbridled violence we daily see in so many areas of life – that conditions could deteriorate and result in protracted conflict, including of racial forms, which could destroy SA, with all its beauty and rich history. We have a country worth fighting for, but there will be nothing to fight for unless the white elite and the small black elite born after 1994 come to the realisation that they and their children will have no future unless the wealth they possess is shared with and redistributed in some form to the mostly impoverished and unemployed black working-class majority.

How that is done is another matter to be decided and perhaps also fought for, but that it must be the goal is beyond any doubt. The high number of white people killed in crime, either on their farms or in their homes in the cities since 1994, must tell them that there simply is no other way forward. Equally the fighting spirit and resilience of black people in SA are both locally and globally acknowledged. They will not rest and there will be no peace in SA until and unless the enormous wealth it possesses is equitably shared by all. In that regard they have suffered under both 'racial capitalism' during apartheid and under a black majority-led neoliberal ANC government, which in some critical areas of life has made conditions worse than they were under apartheid.

This situation wields together enough political and moral authority for a fundamental change in the conditions of life of those people. There cannot be a more noble fight to wage on the one side and to yield to on the other, especially given our history. The enormous resources of this country remain in white hands, which is the main reason for black poverty and multiple social injustices. Unless in one way or another that wealth is redistributed so as to end such conditions of life for the majority of people in SA, or at least secure major changes, we might soon have a revolution that will sweep away a social order whose roots can be traced back to the Cape Colony and more directly to the mineral revolution. It is my fervent wish that this book can contribute to that fully justifiable end.

I conclude this book on a note which strikes at the heart of my arguments regarding the historically largely symbiotic relationship between race, racism and capitalist development in SA. Asked whether we have a non-racial society, Shaheen Khan answered:

> The system today is definitely not non-racial as the racial character and designations are still very much in place. Non-racialism is characterised by an understanding that the concept of 'race' is not biologically or scientifically valid and that 'race' exists as a social category to divide people so as to facilitate the system of exploitation and oppression. The 'New' South Africa as a capitalist system cannot be non-racial as it is based on a system of exploiting cheap black labour.

In this book I showed how and why that is still the dominant and defining reality in SA today.[76]

I have argued too that until and unless the capitalist system, which is ultimately still based on race, is transformed, whether we prefer to talk of the creation of an anti-racist or non-racial society, it will not materialise. We have seen throughout this book what 26 years of 'non-racialism' have delivered in this country. The sooner the capitalist class, both white and black, also comes to that realisation that the poverty, multiple social injustices and raging inequalities, which in many respects have worsened over that period, will likely deteriorate further, especially after the impact of the Covid-19 crisis and the 4IR, whose effects more fully lie in the years ahead, the better. How we navigate that future nobody can say in advance, but one thing is very clear: there will be little or no future worth speaking about until that reality dawns upon us and until we do something about it.

Endnotes

1. See Darcy du Toit, *Capital and Labour in South Africa: Class Struggles in the 1970*, (London and Boston: Paul Keagan International, 1981). See also Geoffrey Wheatcroft, *The Randlords: The Men Who Made South Africa* (London: Weidenfeld, 1985).
2. Carin Runciman, 'Why changes to South Africa's labour laws are an assault on worker's rights', *The Conversation*, 12 December 2017, at https://theconversation.com/why-changes-to-south-africas-labour-laws-are-an-insult-to-workers-88330. The low hourly minimum wage was enacted alongside two labour laws the ANC government introduced at the same time, limiting the right to strike.
3. Cited in Ebrahim Harvey, 'Workers need a united trade (union) federation', *Sunday Independent*, 6 May 2018.
4. Harvey, 'Workers need'.
5. See J. Steven Stedman, *South Africa: The Political Economy of Transformation* (Boulder and London: Lynne Rienner Publishers, 1994).
6. Saul Hansell 'Clive Menell, 65, mining executive in South Africa', *New York Times*, 27 July 1996, at www.nytimes.com.
7. I respect the role Ramaphosa played in the trade union movement. Though I have big differences with the policies he has advocated in SA, he was very helpful when in 2003 I was invited to a socialist conference in Cuba but as a result of studying full-time at the time I could not pay for my flight and accommodation and asked him if he could pay for those expenses, which he gladly did.
8. Paragraph based on 'Whites still earning three times more than blacks in SA', 15 November 2019, at https://m.fin24.com.
9. Andries Bezuidenhout, 'Has South Africa's labour movement become a middle class movement?', *The Conversation*, 30 November 2020.
10. Harvey, 'Workers need a united trade federation'.
11. 'National minimum wage increase to R21.69', 10 February 2021, www.sanews.gov.za
12. Harvey, 'Workers need a united trade federation'.
13. See 'The struggle for a living wage (in) the quest to restructure our economy', at http://www.cosatu.org/show.php?ID=63.
14. See Kaveel Singh, 'Ramaphosa thanks Cosatu for national minimum wage, vows to fight for effective implementation', 2019, at https://news24.com.
15. Harvey, 'Workers need a united trade federation'.
16. See Lukanyo Mnyandla, 'Mboweni set for fight with unions over cuts', *Business Day*, 27 February 2020.
17. Mnyandla, 'Mboweni set for fight'.
18. 'Meet the South African bosses who earn around R140,000 a day', 3 June 2019, at businesstech.co.za.
19. 'Mixed reaction to new minimum wage', 26 February 2020, at www.ecr.co.za.
20. 'Unions slam "paltry" rise in minimum wage', *Business Day*, 20 February 2020.
21. Kate Wilkinson, 'Guide: Black ownership on SA's stock exchange – what we know', 29 August 2017, at https://africacheck.org.
22. Wilkinson, 'Guide: Black ownership on SA's stock exchange – what we know'.
23. Cited in Patrick Bond, 'Neoliberalism? African authoritarianism? Disorganised dissent?' *Class History and Class Practices in the Periphery of Capitalism*, 34 (2019), pp. 89–116.
24. See Dominic Brown, 'PIC: The financing of a black capitalist class', *Daily Maverick*, 1 July 2019.

25 Interview with Zwelinzima Vavi, 23 November 2018, Johannesburg.
26 Interview with Saki Macozoma, 10 December 2017, Johannesburg.
27 Jeremy Cronin, Alex Mashilo and Malesela Maleka, 'Chris Malikane and the Gupterisation of Marxism', at https://www.politicsweb.co.za/opinion/chris-malikane-and-the-gupterisation-of-marxism; Oupa Lehulere, 'Cronin and company harness Marxism to the service of white monopoly capital', 2017, at http://khanyajournal.org.za/cronin-company-harness-marxism-to-the-service-of-white-monopoly-capital.
28 Brown, 'PIC'.
29 Brown, 'PIC'.
30 Mark Gevisser, 'State capture: The corruption investigation that has shaken South Africa', *The Guardian*, 11 November 2019.
31 See Asghar Adelzadeh, 'From the RDP to Gear: The gradual embracing of neoliberalism in economic policy', *Transformation*, 31 (1996).
32 Angelo Fick, 'Ethnic boxes perpetuate colonialism', *Mail & Guardian*, 13 July 2018.
33 See Bekezela Phakathi, 'No need to change constitution for land expropriation, says think-tank', *Business Day*, 30 January 2020.
34 Phakathi, 'No need to change'.
35 Chantall Presence, 'Lack of will to blame for slow pace of land reform, MPs told', 4 September 2018, at www.iol.co.za.
36 Lucas Ledwaba, 'Land expropriation decision an EFF victory, but what about the landless', *Mail & Guardian*, 6 December 2018.
37 Mmatshilo Motse, 'Bound to the land in inextricable connections', *Sunday Independent*, 16 December 2018.
38 See Thebeka Ngcukaitobi, 'What section 25 means for land reform', *Mail & Guardian*, 13 December 2019.
39 See 'Freedom Charter', at https://en.wikipedia.org.
40 See 'Review of land acquisition and willing acquisition and willing buyer seller principle: Briefing by the Department of Rural Development; Committee report on joint oversight visits to the Northern Cape, Limpopo, Free State and Mpumalanga: discussion', at https://pmg.org.za.
41 Mvuso Msimang, 'Before criticising, check facts', *City Press*, 7 October 2018.
42 John Lamola, 'Mbeki's utter nonsense', *City Press*, 30 September 2018.
43 Mary de Haas, 'Speaking with forked tongues on land policy', *The Star*, 3 November 2018.
44 Sam Sole, 'Xolobeni: The mine, the murder, the DG – and many unanswered questions', 30 June 2019, at www.dailymaverick.co.za.
45 De Haas, 'Speaking'.
46 Ebrahim Harvey, 'Xolobeni ruling a triumph', *The Star*, 27 November 2018.
47 Harvey, 'Xolobeni ruling'.
48 Kathleen Wooton, 'Land rights holders square up to Ingonyama Trust', 14 November 2019, at www.dailymaverick.co.za.
49 Wooton, 'Land rights holders'.
50 Aninka Claassens, '"Bantustan Bills" trample on the rights of rural people', *Daily Maverick*, 11 April 2019.
51 Claassens, 'Bantustan Bills'.
52 Claassens, 'Bantustan Bills'.
53 Patric Tariq Mellet, *The Lie of 1652: A Decolonised History of Land* (Cape Town: Tafelberg, 2020).

54 Mellet, *The Lie of 1652*, p. 313.
55 Ebrahim Harvey, 'Women still at the bottom of the heap', *Business Day*, 14 August 2005.
56 Barbara Creecy, 'Tackling climate change', *The Star*, 24 February 2020.
57 Ahmed Mokgopo, 'Climate change is a threat to the public and public money must be harnessed to fight it', *Sunday Times*, 22 December 2019.
58 Sara Evans, 'SIU probes R139 billion rot at Medupi and Kusile – report', 2019, at https://mfin24.com.
59 Cited in Gayle Edmunds, 'Apocalypse now? From climate change to climate crisis', *City Press*, 22 December 2019.
60 Edmunds, 'Apocalypse now?'
61 See 'Eskom applies for emission exemptions at Medupi and Matimba power plants', *Business Day*, 12 December 2019.
62 'Eskom applies for emission exemptions'.
63 Sipho Kings, 'The decade that decides our fate', *Mail & Guardian*, 20 December 2019.
64 All quotations in this paragraph from Kings, 'The decade that decides'.
65 Kings, 'The decade that decides'.
66 The 'just transition' discourse has its roots in a critique of the destruction wrought by the fossil fuel-based energy industry which was primarily responsible for the worsening global climate change crisis. The just transition programme has progressively expanded its parameters over the past decade into a broad vision of environmental justice – and in South Africa with a more comprehensive anti-capitalist perspective and programme. See Vishwas Satgar, *The Climate Crisis: South African and Global Democratic Eco-socialist Alternatives*, especially chapters by Vishwas Satgar, Hein Marais and Jacklyn Cock (Johannesburg: Wits University Press, 2018).
67 Vishwas Satgar, 'From the National Question to the Eco-cide Question', in *Racism after Apartheid: Challenges for Marxism and Anti-Racism*, ed. Vishwas Satgar (Johannesburg: Wits University Press, 2019), pp. 194–216.
68 Satgar, 'From the National Question', p. 195.
69 Mokgopo, 'Climate change is a threat'.
70 Jonny Steinberg, 'Black public housing edged out by white suburbanites', *Business Day*, 29 November 2019.
71 Patrick Bond, *Unsustainable South Africa: Environment, Development and Social Protest* (Pietermaritzburg: UKZN Press, 2002), p. 128.
72 Elisabeth Peyroux, 'City Improvement Districts in Johannesburg: An examination of the local variations of the BID model', at https://www.researchgate.net/publications/265148761.
73 Henri Lefebvre, *Critique of Everyday Life* (London: Verso, 2014).
74 'Is it even possible to lock down townships and informal settlements, asks Prof', at http://www.702.co.za/articles/379199/.
75 'Has South Africa lost R700 billion to corruption since 1994?', 12 February 2018, at https://africacheck.org/reports/has-sa-lost-r700-billion-to-corruption-since-1994. The report, however, stated that the figure of R700 billion is not very reliable. But even if it was far less, say R65 or R60 billion, it would be an enormous sum of money lost to corruption and fraud, which could have been spent on water, sanitation and electricity infrastructure in black townships.
76 Interview with Shaheen Khan, email correspondence, 14 February 2018.

Bibliography

Adhikari, M. (2005), *Not White Enough, Not Black Enough: Racial Identity in the South African Coloured Community*, Athens: Ohio University Press & Cape Town: Double Storey Books.

Alexander, A. and A. Mngxitama (2011), 'Race and Resistance in Post-Apartheid South Africa'. In S. Essof and D. Moshenberg (2017), *Searching for South Africa: The New Calculus of Dignity*, Pretoria: Unisa Press.

Alexander, N. (1979), *One Azania, One Nation: The National Question in South Africa*, London: Zed Press.

—— (2002), *An Ordinary Country: Issues in the Transition from Apartheid to Democracy in South Africa*, Pietermaritzburg: University of KwaZulu-Natal Press.

—— (2013), *Thoughts on the New South Africa*, Johannesburg: Jacana Media.

Alexander, P., T. Lekgowa, B. Mmope, L. Sinwell and B. Xeswi (2013), *Marikana: Voices from South Africa's Mining Massacre, the Mountain and a Case to Answer*, Ohio: Ohio University Press.

Anciano, F. (XXXX), 'Non-racialism and the African National Congress: Views from the branches', *Journal of Contemporary African Studies*, 32, 1, pp. 35–44, DOI: 10.1080/02589001.2014.900308.

Bahn, P. (ed.) (2007), *Ancient World in a Pocket*, New York: Barnes & Noble Books.

Banton, M. (1987), *Racial Theories*, Cambridge & New York: Cambridge University Press.

Barnard, N. (2015), *Secret Revolution: Memoirs of a Spy*, Cape Town: Tafelberg.

Barzun, J. (1938), *Race: A Study in Modern Superstition*, Harcourt: Brace & Company.

—— (2001), *From Dawn to Decadence*, London: Harper Collins Publishers.

Benedict, R. (1983), *Race and Racism*, London: Routledge & Kegan Paul.

Bernal, M. (1991), *Black Athena: The Afroasiatic Roots of Classical Civilisation*, London: Vintage Books.

Biko, H. (2013), *The Great African Society: A Plan for a Nation Gone Astray*, Johannesburg & Cape Town: Jonathan Ball Publishers.

Biko, S. (2004), *I Write What I Like*, Johannesburg: Picador Africa.

Bond, J. (1971), *They Were South Africans*, London & New York: Oxford University Press.

Bond, P. (2000), *Elite Transition: From Apartheid to Neoliberalism in South Africa*, Scottsville: University of KwaZulu-Natal Press (UKZN) Press.

——(2002), *Unsustainable South Africa: Environment, Development and Social Protest*, Pietermaritzburg: UKZN Press & London: Merlin Press.

—— (2003), *Against Global Apartheid: South Africa Meets the World Bank, IMF and International Finance*, Cape Town: UCT Press & London: Zed Books.

—— (2004), *Talk Left Walk Right: South Africa's Frustrated Global Reforms*, Scottsville: UKZN Press.

—— (2014), 'Contradictions Subside Then Deepen'. In J.S. Saul and P. Bond, *South Africa, The Present as History: From Mrs Ples to Mandela & Marikana*, Johannesburg: Jacana Media and London: James Currey.

Bonner, P. (2012), 'Fragmentation and cohesion in the ANC: The first 70 years'. In A. Lissoni et al. (eds) *One Hundred Years of the ANC: Debating Liberation Histories Today*, Johannesburg: Wits University Press.

Boxer, C.R. (1965), *Four Centuries of Portuguese Expansion*, Johannesburg: Wits University Press.

Bradford, S. (1973), *Portugal*, London: Thames & Hudson.

Buhlungu, M.S. (2001), 'Democracy and Modernisation in the Making of the South African Trade Union Movement: The Dilemma of Leadership, 1973–2000', PhD Thesis submitted to the Sociology Department of the University of the Witwatersrand.

Bundy, C. (1988), *The Rise and Fall of the South African Peasantry*, Cape Town: David Philip and London: James Currey.

—— (2019), The Challenge of Rethinking Mandela, *Journal of African Studies*, 45 (6), 997–1012, at https://doi.org/10.1080/0305070.2019.1697553.

Carr, E.H. (1945), *Nationalism and After*, London: Macmillan.

Clare, J. (2010), *Captured in Time: Five Centuries of South African Writing*, Johannesburg and Cape Town: Jonathan Ball Publishers.

Clark, S. (ed.) (1993), *Nelson Mandela Speaks: Forging a Democratic Non-Racial South Africa*, Johannesburg: David Philip.

Commins, S. and R.N. Linscott (eds.) (1947), *Man and the State: The Political Philosophers*, New York: Random House.

Davidson, B. (1992), *The Black Man's Burden: Africa and the Curse of the Nation State*, London: James Currey.

Davis, R.C. and R. Scheleifer (1991), *Criticism and Culture*, Essex (England): Longman.

Du Toit, D. (1981), *Capital and Labour in South Africa: Class Struggles in the 1970s*, London & Boston: Keagan Paul International.

Edgar, R.R. and L. Ka Msumza (2015), *Anton Lembede, Freedom in Our Lifetime*, Cape Town: Kwela Books.

Elphick, R. and H. Giliomee (1989), 'The origins and entrenchment of European dominance at the Cape, 1652–c.1840'. In. R. Elphick and H. Giliomee (eds), *The Shaping of South African Society*, 1652–1840, 2nd edition, Cape Town: Maskew Miller Longman.

Essof, S. and D. Moshenberg (2011), *Searching for South Africa: The New Calculus of Dignity*, Pretoria: Unisa Press.

Etherington, N., 'Religion and Resistance in Natal, 1900–910'. In Lissoni et al., *One Hundred Years of the ANC: Debating Liberation Histories Today*, Johannesburg: Wits University Press, 2012.

Everatt, D. (2009), *The Origins of Non-Racialism: White Opposition to Apartheid in the 1950s*, Johannesburg: Wits University Press.

Fanon, F. (1989), *Studies in a Dying Colonialism*, London: Earthscan Publication.

—— (1990), *The Wretched of the Earth*, London & New York: Penguin Books.

Fatton, R. (1986), *Black Consciousness in South Africa: The Dialectics of*

Ideological Resistance to White Supremacy, New York: State University of New York Press.

Feuer, L.S. (1984), *Marx and Engels: Basic Writings on Politics and Philosophy*, Fontana/Collins: London.

Fine, R. and D. Davis (1990), *Beyond Apartheid: Labour and Liberation in South Africa*, Johannesburg: Ravan Press.

Frederikse, J. (1990), *The Unbreakable Thread: Non-Racialism in South Africa*, Johannesburg: Ravan Press.

Friedman, S. (2015), *Race, Class and Power: Harold Wolpe and the Radical Critique of Apartheid*, Pietermaritzburg: UKZN Press.

Gates, H.L. (1985), 'Editor's Introduction: Writing "Race" and the Difference It Makes', in H.L. Gates (eds.) *'Race', Writing and Difference*, Chicago and London: University of Chicago Press.

Gerhart, G. (1978), *Black Power in South Africa: The Evolution of an Ideology*, Berkeley: University of California Press.

Giliomee, H. (2003), *The Afrikaners*, Charlottesville: University of Virginia Press.

Gordon, L.R. (2015), *What Fanon Said: A Philosophical Introduction to His Life and Thought*, Johannesburg: Wits University Press.

Gordon R.J. (1992), *The Bushman Myth: The Making of a Namibian Underclass*, Boulder, San Francisco and Oxford: Westview Press.

Graham, P. and A. Coetzee (eds.) (2002), *In the Balance: Debating the State of Democracy in South Africa*, Cape Town: Idasa.

Grayling, A.C. (2009), *Ideas That Matter: A Personal Guide for the 21st Century*, London: Weidenfeld & Nicolson.

Greenberg, S.B. (1980), *Race and State in Capitalist Development: South Africa in Comparative Perspective*, Johannesburg: Ravan Press & New Haven: Yale University Press.

Habib, A. and K. Bentley (2008), *Racial Redress and Citizenship in South Africa*, Cape Town: HSRC Press.

Hain, P. (2018), *Mandela: His Essential Life*, London and New York: Rowman & Littlefield.

Harvey, E. (2002), 'Popular Control over Decision Makers', in P. Graham and A. Coetzee (eds.), *In the Balance: Debating the State of Democracy in South Africa*, Cape Town: Idasa Press.

—— (2008), 'The Commodification of Water in Soweto and Its Implications for Social Justice', PhD Thesis submitted to the University of the Witwatersrand.

—— (2012), *Kgalema Motlanthe: A Political Biography*, Johannesburg: Jacana Media.

Herd, N. (1966), *1922: The Revolt on the Rand*, Johannesburg: Blue Crane Books.

Hitchens, C. (2006), *Thomas Paine's Rights of Man*, London: Atlantic Books.

Hlongwane, K. A, S. Ndlovu and M. Mutloatse (2006), *Soweto '76, Reflections on the Liberation Struggle*, Johannesburg: Pan Macmillan.

Hommel, M. (ed.) (1989), *Contributions of Non-European Peoples to World Civilisation*, Johannesburg: Skotaville Publishers.

Huds, P. (2018), Racism and the Logic of Capitalism: A Fanonian Reconsideration, at https://www.historicalmaterialism.org/articles/racism-and-logic-of-capitalism.

Innes, D. (1984), *Anglo American and the Rise of Modern South Africa*, Johannesburg: Ravan Press.

Jansen, J. (2017), *As by Fire: The End of the South African University*, Cape Town: Tafelberg.

Johnson, R.W. (2009), *South Africa's Brave New World: The Beloved Country since the End of Apartheid*, London: Penguin Books.

Jordan, P. (2017), *Letters to My Comrades: Interventions and Excursions*, Johannesburg: Jacana Media.

Karis, T. and G. Gerhart (1997), *From Protest to Challenge: A Documentary History of African Politics in South Africa*, Vol. 5, Nadir and Resurgence, 1964–1979, Bloomington: Indiana University Press.

Keegan, T. (1996), *Colonial South Africa and the Origins of the Racial Order*, Cape Town and Johannesburg: David Philip

—— (2016), *Dr. Philip's Empire: One Man's Struggle for Justice in Nineteenth-Century South Africa*, Cape Town: Zebra Press.

Krikler, J. (2005), *The Rand Revolt: The 1922 Insurrection and Racial Killing in South Africa*, Cape Town and Johannesburg: Jonathan Ball Publishers.

Kuljian, C. (2017), *Darwin's Hunch: Science, Race and the Search for Human Origins*, Johannesburg: Jacana Media.

Lalu, P. (2009), *The Deaths of Hintsa: Post-Apartheid South Africa and the*

Shape of Recurring Pasts, Cape Town: HSRC Press.

Lefebvre, H. (2014), *Critique of Everyday Life*, London: Verso.

Legassick, M. (2007), *Towards Socialist Democracy*, Scottsville: University of KwaZulu-Natal Press.

—— (2013), *Hidden Histories of Gordonia: Land Dispossession and Resistance in the Northern Cape*, Johannesburg: Wits University Press.

—— (2017), 'The Marxist Workers Tendency of the African National Congress', in Webster and Pampallis, *The Unresolved National Question: Left Thought under Apartheid*, Johannesburg: Wits University Press.

Lemon, A. (1995), *The Geography of Change in South Africa*, Chichester: John Wiley & Sons.

Lipton, M. (1985), *Capitalism and Apartheid, South Africa, 1910–1986*, Cape Town: David Philip.

—— (2007), *Liberals, Marxists and Nationalists: Competing Interpretations of South African History*, New York: Palgrave Macmillan.

Lissoni, A, J. Soske, N. Erland, N. Nieftagodien and O. Badsha (eds.) (2012), *One Hundred Years of the ANC: Debating Liberation Histories Today*, Johannesburg: Wits University Press.

Lukacs, J. (2011), *The Future of History*, New Haven & London: Yale University Press.

MacDonald, M. (2006), *Why Race Matters in South Africa*, London & Cambridge, MA: Harvard University Press.

Maharaj, M. (ed.) (2001), *Reflections in Prison*, Cape Town: Zebra & Robben Island Museum.

Malcolm X. (1970), *By Any Means Necessary*, London & New York: Pathfinder.

Mangcu, X. (2012), *Biko: A Biography*, Cape Town: Tafelberg Publishers.

—— (2015), *The Colour of Our Future: Does Race Matter in Post-Apartheid South Africa?* Johannesburg: Wits University Press.

Marais, H. (2011), *Pushed to the Limits: The Political Economy of Change*, Johannesburg: Jacana Media.

Maré, G. (2014), *Declassified: Moving beyond the Dead End of Race in South Africa*, Jacana Media: Johannesburg.

Maré, G. (2017), 'The National Question confronts the Ethnic Question'. In E. Webster and K. Pampallis (eds), *The Unresolved National Question:*

Left Thought under Apartheid and Beyond, Johannesburg: Wits University Press.

Marks, S. (1986), *The Ambiguities of Dependence in South Africa: Class, Nationalism and the State in Twentieth-Century Natal*, Johannesburg: Ravan Press.

Mbeki, M. (2009), *Architects of Poverty: Why African Capitalism Needs Changing*, Johannesburg: Picador.

Mbembe, A. (2017), *Critique of Black Reason*, Johannesburg: Wits University Press.

McCoskey, D.E. (2012), *Race: Antiquity and Its Legacy*, Oxford & New York: Oxford University Press.

McDonald, D.A. (2002*)*, *Environmental Justice in South Africa*, Athens: Ohio University Press & Cape Town: UCT Press.

—— and J. Pape (2002), *Cost Recovery and the Crisis of Service Delivery in South Africa*, Cape Town: HSRC Press & New York: Zed Books.

—— and G. Ruiters (2005), *The Age of Commodity: Water Privatisation in Southern Africa*, London: Earthscan.

McDonald, M. (2006), *Why Race Matters in South Africa*, Cambridge, MA: Harvard University Press.

McKaiser, E. (2012), *A Bantu in My Bathroom: Debating Race, Sexuality and Other Uncomfortable South African Topics*, Johannesburg: Pan Macmillan & Bookstorm.

—— (2015), *Run, Racist, Run: Journeys into the Heart of Racism*, Johannesburg: Bookstorm.

Meli, F. (1988), 'South Africa and the Rise of Nationalism', in M. van Diepen, *The National Question in South Africa*, London: Zed Books.

Meredith, M. (1997), *Nelson Mandela: A Biography*, London: Penguin Books.

Miles, R. (1989), *Racism*, London & New York: Routledge.

Mirza, H.S. (1992), *Young, Female and Black*, London & New York: Routledge.

Mngxitama, A., A. Alexander and N.C. Gibson (2008), *Biko Lives! Contesting the Legacies of Steve Biko*, New York: Palgrave Macmillan.

Montague, A. (1972), *Statement on Race*, London & New York: Oxford University Press.

—— (1974), *Man's Most Dangerous Myth: The Fallacy of Race*, New York: Oxford University Press.

Moore, C. (1988), *Castro, the Blacks and Africa*, Los Angeles: University of California Press.

Motala, E. and S. Vally (2017), 'Neville Alexander and the National Question', in E. Webster and K. Pampallis (eds.), *The Unresolved National Question: Left Thought under Apartheid*, Johannesburg: Wits University Press.

Mudimbe, V.Y. (1988), *The Invention of Africa: Gnosis, Philosophy and the Order of Knowledge*, Bloomington: Indiana University Press & London: James Currey.

Muller C.F.J. (ed.) (1986), *500 Years: A History of South Africa*, Pretoria & Cape Town: Academica.

Munger, E.S. (1967), *Afrikaner and African Nationalism: South African Parallels and Parameters*, London: Oxford University Press.

Musson, D. (1989), *Johnny Gomas, Voice of the Working Class: A Political Biography*, Cape Town: Buchu Books.

Naidoo, J. (2010), *Fighting for Justice: A Lifetime of Political and Social Activism*, Johannesburg: Picador.

Nasson, B. (2016), *History Matters: Selected Writings, 1970–2016*, Cape Town: Penguin Books.

Ndletyana, M. (2008), 'Affirmative Action in the Public Service', in A. Habib. and K. Bentley (2008), *Racial Redress and Citizenship in South Africa*, Cape Town: HSRC Press.

Nieftagodien, N. (2012), 'Popular Movements, Contentious Spaces and the ANC, 1943–1956', in Lissoni et al., *One Hundred Years of the ANC: Debating Liberation Histories Today*, Johannesburg: Wits University Press.

Oakes, D. (1988). *Illustrated History of South Africa: The Real Story*, Cape Town: The Reader's Digest Association of South Africa.

Odendaal, A. (2012), *The Founders: The Origins of the ANC and the Struggle for Democracy in South Africa*, Johannesburg: Jacana Media.

Padayachee, V. and R. van Niekerk (2019), *Shadow of Liberation*, Johannesburg: Wits University Press.

Painter, N.E. (2010), *The History of the White World*, New York and London: W.W. Norton.

Pakenham, T. (1990), *The Scramble for Africa*, Johannesburg: Jonathan Ball.

Pallister, D., S. Stewart and I. Lepper (1987), *South Africa Inc: The Oppenheimer Empire*, Johannesburg: Lowry Publishers.

Pauw, P. (2017), *The President's Keepers: Those Keeping Zuma in Power and out of Prison*, Cape Town: Tafelberg.

Pinnock, D. (2007), *Writing Left: The Radical Journalism of Ruth First*, Pretoria: University of South Africa.

Plaut, M. (2016), *Promise and Despair: The First Struggle for a Non-Racial South Africa*, Johannesburg: Jacana Media.

Price, R.M. (1991), *The Apartheid State in Crisis: Political Transformation in South Africa 1975–1990*, New York & Oxford: Oxford University Press.

Ramirez-Faria, C. (1991), *The Origins of Economic Inequality between Nations: A critique of Western Theories on Development and Underdevelopment*, London: Unwin Hyman.

Rattansi, A. (1989), *Ideology, Method and Marx*, London & New York: Routledge.

Ray, M. (2016), *Free Fall: Why South African Universities are in a Race against Time*: Johannesburg: Bookstorm.

Robinson, C.J. (1983), *Black Marxism: The Making of the Black Radical Tradition*, London & New Jersey: Zed Books.

Roediger, D.R. (2007), *The Wages of Whiteness: Race and the Making of the American Working Class*, Verso: London.

Ross, R. (1994), *Beyond the Pale: Essays on the History of Colonial South Africa*, Johannesburg: Wits University Press.

Roux, E. (1964), *Time Longer than Rope: The Black Man's Struggle for Freedom in South Africa*, Wisconsin & London: University of Wisconsin Press.

Ruiters, G. (2002), 'Commodified Water, Race and Social Justice', PhD Thesis submitted to John Hopkins University.

Said, W.E. (1993), *Culture and Imperialism*, Vintage: Great Britain.

Sampson, A. (1987), *Black and Gold: Tycoons, Revolutionaries and Apartheid*, London: Hodder & Stoughton.

—— (1999) *Mandela: The Authorised Biography*, London: HarperCollins Publishers.

Satgar, V. (2019), 'From the National Question to the Eco-cide Question', in Satgar (ed.) *Racism after Apartheid: Challenges for Marxism and Anti-*

Racism, Johannesburg: Wits University Press.

Saul, S.J. (2014), 'The Apartheid Endgame, 1990–1994', in J. Saul and P. Bond, *South Africa: The Present as History*, Jacana Media: Johannesburg.

Saunders, C. (1988*)*, *The Making of the South African Past: Major Historians on Race and Class*, Johannesburg & Cape Town: David Philip.

Schreiner, H., P. Baron and S. Fonn (2007), 'The Promise and the Practice of Transformation in South Africa's Health System', in S. Buhlungu et al. (eds*.)*, *State of the Nation 2007*, Cape Town: HSRC Press.

Seekings, J. and N. Nattrass. (2006), *Class, Race and Inequality in South Africa*, Scotsville: KwaZulu-Natal Press.

Shivambu, F. (2014), *The Coming Revolution: Julius Malema and the Fight for Economic Freedom*, Johannesburg: Jacana Media.

Simons, J. and R. Simons (1983), *Class and Colour in South Africa 1850–1950*, London: International Defence & Aid Fund for Southern Africa.

Sivanandan, A. (1990), *Communities of Resistance: Writings on Black Struggles for Socialism*, London & New York: Verso.

Smith, D. (1990), *Capitalist Democracy on Trial: The Transatlantic Debate from Tocqueville to the Present*, London & New York: Routledge.

—— (1995), 'Redistribution and Social Justice after Apartheid', in A. Lemon, *The Geography of Change in South Africa*, Chichester: John Wiley & Sons.

Soske, T. (2012), 'Unravelling the "Doctor's Pact": Race, Metonymy and the of Nationalism in History', in Lissoni et al., *One Hundred Years of the ANC: Debating Liberation Histories Today*, Johannesburg: Wits University Press.

Soudien, C. (2008), 'Robben Island University Revisited', in Lissoni et al., *One Hundred Years of the ANC: Debating Liberation Histories Today*, Johannesburg: Wits University Press.

—— (2012), *Realising the Dream: Unlearning the Logic of Race in the South African School*, Cape Town: HSRC Press.

—— (2016), 'Non-Racialism's Politics: Reading Being Human through the Life of Neville Alexander', in A, Zinn (ed.), *Non-Racialism in South Africa: The Life and Times of Neville Alexander*, Stellenbosch: Sun Media.

—— (2019) *Cape Radicals: Intellectual and Political Thought of the New Era Fellowship, 1930s–1960s*, Johannesburg: Wits University Press.

South African Human Rights Commission (SAHRC) (2006), *Reflections on Democracy and Human Rights: A Decade of the South African Constitution*, Johannesburg: SAHRC.

Southall, R. (2006), 'Black Empowerment and Present Limits to a More Democratic Capitalism in South Africa', in S. Buhlungu, J. Daniel, R. Southall and J. Lutchman (eds.) *State of the Nation, South Africa 2005–2006*.

—— (2012), 'The ANC: Party Vanguard of the Black Middle Class', in Lissoni et al., *One Hundred Years of the ANC: Debating Liberation Histories Today*, Johannesburg: Wits University Press.

Sparg, M., J. Schreiner and G. Ansell (2001), *Comrade Jack: The Political Lectures and Diary of Jack Simons, Novo Catengue*, Johannesburg: STE Publishers.

Stedman, J.S. (1994), *South Africa: The Political Economy of Transformation*, Boulder: Lynne Rienner Publishers.

Suckling, J. and L. White (1988), *After Apartheid: Renewal of the South African Economy*, York: Centre for Southern African Studies, University of York and London: James Currey.

Sullivan, B. (2001), *Africa through the Mists of Time*, Johannesburg: Covos Day Books.

Suttner, R. (2015), *Recovering Democracy in South Africa*, Johannesburg: Jacana Media.

Swan, M. (1985), *Gandhi: The South African Experience*, Johannesburg: Ravan Press.

Swilling, M., R. Humphries and K. Shubane (1991), *Apartheid City in Transition*, Oxford: Oxford University Press.

Tate, C. (ed.) (1989), *Black Women Writers at Work*, England: Old Castle Books.

Terkel, S. (1993), *Race*, London: Minerva.

Terreblanche, S. (2012), *Lost in Transformation: South Africa's Search for a New Future since 1986*, Johannesburg: KMM Review Publishing.

Ticktin, H. (1991), *The Politics of Race Discrimination in South Africa*, London: Pluto Press.

Todorov, T. (1985), 'Race, Writing and Culture', in H.L. Gates, *'Race', Writing and Difference*, Chicago and London: University of Chicago Press.

Tomlinson, J. (1999), *Globalisation and Culture*, Oxford: Polity Press.

Tosh, J. (1999), *The Pursuit of History*, London and New York: Longman.

Trewhela, P. (2009), *Inside Quatro: Uncovering the Exile History of the ANC and SWAPO*, Johannesburg: Jacana Media.

Trotsky, L. (1977), *The History of the Russian Revolution*, London: Pluto Press.

Troyna, B. and R. Hatcher (1992), *Racism in Children's Lives*, London: Routledge.

Turok, B. (2001), *Readings in the ANC Tradition, Policy and Praxis, Vol. 1*, Johannesburg: Jacana Media.

—— (2008), *From the Freedom Charter to Polokwane: The Evolution of ANC Economic Policy*, Cape Town: New Agenda.

—— (2010), *The Historical Roots of the ANC: Understanding the ANC Today*, Johannesburg: Jacana Media.

Uhlig, M.A. (ed.) (1986), *Apartheid in Crisis*, London: Penguin Books.

Vail, Leroy (1989), *The Creation of Tribalism in Southern Africa*, London: James Currey & Berkeley: University of California Press.

Vally, H. and M. Isaacson (eds) (2012), *Enough is a Feast: A Tribute to Dr Neville Alexander*, Johannesburg: Foundation for Human Rights.

Van der Ross, R.E. (2008), *The Black Countess*, Cape Town: Ampersand Press.

Van Niekerk, R. (2017), 'African National Congress: Social Democratic Thinking and the Good Society 1940–1962', in Webster and Pampallis (eds.), *The Unresolved National Question: Left Thought under Apartheid*, Johannesburg: Wits University Press.

Van der Westhuizen, C. (2007), *White Power and the Rise and Fall of the National Party*, Cape Town: Zebra Press.

Van Diepen, M. (1988), *The National Question in South Africa*, London and New Jersey: Zed Books.

Walvin, J. (2008), *The Trader, the Owner, the Slave: Parallel Lives in the Age of Slavery*, London: Vintage Books.

Wasserman, H. and S. Jacobs (2003), *Shifting Selves: Post-Apartheid Essays on Mass Media, Culture and Identity*, Cape Town: Kwela Books.

Watson, R.L. (1990), *The Slave Question: Liberty and Prosperity in South Africa*, Johannesburg: Witwatersrand University Press.

Webster, E. and J. Mawbey (2017), 'Revisiting the National Question', in E. Webster and K. Pampallis, *The Unresolved National Question: Left Thought under Apartheid*, Johannesburg: Wits University Press.

Wheatcroft, G. (1985), *The Randlords: The Men Who Made South Africa*, London: Weidenfeld.

White, J. (1985), *Black Leadership in America: From Booker T Washington to Jessie Jackson*, London and New York: Longman.

Wilson, H.S. (1994), *African Decolonisation*, London: Edward Arnold.

Wise, T. (2008), *White like Me: Reflections on Race from a Privileged Son*, New York: Soft Skull Press.

Wolpe, H. (1989), *Race, Class and the Apartheid State*, London: James Currey and Paris: OAU, Inter-African Cultural Fund & Unesco Press.

Wood, G.S. (2008), *The Purpose of the Past*, New York: Penguin Press.

Worden, N. (1994), *The Making of Modern South Africa: Conquest, Segregation and Apartheid*, Oxford: Blackwell.

—— (ed) (2012), *Cape Town between East and West: Social Identities in a Dutch Colonial Town*, Johannesburg: Jacana Media and Hilversum: Uitgeverij Verloren.

Zegcyc, A. (ed.) (2001), *Social Identities in the New South Africa, after Apartheid*, Cape Town: Kwela Books.

Zinn, A. (ed.) (2018), *Non-Racialism in South Africa: The Life and Times of Neville Alexander*, Stellenbosch: Sun Media.

Index

This index is arranged word by word.

4IR *see* Fourth Industrial Revolution

A

Abdurahman, Abdullah 169, 170–172, 182
affirmative action (AA) *see* black economic empowerment
Africa as a source of wealth 46–47, 49
African Claims (1943) 31, 184
African Democratic Party (ADP) 185
African National Congress (ANC)
    branches 325–326, 327–328
    and broad church myth 192–193
    and capitalism 62, 198, 264–265
    and Coloured community 220, 221, 223, 225–227, 231, 232–235, 236, 238, 245
    founding 115, 284
    and gender 35, 137–139
    history of 146–148, 151, 152–153, 154–155, 170, 175–177, 179, 181–190, 204–205, 218, 272–273; *see also* membership
    Kabwe conference (1985) 159, 173
    leadership 27, 270–271, 274, 275, 326
    membership 155–157, 158, 159–160, 162–163, 164–165, 166, 167, 172–173, 177, 180–181, 188, 204, 94, 325; *see also* African nationalism and chauvinism
    Morogoro conference (1969) 159, 172, 180, 207
    and negotiations 19–20, 21–22, 25, 36, 53, 62, 126, 133, 198, 202, 207–208, 210, 211, 214, 215–216, 217–218, 219–220, 253, 272, 275, 276, 382
    policies 24, 27, 35–36, 37, 81, 117, 137, 139–140, 172, 188, 199, 200, 210, 275, 279–280, 284–285, 327, 345
    and race and racism 18, 29–30, 34, 39, 289–290
African National Congress Youth League (ANCYL) 35, 156–157, 160, 185, 186, 187, 204, 298–299
African nationalism and chauvinism 36, 37, 68–69, 85–87, 93, 97–99, 118, 132, 140, 153, 154, 155–157, 158, 164–168, 169, 173, 177–178, 186–187, 188, 203, 204–206, 221–222, 227–228, 229–230, 231–232, 239, 240, 244, 251–252, 267–269, 270, 271–272, 274, 285, 290, 291, 295–296, 298, 299–300, 301, 310, 333–334, 339, 340, 352, 373, 382
African People's Organisation (APO) 166, 169–172, 182

Afrikaner capitalism 228, 380
Afrikaner nationalism 96, 373, 380
Aggett, Neil 341
agriculture 128, 388, 389–390
air pollution 397, 398–399
Alexander, Neville 161, 245
Alexandra bus boycott (1942–1943) 184, 185
Anglo American Corporation (AAC) 22, 25, 125, 198, 201–202, 228, 254 n.2, 371, 372, 373, 383
Anglo-Boer War (1899–1902) 124–125, 149
apartheid
  abolition of 25, 55, 101, 260
  and blame 30
  and cultural deprivation 87
  and reparations 215
  terminology and legislation 39, 77, 95–96
arms deal 381
Association of Mineworkers and Construction Union (Amcu) 315, 323
Azanian People's Organisation (Azapo) 86, 231, 246, 283, 287, 374

B
Baloyi, R.G. 185
Baloyi Commission of Enquiry (2019) 393
Berlin Conference (1885) 49
Biko, Steve 85, 87–88
black billionaires 273
black consciousness 86, 87, 186, 246, 271, 283
black economic empowerment (BEE) 39, 75, 131, 193, 200, 206, 230, 232, 240, 247, 274, 278, 279, 291–292, 295, 321, 341, 367–368, 371–372, 374, 376
black elite and middle class 25, 27, 29, 36, 39, 75–76, 80, 82, 124, 131, 136, 140–141, 148–149, 150–152, 153, 162, 165, 179, 182–183, 193, 211–212, 215, 216, 229–230, 247, 250, 251–252, 272, 273, 274–276, 280, 299, 307, 345, 346, 370–371, 372, 375–376, 377–378, 382, 383
Black First Land First (BFLF) 374
black nationalism *see* African nationalism
and chauvinism
black working class *see* working class, African
black working class women 135–137, 138–139, 175
Bosasa 206, 381
Botha, Louis 122
Botha, P.W. 202
Britain 54–55, 126
  and South Africa 114–115, 120, 122–123, 124–125, 184
British imperialism 19, 23–24, 26–27, 48, 52, 55–56, 57, 149
Bunting, Brian 275
Buthelezi, Mangosuthu (Gatsha) 240

C
cadre deployment 270
Cape Colony 19, 35, 48, 50, 54, 55, 68, 107, 109–113, 114–116, 117, 118–119, 121, 231, 379–380
Cape Dutch architecture 128
Cape Flats 297
Cape franchise 26, 32, 56, 122–123, 125, 147, 148, 149
capitalism 20–21, 22–25, 26, 28, 34–35, 52, 53–55, 57, 60–62, 68, 77, 81, 88, 95, 100–104, 130, 152, 190–192, 206, 218–219, 250–251, 263, 282, 311, 321, 359, 378–379, 389, 402–403, 408, 409–410, 411
caste system *see* race and racism, India
cholera 248
circumcision 222, 223
civil rights 126
civil society 310, 391, 403
civilisation 53
class and class struggle 74, 81–82, 84, 86–87, 89, 97, 112, 132, 165, 254, 264, 279, 283, 341, 400–401
climate change 395, 396–398, 399, 401, 403, 404
clothing and textile workers 135
coal-fired power stations 397, 399, 400, 404
colonialism 59, 80, 128–130, 132–133, 150, 169, 335–336

of a special type (CST) 31
Coloured community 117–118, 119, 157–160, 161, 167, 168, 177, 180, 203, 219, 220, 221, 223, 225–227, 231, 232–236, 237–239, 241, 243–245, 289–290, 295, 297–298
Coloured Labour Preference Policy 225, 226
Coloured Question *see* Coloured community
Comintern 31
Communist Party of South Africa (CPSA) 184, 187, 188; *see also* South African Communist Party
comprador bourgeoisie *see* black middle class
Comprehensive Sexuality Education (CSE) curriculum 224
Congress Alliance 187–188, 189–190
Congress of Democrats 157
Congress of South African Trade Unions (Cosatu) 97, 189, 208, 210, 213, 214, 216, 219, 276, 280, 310, 319, 323, 363, 364, 365–366, 373–374, 403, 404
Congress of Traditional Leaders of South Africa (Contralesa) 223, 240
Constitution (1996) 26, 31, 140, 167–168, 253, 285, 305, 311, 330–331, 360–361, 364–365, 383, 384–387, 388–389, 390
Convention for a Democratic South Africa (Codesa) 210, 371
Copelyn, Johnny 319–320
coronavirus pandemic 38, 375, 407–408
corruption 30, 218, 237, 269, 270, 273, 274, 276, 280, 299, 300, 306–307, 311, 324, 325, 326, 328, 348–352, 353–355, 355 n.1–2, 376, 378, 379, 380–381, 397, 408–409
Covid-19 *see* coronavirus pandemic
culture 87–88, 91
traditional 173, 174–175, 222, 223–224, 240, 309–310

D
Da Gama, Vasco 48, 107
Dart, Raymond 134

De Klerk, F.W. 202, 211
debt 215, 216
Defiance Campaign 187
Democratic Alliance (DA, formerly Democratic Party) 116, 127, 234–235
Dexter, Phillip 246
Dias, Bartolomeu 47–48, 107
Dlamini-Zuma, Nkosazana 312
domestic workers 135, 136–137, 360, 367
Duarte, Jesse 290
Dube, John Langalibalele 152, 153–154, 159, 179
Dudley, Richard 221
Dutch East India Company (DEIC) 50, 109, 110–111, 114, 379

E
eco-cide 401, 402
economic development 53, 60, 127–129, 130
Economic Freedom Fighters (EFF) 37, 187, 231, 293–294, 295, 296–298, 299–300, 332, 333, 341, 353–354, 374, 383, 386, 404, 409
education 174, 175–176, 189, 203, 235, 236–239, 249, 269, 270, 330–333, 342–343, 366, 409
decolonisation of 334–335, 336–337
Eldorado Park (Gauteng) 227, 232, 233, 234, 235, 236, 289, 290, 298
elections 349
general 294–295
general (1994) 212–213, 218, 220, 226, 245, 348, 383
local government 269, 294
electricity 247, 253, 306, 307, 397, 407, 409. *See also* coal-fired power stations; Eskom; meters, pre-paid
Employment Equity Act (1998) 278
epistemology 29, 394
Esidimeni scandal *see* Life Esidimeni
Eskom 306, 307, 381, 398–399, 400
Europe 51, 58–59, 63
expropriation without compensation (EWC) 383, 388

F

Fanon, Frantz 229–230
Farlam Commission of Enquiry 317, 318, 320
farmworkers 135, 137, 159, 360, 367
Fees Must Fall movement *see* student uprisings
floods 399
Fourth Industrial Revolution (4IR) 31, 57, 60, 62, 323, 394, 403
Freedom Charter (1955) 31, 157, 161, 183, 184, 187, 188, 198–199, 200, 201, 215, 221, 272, 273, 276, 284, 288, 305, 330, 361, 365, 389–390, 391
Frontier Wars 113
Funamalungelo Society 151

G

gang warfare 297
Gatvol Capetonian 233
Gear *see* Growth, Employment and Redistribution
gender 35, 135, 137–139, 174–175, 395–396
 and violence 137–138, 396; *see also* rape
Ghana 24, 26
Glen Grey Act (1894) 121
Golding, Marcel 319–320
Good Party 385
Gordhan, Pravin 294, 300–301
Group Areas Act (1950) 253
Growth, Employment and Redistribution (Gear) 138, 200, 209–210, 211, 248, 309, 319, 327, 366, 381, 385, 386, 388–389
Gumede, Josiah 151, 179, 184
Gupta family 378, 380, 381, 382

H

Hani, Chris 207
health services 81, 191, 293, 309, 313; *see also* hospitals
Helen Suzman Foundation 385
High Level Panel on Land Reform (Motlanthe) 393
historical materialism (Marx) 17, 18, 53, 74–75, 229, 322–323, 378–379
history (as concept) 63, 128, 145–146
HIV/Aids 223, 307–310, 311–313
Holland 49–52
 and South Africa 109–110, 112
hospitals 141, 269, 270, 346, 366, 409
housing 249, 315, 316, 365, 366, 387, 405–406, 409
Hulett, G.H. 147
Human Rights Commission 393
humanism 287–288

I

Immorality Act (1927) 253
independent left 203–204, 211, 255 n.13, 257 n.79, 291, 310–311
Indian community 158–159, 161, 168, 177, 180, 187, 203, 219, 293, 294, 295, 296, 298, 300–301
indigency 138
Industrial and Commercial Workers' Union (ICU) 176
Industrial Revolution 58
Ingonyama Trust 240–241, 392–393
Inkanyiso yase Natal (newspaper) 151
International Monetary Fund (IMF) 214, 390

J

Jabavu, John Tengo 170
Jim, Irvin 231
Johannesburg 123, 406–407
Johannesburg Stock Exchange (JSE) 369, 370, 371, 373, 374, 377
Johannesburg Water and City Power 199
Jordan, Pallo 390
just transition 400, 402, 414 n.66

K

Kasrils, Ronnie 213, 214–215, 246, 247–248, 273
Khoisan Leadership Conference 256 n.60
Khoisan people 109–110, 112–113, 115–116, 117, 118–119, 132, 133–134, 158, 163–164, 167, 180, 186, 232, 239, 241, 242–244, 379

kholwa 151–152
knowledge 59, 223

L

land 179, 240–241, 285, 384–388, 389–390, 391, 392–395. *See also* expropriation without compensation; property
Lembede, Anton 185–187, 298
Letseleba, W.P. 147
Liberal Party 116
liberalism 85, 115–117, 119, 125–126, 181–182
liberation movements 229
Life Esidimeni 346–348, 349, 350
living wage *see* minimum wage
Lonmin 314, 315, 316, 318, 320, 322, 323, 372
Luthuli, Albert 85, 163, 177
Lutuli, Martin 147

M

Macroeconomic Research Group (MERG) 212
Madikizela-Mandela, Winnie 208
Madonsela, Thuli 325, 378
Magashule, Ace 324
Mahlangu, Qedani 347, 348
Makgoba, Malegapuru 347, 348
Makhura, David 292–293, 348
Malema, Julius 293–294, 296, 299–300, 353–354
Mandela, Nelson 19, 20, 22, 36, 161, 167, 179, 183, 197, 198, 200, 201–202, 207–208, 210, 211
Mantashe, Gwede 325, 392
Manuel, Trevor 183, 234, 327, 373
Manyi, Mzwanele (Jimmy) 234, 297
Marikana massacre (2012) 313–315, 316–319, 320, 321–322, 324, 329, 372
Marxist Workers Party 409
Marxist Workers Tendency group (of the ANC) 271, 302 n.16
Mass Democratic Movement (MDM) 214, 276, 293, 310
Masters and Servants Ordinance 118
Mbeki, Thabo 200, 209, 219, 247, 307, 312, 320, 390
Mboweni, Tito 140
media 300, 353, 394
Menell, Clive 361
meters, pre-paid 137, 200, 248, 406
migrant labour 121, 126, 217, 263, 314, 318
Milner, Alfred 124
minimum wage 359–360, 361, 362, 363–364, 365, 367, 368, 369
mining industry 21, 48–49, 92, 99, 101, 108, 115, 119–120, 122, 123, 124, 127, 176, 182–183, 281, 313–318, 320–321, 322, 323, 391–392
minorities (concept) 167, 178, 227, 232
miscegenation 117
missionaries 150, 154, 281
MK *see* Umkhonto we Sizwe
modernism 130–131
Momberg, Jannie 276
Momoniat, Ismail 37, 293, 295, 298
Motlanthe, Kgalema 294, 385
Motsepe, Patrice 252, 272
Mpofu, Dali 37, 296–299, 320
Mthembu, Jackson 326
Mthethwa, Nathi 314
municipal services 246–247, 248, 251, 253–254, 263–264, 269–270, 284, 306, 319, 352, 355, 391, 407
Municipal Systems Act (MSA, 2000) 138, 247–248, 264, 390, 406

N

Naidoo, Jay 209, 213, 246, 276, 318–319, 320
Natal Indian Congress (NIC) 157, 166
Natal Native Congress (NNC) 147
National Convention (1908–1909) 56, 148
National Democratic Revolution (NDR) 27, 36–37, 127, 189, 216–217, 218, 219, 221, 250, 251, 261–262, 263, 271
National Forum 283, 286, 287
National Health Amendment Act (2013) 349
National Minimum Wage Act (2018) *see* minimum wage
National Party (NP)
and capitalism 20, 21, 22, 52, 96, 102, 202–203

and elections 220, 226
and negotiations 19–20, 21–23, 52–53, 126, 198, 202, 207–208, 215–216, 218, 253, 272
National Prosecuting Authority (NPA) 378
National Question (NQ) 37, 93, 153, 157, 181, 219, 222–223, 231, 232, 239, 243, 245, 259–260, 261, 263, 265, 266–268, 271, 272, 285, 295, 298, 333, 334, 401–402
National Union of Metalworkers of South Africa (Numsa) 231, 271, 289
National Union of Mineworkers (NUM) 315, 320, 323, 360
nationalisation 198, 199, 200, 211, 220, 273, 276
nationalism 70, 72–73, 161, 166, 229, 241, 274, 296, 299, 352
nationhood 288
Native Recruitment Corporation 115
Natives Land Act (1913) 179, 385, 389
Ndlambe, *Chief* 132
neo-colonialism 24, 25–26, 79–80, 230
neoliberalism 202, 206, 211, 218
Netherlands *see* Holland
Ngqika, *Chief* 132
Nkandla scandal 324, 325, 326–327, 328
Non-European Unity Movement (NEUM) 204–205, 335
non-racialism 277, 278, 280–284, 285–286, 287–289, 290–291, 292, 382
Ntantala, Phyllis 141–142

O

offshore listing 183, 215, 373
Ohlange Institute (Inanda) 154
Olver, Chippy 250
Oppenheimer family 22, 25, 125, 198, 373, 383

P

Pan Africanist Congress (PAC) 87, 165–167, 186, 187, 210, 246, 271, 374
passes 163–164
patriarchy 136, 137, 142, 174–175, 224, 395–396

pension schemes 216
Permanent Revolution theory (Trotsky) 217, 302 n.30, 402
Philip, John 115, 116, 150
Portugal 47–48, 49–50, 57, 107–108
privatisation 319
Programme of Action (ANCYL, 1949) 187
Progressive Party 116
property 25, 116, 140, 151, 321, 388, 389; *see also* expropriation without compensation; land protest and violence 25, 30, 81, 126, 261, 265–266, 289, 343, 410
Public Finance Management Act (PFMA, 1999) 309
Public Investment Corporation (PIC) 376, 381, 382
public sector wage bill 365–366

R

race and racism 42–43, 59–60, 62–63, 70–71, 72–74, 74–75, 77–79, 82, 88–89
  Ancient Greece and Rome 41, 42–45, 71
  Britain 50, 54, 69–70, 74, 83
  Holland 31, 50
  India 31, 41, 70, 104
  scientific 73, 76–77, 90, 91, 133–134
  South Africa 18, 19, 20–21, 27–28, 33–35, 38–39, 41–42, 52, 67–69, 77–79, 80–81, 83–87, 93, 94–105, 108, 111–112, 126–127, 131, 133, 139, 140, 161, 173–174, 178, 239–240, 244, 264, 266, 273–274, 278–279, 280, 281, 294, 295, 297, 300–301, 334, 339–342, 344–345, 376–377, 382–383, 400–401, 409–410, 411
  Soviet Union and eastern Europe 71
  Spain and Portugal 31, 45, 46, 47, 50
  USA 74, 93–94, 343
  See also African nationalism and chauvinism; racialism
racialism 90–91, 92–94
Radebe, Mark 147
radical economic transformation (RET)

300, 370, 371, 374, 375
Ramaphosa, Cyril 25, 240–241, 252, 272, 290, 314, 315, 316, 317, 318, 319–320, 321, 325, 326, 329, 361, 363–364, 367, 372, 386, 412 n.7
rape 224
Reconstruction and Development Programme (RDP) 31, 208–209, 212, 213, 248, 249, 276, 305, 361, 381
Relly, Gavin 198
Rhodes, Cecil John 121, 125, 128, 149
Riekert Commission 102, 202
Russia 210, 211, 327

S
San 32, 46, 48, 52, 109–110, 118; *see also* Khoisan people
sanctions 22
Sanlam 372
Seme, Pixley 152, 169, 179
sewerage systems 406
Sexwale, Tokyo 252, 272
Shaik, Schabir 324
Shaka 132
Shanduka 318
Shivambu, Brian 354
Shivambu, Floyd 293, 295, 299, 354
Sisulu, Lindiwe 234–235
Sisulu, Walter 179, 208
slavery 60–61
    in Ancient Greece and Rome 42, 43
    Atlantic trade 45, 46, 57
    in South Africa 48, 68, 109, 117, 119, 158
Slovo, Joe 213
Sobukwe, Robert 165–167, 298
social cohesion 286
social grants 294, 295, 367, 407
social justice 249, 263–264, 273, 286
social media 232, 267, 280
social movements 210
socialism 127
Socialist Workers Revolutionary Party (SWRP) 231, 289, 324, 403, 404, 409
socioeconomic crisis 23, 24, 30–31, 35, 79, 94, 126, 192, 230–231, 254, 255 n.10, 265, 279–280, 292, 378, 405

Soga, Tiyo 148–150
South African Airways 306
South African Communist Party (SACP) 31, 36, 166, 205, 208, 210, 211, 213, 216, 217, 231–232, 247, 250, 251, 275–277, 299, 310, 404; *see also* Communist Party of South Africa
South African Congress of Trade Unions (SACTU) 189, 219
South African Democratic Teachers' Union (SADTU) 235, 236, 237, 238
South African Federation of Trade Unions (Saftu) 231, 403
South African National Civic Organisation (Sanco) 208, 213
South African Native Convention (1909) 162, 172
South African Native National Congress (SANNC) *see* African National Congress
South African Police Service 314, 318, 322, 378
South African Reserve Bank 212, 285, 351
Soviet Union *see* Russia
Soweto student uprisings (1986) 101
Sparrow, Penny 139
Spoor, Richard 392
state capture 378, 380–381, 394
state-owned enterprises (SOEs) 206, 274, 306, 378, 380, 381
student uprisings 329, 330, 331–335, 336–339, 340, 342, 343, 345, 346; *see also* Soweto student uprisings
sunset clauses 213

T
Tabata, Isaac 204
Tambo, Oliver 164, 179
Tatane, Andries 317
taxi drivers 224
Teachers League of South Africa (TLSA) 335
Telkom 246, 319
Tobias, Philip 133–134
Tobin tax 362
trade unions 203, 280, 323, 328, 362–363, 403–404
Traditional and Khoisan Leadership Act

(2019) 241, 243, 393
Traditional Courts Bill (2019) 393
traditional culture and leaders *see* culture, traditional
Transvaal 92, 120–121
Transvaal Indian Congress (TIC) 157
Transworld Energy and Mineral Resources (TEMR) 392
Treatment Action Campaign (TAC) 308
trickle-down economics 282
Truth and Reconciliation Commission (TRC) 134–135
Tshabalala-Msimang, Manto 308
Turok, Ben 207
two-stage theory of revolution *see* National Democratic Revolution

U
ubuntu 152
Umkhonto we Sizwe (MK) 202, 207
unemployment 138, 362, 407
Union of South Africa 122, 161, 284, 380
United Democratic Front (UDF) 212, 219–220, 283, 286–287
universities 337–338, 342–344
Urban Development Strategy (UDS) 246–247
Urban Foundation 25, 28, 197–198, 361, 373
urbanisation 92, 179–180

V
Vaal River 406
Van der Stel, Simon 117
Van Goens, Rijckloff 117
Van Riebeeck, Jan 32, 48, 50, 109, 110
Vavi, Zwelinzima 373–374, 403
VBS Bank 350–352, 353–354, 355

W
Waddell, Gordon 22
wage gap 362, 364, 367
water and sanitation 175, 191, 200, 247, 248, 249, 253, 291, 409
Watson, Gavin 381

wealth redistribution 410–411
wealth tax 215, 362–363
Western science 334–335
white community and nationalism 140, 260, 266, 293, 329, 400, 405, 408; *see also* whiteness
white monopoly capital (WMC) 22, 23, 28, 39, 75, 97, 124, 182, 191, 201, 202–203, 210, 321, 369–375, 376–377, 383, 405
whiteness 42–43, 112
Wiehahn Commission 102, 202
Witwatersrand Native Labour Association 115
Workers List Party (WLP) 246
Workers Organisation for Socialist Action (Wosa) 245–246
working class 366–367, 368–369
 African 12, 14, 27, 30, 34, 35, 39, 75, 76, 79, 94, 97, 102, 124, 141, 188–189, 190, 207, 218–219, 252, 260–261, 265, 269, 274, 280, 305–306, 345, 362, 365, 371, 377, 381–382, 397, 410
 Coloured and Indian 159, 160, 171, 227, 233, 243, 362
 industrial 168
 white 113–114, 120, 162, 177
 See also clothing and textile workers; domestic workers; farmworkers
World Bank 250, 282, 390
The Wound (film) 222

X
xenophobia 292
Xolobeni (Eastern Cape) 391–392
Xuma, A.B. (Alfred Bitini) 184–185, 205, 231

Z
Zille, Helen 129, 130, 131
Zondo Commission of Enquiry (ZCE) 205, 206, 324, 380–381, 382
Zuma, Jacob 158, 324–325, 326, 328–329, 370, 378, 381, 383
Zwelithini, Goodwill 240–241, 292